SERVANTS

SERVANTS

A Downstairs History *of* Britain
from the Nineteenth Century
to Modern Times

Lucy Lethbridge

W. W. Norton & Company
New York • London

For information about special discounts for bulk purchases, please contact
W. W. Norton Special Sales at specialsales@wwnorton.com or 800-233-4830

Manufacturing by RR Donnelley, Harrisonburg
Production manager: Devon Zahn

ISBN 978-0-393-24109-9

W. W. Norton & Company, Inc.
500 Fifth Avenue, New York, N.Y. 10110
www.wwnorton.com

W. W. Norton & Company Ltd.
Castle House, 75/76 Wells Street, London W1T 3QT

1 2 3 4 5 6 7 8 9 0

For my parents, and in memory of Blanche Hole

Contents

Preface

In 1901 the Earl of Derby, viewing the prospect of hosting the new King, Edward VII, and forty of the King's friends at Knowsley Hall, near Liverpool, was overheard to say of the arrangements the visit would require: 'that makes sixty extra servants and with the thirty-seven who live in, nothing could be simpler . . .' Entertaining on such a grand scale was the very fabric of Edwardian country house life; in many cases, by the turn of the century, after mid-Victorian agricultural depressions had caused a sharp decline in the value of farming land, lavish entertaining was even its *raison d'être*. Lord Derby's quota of thirty-seven indoor staff was hardly excessive for the times: the Duke of Devonshire found that two hundred servants were the barest minimum necessary to look after the needs of a house party of fifty people.

The idea of the perfect servant – silent, obsequious, loyal – is a central component of the many myths of England's recent past; servants underpin the ideal, never quite attainable, of a perfectly ordered life. Tracing the classes down through their many gradations, we find servants at almost every level except the very poorest. In 1911, 800,000 families in Britain employed servants, but only a fifth of them retained a staff of more than three; the vast majority were served by a single domestic, very likely a girl in her early teens, someone like the poor skivvy described by H. G. Wells in *Kipps*, 'who has to go up and down, up and down and be tired out'. Yet, as people in their own right, servants remain elusive. For the researcher into domestic service, they emerge in tantalising glimpses, mentioned only in passing in the memoirs or autobiographies of their employers, or given comic working-class characteristics. They were witnesses at first-hand of vast social changes but rarely were they able to be active participants; they were adjuncts of the action rather than shapers of it.

From the mid-nineteenth century to our own day, the relationship has been difficult to pin down. With starched uniforms, green baize doors, electric bells and separate servants' quarters, the Victorians reinforced the separation between the domestic workings of a home and the sanctity of the family at its centre. The relationship between the server and the served became the often-resented demarcation of below stairs and above. The author and politician Christopher Hollis, writing in 1929, thought that the inequality between servant and master which beleaguered so many British homes was a 'special vice of Victorian England. The Continent has never properly had it. The Middle Ages certainly did not have it. The Shakespearean masters and servants knew nothing of it, nor did the masters and servants of Sir Walter Scott. In the seventeenth century the Pepys' sent for their servants to join in their games as a matter of course . . .' Below the surface of the social changes of the twentieth century, this inequality, right at the heart of the family home, began to chafe.

Yet servants also squeeze awkwardly into the big narrative of twentieth-century labour history. Despite the great numbers of working-class women employed as domestics, servants have been viewed as standing outside working-class political movements. Although service, particularly in large country houses, was often seen as a way of gaining protection and patronage, career servants were despised by members of their own class as 'flunkeys', propping up a hated system of privilege and dependency. As the butler John Robinson put it in 1890: 'The paralysing influence of the servant's environment has prevented his calling very loudly for more freedom.' It was as if the demeanour of servantliness, once assumed, was impossible to shake off. No wonder employers and domestic advice manuals stressed the 'innate' nature of the 'good' servant, the spiritual communion between hard domestic labour and Christian virtue. As the 1853 manual *Commonsense for Housemaids* suggested: 'A really good housemaid should never be able to be alone in a room with a table without giving it a good rub, or, if the room is occupied, without wishing to do so. Tables and chairs should be to her objects of deep interest; after her own family and the family of her mistress, they should claim the next place in her affections.'

Housework, to that paragon of 1930s fictional femininity, Mrs Miniver, was properly intended to be the 'low distant humming in the background' that allowed Mrs Miniver not only to take her place in the world but to concentrate on the interesting complexities of her inner life – those complexities that only freedom from humdrum domestic labour could facilitate. The having of servants was a precondition of much that has been considered important in all the classes: ceremonial, tradition and leisure for the upper classes; status, hygiene and respectability for the middles; the 'conspicuous consumption' of goods and leisure that marked an age of industrial wealth.

In this book I have gathered together voices, heard and unheard, published and unpublished, of domestic servants. Every example of oppression and ill-treatment on the part of employers can be countered by another of reciprocal friendship and loyalty. Some servants were crushed by the experience, others were rebellious, some were proud. Their accounts are testaments to personalities that were often given little room to shine in their own right but were witnesses of the social changes that have taken place in the British home over the last century: changes in the way we live, in the way we run our homes and our attitudes to family, money, work and status.

PART I

The Symbolic Pantomime

Chapter 1

'A Sort of Silence and Embarrassment'

In 1901, in a slim volume published to mark the accession of Edward VII, the author, identified only as 'One of His Majesty's Servants', sketched an idyllic picture of domestic life in the royal houschold, stressing the new monarch's domestic rectitude, and his homely side, hitherto unknown to his subjects: 'Few people outside the Royal Family and the circle that is honoured by the King's intimate friendship are aware of the high standard of domestic life that he has always set himself and observed.' Not only, wrote the author, did the marriage of King Edward VII and Queen Alexandra have the savour of 'the once-upon-a-time fairy period or the poetic middle ages', but the royal couple loved nothing more than to 'meet for tea', that cosiest of occasions heralding a gargantuan command performance with a 'seemingly inexhaustible supply of cakes both hot and cold, sandwiches of all kinds, rolls and jams'.[1]

To celebrate the sanctity of the English teatime, in 1902, Queen Alexandra invited 10,000 of London's 'maids-of-all-work' to tea parties across the capital to mark the Coronation. The teas were orchestrated by the Office of the Bishop of London and *The Times* reported that between 10 July and 2 August, although it poured with rain almost incessantly, the girls gathered for 'tea, white and brown bread and butter, jam, lettuces and watercress, seed cake, iced plum cake and strawberries'. These were the tweenies, the skivvies, the slaveys, the grafters: girls who slept in basement kitchens next to the stove, or in tiny bedrooms under the eaves, where it was either freezing cold or oppressively hot. From Norwood, Tottenham, St Pancras, St Albans and Camberwell they came, and were entertained with music, 'fancy sketches' and similar treats by the ladies of the local branches of the Metropolitan Association for Befriending Young Servants ('MABYS') and other benevolent institutions. The Bishop of London, Arthur Winnington-Ingram, stood on a table in the Zoological Gardens in Regent's Park to address the throng and reminded them of their vital role in the development and expansion of the Empire. One thousand teas were served in the gardens of the Bishop's Palace in Fulham. 'We carried it off as well as we could,' remembered the Bishop, 'except that a thousand girls insisted on kissing the band, but as the band did not seem to mind there was no harm done.'[2] The maids-of-all-work, most of whom would have half a day off a week at most, were permitted, 'contrary to the custom at gatherings of this kind', to wear their own clothes rather than their usual uniform of cap and apron. It was reported that they raised their cups to the King and wished the new monarch well.[3]

No aspect of the home spoke quite so eloquently to the English middle-class idea of the ordered life than the presence of servants. From the bustling subterranean townships employed on the landed estates, to the maid-of-all-work who did for the rapidly expanding middles, as representatives of the nation's sense of natural and social order, the deferential servant was as necessary to the English pyramid of social life as the squire or the parson. Foreign visitors to England often marvelled at the efficiently orchestrated hospitality for which the English had become famous. In 1832, on a year-long tour round England, the Prussian Prince Puckler-Muskau reported that: 'The treatment of servants is as excellent as their performance of their duties. Each has his prescribed field of activities; in which, however, the strictest and most punctual execution of orders is expected of him ... At the same time the servants enjoy a reasonable freedom, and have certain portions of time allotted to them, which their master carefully respects. The whole treatment of the servant classes is much more decorous, and combined with more *égards* than with us; but then they are so entirely excluded from all familiarity, and such profound respect is exacted from them, that they appear to be considered rather as machines than as beings of the same order.'[4]

The labour which facilitated such an impression of effortlessness was, on the whole, silent, subservient and multitudinous. There was perceived to be an upward momentum for the good servant, a seat at the head of the servants' table. 'Servants, in my childhood,' wrote Susan Tweedsmuir of her youth in a country house at the turn of the century, 'came young to a large house, worked very hard, were promoted, worked less hard as the years went by; were caught up into an empyrean where they had a sitting room of their own. They then wore a black silk dress and were waited on by the under-servants.'[5] Most young servants in households of this size learned the job by waiting solely on the upper-servants. At Welbeck Abbey, in Nottinghamshire, where the fifth Duke of Portland, an eccentric recluse, maintained an enormous entourage of ninety indoor serv-ants to attend him, the ten senior upper-servants had ten under-servants to wait on them in turn. In the larger houses, the system was sufficiently capacious to take in servants whose role was never made explicit. There seems rarely to have been a sense that there were *too many* servants and any stray parties were given vague job titles covering just about anything required of them, or were referred to as apprentices – sometimes for years. A 'useful maid', for example, halfway up the ladder to being a lady's-maid, was often used to accompany young girls to parties. The 'odd man', a vital fixture on an estate, was a manservant who never quite made the grade required to be a front-of-house type and was therefore used for pretty well everything, from carrying heavy luggage to helping with the cleaning. Huge houses could sustain great numbers of the very old and the very young and with their work went the rituals of their particularity, the vital necessity of which no-one thought of questioning. Lady Diana Cooper, who grew up in Belvoir Castle, Rutland, remembered the 'gong man' whose only job was to summon the household to meals by walking the corridors three times a day banging a gong: 'He would walk down the interminable passages, his livery hanging a little loosely on his bent old bones, clutching his gong with one hand and with the other feebly brandishing the padded-knobbed stick with which he struck it.'[6]

The idea that the country estate – supported by farms, orchards, gardens and well-stocked lakes – constituted a microcosm of the natural and social order, had taken root deep in the English imagination. By 1900 the country estate became imbued with a nostalgia captured in the pages of *Country Life*, a weekly magazine which had been established in 1880 precisely to feed a nation's longings for the ideal country house. Like Edward Ponderevo, the self-made millionaire of H. G. Wells's novel *Tono-Bungay*, the new-rich quickly learned the social cachet of the old over the showy glitter of the new: 'Their first crude conception of dazzling suites of the newly perfect is replaced almost from the outset by a jackdaw dream of accumulating costly discrepant old things.'[7]

The great estates became the symbols of an Englishness where effortless caste superiority was preserved by the trappings of patronage and rich Americans fell over themselves to marry their daughters to aristocratic families who, in turn, were in need of funds. The writer Ralph Waldo Emerson, on a visit from the New World, was among those seduced by the English milord's resistance to strenuous effort of any kind: 'They have the sense of superiority, the absence of all the ambitious effort which disgusts in the aspiring classes, a pure tone of thought and feeling, and the power to command, among their other luxuries, the presence of the most accomplished men at their festive meetings.'[8]

For many of those American heiresses who did marry into the aristocracy it was often their spouses' practical incompetence – being stumped by the simplest of daily tasks – that proved most perplexing to their new brides. When sitting beside a dwindling fire, a poker at their feet, it was usual to ring for a footman to poke the fire using the very same poker. Yet at the same time, they often went to great lengths rarely to encounter most of those who did the work for them, never to brush up against the spectacle of manual labour itself. 'If someone walked into the room and all they wanted was a handkerchief you had to stop whatever you were doing and walk out until such time as they did this,' remembered an Edwardian maidservant.[9] Lord Curzon, whose intellect was regarded as one of the glories of the Empire, was so baffled by the challenge of opening a window in the bedroom of the country house in which he was staying (no servants being available so late at night), that he simply picked up a log from the grate and smashed the glass.

So deep was felt to be the *Englishness* of the master-servant relationship that domestic technology was far slower to catch hold in Britain than in America or Continental Europe. Although, in 1906, King Edward VII's yacht was fitted up 'with a complete electric outfit, including soup and coffee boilers, hotplates, ovens, grills and hot closets', on the whole, the upper classes distanced themselves from the pursuit of technological progress, preferring to maintain the superiority of traditional elbow grease over brash, modern contrivances. The idea of 'labour-saving' was anathema – and even the royal laundry, an astonishingly elaborate set-up with steam apparatus and fed by its own private railway, was staffed not only by fleets of laundresses but by thirty-four royal engineers. The most basic technological amenities were not seriously to take root in the majority of English country houses until well after the First World War, and sometimes beyond the Second. In fact the more labour-intensive the house was seen to be, the more it was seen as upholding the values of the old world order. Although there were some significant changes made to English houses in the late nineteenth century, human effort was on the whole considered vastly preferable to modern amenities. Houseguests shivered in the cold of country houses where, recalled Lady Cynthia Asquith, 'you perambulated long, icy passages in search of the nearest bathroom – if there was one'.[10] Labour was cheap: the servant problem was a problem for the cash-strapped, not the rich. At Beech Hill Park, a vast Victorian house in Epping Forest, there was a hall entirely covered in mosaic that had to be washed with milk by hand every week by five maids; yet there was no telephone in Beech Hill and it was lit entirely by candles until the late 1940s.[11]

A general distrust for new technologies percolated through the classes. Leslie Stephen, father of Virginia Woolf and Vanessa Bell, wondered why he should install a hot water system in his London house when he could always employ two or three girls to carry the bath water up and down stairs as required. Too much newness became regarded as vulgar: Mrs Loftie, author of books of advice on interior design, warned against gas, a form of lighting which had once been embraced by the fashionable but by the early twentieth century had become *too* popular and was now associated with trade showrooms and other iniquities. 'Nothing can compete with the gasolier in tawdry deformity,' she cautioned.[12]

In 1912, the *Illuminating Engineer* expressed the view that gas was a 'middle-class luxury. It never invaded the marble halls of the West End; and of course, the poor could not get it. It was admitted to the rich man's kitchens and domestic offices, and its attractions beckoned the workman to his only club, the corner pub. As a domestic light in the fullest sense of the word, it was almost as sure a sign of respectability as the keeping of a gig.'[13] In grand houses, gas lamps were generally confined to the servants' hall, where they enabled the staff to work till late at night; gas was considered too smelly and too damaging to antique furniture to be used in other parts of the house. The inimitable patina of age became central to the national idea of Englishness, and to this idea, new technology was often considered positively threatening. The American economist Thorstein Veblen noted in 1892 how the attraction of old-fashioned beeswax candles to illuminate evening dinner parties was suddenly revealed when gas and electric lighting became widely available to the middle classes. The reason was said to be the flattering rosy glow that candles cast, but behind it lay a snobbery about industrial mass production. The lady of a house in Wigmore Street was typical: her new maid, Elizabeth Banks, reported in 1891 that there were gas fittings but her mistress declined to use them, preferring to use candles that her maid had to clean up afterwards. 'In the halls, on the stairs and in every room of the house, from the kitchen to the fifth floor, candle grease was liberally sprinkled, and my brown paper and flat iron were in constant demand.'[14]

The stateliest homes still relied on lamp men, whose job for generations had been to patrol the corridors of English country houses, lighting and tending the oil lamps or candles that were the only source of light. Lamp men were retainers of the old sort, associated with homes that had no need of flashy modern accoutrements that needed only the turn of a switch. Trimming, cleaning and maintaining the lamps was an arduous daily job: at Erddig in Wales, the Yorkes had forty oil lamps requiring constant attendance, for a dirty lamp created clouds of soot. 'An Old Servant', the author of an anonymous little memoir written in the First World War, described 'strings of soot hanging from the ceiling all over the room; everything was thick with greasy soot' when a lamp was inadequately cleaned.[15] At Badminton House, seat of the Duke of Beaufort, the lamp man was totally blind and felt his way expertly about the corridors – and was still doing so in the 1920s. At Belvoir Castle there were at least three lamp and candle men who laboured continuously at snuffing wicks, filling lamps and cleaning and de-waxing glass – a full-time job. 'Gas was despised, I forget why – vulgar I think,' was how Lady Diana Cooper remembered it.[16] Gordon Grimmett, who in 1915 went to work as a lamp boy for the Marquess of Bath at Longleat, where there was no electricity, put this distaste for technological innovation down to the ruling classes' immunity to discomfort: 'The English public school system had instilled in them the virtues of a spartan life, and early principles, it seemed, died hard. It was all right for the foreign aristocracy, they were a soft lot, that was why the British Empire was there and would always remain there. It was also why every day I had to collect, clean, trim and fill four hundred lamps.'[17]

In 1900 domestic service was the single largest occupation in Edwardian Britain: of the four million women in the British workforce, a million and a half worked as servants, a majority of them as single-handed maids in small households. Hardly surprising then that the keeping of servants was not necessarily considered an indication of wealth: for many families it was so unthinkable to be without servants that their presence was almost overlooked. When the actress Dame Sybil Thorndike, who was a daughter of a Canon of Rochester Cathedral, described in an interview her childhood in the late nineteenth century, she several times repeated that the family, who kept four servants in residence, was 'very poor'.

Yet, despite their constituting the largest working group, the records on servants are often hazy, their lives rendered indistinct. Servants were simultaneously visible, their presence a sign of status, and invisible, the details of their individual experience subsumed into that of their employers; and it was employers who controlled the historical record. Take the case of Alice Osbourn. In 1901 she was a member of the Baldwin household at Rectory Farm House in the village of Taplow, Buckinghamshire. In the national census of that year she is described as a nursery governess aged twenty-one. Alice, we can assume, had been employed to look after the Baldwins' two young sons, Jim and Harold. Also listed at Rectory Farm House is a woman from nearby Cookham, Ellen Godfrey, aged thirty-five, and described as a 'cook domestic'. Alice's entry is scant: it tells us only that she was born in Warwick, as was her employer, Walter Baldwin, who ran the family paper mill in King's Norton, near Birmingham.

Though modest in comparison to nearby Taplow Court (the home of Lord and Lady Desborough) and Cliveden House, the magnificent home of the Astors just a mile away, Rectory Farm House was a substantial property with huge bow windows and a large garden. We can assume that the administration of the household was largely undertaken by Alice and the cooking and tidying by Ellen Godfrey. It is likely there was a daily woman who came to do 'the rough' – the scrubbing, elbow grease and heavy work.

Fragments of Alice's daily life survive in print only through the journals that she kept from 1906, five years after the census was taken. That January she started a new diary, purchased from the department store Peter Robinson, and began a careful daily record of the weather, in which she always took a punctilious interest, of the provisions ordered for the household, delivered from London shops such as the Army and Navy Stores and from local suppliers, and of various other household duties. In that first week of 1906, Alice ordered twelve eggs, one pheasant and a pound of butter; on 2 January, more butter and seven chocolate cakes; the next day, a chicken, two lettuces, one haddock and a small plaice (the chicken, she noted, was expensive at five shillings and the young Grenfells, Lord and Lady Desboroughs' children, had come to supper and eaten too much of it). That same week Alice travelled to Maidenhead to have a fender repaired, oversaw the sweeping of the nursery chimney and booked the man who came to oil the clocks.

Most important of all for Alice, however, was the presence of Daphne Baldwin, the adored only daughter, born in 1903 when Mrs Baldwin was thirty-nine. The infant Daphne's every ailment, her every requirement for food or clothing is faithfully documented in Alice's diary. Although she had been enrolled in a local school, Daphne's earaches, her constipation and her headaches kept her at home much of the time.

As each year unrolls, a picture of Edwardian life at Rectory Farm House emerges from Alice's bare facts; occasionally she even allows herself to hint at feelings of impatience or worry. The family, who also had a London house in Ladbroke Grove, seem to spend weeks at a time in Brighton; occasionally Walter Baldwin makes a business trip to Birmingham. The two boys come home for the school holidays bringing piles of clothes to be washed and mended. In 1912, when nine-year-old Daphne was sent to Roedean, Alice makes dozens of lists in her diary of school uniform requirements, all jotted down and meticulously cross-referenced.

By 1911 a new national census records that Ellen Godfrey has left the Baldwins and been replaced by Emily Johnson, aged fifty-five, a 'housemaid'. Alice is now described as a 'cook', though she makes no reference in her diaries to doing any actual cooking. Perhaps no-one asked Alice how she wanted to be described when the census forms were filled in; perhaps Mr Baldwin, taking his fountain pen to the entries, thought 'cook' would do as well as 'nursery governess'. Other staff come and go. In 1912 'yet another' parlourmaid walks out; 'she does not think that Taplow suits her', writes Alice. There may have been more people living at Rectory Farm House than is apparent from the census: a fluid population of resident and non-resident servants flowing in and out. The entries show other conflicting information. In 1901, Walter's wife Liley

Baldwin's birthplace is listed as Rutland, but by 1911, whoever filled in the census form has changed this to Bridgnorth, Shropshire. Furthermore, in 1911, Alice's census entry records her age as thirty-seven – which would mean that she had aged a miraculous sixteen years in a single decade.

Alice Osbourn's diaries give us only partial and inconclusive glimpses of her life with the Baldwins and her relationship to them is as difficult to pin down as any intimacy. Yet the uncategorisable nature of the servant-master bond, so convenient for the master, was beginning by the turn of the century to chafe; many servants felt bitterly their exclusion from the social changes brought about by the Industrial Revolution. The idea that English society was bound by a complex and essentially benevolent social web that held the classes together in mutual co-dependency was one of the most potent myths of Edwardian England, at a time when inequalities were in real life stark. The upper and middle classes enjoyed improvements in diet, sanitation and medicine and a concomitant rise in life expectancy. At the turn of the century they could expect to live for nearly sixty years, while the life expectancy of the poorest of the working classes, whose diet chiefly consisted of tea, bread, and dripping, had not risen at all for three centuries, and remained at just thirty years. An awkwardness settled over a domestic relationship that was both startlingly intimate and distant – and in the ever-expanding middle classes it often became suffused with suspicion and guilt. G. K. Chesterton, reflecting on his own comfortable, middle-class childhood in Kensington remembered that: 'One peculiarity of this middle class was that it really was a class, it really was in the middle. Both for good and evil, and certainly often to excess, it was separated both from the class above it and the class below. It knew far too little of the working classes, to the great peril of a later generation. It knew far too little even of its own servants.' Hanging over the subject of servants was, recalled Chesterton, 'a sort of silence and embarrassment'.[18]

Chapter 2

The Dainty Life

In the last year of the nineteenth century, Mrs Alfred Praga, a working journalist and author of self-improving guides for the struggling housewife, published *Appearances: How To Keep Them Up on a Limited Income*, taking as a template her own domestic experience. Mr Praga's work as a lawyer earned him a modest £300 a year and his wife's book charts her struggle to maintain the necessary appurtenances of gentility in their small house in *démodé* West Kensington. It is an upbeat book, designed to give hope to those women, like Mrs Praga herself, who, teetering on the abyss of genteel poverty, could live a 'dainty life' in which effort and domestic order might be rewarded by social acceptance.

In Mrs Praga's world, servants continued to be the single most important indicator of social status, crucial players in the dinner, the tea party, the demands of entertaining, who's in, who's out, the correct placement of oneself and one's family in the great web of society. As the pseudonymous 'Member of the Aristocracy' counselled: 'So much depends on the constant cooperation of well-trained servants. Without it, the best bred of hostesses is placed at a disadvantage.'[1] For Mrs Praga, therefore, doing the cooking or cleaning herself was out of the question: keeping a resident cook and a house-parlourmaid – young (aged somewhere between twelve and fifteen), wet behind the ears and needing some training-up, need only cost £15 a year (£10 for the cook and £5 for the maid) plus board and food. Mrs Praga thought her fourteen-year-old house-parlourmaid rather 'stupid', but this deficiency was happily outweighed by the vital qualities of her being cheap and also 'deft and low-voiced and soft-footed', which would render her pleasantly unobtrusive.

It would not have been practical in Mrs Praga's small house to ask her servants to turn their faces to the wall when encountering their employer, as they might have had to do in a grander establishment, but near-invisibility was nonetheless desirable if you could manage it. (Non-creaking shoes with elastic sides were recommended footwear for indoor servants – though John James, a young manservant, was told by an early employer that as he had the heavy step of a manual labourer, 'it was very evident that I was not cut out for indoor service'.[2])

In 1909 the liberal politician and historian Charles Masterman concluded that one of the hallmarks of the Edwardian age was its taste for 'ineffectual pleasure' and, above all, waste, excess and superfluity. 'Where one house sufficed, now two are demanded; where a dinner of a certain quality, now dinner of superior quality; where clothes or dresses, or flowers, now more dresses, more flowers.'[3] 'We old servants,' wrote the anonymous memoirist of service, 'hope that waste is now a thing of the past, for surely everyone now will be more and more careful. Surely the waste will be stopped now, for we have seen waste on the top of waste in some of the best situations.'[4] For the middle-class housewife like Mrs Praga, struggling to keep up with the demands of fashion, waste was not affordable, a sign of status though it may have been, and she waged against it an unending battle. Mrs Praga's home economies were conducted on a micro-industrial scale, the tiniest expenditure rigorously noted down in her housekeeping logbooks. The exercise of thrift formed the crucial distinction between a competent middle-class housewife and a lazy one, and suggested a moral life similarly well organised. Mrs Praga took account of every egg and every stock bone used in the kitchen; nothing was left to chance. Because laundry, which generally had to be outsourced expensively and every week, was the smaller household's most pressing expense, she took particular care to buy her servants dresses in dark grey material – 'I never allow my servants to wear light prints' – to save on the washing bill.[5]

Down through the ranks of English society, households of every calibration of middle class calculated how many servants they could afford. In 1900 the *Cornhill Magazine* ran a series for the new century, setting out model budgets that would sustain the standards of living to which modest, middling and affluent households in London might aspire. The span of the social categories that the magazine identified as requiring their advice, from the modest and clerkly lower-middle class on £150 per annum, to the extremely affluent on £10,000, demonstrates the huge expansion of the English middle class during the preceding century. By 1900, this class, loosely embracing business, professions and commerce, had tripled in size and now challenged the monopoly of power, both political and financial, that had been for centuries held by the landed classes.

Despite being what the *Cornhill* article described as 'the backbone of the commonwealth', the lower-middle class, content with a 'snug little suburban' home in the new sprawls of Leytonstone or Forest Gate, would be hard pressed to afford help in the house – but then, as the author of the article is at pains to suggest, it would be quite inappropriate for the housewife on such a budget to even think of seeking help. The purveyors of advice on household economy often counselled that those on the most modest incomes should be content to do their housework themselves: one of the features of advice on domestic service is the way in which those who employ domestic help view housework in the light of a moral endeavour for people poorer than themselves. In the bracket of those surviving on an income at the lowest level, the *Cornhill* included 'the wives of managing clerks to solicitors, teachers in London board schools, younger reporters on the best metropolitan newspapers, second division clerks in the Colonial office, organists, curates and sanitary inspectors'. They should know their place, and for them, as they would find on £150 a year, keeping house, scrimping, saving, making things last and taking in lodgers, it was morally improving. A few pennies were permitted to cover the occasional employment of a laundress and a woman to help with 'the rough', but 'plain living will be a matter of course'.[6] Even in the high summer of Edwardian excess, 'plain living' was most people's lot.

Yet even plain living allowed for some leisure, a development that many literary commentators found monstrous and unnatural. The journalist T. H. Crosland was almost hysterical at the thought of it, scoffing in 1905 at the suburban pleasures of 'penny buses, gramophones, bamboo furniture, pleasant Sunday afternoons, Glory Songs, modern language teas, gold, tennis, high school education, dubious fiction, shillings worth of comic writing, picture postcards, miraculous hair restorers'.[7] But the lower-middle class was growing in confidence and their hobbies, interests and customs would come to dominate popular culture. This was the age of the clerks, the boom time of the small shopkeepers, people like the family of the novelist V. S. Pritchett whose father, son of a Victorian nonconformist preacher in Yorkshire, was a travelling salesman, then a dealer in novelties and fancy handbags; 'for suddenly money was about, commerce was expanding, there was a chance for the lower middle class. They would have a slice of the money the middles had sat so obdurately on for so long.' Money, or at least the conspicuous making of it, no longer carried the taint of sin: 'The difference between "goods" and "the good" was fading.'[8]

Inching up *Cornhill*'s ladder of the middle classes was 'a younger son with a narrow berth in the Civil Service' on a start-up income of £800 a year. After paying a recommended rent of, at the very most, £130 a year, there should be plenty left over for two servants: 'Two is the right number: a cook at £20 a year and a house-parlour-maid at £18. With two such servants, if they are well-meaning and fairly intelligent, a woman can have her household conducted with order and daintiness, if she chooses, which means that she must be willing to supervise and interest herself in the details of the establishment.' Tight control of the household finances was required to maintain help, even at the next budget level of £1,800 a year, but with the wages of four resident servants still only amounting to £130, it was laundry, lighting, repairs, insurance and clothing for man and wife (which alone came to £200) that made the largest inroads into the household budget. At this level, suggested the *Cornhill* author, skimping on servants could even prove to be a false economy: 'I am inclined to think that in early married life, a lady's-maid, besides being a great comfort, partly pays for herself by the saving of dressmakers' bills, and turning old things into new.'[9]

Far more costly than their wages was servants' food and their traditional 'beer money' (rarely now, except in large country houses, actually consisting of beer – a traditional perk that had emerged from the custom on rural estates of brewing their own ale and because it was considered preferable in the eighteenth century for servants to drink beer than to be tempted to pilfer expensive tea). Mrs Praga's mother worried about the cost of her daughter's two maids: 'It's not their wages – it's their food!' There was also their 'washing money' to be spent on the regular laundering of aprons, caps and uniforms. Then there was the duty, in 1900 a matter for individual conscience rather than law, of paying your employee's medical bills. Mrs Earle in the *Cornhill* warned her readers that, including wages, 'every maid represents an additional £60 or £70 a year, and every man servant another £70 or £80'. Their own spending money was the very least of the expense.

A family in the comfortable, professional regions of the middle class then, on an income of between £1,000 and £3,000 a year, could expect to employ, without conspicuous struggle, a butler, two maids, a cook and a governess or nanny. But even this was nothing to the splendours to be enjoyed in the very uppermost echelons of the middles. At the top of the *Cornhill* budgets was a household that could command an annual income of £10,000. As the family probably kept two establishments, the needs of survival were secondary to the requirements of fashion and status. It was recommended, for example, that a gentleman's sporting pursuits, so crucial to his position as a man of leisure, should be allotted one-fifth of the entire household outgoings. Wages for the recommended twelve to fourteen servants still added up to a not princely £400 a year – slightly less than the suggested amount for annual charitable donations and half the amount that it was reckoned the family should put aside in savings; even the cost of the upkeep of the family's horses came to £600.[10]

Prosperous upper-middle-class homes, emulating on limited budgets the establishments of the aristocracy, were peopled to bursting by family and retainers. 'In our day,' recalled Beryl Lee Booker on her affluent Edwardian childhood, 'the family of five, parents and three children, needed eight servants to look after them. A nurse, nursery-maid, lady's-maid, housemaid, between-maid, cook and kitchen-maid. These maids seethed about the place gossiping and making work for one another.'[11] Houses needed therefore to be built on a scale that could accommodate the human machinery of domestic life and there was a boom in speculative building after 1900. The number of newly built houses more than doubled from about three and a half million in the middle of the nineteenth century to just over seven and a half million by 1911.

Suburbs, garden cities and blocks of flats were the newest aspects of this rage for development, and with them came increased demand for maids-of-all-work or the 'general'. In 1900, a correspondent to *The Lady* pointed out: 'The general is more in request among the well-to-do class now than she was at one time, and the reason for this is the rapid growth of ... those enormous barracks called flats, the courts and mansions that are so fast springing up in all parts of London and its suburbs.'[12] The same writer suggested that the flats would encourage relationships between mistress and maid that were, quite literally, on the level and empathy would surely follow, 'the space, being so much more limited, they are, as it were, thrown into contact with one another which produces very often mutual liking and consideration'. In reality, proximity led less to improved relations than to a decline in servants' living standards. *The Lancet* in 1906 campaigned for improvements in servants' quarters in flats, finding that the 'compact' accommodation advertised as maids' rooms was generally an airless cupboard off the kitchen, 'hardly large enough to contain cubic air space for one person, certainly not sufficient for the two poor girls whom it is supposed to accommodate'.[13]

It is the 'villa', however, that best illustrates the ascendancy of Victorian and Edwardian domestic life: protected from the gaze of the outside world by hedges, walls, windows, blinds; and inside, a family sealed off from its servants and their labours by a complicated arrangement of tradesman's entrances, back staircases and basements. A proliferation of small passages separated the kitchen, pantries and scullery regions from the main rooms of the English house. The semi-rural outskirts of London such as Penge, Dulwich, Forest Hill and Finchley were soon a mass of 'pretty and convenient villas'[14] – though the Edwardian idea of 'compact' was flexible. When the architect C. J. Richardson, author of *The Englishman's House*, designed what he called a 'suburban villa' as an example of 'compactness of arrangement and economy of space', it was over 6,000 square feet in size and had seventeen rooms, including an enormous attic specifically designed as sleeping quarters for the servants.[15]

If there was a unifying feature that encompassed the suburban villa and the well-appointed Mayfair townhouse, it was the importance of maintaining discretion and the separation between the family at the epicentre of the home and the servants behind the scenes. This idea of privacy had taken root in the mid-nineteenth century. In 1864, drawing up his list of the key ingredients for a 'gentleman's house', the architect Robert Kerr made privacy his number one criterion (rating it above spaciousness, comfort and convenience, elegance – even light and air), advocating a complete distinction between the family apartments and those of the servants. There was to be absolutely no allowance of any smells or noises to issue from the kitchen regions. This resulted in mazy networks of stairs, doorways and passages forming a partition from one side of the house to the other. Bulky Victorian additions to Georgian houses created a division under one roof between two communities that had not been envisaged in the eighteenth-century home, or indeed in the homes of preceding centuries. These cumbersome new wings created, thought Susan Tweedsmuir, looking back at her family home, Moor Park in Hertfordshire, 'the maximum amount of flights of steps, long passages and in fact everything that was as un-labour-saving as possible'.[16]

Strategies had to be devised to maintain the privacy of one part of the house from the other. The introduction of bells came with the increased distances that needed to be travelled: hand bells had been popular in the eighteenth century, but then, as the servants' areas of operation became housed further from the main hub of the house, more complicated bell systems were installed that linked distant rooms via networks of wires and pulleys. The 'speaking tube' was another popular, pre-telephone device by which the servant could receive orders from upstairs. Electric bells were still commonly installed in newly built houses up to the 1930s but as they were temperamental and dependent on batteries they were never as popular as the old rattling, squeaking kind which juddered querulously on the wall. The dumb-waiter, the lift that carries food or dishes from floor to floor, was another Victorian development which saved time tramping long, unheated passages carting hot dishes. Servants, as always, had to be 'invisible and inaudible' while going about their work.[17] Hidden doorways on the landings of large staircases or behind false bookshelves provided a quick exit for the housemaid disturbed at work by her employer. 'It is very difficult to be a housemaid, to do your work well and never to be seen, and gentlemen fifty years ago did not care to see her often,' wrote the anonymous author of *Domestic Service*.

The design of the home was also rigorously divided between women's space and men's; women had sitting rooms (for receiving callers), boudoirs and dressing rooms while men had billiard rooms, studies, libraries and smoking rooms (and gun rooms for the field sportsman). The servants, of course, had their own warren of sculleries, washhouses, attic bedrooms (probably shared), kitchens, pantries, larders and store rooms; in large houses the sexes were separated by corridors of bedrooms for men and for women – for both servants and guests. By the turn of the new century, kitchens had become smaller in newly built houses and therefore could not always accommodate the table and chairs that customarily offered a respite for the servant – so architects often incorporated a tiny maids' sitting room in their designs. But the traditional middle-class house was still specifically designed for the maintenance and separation of two worlds under one roof, on the model of the country house.

While the fashionable aesthetic of the new home had become simpler and more austere, more self-consciously 'artistic', popular taste continued in the tradition of the fringes and stuffed chester-fields of the Victorian parlour. The home was a showcase for the consumables whose market continued to expand with the speed of the Industrial Revolution. Walter Pritchett, with his fancy goods showroom in London, knew his customers: 'Their very houses looked overfed with hangings, bric-a-brac and cushions . . . They were, above all, a race who draped themselves.'[18] Fringes, antima-cassars and other Victorian dust-gatherers were out of fashion among the Aesthetes – even considered morally degenerate by the champions of the new call to authenticity of materials and truth to function. Nonetheless, the late-Victorians and Edwardians were on the whole still wedded to bits and pieces: the fashionable ladies' morning room still contained a mass of little tables and displays of trinkets. 'There may be a hundred or more of these,' wrote Eric Horne of his days as a footman in the 1890s, 'consisting of minia-ture silver ships, coaches and horses, scent bottles, cigarette cases, inkstands and candlesticks, hand mirrors, comfit boxes, in fact miniature silver and gold ornaments by the dozen.'[19] Wildlife, flow-ers and classical scenes were fashionable decorative features in pictures or textiles. William Morris's wallpaper designs were very popular among those of an Aesthetic bent, as were Persian rugs and friezes of birds or mythical figures or beasts.

Elizabeth Banks, a journalist from New Jersey who posed as a housemaid for a series of undercover articles in the late 1890s on London life, started her investigations with an interview in 'a pretty little house in Kensington' with the name 'Ellsmore Lodge' made out in shining brass on the door. The dining room was furnished in the latest style, 'covered with Japanese matting, with a large crumb-cloth in the centre, and other rugs scattered about. The furniture was of beautiful old English oak and leather and many pictures of game, fruit, fish, horses and dogs hung on the walls.'[20] It was a time of experimentation in interior design: there was a new emphasis on the home as a vehicle for the expression of individual taste and style – with often startling results. When fourteen-year-old Margaret

Thomas, wearing her mother's cut-down grey dress, went to be interviewed for her first job in service in Portland Square, London, she was amazed by the morning room, painted in pale blue with, hanging from the ceiling, dozens of golden cages full of canaries.[21]

In contrast to the Victorians, who liked to keep the windows of the house closed and the rooms in a year-round, coal-grimed fug, turn-of-the-century scientific discoveries about the spread of germs and disease brought with them a new evangelism on the benefits of fresh air. 'The first thing the servants should do in the morning, before they begin their work,' wrote Mrs Eustace Miles in *The Ideal Home and its Problems*, in 1911, 'is to open all the windows wide, and let in the sweet early morning air. This refreshes their minds as well as their bodies, and drives out all impurities in consequence of the shut-in rooms and closed doors of the night.'[22] The home became viewed as a laboratory for the new science of hygiene and health. The work of nineteenth-century scientists and supporters of germ theory, such as Joseph Lister, with his pioneering work on antiseptics, and Louis Pasteur, the microbiologist who developed vaccines, had led to a mania for sterilisation – increasingly interpreted by housework pundits not only as a key to public health but also to private virtue and inner purity. The *Cassell's Household Guide* warned that dust was 'impregnated with millions of more or less deadly microbes'. Germs were 'disease seeds', the unseen enemy, 'breeding' in mould, bad food or unhealthy bodies and passed by unsavoury human contact or stale air. A public health pioneer recommended a mass cleansing of 'every sink and drain, every waste pipe and outlet, every gully-hole and exhaust channel, every lavatory and bathroom, every dustbin and refuse receiver, and every outhouse that provides [germs] with a central point from which to radiate'.[23]

The division between the rich and the poor, 'the great unwashed', was now marked in the public mind even more clearly by the gulf between their abilities to keep themselves rigorously clean. The poor, of course, crushed into tiny living spaces with shared latrines and water sources, had the disadvantage and were therefore viewed as spreaders of disease. Cleanliness joined thrift and temperance as

one of the disciplines on the path to virtue. 'Where dirt has been
driven out, purity and enlightenment have found a congenial home,'
wrote Phillis Browne, a late-nineteenth-century housekeeping
authority, about Port Sunlight, the workers' model village created
by soap magnate Lord Lever near Liverpool.[24] The boiling of milk,
water, vegetables (a minimum of ten minutes was recommended by
most domestic science textbooks) and laundry was the first step in
the battle against the deadly microbial horde. Families often travelled with their own portable sterilisers, and it was considered
prudent to take one's own silver, linen and china as a precaution
against infections from tableware in public restaurants. White, the
colour of purity, became the choice for bathrooms and kitchens as
it showed up every speck of dirt. Nursemaids and nannies had to be
particularly vigilant: 'baths, basins and other toilet requisites need
constant attention and great stress should be laid on the fact that the
cloths used for each thing should be kept for that and that alone.
Each cloth should be clearly marked and have a separate peg, so
that there is no fear of their getting mixed.'[25]

'Mrs A. D.', a former nursemaid at Charlton-on-Otmoor, in
Oxfordshire, had to scrub all the children's quarters every day with
milk and water; and then 'when the eggman was expected I had to
go and help wash all the eggs. Had a box on the ears if I didn't do it
properly.'[26] One woman, in her first job as a kitchen-maid in 1905,
had been reduced to tears when, as her granddaughter recalled: 'Her
mistress being on one occasion unkind enough to bring a knife
down on my grandmother's fingers for touching with her fingers, at
the time of preparation, meat the children were to eat.'[27] Among the
duties of lady's-maids was the nightly washing of their employer's
loose change, the coins having been handled by who knows how
many undesirables before it made its way into her purse.

The new subject of 'Domestic Science' was taught in state elemen-
tary schools from the 1890s, serving the dual function of providing
a training in hygiene and giving a gloss of science to the job of
domestic service in the hope that more girls could be persuaded to
take up the work. Textbooks stressed the importance of fighting the
bacterial invaders of the safe and healthy home. Regularity was the

key to conquest and its imposition the aim of every housewife who saw herself fighting a daily battle against the chaotic individualism of her servants. The regular life was as much an exhortation to moral order as to physical cleanliness. 'Disorder can only be avoided by daily routine and the deliberate determination not to have the routine interfered with,' in the words of one textbook. Instruction as to the frequency, duration and regularity of healthful housekeeping habits amounted almost to mania. Books of advice offered strict guidelines on how often one should wash hair, windows, carpets, stair-rails and fingernails: absolutely no item of body or home was left to chance. In 1910 a science degree for women was introduced at King's College, London, which would, reported Lucy Soulsby, the author of *Home is Best*, 'bear on the likely needs of a woman's future life, whether as Householder, Housekeeper, Inspector or Municipal Worker'.

This new science of domestic life was designed in part to give women power over their daily lives, to send them out in the world brandishing a knowledge that would endow domestic work with dignity and scientific purpose. But it did not obviate the need for servants: it reinforced it. The students of domestic science classes were destined to become domestics; those women who took the science degree at King's College were destined to manage domestics. Although Mrs Soulsby and the other champions of domestic science rightly recognised that women needed control over the maintenance, budgeting and cleaning of the home, this was chiefly in order that they might better instruct others to do the work for them. Moreover, by stressing the 'beauty' of skilled housework, they hoped that its superior womanly qualities would make it a more appealing career for the more educated working-class girl. 'As yet, both in village and town,' wrote Mrs Miles, 'there is a crying need in England for sensible women and girls who know the elements of cooking, hygiene, care of children.'[28]

Chapter 3

'A Seat in the Hall'

Appearances always started at the front door, its doorstep buffed to a shine by a housemaid pounding the step with a 'donkey' – whitening – stone at first light. The front door was the portcullis of the Edwardian house: tradesmen and other necessary undesirables went round the back, through an entrance created especially for them, or down the steps into the basement; only the initiated were permitted to step over the threshold into the hall. The footman only opened the door if there were more than one footman kept; the butler opened the door if there were only one footman (or none) and the parlourmaid opened the door if there were neither a butler nor a footman. These were display servants and were therefore chosen with an eye for their physical attributes.

The Duties of Servants in 1890 stressed that 'only a girl possessed of a very attractive appearance, tall rather than short, smart in her dress and deferential in her manners should undertake the duty' of opening the door. In households like Mrs Praga's, where the maid was a house-parlourmaid – double the work for less money – in the afternoon, the time of day when paying calls was customary, the girls would change to black dresses with white cuffs, caps and collars to open the door to callers and, later, to wait at dinner. The single-handed girl playing two parts had to be always on the alert, as 'Mrs A.' remembered of her days in service to an elderly doctor in Oxfordshire: 'I was house-parlourmaid and no matter where I was I used to have to listen and all the time that if Dr P was going out, I used to have to go down . . . I used to have to go down to help him on with his coat and hat.'[1] All this theatre cost the more modest household dear. Every inch of material for her maid's uniform was measured and accounted for; 'not without a pang' did Mrs Praga therefore forgo the trailing streamers ('the sinuous, floating fila- ments of a jellyfish' as William Plomer described them in his novel *Curious Relations*, his hero Lord Portmeirion lunging hopelessly to clutch at them[2]) that would have adorned the fashionable parlour- maid's cap. Neither could she afford to pay for stature. For £5 a year, Mrs Praga had to make do with her house-parlourmaid Mary who was, alas, 'only of average tallness'. On the other hand, as Mary's employer noted with relief, this meant she 'did not require very large aprons'.

Elizabeth Banks found when she went for interviews that the height question was taken seriously and not always simply for appearances' sake. Mrs Green in Marylebone Road told 'Lizzie' that she would not do because she was too short for practical use. 'You see, a parlourmaid must have long arms in order to reach things on the table, and a housemaid should also be tall, else how can she put the linen away on the top shelves and wash the looking-glasses in the drawing room?' Eric Horne, whose experience of service was at the higher end of the scale, wrote: 'Did anyone see a cross-eyed servant? No, they are as scarce as dead donkeys. A servant must be absolutely perfect in form, disposition and action. Short girls were destined to be firmly below stairs or employed in poorer households.' 'I never got any higher than a house-parlourmaid,' reflected one maid, because 'I wasn't tall enough.'[3] James Hughes was overlooked as a footman in a household which liked to dress their footman in knee breeches and powder, 'cos I weren't big enough'.[4]

It was hardly surprising that most servants, some of them formerly of the orphanage or the workhouse, poorly fed and many barely pubescent, fell far short of the ideal height requirement for front-of-house work. The extent to which Britain's poor were stunted by disease and malnourishment was made fully apparent after the outbreak of the Second Boer War, when recruiting offices reported that a majority of working-class recruits were unfit for active service, their diet consisting for the most part of little more than the 'staples' of bread, dripping and tea; leftovers, sold off cheap, constituted rare treats for the poorest, including bruised fruit, broken biscuits and offcuts of meat. Lillian Westall found work as a maid-of-all-work almost impossible: just carting buckets of hot water up and down stairs needed almost the strength of a grown man – and a single maid in a small household would need to carry an estimated three tons of water a week. 'This sort of work needed the stamina of an ox and years of semi-starvation meant I hadn't this sort of strength.'[5]

Acute social antennae were required from the servant whose job it was to open the door: they needed to understand the details of dress, voice or manner, for instance, which marked the gentleman from the almost-gentleman or the respectable from the straightfor-wardly vulgar. The caste rules of admission were complex and only the properly bohemian or the absolutely aristocratic could flout them convincingly. The romantic novelist Elinor Glyn, in 1892 about to embark on marriage to a spendthrift landowner, was briefed early on by her prospective mother-in-law: 'Army or naval officers, diplomats or clergymen might be invited to lunch or dinner. The vicar might be invited regularly to Sunday lunch or supper if he was a gentleman. Doctors and solicitors might be invited to garden parties, though never, of course, to lunch or dinner. Anyone engaged in the arts, the stage, trade or commerce, no matter how well connected, could not be asked to the house at all.'[6]

Mrs Edith Waldemar Leverton, author of *Servants and their Duties* (1912), listed some of the pitfalls for the unwary servant. 'Most mistresses intimate to their servants whether they are prepared to receive visitors or not, but in many cases it is necessary for the domestic to use his or her own discretion, as to whether the lady of the house is willing to receive the caller in question. This is not always easy to do. I have had a gentleman, canvassing for an order of tea, shown into the midst of a friendly little tea party in the drawing room; likewise have I had a guest whose appearance was a trifle "horsey" refused admission to a reception because my maid mistook him for his own groom.'[7]

Mr Brownlow, whose wife in 1892 employed 'Lizzie' Banks as a parlourmaid, was shocked to learn that Lizzie was unable always to spot at a glance who was a friend of the family and who a creditor. 'Mr Brownlow met me in the hall, and said: "Lizzie, do you know the difference between a friend of the family and a bill-collector?"' To her reply that she thought she did: 'Well, now, you must not let any collectors get into this house for the next month. I'm in Paris, see? Don't wait until they tell you what they want, but you must be able to spot them on sight and say at once that I'm not in London. That last girl of ours got me in more trouble by her stupidity in letting tax-gatherers and dressmakers and tailors into the house. Said she didn't know how she was going to tell what they wanted when they wouldn't give their business. To be a good parlourmaid you must be a mind-reader.'[8]

To accommodate callers whose purpose was not social – a seam-stress come for a dress-fitting perhaps, or a salesman, or a secretary waiting for an interview – the hall chair, which was small, hard and especially designed for the caller who had to sit and wait rather than be ushered straight in, was lined against the wall. 'If you consider them at all doubtful,' was Mrs Waldemar Leverton's advice to a parlourmaid, 'give them a seat in the hall.'[9] These little chairs were decorative because they had to function as adornment but they were rarely upholstered and were therefore impossible to loll on, demanding the straight back and appearance of slight constraint that immediately denoted the visitor there on sufferance; or some-one perhaps of the in-between classes listed as 'hall-chair users' by an American authority on interior design: 'messenger types, book agents, the census man, and the bereaved lady who offers us soap'.[10]

By the turn of the twentieth century, the practice of paying social calls was largely confined to the period between three and six in the afternoon, although to further complicate matters, they were still generally known as morning calls. During this period, the parlour-maid had to change out of the standard print or plain dress she used for tidying and cleaning the drawing rooms in the morning and, in time to serve lunch, into a dark-coloured dress with white cuffs and collar – and, of course, a cap, with or without streamers. Twelve-year-old Eveline Askwith, working for a vicar in Harrogate in 1903, was required to substitute her white morning aprons for embroidery-trimmed ones when opening the door to afternoon callers.[11]

The rules on calling were fiendishly complex. If the lady or gentleman making the call arrived by carriage, they had to send their servant to ask if the lady of the house was at home; if they arrived on foot, they went themselves to the door. If they were told that the lady was not at home, the visitors left cards. A lady visitor left three cards, one of her own and two of her husband's – for the husband called on both the master and the mistress but she only called on the mistress. If there was no-one at home or receiving visitors, then the visitor's card was left on a silver tray in the hall. The parlourmaid, butler or footman wore white gloves to touch the card and always presented it to their mistress on a salver. The author of an 1896 manual on etiquette hinted at the near-sacred nature of the calling card – 'these magic bits of paste-board' – reminding her readers that the card is 'made to take the place of oneself'.[12] A woman who in 1908 was a servant in a two-servant home, remembered in an interview sixty years later the elaborate charade of her impecunious mistress's 'At Homes' on the first Tuesday of every month: 'And the funny thing was they used to leave their cards on a tray on the hall table, I think it was – I don't know why – but one of her own cards and two of her husband's – visiting cards – so that each lady would leave three. Anything very important they used to leave there so that people could see it.'[13]

If the mistress was At Home and receiving, the servant led the visitor to the drawing room and announced them formally. A gentleman carried his hat, stick and gloves upstairs with him: 'To leave his hat in the hall would be considered a liberty and in very bad taste,' according to *The Manners and Rules of Good Society*. It was not done to linger or to settle in for a long conversation and calls, probably to the relief of all involved, were not supposed to last longer than fifteen minutes. Conversation was light; other forms of entertainment such as producing photographs or one's own artistic efforts was considered bad form. Tea, the only refreshment on offer, would be served at 4.30 on the dot.[14]

Small activities filled the daily life of the Edwardian lady, many of them diversions, some of them accomplishments. 'I play seven instruments and all of them perfectly!' was the furious retort of Mrs Binns when asked by a housemaid if it were true that 'ladies had nothing to do all day but lie on a sofa and read novels'.[15] Housemaid Gertie, employed on the Somerleyton estate, Suffolk, used to polish the bedroom fireplaces in the middle of the morning while her mistress, Lady Somerleyton, lay in bed watching her. 'She had curtains all round her bed. You didn't speak unless she spoke to you. I used to be terrified but you got used to it. I can see her now. This would be at ten, half past ten – she'd lay in bed half the day, 'cause she was old then. Downstairs she had a boudoir – that was her sitting room, that was all blue and white, beautiful.'[16] Then there were the charity jumble sales, whist-drives and bazaars. Bridge-playing became so fashionable in Edwardian drawing rooms that for many it became an obsession, and it filtered down to the servants' hall where a little light gambling on the bridge table became a well-known fixture of the housekeeper's room where the upper-servants gathered: a 'sweet pastime of the Upper-Ten', in the words of a contemporary song.

For the aspiring middle classes it was crucial to master the art of the dinner party, for cementing one's place in the world or for currying favour on your husband's behalf with his work colleagues. They were also a major expenditure. The simplest Edwardian dinner party included two kinds of soup, two fish dishes, two or three meat dishes, two or three savouries and the same number of sweets. The pundits recognised that dinner parties were prickly social territory. 'People are very thin-skinned and rather touchy on the subject, and a guest would prefer to eat of a dozen bad dinners at his friend's table than to offer the faintest suggestion as to how those dinners might be improved.'[17] Most importantly of all, everything had to be in order in the servants' hall; a clumsy or inexperienced servant could throw the whole enterprise.

At Tapton House in Chesterfield, Mrs Markham kept detailed notes of dinner party successes and failures so that 'Lessons Might Be Learned'. On one occasion, for example, she noted: 'Another tiresome dinner spoiled entirely by bad WAITING ... plates COLD TOO to add to annoyance.'[18] For a single-handed parlour-maid, serving a dinner party was a nightmare. Lizzie Banks had 'proudly mastered the knack of folding serviettes in the shape of a boat, but try as I would I found myself unable to manage a cork-screw'.[19] Lillian Westall remembered: 'We had strict instructions never to touch a plate with our fingers, always they had to be held by serviettes. The plates were examined keenly for finger marks and they came back at once if one was found.'[20]

Elsie, the gentle, sweet-natured house-parlourmaid in the Arnold Bennett story *Elsie and the Child*, trying to be both invisible and silent as she stacks the plates at her socially aspiring employer's dinner party, is thrown into a sweating agony when she accidentally spills a drop of red wine on the tablecloth. 'Another dreadful moment! For some time afterwards she could see nothing but the red stigmata on the white tablecloth, and she could see them even through the mound of salt under which the master buried them.'[21] Elsie, like so many general servants, finds mastering the rules of presentation almost impossible, because they have been devised to be upheld by legions of staff and to be therefore inimitable in the single-servant household. A vast array of implements, each one designed for a particular purpose, had to be memorised: celery goblets, cucumber trays, custard glasses, muffineers, long spoons for prising out the marrow from bones ('How I laugh today when I see them with the dog, licking out the marrowbone ...!' declared a cook, Miss Ellery, fifty years later[22]).

Silver knick-knacks and tableware made a resplendent show on the dining tables of the fashionable home. A bride's wedding presents might include bon-bon baskets with matching spoons, pickle forks, sandwich boxes and menu stands – all in silver. The table would be decorated with vases of flowers, an ornamental cup perhaps in the centre; an array of silver animals often disguised other functions – a hound and a fox filled with salt and pepper or a silver bear holding a mustard pot. Folded napkins came in many variations but were commonly upright in a mitre shape; there were no napkin rings. Sometimes there would be decorative holders beside each place with the name card in each. A large dinner party might require every place to be set with twelve pieces of silver. Vegetables (never fewer than four kinds) were generally served in elaborate forms that hid almost completely their original nature. Tomatoes were skinned, scooped out and cut into flower shapes; game chips were cut into perfectly matching circles; the hearts of globe artichokes were trimmed into perfect spheres; boiled spinach was pureed and then, using moulds, arranged in perfect pyramids. Fashionable meat dishes were often expertly arranged after cooking to look as though their raw material was still alive: rabbits propped up with wires after roasting to look as if they were standing on their hind legs with their ears up; lobster mousse was time-consumingly moulded into intricate pink lobster shapes.

Mrs Praga, who counted the cost of each daily mutton chop, recognised the importance of the dinner party in aiding her husband's career. She suggested meticulous pre-planning. 'Thoroughly dainty cooking of the French bourgeoisie sort' was the desirable outcome, but each dinner party resigned the Pragas to days of austerity to return their budget to balance. Large houses, however, particularly in the country, both upstairs and downstairs, consumed vast quantities. Gertrude Pitt in Buckinghamshire went to work for a house where half a pound of butter went with the potatoes at every serving and peas never had less than half a pint of cream poured over them. At Tapton House, according to Mrs Markham's account books, twelve people sat down in 1893 to 'a midday meal which consisted of gravy soup, turbot with lobster sauce, sweetbreads macedoine, soubise cutlets, haunch of venison, calf's head, four grouse, neapolitan cake and jelly with fruit'. Her daughter Violet Markham was later to look back longingly on 'generous days when you took a pint of cream, a pound of butter and a dozen eggs as a mere preliminary to the business in hand'.[23] Even in the more restrained atmosphere of Rectory House Farm, Taplow, Alice Osbourn's diary records that in one week in 1906, the

Baldwin household got through seventy-seven eggs in five days. The Marquess of Ailesbury's cook produced breakfasts every day that included marbled rabbit, brawn, pigs' feet and galantine. She 'often skinned thirty rooks before breakfast for a rook pie for dinner'. Even in a medium-sized country house like Pilgrims Hall in Essex, home of a prosperous solicitor, James Lawrence, and his family, an ordinary weekday breakfast consisted of 'variations on eggs and bacon, kippers, dried haddock, fishcakes, kedgeree and kidneys'. (More than half a century later, Lesley Lawrence marvelled at the quantities of food they had consumed then and yet how rarely one saw a fat child – 'they were regarded as freaks poor things'.[24])

For servants in households such as these, there were meals below stairs beyond anything they could possibly have imagined before they went into service. When Rose Gibbs, working as a scullery-maid for the first time in Box Hill, Surrey, saw the food laid out in the servants' hall, she 'just stood and cried, wondering if my mother and father had any food. The butter was made in the estate dairy, the vegetables were homegrown, and the fruit in the summer included strawberries, raspberries and loganberries, peaches and apricots.'[25] Charles Washington, a second footman in a large country house, once accompanied Maisie, the stillroom maid, to her home in Wales where her miner father had been laid off with illness. The family was so poor that they were living off only bread and potatoes. 'Feeling rich', Washington bought them two pounds of scrag-end of beef, at which Maisie's mother wept while her father fell to his knees and gave thanks to God.[26]

Chapter 4

Centralising the Egg Yolks

'Don't you think George that a few sheep, with lambs gambolling about, would make the fields look furnished?' enquired a duchess to her butler, Albert Thomas. 'So I saw to it that the sheep and lambs were there by the following morning.'[1]

Whimsical requirements out of season and out of sense have always been a perk of the rich. It seems often to have been the case that the grander the employer and the more eccentric the request, the more indulgently they were viewed by their servants. The lack of any practical common sense, the batty obsessions that were nourished and exaggerated by time and leisure, were sources of amusement as well as irritation. Many servants seem to have looked on their employers with a kind of pity for their deficiencies when it came to the skills of basic survival. The butler Ernest King's first employer Charles Chichester liked to dabble in cooking and often ventured into the kitchen to prepare idiosyncratic meals for his servants: 'How hurt he was', that none of them wanted to eat his 'fawn pie or, during Lent, his salted cod soaked in a rainbutt'.[2] Every year, Chichester would invite all forty-eight of the cab drivers of Barnstaple to a dinner, cooked by himself, to thank them for ferrying so many of his guests from the station to the house.

The grander flights of theatrical fancy, however, are only the entertaining extreme of daily lives conducted with a degree of metronomic regularity that sometimes bordered on the obsessive. Small habits became magnified into neuroses and an eye for detail easily tipped into a mania for control. King George V, who made a fetish of order, correct dress and punctuality, had all the rooms in his homes photographed so that no object could ever be displaced by a careless housemaid. Waldorf Astor could not bear to drink milk from any cow but his own – so the cow accompanied the family when they travelled to Scotland by train. Eric Horne's first employers, the strange Gladstone twins, nephews of the Prime Minister, lived in the same house, in different wings, drove in different carriages, hardly spoke to one another, ate at the same table but were served different food – always fish. One of them went for a walk every day, whatever the weather, and always set out wearing five overcoats, as he grew hotter flinging them off one by one to be picked up by a footman following at a discreet distance behind him. The Duke of Portland, his inclinations intensified by extreme solitude into madness, required a chicken to be constantly turning on a spit in the kitchens, day and night, so that if he should ever feel like a plateful it was ready for him.

The American heiress Consuelo Vanderbilt, trapped from 1895 inside a chilly marriage to the ninth Duke of Marlborough, left a memorable portrait of her early years at Blenheim Palace, in which the maintenance of display, directed into minutiae of a crushing self-indulgence, had become for both the Duke and his servants an end in itself. The Duke was obsessed by minute details that concerned his own status. Meals, course after course served in near silence, were a particular ordeal. 'Considering,' the Duchess was told by her husband, 'that it is the only pleasure one can count on having three times a day, every day of one's life, a well-ordered meal is of prime importance.' At her end of the table, the Duchess took up knitting to kill the boredom. 'We seemed to spend hours discussing the merit of a dish or the bouquet of a vintage. The maître d'hôtel had become an important person to whom at meals most of my husband's conversation was addressed.' Meals for just the two of them were served by at least eight members of staff – and a menu of seventeen different choices for each course produced at every meal. 'How I learned to dread and hate those dinners, how ominous and wearisome they loomed at the end of a long day. They were served with all the accustomed ceremony, but once a course had been passed the servants retired to the hall; the door was closed and only a ring of the bell placed before Marlborough summoned them. He had a way of piling food on his plate; the next move was to push the plate away, together with knives, forks, spoons and glasses – all this in considered gestures which took a long time; then he backed his chair away from the table, crossed one leg over the other and endlessly twirled the ring on his little finger . . . after a quarter of an hour he would suddenly return to earth, or perhaps I should say to food, and begin to eat very slowly, usually complaining that the food was cold!'[3]

It was not only the very rich whose perspective was skewed by habit. All sorts of desires become elevated to necessities when there is someone to do the hard labour of realising them for you, and these daily routines are rendered almost surreal in the accounts of those who suffered them. 'Mrs B.', a housemaid in Oxfordshire, had to make the beds afresh with new linen every day: 'if you made one little crease on a pillowcase that was thrown aside – "Her Ladyship can't sleep with creases on a pillowcase" – so I had to be careful how I put the pillowcases on, I had to learn that bit'.[4] The reminiscences of cooks and kitchen-maids of the period are full of the tedium of presentation; of learning, for example, the common breakfast requirement of centralising the egg yolks. Eveline Askwith, in her vicar's household in Harrogate, was one of many who had to master the art of stirring the breakfast eggs continuously while they were boiling – so that the yolks were positioned perfectly in the middle of the white; if they were off-centre, they were sent back, and the process started all over again. Eveline's mistress's dog was fed sponge fingers at 5 p.m. on the dot. Ernest King worked for a couple who 'had eight chipolatas every Sunday morning for breakfast. She would have three and he five. She would arrange the sausages in a triangle, then take a boiled egg and cut it in half with a letter opener. She thought a knife wasn't good enough, the blade too wide . . . Her husband would cut his chipolatas into inch lengths, then pick them up and dip them in his egg.' No wonder Ernest King concluded 'that to cope with this and other eccentricities I should need a course in psychiatry'[5].

Even Thomas Hardy, born in Dorset poverty, developed a fixation in later life for cobwebs. His parlourmaid, Ellen Titteringham, described him as 'a quiet, shabby little sparrow', incorrigibly stingy, who patrolled the night-time corridors of his house, Max Gate, in the 1920s with a lantern, searching for webs she might have missed. 'A gloom filled the entire atmosphere,' she remembered, unsurprisingly.[6] Arnold Bennett's Elsie, accepting completely her subsidiary role in the theatre of the Rastes' life, nonetheless wondered at the curious and time-consuming demands of her middle-class employers: 'A strange caste; they were unhappy if they could not have a bath every day! And they would not eat simply; their meals were made as complicated as a church service, with all sorts of cloths, glasses, cutlery and silver which had to be arranged in a very particular way.'[7]

Time-keeping was adhered to with military precision: in fact it was the hallmark of the well-run home. 'The besetting fear of my debutante self,' remembered Lady Cynthia Asquith, who was presented at court in 1907, 'is that I should be late for dinner.' Half an hour after the sounding of the dressing gong, the guests had to be assembled for dinner itself: 'No joke to find yourself the impatiently waited-for last-comer.'[8] Gongs for lunch went twice with ten minutes between them – to give a space for hand-washing. Most houses still had daily prayers for family and servants: 'About quarter past ten, the bell rang, and wherever you were in the house we had to run to the top and put a clean apron on, you used to run downstairs very quickly and we all had to line up in the drawing room.'[9]

For children, sticking to a daily schedule was considered part of the vital work of building character. 'Everything happened to the minute,' remembered nursemaid Sarah Sedgwick, in 1900 one of five nursery staff dedicated solely to the welfare of a toddler and a baby in a house near Doncaster (and in the winter a footman 'who came up every two hours to make up the fires').[10] 'At ten sharp we were out with the prams, and pushed them until half-past twelve. Luncheon was one o'clock. Then from two until half past three another walk with the prams, the nursemaids in their customary going-outside uniforms.' Fresh air, light exercise (though generally weighed down with layers of elaborate and uncomfortable clothing) and bland but wholesome food at regular intervals, marked the hours of the middle- and upper-class child's domestic day. Food for children under six was generally pureed or minced; vegetables and meat were strained through sieves until almost liquid. Quantities of cream, buttermilk and milky puddings were considered far more nutritious than spice or flavour, so rice pudding, semolina, junkets and milk jellies featured prominently on the menu of an Edwardian child. Tea in the afternoon of course was groaning with cakes and biscuits and, always to be eaten first, 'little tiny slivers of bread and butter that you could blow away just like that'.[11]

Children, who in previous generations had been viewed as little more than adults in formation, now inhabited a world of their own, their health and moral welfare monitored daily by an army of ever-vigilant nannies and nursemaids. Uniforms for servants in charge of children reflected the preoccupation with purity; starched, white, spotless, they resembled those of Florence Nightingale's regiment of nurses: 'In the house we always wore white, even white shoes and stockings, outside we wore grey costumes with white blouses and black shoes and stockings.'[12] Whatever the season, the wealthy child never wore the same clothes in the morning as they wore in the afternoon, and of course there was a complete change from top to bottom when the dressing-up to go downstairs took place, when they were brought down to be presented briefly to their parents ('from that separate sphere, the nursery, they would stump in their sashes and necklaces of coral or amber beads'[13]) before returning upstairs and undressing again to go to bed. And more than that, clothes were rarely worn twice but had to be laundered in the evening, frills starched and ribbons taken out of the elaborate underwear and ironed separately before being threaded back in. It was not the monotonous mincing and pureeing of special foods or even the endless two-hour morning and afternoon walks in all weathers (fresh air being an article of faith for the upbringing of the Edwardian child); it was, remembered Sarah Sedgwick, 'the way the children had to be turned out that made so much work'.[14]

Mrs Panton, who took the brisk view that a new baby is 'a profound nuisance to its relations at the very first', recommended outsourcing childcare to professionals at the earliest opportunity. Working-class women, almost certainly mothers themselves (by the end of the nineteenth century it was estimated that the average working-class married woman aged forty had borne between seven and fifteen children) had for generations been the wet-nurses and nursemaids to yet more generations of children. But as the urban middle-class home began to seal itself off from the world of the poor during the nineteenth century, these women became viewed as less than suitable as primary child-rearers. The enormous expansion in the number of toiling little nursemaids, children themselves, who worked in the middle-class home, were testament to the growing distance between the daily life of middle-class parents and their children: there were 5,937 nursemaids employed in 1851; by 1871 the number had risen to 75,491. But nursemaids were the servants of the nannies; and nannies of a more professional type became increasingly desirable, qualifications beyond childminding being sought after.

The establishment in 1892 of the Norland Institute raised the status of their nursery nurse and nanny to the level of educational mentor and moral guide. The Institute's first principal, Isabel Sharman, observing that 'nowhere but in England does the child live such a separate and distinct nursery life',[15] looked to the teachings of the German educationalist Friedrich Froebel to inject some helpful educational play into the rigid routines of the English child. Recruited among girls not quite academic enough to become teachers, Norland students were always to be considered, at the insistence of the Institute's founder Mrs Emily Ward, 'gentlewomen'. They would not eat with the servants and were instructed that on arrival in a new home they should place their silver hairbrushes ostentatiously on their chest of drawers to make evident their superiority to the servants' hall. Norland nurses did not clean, wipe, launder or sweep: their concern was solely the tending of their charges' moral and psychological development.* Nonetheless, the work clearly crossed into domestic labour, without this being specific, and Nurse Christine Tisdall in 1895 received a glowing reference from an employer in Edinburgh who praised her abilities 'to perform the duties of a servant in the spirit of a lady and without causing friction in the household'.[16]

Mrs Beeton, whose *Household Management* was on the shelf in most kitchens, had once likened the housewife to 'the commander of an army'. Routine, like a military campaign, kept chaos at bay and spread its benevolent order on both mistress and servant. Or so the thinking went. In H. G. Wells's short novel *Marriage*, the newlywed Marjorie Pope dreams of her ideal home, so much more efficiently run and well appointed than her parents' disorderly, frugal gentility: 'Everything in the place was bright and good and abundant, the servants were easy and well mannered and free of resentment, and one didn't have to be sharp about the eggs and things at breakfast in the morning, or go without.'[17] In Marjorie's dream home, regularity, provided by obedient servants, is comfort, but it is also, she believes, an aid to her own moral development, bringing out the best in her, preventing her being 'sharp'. In Marjorie Pope's case, trying to achieve the perfectly regular home eventually drags her into a spiral of debt and disaster. The imprisoning standards that denoted the well-managed Edwardian house were often a mere façade behind which lay financial struggle and social insecurity.

---

* Norland nurses were also responsible, in 1907, for the first crèche for working-class children, enabling working women, mainly from the laundry industry, to leave their children all day in professional care. The first crèche was in Hammersmith, London, at the reasonable cost to their mothers of four pence a child or seven pence for two. When they opened a second in nearby Acton, they had 2,436 attendances in six months.

Chapter 5

Popinjays and Mob Caps

It was important to the Edwardian employer that a servant should be immediately recognisable as a servant. In the mid-nineteenth century, with the emergence of cheap, factory-made textiles narrowing the gap between the appearance of the gentry and that of their employees, the maintenance of a visible distinction was seen as crucial. It had been customary since the early nineteenth century for employers to give butlers and other menservants their cast-off clothes, but always at the same time to make sure that the resulting outfit was never quite 'correct' – that the tie was not quite right with the coat or that the coat was slightly out of fashion. Thus the butler looked like a gentleman's gentleman but not a gentleman in his own right. Lady's-maids were warned in *The Duties of Servants* 'never to dress out of your station, nor attempt to rival the ladies of the family. This is of more importance for you to guard against than if you were in any other station as a servant: for your knowledge of stuffs, trimmings and fashions, gives you the means of doing this more successfully than any other servant.'

Any attempt to cross the social boundaries was viewed with hostility. Nineteenth-century publications are full of comic caricatures of servant girls who look ridiculous when they dress up in the bustled and crinolined fashions of their employers. Jane Carlyle in the 1840s found amusing an anecdote of her maid who went out one Sunday wearing a makeshift bustle put together from three kitchen dusters. The fashion-conscious servant became a byword in popular culture for garishness and vulgarity, for aping the lady but ending up looking a fright. When one Edwardian writer wanted to mock victims of extreme fashion, she described them as looking 'like crazy housemaids'.[1] Long after it was not only common but customary for society women to use cosmetics, to cut their hair and raise their hemlines, servant girls who dressed in the latest styles were derided for getting above themselves. At the same time, and in the complicated and excluding way that rules have of evolving sub-sections of the rule book that are even more exclusive, it was assumed a mark of the gentry that they were above the considera-tion of mere clothes: the shabbiness of well-cut clothes was more often than not a hallmark of inner distinction. This worked rather better with men's costume; women were more ambivalent about the appeal of threadbare. One Bonfire Night, Edith Sitwell's grand-mother, Lady Londesborough, seated in a bathchair, with her wild white hair and black clothes, was mistaken by a hapless visiting curate for a 'guy' and he deposited a penny in her lap. This was met with outrage: Lady Londesborough made it a rule never to speak to her servants directly, so she told the footmen, through an interme-diary, that the episode must never be spoken of below stairs.

All servants wore some kind of distinguishing uniform. Even the poorest farm maids were garbed in a herden apron made from old flour sacking that had been washed and boiled. Edith Watkins, daughter of a shepherd in Knighton, Herefordshire, went to work for a local farmer's wife around the turn of the century. She wore her own clothes for work – red flannel petticoats, thick black stock-ings and boots – and a 'very warm' apron. 'You weren't smart unless you'd got a nice apron made of flour sacks: they'd be white when you boiled them, because the flour was white and the sacks were white, beautiful . . . and you were thought to be very smart and very industrious if you wore a nice clean herden apron.'[2]

Regulations on clothing were among the most resented of the small slights that made service increasingly unpopular. It had become, for example, customary to instruct maids not to wear hats to church on Sundays but to wear instead identifying bonnets in case they should be mistaken for one of the family. It was a practice deeply resented: if there was one place a servant should have expected to know he was equal to anyone it was in church. When James Hughes worked as a footman at Gorstage Hall in Cheshire, the maids used to kick their regulation bonnets 'up and down the passageway when we come out of church'.[3] Yet the distinctions were usually as rigidly maintained in church as they were in the house, the staff of grander houses often filing in to take up their place in the pews in order of rank. Miss Spence, a maid at Rendlesham Hall, Suffolk before the First World War, remembered how the staff were instructed to wear 'very plain clothes' to church and how 'furious' Lord Rendlesham was when he spotted a stillroom maid wearing a hat rather than a bonnet.[4] In Northumberland, Lizzie Grange's mistress even instructed her maids to wear their uniform on the train, 'because, they reckoned, the mistress wouldn't like anyone to think that we were the daughters. One of the housemaids said: "You know what's the matter, it's because we're better looking than what the daughters is".'[5]

Few personal idiosyncrasies of style were permitted: facial hair for menservants was discouraged even when their employers sported the latest elaborate fashions in whiskers. Eric Horne had few regrets about his long career as a butler, but in old age he reflected wistfully that in 'all those years in gentleman's service, I had an intense desire to grow a moustache, which of course we were not allowed to do'.[6] Attempts at giving the ubiquitous print dress a few modish additions were certainly not allowed. '[My lady] imposed three conditions on me if I entered her service. First I was to take the pads out of my hair (large chignons being then the fashion); second, I was to cut the tail off my dress (long dresses were then worn); third I was to wear aprons with bibs to them (which were never worn those days).'[7]

It was the custom, in many houses up until the Second World War, to present maids at Christmas with a bolt of cloth with which they could make up their uniform print dresses. When Eveline Askwith wanted to be confirmed, her employer offered to buy her a confirmation dress: instead of the white which all the other girls were wearing, 'I was close to tears when the dress turned out to be a black one.' It would, said her employer, be more useful to wear about the house.[8] Uniforms or work dresses were rarely supplied and if they were, the cost of them would often be taken out of a servant's wages. Boots were the largest clothing expenditure for poorer families. The Fabian social worker Maude Pember-Reeves's 1913 survey of poor households in Lambeth found that over half the meagre clothing budget for a single family went on boots and boot-mending and the cost of those elastic-sided shoes servants were so often required to bring with them often had to be advanced by their employer. One girl in Somerset reported that her shoes cost her her entire first month's wages.

Sartorial distinctions had not always been so important. The eighteenth-century male servant had for a time actually set the pace of fashion and sedentary gentlemen of style had striven to imitate the appearance of the working man. 'Our very footmen are adorned with gold and silver, toupees and ruffles,' reported Soame Jenyns in 1765; 'meanwhile we debase ourselves by a ridiculous imitation of their dresses. Hence are derived the flapped hat, the green frock, the long staff and buckskin breeches.'[9] In 1780, J. W. Archenholz, on a trip to England, had found it embarrassing that when dining with the Duke of Newcastle, 'ten or twelve servants out of livery attended on us, which would naturally make it difficult for a stranger to distinguish between guests and servants'.[10] A memory of his original role as the 'foot man' who ran ahead of a nobleman's entourage to take messages still lingered in the footman's livery, in the short coat or 'coatee' with the sword slash that was worn when he took his place beside the coachman. But by the end of the eighteenth century, among the more practical duties of the footman was his role as the most conspicuous member of the pageant of the grand household, and his individual sartorial tastes were subsumed into a matching entourage. By 1800, an American visitor was vastly impressed by the coordinating livery on display for a royal birth-day celebration: it was 'gaudy and fantastical to the last degree. They wore lace not only on the borders, but on the seams of their garment, and their large cocked hats were surrounded with broad fringes of silver or gold.'[11]

The footman remained the most visible and splendid of the servants in a large Victorian or Edwardian house, an adornment whose chief job, apart from waiting at table and polishing the plate, was to supervise the rooms and activities of the lady of the house. 'My lady's own man,' wrote Eric Horne; 'he dresses in morning livery when he gets up in the morning, with a white necktie. He takes the lady's breakfast to her bedroom door on a tray; takes her dog for a short walk; cleans her boots and shoes. Her fur coats and umbrellas in the front hall are under his care; he cleans her hunting kit.'[12] For a tall, good-looking young man, promotion to the best households could be swift – as discovered by Thackeray's fictional manservant, Mr Charles J. Yellowplush, who reported in his memoirs that he had arrived at the pinnacle of his ambitions: 'two livries, forty pound a year, malt-licker, washin', silk-stocking, and wax candles'. A six-foot footman could expect to be paid more than £10 a year more than a shorter one. The Duchess of Portland at Welbeck Abbey instituted classes in callisthenics and jiu-jitsu for her footmen to ensure that they kept their physiques at the required peak level. It was among the small indignities of front-of-house menservants such as footmen that they were often required to maintain the athletic appearance of men who did active and invigorating work – while in fact much of their job was ornamental.

Liveries became ever more flamboyant, dyed in employers' sporting colours, embroidered with crests and coats of arms. They still incorporated breeches, stockings and buckled shoes for evening wear, and during the day footmen commonly wore a tail coat and a striped waistcoat. It was a convention of livery that horizontal stripes be worn by indoor servants and vertical ones by outdoor servants. In the evening, or for accompanying their mistress to the theatre or to dinner, nothing less than full costume was required. 'Chocolate-coloured coats,' perhaps, 'with red collars and cuffs, scarlet waistcoats and breeches all trimmed with silver brocade, pink silk stockings, buckled shoes, powdered hair when we had visitors.'[13] Frederick Gorst, in his first job as a footman to Lady

Howard in about 1880, was resplendent in 'blue plush knee breeches, white stockings and pumps with silver heels'.[14]

By the mid-nineteenth century, in footmen, the foppish Georgian popinjay lived on in the otherwise sober, dark-suited masculine world of Victorian England. Powdered hair had gone out of fashion for men following the introduction of a powder levy in 1795 but the tradition of powdering remained for footmen and (sometimes) coachmen. Powder was in fact more of a sticky kind of clay made of violet powder mixed with water that, when dried, gave the appearance of having a mask modelled on the head. Powdering was time-consuming and unpleasant and underneath the powder the hair became matted and tangled. It was tiresome to mix up and apply with a huge puff and it stung the scalp when it was on. In extreme cases it caused the hair to fall out altogether.

With liveries beautifully made to fit by the finest tailors, the decorative end of male service had its attractions. When Edward Humphries was eleven years old, 'a raw Devonshire dumpling' from a poor farming family, he went into service as a pageboy at the Almacks Club in Piccadilly in 1900. A smart West End tailor fitted him out with a suit of 'fine black Melton cloth with yellow facings and three rows of black, silk-covered fabric buttons'. He also had 'box calf leather boots, black raincoat and a silk top-hat with a cockade'.[15] The elaborate rows of buttons that adorned the page-boys' liveries gave rise to the music-hall nickname 'buttons'. 'It was a part of the theatre that I hankered after,' wrote Peter Whiteley, footman at Luton Hoo in Bedfordshire; 'with the smell of the greasepaint again in my nostrils I went to be measured at a tailors in Conduit Street, Mayfair.'[16]

To the world outside, however, footmen all too often looked absurd, the embodiments of mincing servitude. A fishwife in Billingsgate once flung a stinking flounder at Frederick Gorst and his fellow footman tripping their way through the market, yelling: 'Blimey! Will you get a look at them flunkies!' Gorst was mortified: 'It left a large, unsightly stain on my fawn-coloured coat.'[17] Urchins, it was reported, deliberately splashed muddy puddle water at foot-men's white silk-stockinged legs – the legs perhaps filled out by the special pads used by footmen to make their calves appear more shapely.

Footmen, despite the splendour of their plumage, were rarely if ever addressed by their own names but by a generic name, saving employers the effort of remembering a new one. In all the places that the cook Margaret Thomas worked, there was always a general name for footmen: 'In one house they were William and another Henry, and where there were three, the first was John, the second William and the third was always Henry.'[18]

By 1900, the job of the male servant, though respected within the world of service itself, to the world beyond was no longer considered entirely manly. Once, domestic service had been a man's work, the household servant the descendant of the members of the sporting and military retinues of the medieval nobleman. The best cooks were men, the front-of-house servants were men, and women were employed only for the most menial tasks or as lady's-maids. But the nineteenth century had seen the increasing feminisation of domestic service. By the 1870s, according to the journalist C. S. Peel, writing in 1929, parlourmaids were already beginning to take the place of footmen and pageboys in even the largest houses, 'and in the nineties it began to be the fashion to keep two, or even three, parlourmaids instead of butler and footmen'.[19] Male indoor service never entirely recovered its appeal.

It was Charles Mayhew's view that the liveried servant, who had once cut such a fashionable dash about town, had been 'made ridiculous' by cartoons in popular periodicals such as *Punch*'s 'Jeames of Berkeley Square'. 'How infinitely superior was the manly and self-respecting lacquey or major-domo of one hundred years ago to the servile and obsequious servant of modern days,' wrote the butler 'John Robinson', in an article in *The Nineteenth Century* in 1892. The article, 'A Butler Speaks', is a poignant call for employers to treat their male servants with proper respect, as trained professionals, as people with feelings. Robinson wrote it in response to the publication of a mocking piece by Lady Violet Greville in the *National Review*, which poked fun at male servants and their 'foibles'. Lady Violet had written in a tone that suggested, wrote

Robinson, that employers thought there was something 'low, mean and degraded' about the very idea of the manservant. The role of the upper-manservant, he wrote, was to be always at the beck and call of his master, to be subject to the same indignities of loss of freedom as other servants. 'His opportunities for self-improvement are usually very small. The hours he may call his own are fitful and rare. His duties may be light, but if he wishes to prove himself a good servant he must always be on the alert.'[20]

The male servant, though he still maintained a high profile in the grander houses, was increasingly in retreat. In 1861 the census tells us that there were 62,000 male indoor servants and 962,000 female servants. But by 1901, the numbers had changed to 47,000 male indoor servants and just under 1.3 million female ones. A tax in 1777 on male servants (brought in to raise funds to fight the Americans in their war of independence) probably sparked the decline.* By the middle of the century, following the agricultural depression of the 1870s, a flood of rural girls came to work in the houses of the city and shopkeepers, clerks and other members of the expanding middle class who had not before employed servants could for the first time employ the single, overworked girl who was to characterise domestic service for the next century.

Yet despite the decline in numbers, male servants still earned considerably more than their female counterparts. A butler in 1912 could take home an average of £50–£80 per annum with three weeks' holiday a year, while a housekeeper could expect to earn in the region of £30–£50. And a 'man cook', by far the most fashionable option in the kitchen (especially if he were French) could earn a really handsome £100–£150, while a female cook, however celebrated and skilled, would be extremely lucky to earn more than £100. (In 1825, Samuel and Sarah Adams, the authors of *The*

---

* This was not the case in Ireland, where the tax was never imposed. Dorothea Conyers from Ireland noted as late as 1920 the willingness of Irish servants to do any work allotted to them: 'Every Irish servant will do everyone else's work cheerfully, the men come in to help the maids polish the floors and shoes, and the maids are quite willing to feed the horses if the men are all out.' (Dorothea Conyers, *Sporting Reminiscences*, p. 131.)

Complete Servant, had paid tribute to the superior mystique of Continental male cooks: 'In the house of fashion, he is generally a foreigner, or if an Englishman possesses a peculiar tact in manufacturing many fashionable foreign delicacies or of introducing certain seasoning and flavours in his dishes.') Furthermore, while men tended to the decorative end of the profession, with hours spent listlessly waiting in the hallway for visitors or contriving complicated dinner dishes, women were the grafters, undertaking the bulk of the heavy manual work. 'How they worked those girls! Up at five to clean and light the fires, to polish the steel grates in the Adam fireplaces, to whiten the hearths and later to take up the brass cans of hot water to the bedrooms. We men only started at seven and could sit down in the afternoons, but the girls had to then darn and repair the linen – and all for eight pounds a year,' remembered Ernest King.[21]

The turn of the twentieth century was not quite the end for the male servant but it was the beginning of the end. 'The parlourmaids will be doing the whole box of tricks,' prophesied butler Eric Horne, gloomily.

Chapter 6

The Desire for Perfection

It is a paradox that while male domestic service began its decline, the figure of the butler continued to reside at the apex of the servants' pyramid. It is difficult to think of any other servant stereotype – pert parlourmaid, red-faced, drunken cook, mincing footman, slovenly scullery-maid – whose characteristics are so deeply embedded and so instantly recognisable today. Butlers seem almost to have colluded in the creation of their own public character. The voice and manner of the butler not only became part of the job but also, for the most part, appear to have become part of the man himself. As the servants' halls imitated the hierarchies found above stairs, the butler, paterfamilias of the servants' hall, led by example, representing the moral and social values of the drawing room to those beneath him. So infallibly discreet were considered the manners and demeanour of the good butler that there are many stories of butlers being mistaken for their employers and vice versa. In fact, the model butler is the model gentleman, his life given over to public service and his general demeanour both dignified and modest. 'Oh they thought a lot of the butlers,' remembered James Hughes: 'If any butler at a place that was a sort of a decent man, he was always welcome down in the village for dancing and whist-drives and always respected.'[1]

Lord Haldane, when Minister of War, was mistaken for a butler, while on his way by train to a weekend in a country house, by a lady's-maid so 'charming, well-dressed and obviously a woman of the world' that he in turn mistook her for a fellow guest. When he realised his companion's mistake he had the gentlemanly good manners to get out of the carriage and walk all the way to the house rather than embarrass her by going to the front door as she swung round to the servants' entrance. Violet Markham, who told this story, found it typical of the world of her childhood, in which the highest ideals of public service upstairs were reflected downstairs in private service. 'Some of the pre-war butlers,' she remembered, 'were remarkable for such distinction, dignity and good manners that I often felt "your excellency" was the only proper method of address when speaking to them. To be taken for one of these superior beings was no reflection even upon a Cabinet Minister. There was a general air of discretion about Lord Haldane not unfitting for one in charge of the cellar keys and other confidential business.'[2]

Accounts of butlers by themselves and others tend to show him as his master's lieutenant, bestowing his beneficent order not only on the household, but on nature, on his country and, like ripples spreading outwards, on the subject peoples of the British Empire. 'I walked right up to the front door, great big thing – bang, bang, bang – and the butler arrives; I thought it was the lord himself,' said a young maid describing the interview for her first job.[3] The celebrated Edwin Lee, for years the Astors' butler at Cliveden, was a figure whose discipline and efficiency was legendary in servant circles and beyond. Lee maintained the highest standards of both behaviour and household order, upstairs and down, and was viewed with awe both by his underlings and by guests. Rosina ('Rose') Harrison, Lady Astor's lady's-maid, described Edwin Lee as 'the most dominating figure in my life . . . His Christian name was the most unimportant thing about him. I can hardly remember it being used; he was known to everyone who visited us as Lee or Mr Lee. Even royalty never had to be reminded of it. There were other great butlers at the time but Mr Lee would be acknowledged by almost all as the greatest.'[4] An under-butler at Cliveden remembered Lee's meticulous appearance:

In the daytime he would wear a black alpaca jacket and a bow tie, but
in the evening of course he'd change to a tail coat, oh yes. Full regalia
then, to match the guests I mean. The footmen were always young
men, and you would know that they weren't the butler, as the butler
was portly and – got a presence, had a presence. He was immaculate,
and he had a wardrobe – a magnificent wardrobe. Yes, he got a
clothes allowance, you see. So he was always well dressed. No, I've
never known the man slovenly in any way, not even when he went
for a walk with his walking stick and his sporting suit. You'd have
thought he was head of the house. In fact, people have met him and
thought he was Lord Astor! He acted like it.[5]

'The office of butler is as ancient as it is responsible,' wrote the
author of *The Duties of Servants*, and indeed the role of the butler,
like that of the footman, emerges directly from that of the roistering
members of a medieval nobleman's entourage. Addressed always as
'Mr' by the other servants and by his surname by the family, the
butler saw to the laying of tables, the replenishment of drinks and
the polishing of the silver. He held the keys to the wine cellar and
the secrets of table service: 'under a butler, plate succeeded plate as
if by magic', remembered Lesley Lewis.[6] In the servants' hall, the
butler (only superseded in importance in houses where they still
kept a house steward) sat always at the head of the table: when carv-
ing the Sunday roast, he would serve first the housekeeper, as his
equal in the servants' hierarchy, then move down the ranks to the
odd man, the scullery-maid and the hall boy.

Like Chinese boxes, dozens of smaller versions stacked within
one larger model, the hierarchy of the aristocratic servants' hall
unfolded:

Supper was the big event of the day when protocol and snobbery
took over. All the staff assembled for this meal except the kitchen
people; they always keep to themselves and eat in the kitchen . . .
First came the butler with the housekeeper; he sat at one end of the
long refectory table and she sat at the opposite end. The butler was
dressed in full evening dress, wing collar, white tie and tails. The

housekeeper wore a black silk dress, sometimes relieved with lace and always jewellery – earrings, necklaces, bracelets, ring brooches and anything else she possessed. Next came the lady's personal maid, dressed much the same as the housekeeper; then the first footman; his uniform was the same as the butler's with one exception – all footmen have yellow and black striped waistcoats – they all sat one side of the table, looking like wasps at a feast; at the end of their row sat the odd job man, the hall boy who waited on us at table under the keen eye of the butler who corrected him if he made a mistake or forgot any small item or spilled water as he filled our glasses. Last, at the end of the row, was the boot boy. On the other side of the table sat the maids, the head housemaid with her three inches of lace on top of her head, and then the other maids according to position.[7]

The midday meal was the main one of the day for the servants: a large joint was usually served for everyone. In the grandest houses, after the lower ranks had been served, the joint 'was ceremoniously removed to the housekeeper's room by a footman who carried it out with great pomp', followed by the upper-servants who continued their meal there. Pudding was always served to the 'upper-ten' (the top-ranking servants) in the housekeeper's sitting room, known popularly as the 'pugs' parlour' (the making of pudding being one of the ancient duties of the housekeeper, though now the duty of the cook or chef). This curious procedure was, remembered the Marchioness of Bath, looking back in the 1950s, 'a strange ritual' which was 'the recognised custom of most large houses'.[8] James Hughes, a former butler, remembered being frustrated by the pudding custom as a junior servant because 'they went up there and you never knew what they had for their sweet'.[9]

Presentation and planning were all important. 'It is the butler's duty throughout the day to see that everything is in place and in order, in readiness for use in the drawing room, morning room, and library; the blinds up or down as the case may be, writing tables in due order, books rearranged, newspapers cut, aired and folded for use, fires attended to by the footman & etc., & etc.'[10] The butler's pantry was his centre of operations. James Hughes found it comical

when some visiting greenhorn thought his butler's pantry actually
had food in it: 'This young fellow said: "By gum, you wouldn't be
short of food then?" I said: "What are you talking about?" He said:
"Well you said butler's pantry." I said: "It isn't a pantry with food
in you dope. It's a butler's workplace."'[11]

The butler was and is still the quintessential career servant. Edwin
Lee had been the son of a struggling tenant farmer in Shropshire,
one of many who went to the wall in the agricultural depression.
Lee chose to go into service in 1900 (against his parents' wishes)
because he saw 'opportunities for advancement I would never have
as a labourer'.[12] Most butlers, like Lee, worked their way up, start-
ing as hall boys, and inching upwards to be under-footmen, then
footmen, then under-butlers. Ernest King was working as an office
boy at the *North Devon Herald* in Barnstaple earning three shillings and sixpence a week, when in 1901 his father died and he
needed to find better paid work in order to take care of his mother.
The editor of the *Herald* was astounded when King announced that
he was to go into service ('learn to bow and scrape and always have
your hat in your hand for the rest of your life!'), but the work was
regular and paid four pence a week more than the newspaper could
offer him. Most important, residential work was 'all found', meaning food, laundry bills and accommodation were included: 'I
became a servant just as others joined the army or went to sea. We
had to eat.'[13]

Arthur Inch liked to quote from the handbook on butlering (by
an author calling himself only 'Williams') which his father, who had
also lived and died in service, carried with him at all times: 'In all
establishments it is his [butler's] duty to rule. In large establishments more particularly, this exercise of judicious power will be
greatly required; for under-servants are never even comfortable,
much less happy, under lax management.'[14] Certainly, the demands
of running a very large household needed years of training. James
Hughes, when approached by a young footman who wanted to
become a butler, told him that unless he could organise a party for
three or four hundred people in twenty-four hours, then he was not
ready for the job. So high were the standards of management in the

well-run wealthy home that the butler needed to develop a passion for detail that often bordered on fetish. It was absolutely crucial that the well-oiled wheels of the home were never on display, that no household necessity or comfort ever looked as though it were not always available in abundance, filled to the brim by invisible hands. Cigarette boxes had therefore to be constantly replenished; soap was always fresh and flowers just picked. 'Efficiency to me is happiness,' wrote Ernest King in the 1950s, looking back on half a century of butlering: 'The aim for perfection I fear becomes a bit of an obsession.'[15]

By the mid-nineteenth century, the indispensable manservant, the opener of doors, the wearer of black suits, the imperturbable front-man and keeper of the gate, emerged in the form that we would recognise today. The acceptable public demeanour for the job of butler was ponderous, solemn, cautiously avuncular, with a steely discipline concealed behind a pedantic attention to correct proce-dure. Real-life butlers too (from the memoirs available to us) seem to have found that the job was most effective if they played to type. In fact an understanding of the butler type, both fictional and real, is a crucial component of the theatre of the front-of-house manserv-ant. Twentieth-century fictional butlers often take their cue from the eponymous butler-hero of J. M. Barrie's 1901 play *The Admirable Crichton*, whose worldly intelligence was hidden behind a lugubri-ous deference. The self-indulgent Lord and Lady Loam, Crichton's employers, are fond of declaring that they treat their servants abso-lutely as social equals – while the servants understand that no such equality can truly exist in the Loams' protected world. It is Crichton who upholds the usefulness, for the purposes of managerial organi-sation, of maintaining strict class divisions; yet when the household is shipwrecked on a desert island, the superior practical skills of the tweeny – 'between-maid' – and the butler make them the overlords. (Kazuo Ishiguro's poignant 1989 fictional depiction of a butler emotionally crippled and stranded in a changing mid-twentieth-century world is the tragic obverse to Barrie's comedy of manners.)

Barrie made Crichton highly attractive to women: both the tweeny and Lady Mary Loam fall for him. But in real life, marriage was generally frowned on for butlers, except in those establishments which could afford spacious married quarters for their staff. There are accounts of butlers settling down and marrying fellow servants – housekeepers or lady's-maids, being from the appropriate stratum. Together their accumulated savings would ensure a comfortable retirement. 'We knew a very nice butler who married a lady's-maid and both had money in the Building Society – and got a nice house . . . where they had their own servants', remembered 'An Old Servant'.[16] Many butlers, however, appeared to have viewed the job as a celibate calling, perhaps because it was so difficult to envisage where the career servant would stand in any society outside the servants' hall. 'The only thing that brings anxiety to a servant is marriage,' reflected the butler William Lanceley, a lifelong bachelor.[17] For Albert Thomas, who did marry, the harsh truth was that 'no-one wants you if you have kiddies'.[18] For young female servants, marriage offered escape – perhaps the only escape – from service, but for male career servants it could be a handicap. There were married butlers of course but often a wife was considered an impediment to advancement. With its implication of divided loyalties, marriage would be 'simply suicidal' warned Eric Horne, another butler-bachelor. Ernest King survived a too-close shave with an amorous housemaid in the 1930s and although he was later to marry when he was firmly established, shuddered to think how close he came to surrendering the duties of perfection: 'Never again did I allow my affections to wander in any house where I worked.'[19]

All was not stern, black-clad self-denial, however. In the grander households, where there were annual servants' balls, the butler would be asked to commence the dancing by waltzing with the mistress. Henry Moat, Sir George Sitwell's irrepressible butler-valet, never allowed his unmarried state to stint his pleasures; the many admiring accounts of Moat stress how attractive he was to women. In 1908 he wrote in characteristic style to the young Osbert Sitwell from Scarborough, where he was on holiday, and asked him to send him, post-haste, a pair of the coachman's livery stockings and a wig as he intended to go to a fancy-dress ball as Leonardo da

Vinci: 'I am all excitement and jumping about the gambols of a skittish young hippopotamus.'[20]

The most conspicuous temptation of the job was the ready availability of alcohol; as a result, butlers had a reputation as heavy drinkers. The pseudonymous John Robinson complained bitterly that the modern manservant had to put up with contemptuous 'surveillance' from employers who checked the wine bottles. This led, said Robinson, to a lack of respect and a loss of trust between upstairs and downstairs which in turn led to unhappiness, loneliness, loss of self-respect and, in the end, to drinking. Ethel Stanbridge was a maid at Burwood House in Bedfordshire: 'The staff,' she remembered, 'were ruled by the butler who was always drunk by lunchtime, everybody knew he was drunk but in Lady Ellesmere's eyes he could do no wrong and he was there for forty years. The lady's-maid was also drunk, part of her allowance was beer at dinner, beer at night and beer when she went to bed and she never missed any!'[21] So notorious were the instances of alcoholic butlers that many insurance companies refused to a butler any form of insurance because of his ready access to alcohol. Ernest King was advised to write down 'valet' as his occupation when applying for insurance.

The compensations of the butler's life were the achievements of a particular and measurable form of excellence. Precision, order and discipline were maintained, often against the odds. Henry Moat, beloved by the Sitwells – 'an enormous purple man, like a benevolent hippopotamus' is how Edith Sitwell later described him – though he behaved towards his employers with a gleeful and affectionate irreverence, retained a high respect for the demands of the job, and for appearances. Mr Ling, the butler at Carden Park, Sussex, where Frederick Gorst was a footman, was a drunk whose chief occupation outside work was contriving elaborate traps for the starlings that he liked to eat roasted. But according to Gorst, he was never less than beautifully turned out and he watched him as, unawares, Ling 'continually fingered a grey silk four-in-hand tie, meticulously arranging the folds and constantly appraising himself in a mirror on the wall'.[22]

The only ambition available to a butler was to be the best butler possible. It was one of the few career choices that, despite financial rewards and security, offered absolutely no prospect of social advancement; quite the opposite. A butler with a gentlemanly mien and a talent for leadership was nonetheless stuck for ever in the servants' hall – and yet not quite of it. A little learning was viewed with suspicion and Eric Horne knew well the limitations it imposed: 'There is a vast abyss between gentry and servants, the more intelligent and well read a servant may be, the less they will have to say to him or her.'[23] The figure of the butler therefore embodies a poignant paradox: that although the career manservant may have all the skills required for leadership, those skills rarely went beyond the meticulous planning of a domestic day. A shopkeeper or a factory worker could conceivably become a millionaire, eventually possibly a Member of Parliament or even a peer, but a butler was for ever cobwebbed in the language and demeanour of deferential butlerese.

Barrie had intended when he first began work on *The Admirable Crichton* to make the romance ignited on the island between the shipwrecked Lady Mary Loam and the butler Crichton end in marriage, the butler's superior intelligence far eclipsing the effete aristocrat who is Mary's fiancé. But even for the purposes of drama such an outcome was impossible to envisage, and Barrie decided against it on the grounds that 'the stalls wouldn't stand it'.

Chapter 7

'Some Poor Girl's Got To Go Up and Down, Up and Down . . .'[1]

In Kent, at the turn of the century, twelve-year-old Daisy Record's father marched her into a job in service saying: 'Well, young lady, you're not gittin' your feet under my table: you git your feet under somebody else's table.'[2] Poor families like Daisy's needed their children to leave home and start earning as soon as they were old enough to work; for women, service was the usual option. It was 'taken for granted', said Rosina Walsh, who was born in 1911, that girls from the families of the rural poor went into service: 'they hadn't the room at home so they were glad to get us out'.[3]

There were few houses in England so poor that they did not employ some kind of household help. Joseph Rowntree, in his famous 1901 study of poverty in York, made servant-keeping the criterion that separated the very poorest from the merely poor. It is hard to imagine any rung of the social ladder being lower than that occupied by the young girl, perhaps aged only ten or eleven, who scrubbed floors or looked after babies for a few pennies. 'Two pence and a cup of tea to some old woman or little girl to mind baby for a few hours is an item which you may find in the poorest budget,' wrote the philanthropist Mrs Bernard Bosanquet, who worked in London's East End.[4] The upper-working-class family of Stella Davies in Lancashire had a maid-of-all-work they called 'fat Ellen', 'a simple soul who slaved away unceasingly'.[5] Servants were the very first definition of status. When Paul Thompson conducted his famous interviews with the last Edwardians during the 1960s and 1970s, he was told by one woman, whose father had been an under-foreman in a factory, that they had afforded a weekly washer-woman; the children were told to call her Auntie Meg to avoid any suggestion that in terms of social class they might all be on the same footing.

Crucial pennies were earned by women and children who took in washing – often for people as poor as themselves. Washerwomen who worked from home were, alongside charwomen, among the poorest paid and lowliest on the many rungs of domestic work. The trade unionist and Labour activist Walter Southgate, born in 1890, lived with his family in the East End. His mother was a washer-woman at a public laundry, where there was 'one of those huge mangling machines' operated manually. 'The pay for a day at the washtub in my schooldays was around three shillings, and a meal was included.'[6] Lillian Westall first went to work in a laundry at King's Cross in 1907 at the age of fourteen, for two shillings a week. She collected the washing on foot, 'walking as far as Highbury and staggering back with a full basket'. Finally, Lillian was promoted to working on a machine to curl stiff shirt collars, but she was so tiny and fragile that she found the speed of the machine impossible and was sacked.[7] Mrs Bosanquet noted: 'Among the higher class arti-sans, the little nurse-girl, the young slavey or general and the peri-odical char-woman are quite frequent; for in this class the daughters of the house on leaving school are generally put out to some trade, and the mother has her hands over full with the cooking, mending and washing, for a family with a standard to maintain; but it is rare to find an adult servant in possession of all her faculties until you come to the shop-keeping class. Domestic service amongst the working classes is carried on by the immature or the aged, the maimed and the halt, or those who are in some other way handi-capped in the battle of industry.'[8]

Domestic service was considered for many a safe berth in a world where disreputable traps lurked for the unwary girl. For rural families in particular, especially those who lived within the patriarchal country estate, service was considered more respectable than other forms of female employment. One village girl started work as a kitchen-maid in 1908 on a salary of £8 a year, but longed for a different career. Seventy years later her daughter recalled that 'she in no way wished to do so, but knew well that it would do no good to protest as there was just no chance of a choice. Years later she told me that she had, at that time, a secret desire to be a dancer or actress. This she had to keep to herself as anything to do with the stage was considered improper in her home. It was my grandfather's wish that none of his daughters should even attend dances. Music and singing by professionals, however, was viewed in quite a different light.'[9]

Newspaper advertisements, registration agencies and word of mouth were the most efficient methods of securing a good place. The *Morning Post* was a popular newspaper for its Situations Vacant columns, as were the *Morning Chronicle* and *The Times*. Some employers stipulated that they would have no Catholics, while others made often mysterious specifications. Lillian Westall's first employer, in Cheyne Walk, London, asked her to open her mouth: 'Let's see your teeth.' 'Whatever she saw, it seemed to satisfy her, for I got the job.'[10]

Demand for servants in wealthy areas outstripped supply (in Westminster in 1900 there were twelve servants to every one hundred residents), as Elizabeth Banks discovered when she advertised for a position as a house-parlourmaid using the name 'Lizzie Barnes' and received hundreds of replies. Several were from bachelors or widowers hoping for 'lady companions'. Many were courteous; most sent stamps for a reply; one even offered to supply references of her own in exchange for those of a prospective employee; another, a Mrs Clifford-Morris, addressed her politely, if absent-mindedly, as 'My dear Miss Burrows'. Some replies were very specific about requirements: one old lady needed a maid 'of a restful appearance' who could rub her arthritic knees; another required a particular expertise in mending, particularly handkerchiefs and stockings. 'One inquisitive person demanded to know

my age, height, position in life, my father's business, if my mother
was a gentlewoman, and whether I was a Churchwoman or
dissenter.' Another subjected her to a 'catechism' about her most
personal life. At an interview in Grosvenor Square, she was told she
would have to cut her hair – 'No fringe allowed!' By the end of a
week, Banks reported, she had called on 'bachelors, widowers and
widows, ladies of title, members of the upper and middle classes,
actresses, literary women and boarding-house keepers'.[11]

Registries or domestic employment agencies were generally the
most efficient form of offering or finding work. Servants' registries
had opened all over the country, many under the auspices of charities
such as the Metropolitan Association for Befriending Young Servants,
which had successfully introduced regulations to an industry that
had until the late nineteenth century been almost entirely unregulated. Mayfair's Masseys and Mrs Hunt's were the best-known agencies; each had opened regional branches and a place on their register
gave a good chance of a satisfactory placement. For girls leaving
home for the first time rumours abounded of white slave traffickers
lying in wait at railway stations, while there were whispers among
employers of gangs running girls who got their fares paid by a new
mistress, then pretended they had 'lost their box'; the girl was bought
a new one, 'whereupon she did a bunk'.[12] It was expected that train
fares would be paid and in railway stations all over Britain girls
waited to be picked up by strangers and taken to a strange home in a
strange city.

For employers unwilling to spend the money on an agency
commission, there were other approaches possible. Mrs Macrae,
author of the 1899 *Cassell's Household Guide*, suggested that if a
housewife in need of a servant bypassed the registry office and
applied straight to the local vicar's wife, then she might get a local
girl, very young and an attendee at Bible classes. Furthermore, such
a candidate would very likely be from a children's home and therefore 'willing and grateful for small kindnesses' – and, of course,
cheap.

In rural areas, many hiring fairs still operated as they had done
for centuries. Mop fairs, held in November at Martinmas, were

where a farming family might find themselves a 'mop' or servant girl, usually to work single-handed. The 'Runaway Mop' fairs then scooped up servants who wanted to change their positions. The hiring fair was a reminder of a lingering tradition of those looser, unregulated servant-master relationships that were woven into the fabric of rural life. The hiring process was straightforward: no character references, no interview, no uniform required. In Cumbria, for example, in 1905, 'the old farmers used to come up King Street and say: "Is tha for hiring lass?" I used to say "Aye." He'd say: "What's tha asking?" We used to say: "What are tha going to give us?" "I'll give you four pound ten." We'd say: "No thank you." We used to walk a bit farther down King Street and another farmer would come up and say: "Is tha for hiring lass?" Perhaps we can get five pound ten off him for the six month. He used to say: "Can you wash, can you bake, can you scrub?"'[13]

Hiring fairs had customarily been riotous occasions in which young men touting for work dressed up in extravagant costumes that sent coded messages about their skills to prospective employers. The *Bridlington Gazette* in 1895 reported: 'The wagoner has a piece of fancily twisted cord in his cap, a bright flower (it may be artificial) in his buttonhole and his jacket is not buttoned – that would not be correct. The proper fastening is two or three inches of brass chain, the better to display a capacious chest. Feathers on some of the bowler hats are suggestive of the fold yard [the sheep enclosure].'[14] But during the 1850s there was a clampdown on girls and boys consorting freely at the hiring fairs and by 1900 mixed hiring had almost completely disappeared – and with it the market for domestic service hiring at the fairs (though a few mop fairs lingered on in the north of England until the 1920s). A handbill in Northamptonshire in 1870 warned of the unregulated dangers of the hiring fair:

Parents! Will you let your children go to Mops and Statute Fairs? . . . To be stared at and picked out – and bound by taking a paltry shilling – to masters about whom they know nothing, and who know no more about them than the car or horse which they judge by

appearance ... tell them that they now have the opportunity of
sending to a Register Office where their names will be put down for
a very small payment and where good character will always insure
good places.[15]

The average age for entering service was fourteen. 'Servants like
birds must be caught when young,' was William Lanceley's sad
advice.[16] In rural areas, many domestics were born into families
who had been in service on the same estate for generations. It was
the coachman father of 'Mrs B.' in Oxfordshire who found her
work as a housemaid: 'I really got the job because they really go
through all the generations to work in a place like that because you
understand there are such a lot of expensive things, they really have
got to know your background and the companion-housekeeper
knew my father anyway as he used to drive them back and forth
sometimes – so I got the job.'[17] Most girls going into service had
themselves been working at home, sometimes for several years. The
care of younger children in a large family fell to the lot of little girls
barely out of infancy. The journalist George Sims, author of the
'Living London' newspaper sketches, glimpsed in the 'rookeries',
the capital's labyrinth of tenement slums, a tired child of eight nursing a baby: 'By the time she marries and has children of her own she
will be a woman weary of motherhood.'[18] Margaret Powell was
fifteen when she became a kitchen-maid, but had been in charge of
giving her brothers and sisters breakfast and then, after school,
cooking the vegetables for the evening meal, since she was seven: 'I,
as it were, took my place in life.'[19] Oxfordshire shepherd Mont
Abbott had a sister, Dora, born in 1900, who went into service as a
'tweeny' – a between-maid – the lowest rung of housemaid, at the
beck and call of all the staff. Dora was 'skivvying as a tweenymaid'
in Oxford by the time she was thirteen and Mont remembered:
'She'd been a second mother to so many of us village children she
looked twice her age.' Dora stayed in service with the same Oxford
family until her death, unmarried, forty years later.[20]

The school leaving age in 1900 had been raised to twelve, but
maids even younger than that could be got cheaply, sometimes for

as little as half a crown a week, if she qualified as a 'partial-exemption scholar' (one of many schemes intended to encourage girls to go into domestic service). This required the child to attend school for only half a day and then go to work for not more than twenty-seven and a half hours a week. In 1903 the American novelist Jack London lived in the East End of London, researching life there for his book *The People of the Abyss*. There he observed the frequency of what he called the 'very frowzy slavey', one of the part-timers that 'Fabian reformers are so vehement about': very young girls, some as young as six, were sometimes paid as little as three shillings a week.[21]

The commonest form of servant was not the starched and capped parlourmaid, but the general dogsbody, cleaner and cook, rarely seen outside the basement where she both worked and lived. Mrs Waldemar Leverton itemised the duties of the general servant over several pages – considerably more than those she devoted to higher servants, or those with particular jobs. Here is her list of what had to be completed before the girl even had her own breakfast:

> As the duties of a general servant are many and varied, she is usually expected to be up at 6 a.m. in the summer and 6.30 in the winter. She opens the windows and airs the rooms, cleans the kitchen range, lights the fire, tidies the dining-room grate and lights the fire, after which she will take hot water to the bedrooms, brush the boots and fill the coal scuttles. It will then be time to cook and serve the breakfast, after which she will clean the front door step, unless it is possible to do this before preparing the first meal of the day. She will then go to the bedrooms, strip the beds, attend to the washstands and make the beds.[22]

When Elizabeth Banks set out to prove, with the brightest of New World intentions, that 'there is nothing incompatible between gentility and domestic work', she was amazed by the work expected of a single-handed servant girl in London. It turned out that the employers held on to the gentility and the servants did all the work. In the household of a Mr and Mrs Allison, residents of Portman

Square, they kept a cook, a parlourmaid and a lady's-maid as well as Elizabeth – 'Lizzie', the housemaid, but lived in a manner which required double that number in attendance. 'It seemed to me that the responsibilities put on my shoulders were tremendous. I was to rise at six in the morning and my first job was to shake and brush Mr Allison's trousers, which I would find hanging on the doorknob outside his room. I was about to inform Mrs Allison that I did not engage as a valet, and was not up in the art of brushing trousers, when I suddenly remembered that I was not a "young lady" but a "young person", expected to do with her might whatever her hands found to do.' After that, her task was to brush Mrs Allison's dress, then take all the family's boots to the kitchen to be shined by the cook. Elizabeth then had to 'sweep and dust four flights of stairs and four halls, clean up and dust the study and drawing rooms, and carry a can of hot water to each person, knocking on the door to wake him or her up'. Then – 'were my ears deceiving me?' – Mrs Allison told her she may have her breakfast. 'So I was to achieve all these Herculean feats on an empty stomach!' Mrs Allison blithely continued:

> 'After you have breakfasted, Lizzie, you must help Annie with the dishes, then make the beds, clean up the washstands, fill the water jugs, sweep and dust the bedrooms, attend to the candlesticks and put everything in perfect order in the sitting rooms. You will get this done by eleven o'clock ... From eleven to three, you will turn out one or two of the rooms, and eat your dinner in the meantime. At four o clock, I want you to be dressed with clean cap and apron. Then you will get the servants' afternoon tea and clear it away, and you can fill up the time until supper with needlework' ... After supper I was to make a round of the rooms again and sew till a quarter past ten.

At that point, an exhausted Elizabeth was permitted to go to bed.[23]

'Where the maids slept I daren't think,' wrote Beryl Lee Hooker of her affluent Edwardian childhood in London. 'Three poor souls dwelt in a box room with a skylight and no fire, and the nursery-maid slept among basket trunks in a fourth den at the side of the cistern.'[24] It was widely considered, even by the most considerate employers, that when it came to their own quarters, a servant would be happiest living in spartan simplicity. For the single maid-of-all-work, this was often airless, dark, damp and unhealthy. Arnold Bennett's Elsie and her husband Joe live in the basement – 'it was a cave, subterranean, and felt like a cave' – cluttered with unwanted furniture discarded by the Rastes upstairs. These dank quarters were a breeding ground for consumption. Mrs Panton, dispensing advice on all matters domestic to housewives in the 1890s, recommended plain, colour-washed walls or 'washable sanitary paper' for the bedrooms of servant girls. A 'simple dhurrie by the bed' would do for carpeting and 'each servant should have a separate bed if possible'.

At the Allisons', Elizabeth Banks found 'three iron bedsteads stood in a row, and in front of each a strip of ragged carpet'. The author and teacher Molly Hughes, furnishing her first married home in 1897, wondered if something fresh and sprigged would be apt for her one servant: 'I had a rooted idea that a servant's bedroom must have pink chintz covered with muslin round her table,' she recalled.[25] But Mrs Panton cautioned her readers that too much prettiness was bad for servants: they were not up to appreciating it and the effect would be only to make them feel uncomfortable. 'I should like myself to give each maid a really pretty room,' she wrote, 'but at the present they are a little hopeless on the subject. No sooner is the room put nice than something happens to destroy the beauty ... and I really believe servants are only happy if their rooms are allowed in some measure to resemble the home of their youth, and to be merely places where they lie down to sleep as heavily as they can.'[26] So a cheap and lumpy mattress, a chilly floor, probably covered in cheap linoleum (invented in 1855) and a spotted mirror were among the few adornments that might have been expected in the home-like room of a general servant. Furthermore, the 'housemaid's closet', which was generally situated near the servants' bedrooms, contained a sink into which the contents of the household's chamberpots (slop pails) were poured and the area was therefore, as the *Hand Book of House Sanitation* warned in 1882, 'subject to a slight though disagreeable odour'.

Even in the domestic service agencies, a rigid demarcation in the surroundings considered suitable for employer and employee was imposed in the waiting rooms, and servants could here get a taste of what they might expect of their quarters. Going to register at the Mayfair Agency, one prospective maid stepped through the door and was at first delighted by 'the elegance of white and gold paint, velvet curtains and delicate chairs, and sofas piled with cushions. I just stood on the thick carpet and stared until a very smart woman came sailing towards me. She knew at once, the same as I knew, that I was in the wrong door.' She was shown briskly into the room for prospective servants and, 'My word, what a different place it was; no thick carpet, no velvet curtains, the floor was covered with brown linoleum and benches lined each side of the room.'[27]

The basement kitchen, with backstairs leading to the servants' bedrooms (in poorer houses the servants slept in front of the range in the kitchen) was the domestic hub of the house. And while in the servants' halls of the great estates staff were generously fed with fresh food from the home farms, in the smaller, scrimping houses where most servants were employed, the food considered suitable was cheap and plain with herrings, bread and margarine featuring prominently. Ann Humpage's mother worked for an elderly couple and their two daughters. 'My mother slept in the attic which she said was never warm and the only day she had a cooked hot meal was on a Monday when the washerwoman came, otherwise she just ate anything left over from the family meals. When she had a day off, the dishes were left for her to wash when she came back.'[28] The former King's Cross laundrymaid Lillian Westall left a nursemaid's job in Palmers Green to 'better herself' in the household of a dentist in Chiswick: 'The meals I remember well. For breakfast I had bread and dripping. There were often mice dirts on the dripping to be scraped off first. Dinner was herring, every day; tea was bread and marge.'[29]

Cleaning technologies were viewed with suspicion – elbow grease being preferred over newfangled shortcuts. In rural houses, they still used a cockscomb to clean the flue and a deep suspicion persisted of machinery or cleaning agents that took the hard labour out of work and encouraged idleness. 'Now Edith, you're getting lazy,' admonished Edith Hall's employer when she suggested using a soapy water wash instead of a traditional soda water scrub so harsh it took the pattern off the linoleum.[30] There was a marked reluctance among many employers to give way to servants' requests for more up-to-date or convenient tools for cleaning. Elizabeth Banks's employer, Mrs Allison, refused to buy her a brush to sweep into difficult corners so Banks was forced to use her own clothes' brush for the job. The use of cloths was discouraged in washing-up as it was believed that bare fingers could more effectively dig into the creases of a jelly mould or the corner of a baking tin. In Dorset, Lady Gray, who employed Edna Wheway as a kitchen-maid, returned from a holiday in Jamaica bearing the husk of a coconut. This, she suggested, cut in half, would make Edna an excellent scrubbing brush for the stone flags of the kitchen. 'The thick coir made a terrible scratching sound on the stone but I had my orders so did not question why.'[31]

Most cleaning was still done using manual labour and tools that would have been as familiar to a maid in 1700 as they were in 1900. The vast majority of brooms and other brushing implements were made of the same rough materials that they had been for centuries: mops fashioned out of rags; brushes from hogs' bristles and brooms from birch or heather. Dust was considered one of the deadliest interlopers in the healthy home. There were justifiable concerns that the traditional damp duster method of the housemaid simply spread the dust around rather than removed it permanently, but the invention of the vacuum cleaner by the American Cecil Booth in 1901, though it rightly promised a cleaning revolution, took many years to make its way into the daily life of British households. The first vacuum cleaner was enormous and was attached with suction pipes to a machine, pulled by horses, which was parked on the pavement outside the front door.

It was 1910 before a range of practical domestic vacuums appeared on the market and these included the 'Baby Daisy', a nippy model that needed two strong servants to operate it. At about £6 each in 1914, the cost of a reasonably portable vacuum cleaner came to about half the annual wages of a general maid. The first vacuums were temperamental and could not manage anything larger than a dust microbe. At Lyme Park, Cheshire, they had one of the first Hoover models: 'Oh they had one of the first Hoovers up there, and it was always going wrong because the housemaids used to pick all the hairpins up with it.'[32] Larger houses which generated their own electricity found that vacuums were greedy on power and would wear out the generator battery: at footman Fred Collett's post in Goring, the chauffeur, also in charge of the electricity accumulators, cautioned less use of new cleaning technologies to save energy.

More immediately popular was the mechanical carpet sweeper which had been introduced to Britain from the United States as early as 1876. Speculation that the British servant would imminently be replaced in the middling home by a biddable machine continued through the twentieth century, but for the most part the idea was treated rather as a light-hearted joke, in the spirit of a letter to *The Lady* in 1900, which referred teasingly to the 'ever-ingenious Americans who have already invented labour-saving machines and will now turn out mechanical maids, only needing to be oiled and wound up daily'.[33] So deeply was the idea of service embedded in the British psyche that it would be another fifty years, when there were simply no more servants to be employed, until technology would really take its place in the home.

Cleaning agents too were still, for the most part, as they had always been: a combination of elbow grease and various forms of scouring agents, soaps and other ingredients. Sand, scattered on kitchen floors and staircases and then swept up, absorbed grease and droppings, as well as mud brought in from outside. Tea leaves were commonly scattered on rugs and carpets to freshen them before they were swept or beaten out. Soda, a necessary cleaning alkali, had been increasingly popular since the mid-nineteenth century for its grease-dissolving properties, and was now a staple of most households. Just mixing up most cleaning preparations was an arduous job. Chloride of lime, used for cleaning floorboards, had to be stirred daily for several days before it could be used; blacking, indispensable for daily application to iron grates and ranges, as well as for polishing boots, was purchased as a powder in greaseproof paper and then mixed with vinegar or water before it was rubbed in; polish was made from boiling linseed oil with vinegar and water. An Oxfordshire former maid remembered how she had to 'sweep the floors – no Hoovers of course – dustpan and brush. Rugs. And mops with beeswax and turpentine. The beeswax had to be soaked in turpentine in jars the night before then it melted and you had a stick and put it on the rag – all the floors were done with beeswax – all on the knees.'[34]

At Pilgrims Hall, Essex, the storeroom contained supplies ordered in vast quantities every six months from the Army and Navy Stores: 'yellow bar soap for rough scrubbing, soft soap like green jelly for washing-up, floor polish, furniture polish, metal polish, boot polish . . .'[35] The keys to the storeroom were the passport to the inner sanctum, as far as a well-sized household was concerned. 'Oh yes, everything was keys, the storeroom was all keys.'[36] In large houses, it was the housekeeper, rustling in black silk, who measured out the required foodstuffs as the cook ordered them. But in most homes, it was the mistress of the house who controlled the cupboard and its supplies.

Though latex gloves were pioneered in America before the First World War for use in hospital surgery, it would not be until the 1960s that rubber gloves were manufactured for ordinary domestic use. Edna Wheway cleaned fifty copper pots and pans every week with green carbolic soap; her hands became so badly chapped in cold weather that trying to grip the feathers of the pheasants she had to pluck made her weep with pain. Many servant girls recalled how ashamed they were of their hands – rubbed red and raw by silversand, vinegar and boiling water. 'I always had to wear white gloves, me hands were too common looking . . . The water was very hard and me hands used to be raw with chaps and whatnot, so I had to wear white gloves so they didn't look so common.'[37] Footmen's hands were 'hard as boards', remembered Ernest King. 'Cleaning plate is hell. It's the greatest bugbear behind the green baize door, the hardest job in the house. When I began this work, rubbing the silver, the spoons and the forks occasionally getting a prong in my thumb, my fingers grew fearfully sore and blistered, but in those days if you complained you were just told to get on with it and you did. The blisters burst and you kept on despite the pain and you developed a pair of plate hands that never blistered again.'[38] Laundress Annie Wilkinson's hands were burned hard after years of pulling goffering irons* – hot metal tubes around which silk ribbons and other delicate bits of lace were wound to be pressed – out of boiling water. Glymiel jelly was one of the recommended treatments for blistered hands; it had to be applied every night and the hands were then covered with gloves. But the employer of Kate Taylor, at thirteen a general servant in a farmhouse, took a tougher approach: 'I had to help out with the dairy work. If she [the farmer's wife] saw me flinch when I was getting dairy utensils out of the boiling sterilising water, she would push my whole hand in saying that was the only way to get hardened.'[39]

Depending on the size of the house, the cooking area of the kitchen was only one part of the warren of small rooms that made up the servants' quarters. The German architect Herman Muthesius, in his history of English domestic architecture, commented on the peculiarly English custom of dividing kitchen labour between wet (cleaning) and dry (food) work. 'Even in the smallest cottage the English kitchen is unthinkable without its attendant scullery.'[40] A slate-shelved larder kept meat, fish and milk cool before the days of refrigeration; the pantry was where silver was cleaned and the scullery was where the washing-up was done in enormous sinks full of hot, greasy water. It was the scullery-maid's responsibility to tackle the mountain of dish-washing, using soft soap which made everything horribly slippery, and soda to cut the grease; it is hardly likely that she would have warmed to the cheery advice given to her in 1903 in *Friendly Leaves* (the journal of the servants' charity the

---

* They were still using goffering irons, twelve of them, in the Castle Howard laundry forty years later, in 1940.

Girls' Friendly Society) that suggested she look upon her 'true and dextrous' work as 'the finest pianist might view his keys'.

The scullery was also where the raw materials of the Edwardian meal were prepared: 'Food was usually delivered to the cook in a fairly rough state. Vegetables came in with earth and waste matter on them and all birds were plucked and drawn in the scullery, eggs sometimes being extracted from inside the chickens. Hares and rabbits were skinned and gutted, and large codfish with staring eyes had to have their heads cut off. The scullery was no place for the squeamish.'[41] Eels, always popular in Edwardian dishes, had to be skinned alive. Miss Ellery, who had been both kitchen-maid and cook, was regularly skinning eels in the 1930s: 'Well, they was fresh. You used to put your hands in plenty of salt, and catch hold the top, put it on the top of sort of a cooking table, and you have a two pronged fork and stab it in, and then hit it down with a heavy weight, and then cut the skin round and down and pull it right through.'[42] Among the traditional perquisites of the cook and other kitchen staff were rabbit skins, tea leaves (which could be re-used) and dripping: a man would come round weekly to collect the skins which could sell for as much as eight pence each; dripping could raise sixpence per pound. The sale of used corks was another lucrative kitchen sideline. At Rectory Farm House, Alice Osbourn reminded the cook to save all the old bread for the ferrets.

The kitchen was a breeding ground of rising damp, stinking drains, smoking stoves, black beetles, ants and other intruders and, above all, the ever-present problem of 'odours'. The green baize door, designed in the nineteenth century to protect the family from any unpleasant smells issuing from the kitchen regions, only dispensed with the problem in houses large enough for the two communities to live together without contact; in most houses the rooms were too uncomfortably close to shut out the smell of cooking altogether. Kitchens in large houses continued largely unchanged by modern innovation. Mrs Crosby, who started work as a scullery maid aged fifteen, was amazed even in 1912 by the ancient kitchen at Nuthall Temple in Nottinghamshire. Apart from the gas flares lighting the flagged passages, it was based on an almost medieval

model, with the fireplace, so inseparable from the traditional
English notion of 'hearth and home', still at its centre:

> The huge kitchen with its centre table and surrounding ones all
> round, shelves of copper pans and moulds, a large window looking
> out onto two courtyards with outbuildings for the game shoot and
> home killed sheep . . . the coal range in the far end of the kitchen had
> two large ovens on each side and had chimney fittings of brass, spits
> for baking bread and cooking large meat joints in front. The scullery
> was below ground level with a shallow round sink and a hole in the
> back to the outside, facing the lawns and the lake. Two large oak
> metal-banded tubs, one for washing-up all kitchenware and the
> other for rinsing, nothing to help with grease which I collected and
> saved for the man.[43]

Large country houses had stillrooms, where the preparation of
breakfast and tea would take place. Stillroom maids helped the
housekeeper make preserves, confectionery and chutney and in the
grandest houses, where there were two or three stillroom maids,
they learned intricate arts such as making butter sculptures, crystal-
lising flowers and distilling flowers into toilet waters.

In Rectory Farm House, Alice Osbourn wrote out detailed
instructions for the cook (who also seems to have undertaken much
of the cleaning of the kitchen and dining-room areas). By the time
the first breakfast, for Mr Baldwin, was served at 7.20, she was
expected to have lit the kitchen fire, dusted the hall, cleaned the
brass and washed the front door ('clear water only, no soap'). Mr
Baldwin's breakfast was porridge 'which must be very thoroughly
cooked [and] a *very* lightly boiled egg'. Mrs Baldwin, who break-
fasted at eight, had coffee, served '*very* hot', and fried bread and
bacon, after which the dining room had to be turned out and cleaned
and the cobwebs brushed away.

Most kitchens in the average Edwardian house were modestly
sized and rather dingy: facing north was cooler and therefore more
hygienic. The surfaces were generally thickly varnished, which
made them easier to wipe clean. The kitchen might lead to a small

garden, an outside lavatory for the use of the servants, a coal store and a tradesman's entrance. The kitchen itself was dominated by a wooden table which had to be scrubbed exhaustively every day and a cast-iron range which was blacked every morning. All kitchens, from the grandest to the humblest, had a stockpot continually on the boil. 'Almost anything edible went into it to provide the base for soups and sauces,' wrote kitchen-maid Edna Wheway. It was cleaned once a week.[44] As it was used for the household's hot water as well as cooking, the range, traditionally coal-fired (though now sometimes run on gas), had to be watched constantly in case it went out.

After food, laundry was the most expensive consideration in those middle-class households where standards had to be maintained on a tighter budget. Mrs Praga was delighted to find that there was still a copper (a built-in basin in the kitchen under which a fire was lit for boiling water) in her house in West Kensington as it meant that her overworked cook could wash some of the household linen in-house rather than sending it out to be washed in a laundry at extortionate expense. Large machines for mangling and wringing were now common, but the copper, the most traditional method of washing laundry, was still widely used for boiling the water for the first wash – which took place with heavy scrubbing in a wooden tub – and again for the second wash when the linen itself was boiled in it. Mrs Praga's cook was fortunate to have a copper at a time when few people in small houses like hers had running hot water. Rose Stacey, nursemaid for an archdeacon's family in Hampstead, had to do all the household laundry by boiling it in a tin bath on a gas ring in a little pantry at the top of the house.[45]

Annie Wilkinson, for forty years a laundrymaid at Castle Howard, remembered how, before the First World War, she'd 'stood from nine in the morning till five in the evening ironing a court petticoat'.[46] The aristocracy's passion for the old, for the finely crafted and handmade, required the highest and most intensive expertise. 'Lady Mary Fitzwilliam, she was a wonderful old lady, wonderful she was. And she had everything ancient. But I used to laugh: "My Lady, you aren't going to wear that, are you?"

"I am, I am, and don't I look nice in it?"' At Lyme Park, seat of the Legh family, the laundry was sent down by train every week in hampers from their London home. During a shoot, the three full-time laundresses would iron as many as 150 sheets. 'First of all the clothes were scrubbed and then they had a huge copper boiler with a fire underneath and all the whites used to go in there. They had a great big drum that used to rotate. That was the washer, I presume. They came out of the boiler, and they went into there, and that was washing and rinsing. When they were done in there, they used to go in a huge spinner. Then they were taken out of there; hung outside if it was fine. Everything was mangled afterwards, before it was ironed. Everything went through big automatic rollers.'[47]

Cotton, woven in the great textile factories of the industrial Midlands, needed mangling, starching, bleaching and pressing to keep its appearance. For the working-class housewife, washing her own family's clothes took up two full days of the week. 'Wash, wash, wash: it's like washing yer guts away,' was one recollection of the grind of washday.[48] The mother of Elsie Thompson, born in Stoke-on-Trent in 1894, took in laundry for a living. But when it came to their own family washday, she kept the children in bed all day while she washed their clothes, because she did not want the neighbours to know they only had one set.[49] Mrs Stott, born on the outskirts of Lancaster in 1896, came from a long line of laundresses. Her mother took in washing 'for all the big bugs' in the region: 'The washing that they used to do wasn't ordinary washing you know, it used to need goffering. Oh I can see my mother goffering now . . . The [maids'] caps and the aprons and such like, the gowns. The caps had to be goffered and down the sides of the aprons.'[50]

The linen used by servants and their employers, even if laundered at the same time, was kept separate by a complicated system of colour coding. At Lyme Park the three resident laundresses divided the labours: the head laundrymaid was in charge of all the best clothes of the family; the second did some of the higher servants's clothes and the third did the lower servants's clothes and the towels. Mrs Peel recommended that servants should be given red blankets to distinguish them from the blankets used by the family and their guests. The popularity of Whiteley's in Bayswater, one of London's first department stores, was boosted when it introduced into its laundry service separate amenities for washing the linen of servants and their employers.[51]

The stocking of the household linen cupboard itself, with its shelves for sheets, towels, napkins, tablecloths and so on, was a task so complex that elaborate systems were introduced to manage it efficiently. Each new item was marked with a red cross-stitch of the mistress's initial. Grander linen would be ordered with this already in place, but in most households it was the maid's job to see the initial was sewn on. Next to the initial would be embroidered the area of the house where the article would be employed (bathroom, bedroom or dining room), the date it was purchased and the number of each piece in its set: thus 3/6 on a sheet and towel would indicate that it was number three of a set of six.[52]

As it was customary for society ladies to change their clothes three times a day, laundering was a continuous operation. *Etiquette of Good Society* told its readers that on no account were ladies to wear lace in the mornings but that if visiting a friend in the morning it was acceptable for a dress to have embroidery. Tea gowns for afternoon 'At Homes' were deliberately diaphanous so that corsetry underneath could be loosened for a couple of hours. Then there were hats which needed trimming, boots which needed polishing and, always, gloves: 'all gloves are long, and are fastened by many buttons, from six on those worn out of doors to twenty on those worn with evening dress'.[53] Gloves were very often washed after a single wearing, or in the case of those made of kid, carefully brushed with a mixture of turpentine, ammonia and pumice powder.

Underwear (or, as the chic referred to it, *lingerie*), was now for the first time perceived as having an erotic as well as a functional purpose. It was recommended that ladies possessed at least two dozen examples of each kind of undergarment: chemise, knickers (with separate linings, washed daily), corsets, camisoles and stockings with suspenders. Black undergarments, though rather risqué, did not show the dirt and were therefore popular among those watching their budget. Chiffon was expensive, but it was the material of choice for the filmy undergarments in vogue, though it needed careful handling and could not be trusted to the large-scale steaming and mangling of a public laundry. These expensive wisps were washed by hand by a lady's-maid, if there was one, and after undressing would be discreetly wrapped by their owner in decorative chiffon pouches made especially for the purpose (often at a charitable institution). Nancy Astor's pouches, made for her 'by French crippled girls', were embroidered by her maid Rose Harrison with motifs in Lord Astor's racing colours.[54]

Lady's-maids, common only in the wealthier households, occupied a very particular place in the hierarchy of the servants' hall. Even within the upper-ten, they were regarded, by the nature of their job, as being on terms of privileged intimacy with their employer. Like governesses or secretaries, they were generally referred to by only their surname by their mistress and as 'Miss' by the other servants. Perks of the job often included travel and almost always included their mistress's cast-off clothes; they also received commissions from the tradesmen to whom they took their employer's custom. Mrs Earle in the *Cornhill* thought a lady's-maid with superior dressmaking skills a cost-saver, if you could afford one: 'It is fancy things made at home that really pay, not petticoats and underlinen. The lady's-maid, too, must undertake the mending of house linen, an important duty, as very few housemaids can be trusted to do fine needlework at all.'[55]

The lady's-maid also had the job of accompanying her mistress to country house parties where she enjoyed some kudos in the servants' hall and was addressed there by the name of her employer. A *Punch* cartoon of 1895 shows a lady's-maid standing by the train in which her mistress is about to depart, checking a list of items: 'Yes, my Lady, James went this morning with the Hunters, and I've sent on the Heavy Luggage with Charles. But I've got your Pencil-case, the Bicycle, your Ladyship's Golf-Clubs and Hunting Crop and Billiard Cue, the Lawn Tennis Racket, the Bezique Cards and Markers, your Ladyship's Betting Book and Racing Glasses and Skates and Walking-Stick – and if I've forgotten anything I can easily wire back for it from the first station we stop at.'

Like the butler, the lady's-maid was often tasked with transmitting the priorities of her employers to her fellow servants, and seeing on her behalf that the correct protocol was maintained below stairs at all times. The rank was one which expected to be accorded dignity. When Queenie Cox was promoted from scullery-maid to kitchen-maid, 'that meant the lady's-maid could say good morning to me before the scullery maid'.[56] French or Swiss girls were considered the most prestigious lady's-maids, as it was hoped that a little of their Continental elegance might rub off on their employer. Their social position appears to have been more fluid, in part due to the intimacy demanded by the job. If English, they often came from lower-middle-class homes; if from abroad they were readily associated in the popular imagination with saucy underwear and coquettish foreign ways: '*Ecoutez!* I will tell you another little *histoire*,' begins William Le Queux's 1911 novel, *The Indiscretions of a Lady's Maid*.

PART II

The Sacred Trust

Chapter 8

The Ideal Village

Elizabeth Banks was inspired to undertake her 1892 investigation into service to find an answer to the question that vexed the English middle classes: why was it that many girls would do almost anything, even if it meant living off 'porridge in the morning and watercress in the evening with no midday meal', rather than undertake the work of cleaning someone else's home? She visited a young seamstress living in terrible conditions – 'the unwomanly rags, the crust of bread, the straw and the broken chair' – in a lodging-house in Camberwell on eighteen pence a week. When the dismayed Elizabeth offered to find her a job as a housemaid, 'with a nice clean bedroom, plenty to eat, print dresses in the morning, black stuff in the afternoon, with white caps and aprons and collars and cuffs', she was astounded by the girl's outrage at the suggestion: '"Did you come only to insult me?" she demanded, stamping her feet. "I go out to service! I wear caps and aprons, those badges of slavery! No, thank you, I prefer to keep my liberty and be independent."'[1]

The servant-employing classes struggled to grasp why so many girls did not appear to be grateful for the opportunity to get their feet under a more comfortable table than the one they had come from. Was not the home a haven both moral and practical, a place of safety? The nineteenth century had been haunted by the spectre of the lost child of the Industrial Revolution: the chimney sweep, the crossing-sweeper, the pickpocket, the match-seller, the five-year-old child who had gone blind sorting buttons in a sweatshop. In the popular imagination they were perceived as orphaned (even if this were not in fact the case), adrift, alone and prematurely aged by malnutrition, poverty and abandonment. The social reformer Edwin Chadwick's 1842 descriptions of the 'rookeries' or London tenements in *The Bitter Cry of Outcast London* almost single-handedly sparked an age of public health reform. Chadwick's picture of a world of struggle, suffering and hopelessness was entirely cut off from the comfortable family world of the prosperous; nineteenth-century London, he wrote, was a labyrinth of filthy box-like slums, leading one from the other and 'reeking with poisonous and malodorous gases rising from accumulations of sewage and refuse scattered in all directions'.[2]

According to Henry Mayhew, in 1868–9 there were 17,000 known tramps in England and Wales and 17 per cent of them were under sixteen. In 1889, of the 192,000 registered inmates of work-houses, 54,000 were under sixteen. Dr Thomas Barnardo, the most celebrated of all Victorian philanthropists and a fiery street preacher, was moved to set up his first home for children when he discovered eleven young boys, barely clothed, sleeping along an iron gutter open to the elements. The annual accounts of Dr Barnardo's children's homes contain fearful catalogues of the ailments suffered by those picked up on the streets and given refuge: rickets, knock-knees, goitre, spinal paralysis, deaf and dumbness; and lung diseases like consumption, bronchitis, pneumonia and asthma, which were the legacy of the dust inhaled while working long hours in factories. In 1906, Edith, a five-year-old girl, 'nobody's child', was found by Thomas Barnardo wandering the streets apparently completely unwanted – absolutely nothing at all could be discovered of her origins or parentage. Another, a crippled boy of ten, was referred to Barnardo's after the boy's mother, a rubbish-picker, was burned to death by an upturned paraffin lamp.[3]

Efforts were made to contain these wandering, vagrant children by the institution of industrial schools, but the focus of the schools was largely penal and the pastoral work of caring for 'waifs and strays' was left to private charities and individual philanthropic endeavours. By 1878, in London alone, there were fifty philanthropic societies dedicated to the welfare of children.

Many social reformers of the turn of the twentieth century, Dr Barnardo among them, abhorred the demoralising and alienating effects of industrialisation and found a solution in the ideal of the healing hierarchies of a rural paradise lost, the essence of England. If housekeeping inculcated the discipline of thrift and the battle against waste, mass production was the very agent of superfluity and excess. The pre-industrial utopia was enshrined in another kind of social ecology, and at its centre was the mutual dependency that had existed between the classes in the imagined manorial village of the past. 'The village is the expression of a small corporate life,' wrote Sir Raymond Unwin, the architect of the garden cities of Letchworth and Hampstead Garden Suburb, 'in which all the different units are personally in touch with each other, conscious of and frankly accepting their relations, and on the whole content with them.'[4]

In the new garden cities, lych gates, mullions and gables jostled together in harmonious asymmetry, in contrast to the hastily erected tenement sprawls of industrial cities. Alfred Lyttelton MP hailed the garden city as the model of a community in which 'the squire and the parson and those who clustered round the parsonage or the mansion lived together harmoniously with no sign of tyranny or patronage on one side, or of servility or loss of independence on the other'. The garden city was a vision of a very English Eden, both radical and reactionary, espousing the 'practical socialism', the 'muscular Christianity', of its founders, yet at its heart deeply paternalist: it was a heaven of many levels, where public service flourished at the top only if nourished by the wholesome craftsmanship and service of those at the bottom.

In fact, although the English landed estate still exercised considerable rural influence, the English village was already more often than not a hybrid community of cottagers, landlords and incomers. Three miles south of Farnham, Surrey, is the scrubby heathland landscape of a small community known as the Bourne, the subject of George Sturt's 1912 book *Change in the Village*. Sturt was a wheelwright by trade and his book describes vividly a world in which the traditional communal economy had been replaced by a commercial one. This had brought, wrote Sturt, a creeping loss of self-respect in the villagers: 'inferiority had come into their lives'. The Bourne was not an ideal village as the garden-city reformers might have imagined one: there was no benevolent manor, no village green for dancing round a maypole; there was little indication in the Bourne of the happy hierarchies so beloved of the celebrators of 'Merrie England'. The old crafts and skills of the past had been gradually replaced by piecework for minimum wages which left the villagers too exhausted for the traditional rural festivities that well-meaning outsiders wished them to enjoy. They were resolutely unsympathetic to the 'self-conscious revivals of peasant arts which are now being recommended to the poor by a certain type of philanthropist', wrote Sturt.[5]

The greatest visible change in the Bourne during the early years of the twentieth century was the proliferation of suburban villas that had sprung up on the edge of the village. In the new economy of rural life, it was very often the new villa on which village livelihoods now depended. These middle-class households had gardens that needed tending and 'even the cheaper villas . . . need their cheap drudges'. Other traditional sources of income were increasingly insecure: machinery was gradually replacing labourers; large laundries were replacing washerwomen working at home. In villages like the Bourne, where there was no big-house tradition, poorly paid and unprotected drudge work was the only domestic service available. Sturt tells of a struggling farm labourer whose daughter paid half the family's rent from her earnings as a servant girl in a villa. To the argument that working in a middle-class home raised the servant's aspirations, Sturt had a brisk retort: 'The truth is that middle-class domesticity, instead of setting cottage women on the road to middle-class culture of mind and body, has sidetracked them – has made of them charwomen and laundresses, so that other women may shirk these duties and be cultured.'[6]

George Sturt noted too how the diet of the villagers of the Bourne had been debased by cheap and adulterated processed foods; how they struggled to save money as they became more dependent on shop-bought goods. Pineapples and salmon, once the preserve of the very rich, were now available, tinned, to the masses. Margarine was the cheap alternative to butter for the poor. Meat was shipped in refrigerated containers from Argentina and New Zealand. The writer E. V. Lucas complained bitterly about 'beef which, stiff and stark, has voyaged from distant lands and must be thawed before it is cooked'.[7] An ever-higher premium and status was therefore imposed on food that expressed its authenticity, its truth to its state in nature and its agricultural origins. The colour white having become associated with food that had been artificially altered by chemicals, leached of its organic goodness, earthy brown was now the colour of natural wholesomeness. Walter Southgate remembered the milkman dyeing eggs brown in tea or coffee in order to charge more for them. For the author Philip Mason's mother, 'everything had to be homemade; it would have been a disgrace to buy a cake or a pot of jam. It was a waste of money for one thing but, quite apart from that, shop cakes and jam were not as *good*. They did not taste so good and they were adulterated.'[8]

'Everything [should] taste like the thing it is,' was the view of the butler Albert Thomas who worked most of his life on those self-sufficient estates where produce was so abundant that trains travelled daily into London carrying the fruits of the land to their owners' town houses. Superior homes disdained the sealed, wrapped, frozen and canned: game was only considered ready for eating when it had been hung till it was high and crawling with maggots. Rabbits, delivered to the house whole, had to be skinned, have their heads chopped off with a cleaver, their eyes gouged out and the brains removed with a large spoon. Real meat had the inimitable taste of blood, guts and hard work. 'The cook, she would never let me wash the hares, she always reckoned that you washed the flavour down the sink,' remembered Margaret Powell.[9]

In this vision of social order, domestic service was seen as a good in itself – binding the classes together in co-dependent harmony within both the home and the wider community. Dame Henrietta Barnett's plans for Hampstead Garden Suburb, the building of which began in 1903, included spacious lodging houses for the accommodation of daily servants as well as clubs and meeting places where they could productively fill their leisure hours. She also advocated a school of Household Handicraft intended to train both housewives and servants in the skills of running a well-managed, waste-free home, where old skills were re-learned by a generation that had almost forgotten them.

Like Henrietta Barnett, Dr Barnardo's model of perfect community was the ideal village. Barnardo, a member of the Plymouth Brethren (by conversion), was a man of prodigious energy and showmanship, whose work among London's poor sparked a messianic mission to improve the lot of the poorest of Britain's urban children. At his death in 1905, Barnard left behind ninety-six Barnardo's Homes with the care of 8,500 children, and thousands followed his funeral cortège through the streets of the East End. Instead of children being corralled into large institutions, poorhouses, industrial schools or reformatories, where they suffered de-humanising mass washes by hose as well as the obligatory cropped hair and shaming uniforms, Barnardo wanted the children he had rescued to be embraced into the safety of middle-class private life. It was his belief that only the home, the place of safety, regularity and femininity, could save these waifs from destitution: and having no homes of their own, domestic service in someone else's home was the means of their salvation.

The plight of Barnardo's children fired the imagination of the Victorian public and Dr Barnardo used photographs of the 'saved' in their white pinafores contrasted with terrible (routinely faked) pictures of their 'before' state to help raise the funds of which he was constantly short. The key to Dr Barnardo's vision was domestic order and craftsmanship as a bulwark against the dislocation and unnaturalness of urban mass industry. Both boys and girls were taught the domestic disciplines. 'All the household work of the Homes is done by the boys themselves,' wrote Barnardo in the 1890s. 'They are their own cooks and waiters, their own boot blacks and house and chambermaids. They scrub the floors (and we pride ourselves on the floors at Stepney).' And while the boys were also to be trained as tailors, blacksmiths or bakers, the girls were to be trained for domestic service. Dr Barnardo was not interested in creating footmen or lady's-maids: Barnardo girls were destined to be the maids-of-all-work, the good plain cooks of the Christian, middle-class household. As Dr Barnardo wrote: 'Each girl saved from a criminal course is a present to the next generation of a virtuous woman and a valuable servant.'[10]

The doctor, who operated a policy of never turning any child away, was among the few reformers who took an enlightened view of unmarried mothers – those who would never be permitted to register with a domestic employment agency and, if pregnant, would almost certainly have been sacked by their employers without references. Instead he found them domestic work in kindly and carefully vetted homes, and encouraged them to choose other women to bring up their children at a cost of five shillings a week. Dr Barnardo's paid three shillings and sixpence of this expense and the young mothers paid the balance. In 1908, 417 children were found homes under this scheme.

The price paid for this boundless protection was freedom, for Dr Barnardo exercised control over almost every detail of his children's future lives. A young mother who transgressed the rules or 'lapsed into immorality' would find the Barnardo's doors for ever closed to her. The alternative, however, was the complete and ruthless separation of a working mother and her child. At the turn of the century, Jenny, a maid in a household in Eaton Square, London, had a child by a policeman who abandoned her. Later, in the 1920s, having worked for two decades for a family in Watlington, Jenny revealed that she had a daughter of her own who had been brought up by her grandmother in Norfolk: 'Her disgrace was kept secret for twenty years and we children never had the slightest suspicion.'[11]

Barnardo's first girls' village in Barkingside was nostalgic in design and conception, a Kate Greenaway picture of village England: rows of half-timbered cottages, each one named after a wild flower, grouped round a simple green or communal garden.

Each cottage was run by a volunteer 'mother' who oversaw the training of the girls in those domestic skills which would secure them placements as servants. They kept goats and ponies, grew their own vegetables, baked their own bread and worked in the communal laundry. Festivities on the green were encouraged with the singing of traditional English folksongs and maypole-dancing. An emphasis was put on cleanliness and all girls had the luxury (unknown in other institutions) of their own bed. Regular daily routine was paramount. They were kept in almost total ignorance of the outside world, being forbidden newspapers and, later, the wireless. The 'mothers', in keeping with the vocational spirit of the work, were unmarried, strictly teetotal and required to be Christians of an Evangelical flavour. Sometimes the 'mothers' were loving and tender; sometimes, as later accounts made clear, they were less so.

The community was known only as 'the Village'. Its residents were removed from the cruel anarchy of the streets, but as an exercise in social engineering, the Village operated by benign despotism and the close management of every detail. As Agnes Bowley, one former resident, put it: 'There was a high fence and wrought iron gates and once they clanged behind you, you were shut in and you didn't feel free.'[12] There was a high level of supervision of the homes in which the girls would be placed as servants. She was always to be permitted to be fully in contact with her Barnardo's 'mother' and she was not to be burdened unreasonably with laundry. Other questions posed to potential employers allowed for little dissent from the Barnardo's view of the virtuous life. An application form completed in 1902 by a woman in Sevenoaks who ran a small school included the questions: 'Are all the members of your family resident at home total abstainers?' and: 'Is family worship observed regularly in the household in the morning and evening?' The Sevenoaks householder felt obliged to state that she and her husband were Church of England and her cook was a Nonconformist; and to promise that on no occasion would she permit her domestic to visit a public house.

Other charities and social reformers also took up the theme of salvation through domestic service. The establishment in 1875 by

Dame Henrietta and her fellow social reformer, Jane Nassau Senior of the Metropolitan Association for the Befriending of Young Servants (MABYS), undertook the training and protection of girls to be cared for and gainfully employed in the safe haven of the home. The MABYS fulfilled a vital function in regulating the means by which girls were employed: '8,000 little charmaids helped and comforted, and scolded and advised, and kept from incalculable temptation and wretchedness'.[13] With care homes, agencies and a vast network of volunteers who visited girls they had placed to make sure they were being well treated, the MABYS was, by the 1880s, the most influential regulator devoted only to the employment and protection of young servants. The girls were treated with kindness, as one might treat those for whom decisions have to be made on their behalf. 'Their fathers have abandoned them or are dead; their mothers are dead, or mad, or drunk; they have no relations, or worse still, only bad ones. They have been kept alive, indeed, by the state; but the state at best is more of an incubator than a parent and this Association for years past has tried to help the children, with some heart and pity to spare for so much helplessness and childish misery.' Successful domestic placements in secure homes could effect, said the MABYS, a transformation both moral and material. One claimant arriving at the office in the Strand, reported Mrs Richmond Ritchie, daughter of the novelist William Thackeray, who chronicled the early history of the MABYS, was 'a sturdy little figure in the usual smart hat and cloth jacket of a "general" with a bright-eyed and unmistakable "out for a holiday" air'.[14] The dreadful temptations of the streets were to be averted by MABYS lodging houses where girls were 'received and harboured' for a time between their places.

By the mid-1880s, the MABYS ran twenty-five branch registry offices, seventeen homes and 800 women visitors, and placed around 5,000 girls in service each year. Members of the MABYS network of volunteer ladies interviewed prospective employers, inspecting both conditions and wages, before they would allow a girl to embark on a job.

The Girls' Friendly Society (GFS), also founded in 1875, by Mrs Mary Townsend, was another charity set up to support young servant girls and was administered through the existing philanthropic networks of the Church of England. As the MABYS declined in influence, the GFS continued to play an important part in the pastoral care of young domestics until the 1950s. The GFS was founded on strongly Church of England principles, with a dash of fashionable medievalism thrown in. Members were referred to as 'maidens', or sometimes 'pilgrims', and the GFS membership as a whole was known as a 'fellowship of girlhood'. Like Dr Barnardo's, the key to the GFS mission was the promotion of the prophylactic virtues of temperance, hygiene and thrift. Clubs all over Britain and the colonies were run by the dauntless ladies of the GFS who established a presence wherever there were girls in service who might need them. Many servants recalled the haven that GFS clubs provided when they were friendless in new jobs in unknown cities. There was also a didactic purpose. 'It's church and it's to keep girls good, to keep you off the street,' recalled housemaid Annie Edwards of the Bible classes held by the GFS in her village. Annie and her classmates had to hunt through the Bible for uplifting quotations: 'It kept you good.'[15]

Outside the home, and the benevolent protection of the GFS and MABYS and Dr Barnardo, even if there was not the degrading horror of the slums, there was widely believed to be moral chaos. Even provincial towns like Oxford were not immune from it: 'girls, sixteen to eighteen, parading the fair alone, dressed in jockey caps ... imitation open jackets and waistcoats, and smoking cigarettes or cigars?'[16] ran a shocked editorial in the *Oxford Times* in 1888 about St Giles' Fair, where unmarried boys and girls freely and dangerously mixed in public. Dolly Davey's father insisted she go into service because the alternative could only be 'larking about with boys'.[17] The philanthropists were full of suggestions as to how to distract the working girl from temptation. Lady Albinia Hobart-Hampden recommended the introduction of household clubs which would deter girls from going out at night, 'on the look out for a lark – and often, I fear, entering the public houses'.[18]

The newspapers were full of tales of the dangers of the streets for women. The campaigning journalist W. T. Stead went undercover in the 1890s to meet a woman who ran a successful London brothel.

He reported that she had told him of procuresses who lay in wait for vulnerable young maidservants, possibly alone in London for the first time, whom they would groom for prostitution. There was a lucrative demand for virgins, Stead was told: once a girl had agreed to the proposition of 'meeting a gentleman' in exchange for a small sum, her virginity was tested by a woman posing as a midwife; she was then taken to a private house where a client paid top price for her. Stead was told that: 'The easiest age to pick them up is fourteen or fifteen ... They begin to get more liberty without getting much more sense; they begin to want clothes and things which money can buy, and they do not understand the value of what they are parting with in order to get it.' Stead painted a picture of desolation, of loneliness, cynicism and corruption. The procuress told him proudly that she had most success with 'nurse-girls', though 'occasionally we get a governess and sometimes cooks and other servants. We get to know the servants through the nurses. Young girls from the country, fresh and rosy, are soon picked up in the shops or as they run errands. But nurse-girls are the great field.'[19]

The poor did not always behave in the manner that their benefactors expected of them. Menella Smedley, a lady philanthropist, reported with amazement that the typical Poor School recruit ('violent and obstinate beyond belief') into domestic service quite often refused to be grateful for the opportunity. 'Sullen, violent and unmanageable. Apathetic when not out of temper. Ignorant of all practical matters and deficient in aptitude for learning. Self-possessed. Hard, untruthful. A good-tempered variety is occasionally to be found but it is very rare.'[20] Lady visitors from the MABYS, sensitive to the behavioural problems of girls who had experienced extreme misery and poverty, were nonetheless often dismayed by their charges' refusal to contemplate domestic service instead of work in a factory or other, less secure, occupations. In 1891 one visitor reported that Annie Towle, working in a laundry, was 'a steady girl but quite determined never to go to service'. When seventeen-year-old Alice Coleman, who had been a prize-winning pupil at the Ashford District School run by the MABYS, became a maid, the Association learned that she was proving troublesome. It

turned out that Alice, like the factory girls from whom those philanthropic ladies had saved her, insisted on spending 'all her money
on fine clothes and painting her face'.[21]

The most important advantage of factory life was freedom.
Factory girls did not have to endure the daily petty humiliations of
being at the beck and call of a condescending mistress; of having no
set hours to call their own, of having pitifully few opportunities to
meet men (or even other women). Dr Barnardo's prescription, in a
letter to one of his former cottage residents, was resignation and
obedience. Signing himself 'Your Sincere Friend', Barnardo wrote:
'I hope my dear girl that I shall hear that you are pleasing your
mistress, and that you are not saucy or bad-tempered or lazy, but
obliging, polite, respectful and hard-working, that you get up early
in the morning, and endeavour throughout the day to please your
mistress as much as you can.'[22] Yet, the reality of life in private service was often far from the wholesome promise of contentment held
out by the Village. 'My hands were raw with scrubbing all the time.
You were the drab, the lowest of the low,' recalled a former
Barnardo's girl who left the Village in 1937.[23]

The factory and the home were two sides of a working divide.
'Some maids, after a long period in service, acquired the accents and
attitudes of their employers and, in their turn, looked down on
factory girls and thought them "common",' remembered Edith
Hall. Factory girls returned the contempt with interest, despising
domestic servants as skivvies, slaveys and 'drain 'ole cleaners'.[24]
Elizabeth Banks described for her American readers a new world of
burgeoning opportunities for young women with 'independence'
their battlecry:

> Everywhere I heard that word. It sounded above the clickety-clack
> of the typewriter while the fingers flew over the keys; the noisily
> turning factory wheels failed to drown it; I heard it over the clink of
> the barmaid's glasses; it mingled with the ring of the telephone bell,
> the whirr of the cash machine and the refrain of the chorus girl. The
> telegraph-operator murmured the word as she took down the letters
> of the various messages, the schoolmistress whispered it as she gave

out the morrow's lesson in arithmetic, the female bookkeeper uttered it while she added up the long column of figures. Even the little sub-editress, earning a salary of $1 a week for stealing copy from the daily journals, seemed imbued with that so-called spirit of independence.[25]

Yet Elizabeth Banks's view is too optimistic: in 1911, nearly twenty years after she conducted her investigations into domestic service, one in seven working women were still employed in some form of service. For the fourteen-year-old school leaver, the 1913 findings of social investigator Barbara Drake were nearer the truth: 'For the girl who belongs to the great majority which is average and commonplace and who misses her vocation to marry, the outlook is a poor one. With no taste and no skill for further work, with little hope of another berth, she is discharged for a trumpery fault; or she is shelved at a lower wage as a counter-hand; or she is driven from the beloved haunts of the City or the Strand, to the limbo of the waitress, the teashop of the suburbs.'[26] Most importantly, working-class women, like middle- and upper-class ones, were still, on the whole, untrained for any occupation but housework. Emily Yeddon charred all her working life: 'We've all had a bit of me mother's life, to work like me mother – and we've all been good mothers, and clean, and done plenty of housework because it were drilled into us we'd nothing else to do only have plenty of good housework.'[27]

It became increasingly difficult, however, to convince girls that paid housework had *moral* superiority. There were complaints that Dr Barnardo insisted on training boys and girls in skills such as cobbling that were so fast being overtaken by new technology that they were almost redundant by the time the children entered the world of employment. The working class during the last part of the nineteenth century had become increasingly politically active and organised: the 759,000 workers belonging to trade unions in 1890 had become 4.1 million by 1914; in 1906, there were twenty-nine Labour MPs and by 1910 there were forty-two. Even on the big estates that embodied the reformers' model of healthy patronage, many servants had scented social change. Factory work offered resistance to the deference of previous generations. At Beech Hill Park, on the eve of the First World War, the daughter of two generations in service with the Edwards family would have none of the bowing and scraping that her parents considered normal: 'their attitude put me off the gentry. If you opened a gate for them, they expected you to curtsey. My mother was used to it; in her time there was nothing else for a girl to do but go into service. You know they even told the servants how to vote! Well, I'm afraid I really didn't want to get into that position so I got a job in a factory which really disgusted Mrs Edwards. She complained to my mother that factory girls were so low, so rude – they would have been to the likes of her!'[28]

By 1900, the vast majority of workers in jam factories and match factories were women. It was hard and terrible work: a girl observed packing cocoa in a factory was described by the reformer Clementina Black in her report on sweated labour as 'absolutely colourless, and although there was no sign about her of any specific illness, seemed exhausted literally almost to death'. They earned about seven shillings a week on average, no more than a maid-of-all-work. Factory girls were denounced in the press as loud, brash and, usually, drunk; accounts almost always include derisory descriptions of their garish 'plumage' and painted faces. In contrast to the demure silence expected of servants, factory girls were popularly characterised by defiant loudness, and Black noted that they 'shout merrily to their mates and sauce the men'.[29] Dr Barnardo, describing an unfortunate encounter with a factory worker, struggled to contain his horror at the sound of her voice, 'indescribable for its roughness, vulgarity and unwomanliness'.[30] Miss Clara Collet, another philanthropic researcher on the factory frontline, reported that the girls she encountered were 'rough, boisterous, outspoken, warm-hearted, honest, working girls'. She added that their 'standard of morality is very low, so low that to many they may seem to have none at all', but found this outweighed by their loyalty and generosity in rallying round friends who 'got into trouble'.[31]

The inhabitants of conservative rural communities tended to

uphold this view of factory work as vulgar and disreputable. Libby Low from Herefordshire, who was born in 1900, remembered that 'going into service was the only thing girls could do. There was only one factory in Knighton and people wouldn't talk to you if you worked there. Well, it was so low to come down to that. You see most of the men were farmers round here and I suppose they wouldn't let their girls go to the factory. Service, they didn't mind that, though there was less money, because I think the factory paid more. They did have girls working there but I didn't know any of them. But they said round here it wasn't good enough work for us.'[32] Estate workers' daughters, raised in the shadow of the big house and with a habit of rising with the lark, were, unsurprisingly, viewed as excellent servant material.

The growth of the suburbs increased the demand for domestics and exacerbated the prickly topic that became widely known as the 'servant problem'. The suburban servant girl (and there was usually just the one) was often characterised by novelists and other observers as truculent and impudent, her mistress as pretentious and over-exacting. T. H. Crosland in 1905 created a composite suburban woman called 'Mrs Scold' and called her downtrodden maid-of-all-work the 'slattern'. Crosland's splenetic loathing of the suburban classes is unusually extreme, but he was not alone in viewing the expanding group of lower-middles as having really no right to servants at all. Having not imbibed from birth the mystical nature of the paternalistic bond, it was thought that they did not know how to behave correctly with staff. It was the suburbans' uppishness that really irked; their refusal to stick to the life Crosland thought they had been born to. Furthermore, at a time of shortage, there would be more servants to go round those who really needed them if the suburbans gave up pretending to a status they would never acquire and knuckled down to their own housework. 'The real reason why servants are so dreadful in suburbia is because, nine times out of ten, they belong to the same class as their mistresses who, not to put too fine a point on it, were born to wrestle not to reign,' he opined. Clearly never having experienced life at Chatsworth, Blenheim or Welbeck, Crosland goes on: 'In a reasonable household servants are employed because they are a necessity. In too many suburban households, on the other hand, servants are a superfluity and an ostentation.'[33]

Clerkly, aspiring types inspired both mockery and defensive outrage. Their efforts at education and self-improving leisure, their apparently cramping notions of acceptable behaviour were a familiar theme of jokes and cartoons. 'For in suburbia,' mocked Crosland, 'we must be consistently and un-deviatingly and abidingly respectable.' But despite the contempt for respectability voiced by aristocrats, bohemians and intellectuals, for the most part the values associated with respectability, such as privacy, conformity and self-improvement, had become the dominant social model. And when it came to servants, respectability had the advantage of producing the conservative, cautious and deferential mindsets that turned independent human beings into good staff, becoming therefore a source of amusing and condescending anecdotes for their employers. Working-class respectability encouraged all the qualities found so pleasing in good service: it did not ask difficult questions, enjoyed order and outward appearances, did not gossip, drink or smoke, or gad about with boys – all the qualities so distressingly lacking in the factory girl. Any measure of sexual expression was in particular ruthlessly frowned on: rules on 'followers' imposed on maids in most houses meant that any expression of sexuality became regarded as 'flighty'. All temptations needed to be controlled – even in houses where men and women servants worked together. 'The housemaids' quarters were nowhere near the footmen's quarters,' remembered Enid Field of her time as a maid in Woburn Abbey, which maintained this distinction in the 1930s: 'You avoided them and they avoided you.'[34]

Putting oneself forward in a brash manner was very unrespectable in her family, remembered May Cosh, born into abject poverty in Cardiff in 1897: 'You weren't allowed to chatter. If you were spoken to directly, you spoke back, but we didn't do any chattering.' May's mother 'didn't believe in' second-hand clothes or tinned food – preferring the added expense of new clothes and fresh food.[35] May does not say whether her mother was in service, but a dislike for tinned food might have been acquired in an upper-class household where fresh produce was plentiful.

Keeping oneself to oneself was another central tenet of respectability, and therefore learning how to discern and to avoid those who would contaminate one by association. Respectability was discipline, boundaries and control – all desirable in good servants. Elsie Thompson from Stoke-on-Trent, a charlady until the age of seventy-one, remembered how much appearances mattered: 'Mother was very particular – we weren't allowed to talk during meals.' Gloves were worn. She didn't believe she was '"low class" because she was respectable'.[36]

The maintenance of respectability, of good behaviour and cleanliness, against the odds, was much lauded. Among the very poor, the possession of even one of those social distinctions allowed you to hold your head up in the world. Charlie Chaplin, for example, as a poor child in London, remembered that having a cooked meal on a Sunday instantly conferred respectability, separated you from the formless, habitless horde. The duty of being respectable fell heavily upon women. 'No figure among the poor,' wrote Anna Martin, a settlement worker in Bermondsey at the turn of the century, 'is so much commended as the hard-working drudge who, in spite of a drunken, worthless husband, keeps her home together and rears her children respectable.'[37] Respectable servants were more likely to uphold the service status quo even if their inner lives, the 'damp souls of housemaids' that T. S. Eliot loftily imagined 'rattling breakfast plates' in basement kitchens, were, alas, deficient.[38]

It was a shock for many servants to discover that the standards of respectable behaviour that they were expected to adhere to were often not as valued by their employers. May Cosh found her first domestic position a revelation: 'I wasn't happy there. I wasn't happy there because they were supposed to be toffs. And their children were ruder than the likes of us that were poor.'[39]

Chapter 9

'Silent, Obsequious and Omnipresent'

In 1902 the living conditions of a 'colonial gentlewoman' stranded on the veldt in the British dominion of South Africa were primitive. An article in *The Nineteenth Century* that year set the scene: 'A four-bedroomed cottage, roughly built of stone, with mud floors, cheaply papered walls, and sparsely furnished. No easily accessible neighbours, oftenest no servant, or what perhaps is almost as bad, a dirty, cheeky, inconsequential *kaffir* maid, whose very language is worse than Greek.'

Wives, potential wives, servants, sisters to help brothers run farms; mothers-in-law to help wives look after children – all were in demand for domestic service in the Empire. 'The greatest impediment to progress in South Africa is the impossibility of obtaining efficient domestic servants,' the article explained. The shortage of wives was blamed on the shortage of servants to lighten the load of running a house in the inhospitable wilds of a new country. But it was thought that if sufficient encouragement could be given to a young British girl with some domestic experience, then it might act as an enticement to the English woman to consider making her home abroad, and participating in the on-the-ground work of colonisation: 'the absolute necessity of providing our children with nice-minded, superior companionship, and ourselves with efficient and congenial assistance in household matters'.[1]

British servant girls were soon in such demand in Canada, New Zealand, Australia and South Africa that there were sometimes sixty employers offering a place for each available girl. In 1890 the Reverend E. M. Tomlinson, Honorary Secretary of the Church of England Emigration Society, reported that the Australians were still 'crying out for domestic servants, and they cannot get enough'. Between 1904 and 1907, more than 16,000 domestic maids went to Canada alone.[2] For many girls, the rewards to be found abroad were tempting: the British, even their servants, enjoyed a status in the colonies that they may not have had in Britain, and all outward bound fares were fully paid. Dr Barnardo was among the most enthusiastic proponents of emigration, believing that it could only do girls and boys good to be taken from the hideous urban slums of Britain into the wholesome farm labour and big skies of a new world. It was an activist of the Girls' Friendly Society who in 1884 founded the British Women's Emigration Society, 'the most practical bit of religious work that anyone can take up'.[3]

A proliferation of charitable associations scooped up troubled, impoverished girls, some as young as thirteen, and shipped them overseas to further the development of domestic settlements. Many, notably those sent to isolated farmsteads, were miserably homesick and a few had to be sent home; but others made their lives abroad, some successfully. There were schemes for rehabilitating prostitutes, and for relieving the hard lot of seamstresses, milliners and those who struggled with the drudgery of piecework. At every stage of the journey they were given the vigilant protection of missionary and temperance societies or organisations pledged to protect them from the danger of white-slave traffickers. The application process was rigorous: only one out of every ten applicants was accepted for the journey. Those who sought emigration to escape a 'past' – prostitution perhaps or an illegitimate child, or having been dismissed from a previous domestic post without a 'character' (reference) – had to pay their own way or negotiate some private transaction that would fund their passage.

On arrival, many girls proved less inclined to toil in another woman's home than their employers may have hoped. They were keen to grab with both hands the advantages offered by life in a new continent. In 1902, Lady Hely-Hutchinson, wife of the Cape Governor, complained that the emigration project of British servant girls was 'a lamentable failure'. They were 'flighty, self-serving, purposeless, ignorant, lazy and inefficient'. More often than not, they were also 'common-minded girls of doubtful morals' who, by the time they were eighteen, would 'refuse to be servants any more but go to the restaurants, bars &c; or marry young men who ought to have wives of a higher class'.[4]

A particularly interesting feature of the emigration of women to the colonies is the number of middle-class women who chose to apply for work as domestic servants; women who could hardly be said to have 'doubtful morals', but whose very gentility and lack of practical experience made them unsuited to domestic work in often primitive conditions. The unmarried woman of small education, who advertised her services as a 'lady-help', also perhaps hoped to snatch at some adventure and a chance to make her life anew, possibly even to find a husband. Emigration as a domestic offered a solution to the crushing limitations of a life of genteel poverty in Britain. The lady-help however, generally not qualified to be a nurse, governess, cook or housemaid, was not what was required in a farming station or a remote mining settlement. There were many complaints of their unsuitability for hard work, that they were 'too delicate to undertake any but the lightest duties'. The verdict of the *Imperial Colonist* in 1904 is sharply poignant: lady-helps in South Africa, it said, were 'unemployed because [they were] unemployable'; they were too often 'decayed gentlewomen' who had 'gone to South Africa with the idea that the inefficient will prosper better here'.[5]

English domestics were less in demand in India. The subcontinent offered fewer opportunities for remaking one's life than did the farming communities of South Africa, Canada and Australia. In fact, the Indian nations had a tradition of complex hierarchies and a rigid caste system that proved to be highly compatible with British traditions and social order. In both its bureaucracy and its ceremonial, the Empire held up a flattering mirror to both the British and the Indian ruling classes. An aristocratic household in Delhi was run with the oiled efficiency of the English country house, its retainers the necessary cogs in the vast machinery of the home. 'The servants scurried about on bare feet, the tails of their turbans and the fullness of their white coats waving behind them as they dodged among the people at the table with fresh dishes. They were silent, obsequious and omnipresent.'[6]

Social certainties and strata were reassuringly upheld in the colonial club with its reinforcing taboos, regulations and exclusions; and these were echoed in the households of the Raj, from that of the Viceroy downwards. As Lord Curzon, whose viceroyalty was the most splendid of them all, put it: 'We are always living half in the present and half in the past. In the conditions and still more in the ceremonies of our public life, the two are blended together with peculiar harmony, so that we cannot quite say where the one ends and the other begins and the spirit of the past seems to be part of the atmosphere we breathe.' As late as the 1930s, when the Viceroy toured the subcontinent, he numbered in his entourage, as a show of power, about two hundred 'inferior servants'. But the households of all colonial employees were designed to be equally a demonstration of the mystical, unifying and ordering principle of the Empire itself. When Star Staunton, a girl brought up in a colonial family, berthed at Bombay for the first time, the servants of her father's house came forward to garland her with marigolds and lilies and jasmine: 'as each man delivered his fragrant burden, he intoned the customary vow of love and loyalty'.[7]

For those who experienced it, nothing would ever again match the Anglo-Indian* household in its pomp. Writing her weekly column in the *Times of India* under the pseudonym 'An Anglo-Indian', an army officer's wife declared that 'one of the follies of Indian life' was 'that you must keep three to do the work of one'.[8] While a British bachelor made do with a small team – perhaps a cook, a gardener and a 'boy' (the term used to describe any middle-aged man of some experience in service who acted as a butler and

---

* I use the term here in its nineteenth-century meaning, of the English in India.

valet) – once he had found himself a wife, the Raj household became a teeming populace of employees.

'The number of servants would have been puzzling to anyone who did not know Indian ways; we took them for granted,' remembered the novelist Rumer Godden and her sister 'Jon', who lived as children in Narayanganj, in what is now Bangladesh, in the years before the First World War. 'Even though we did not have as many servants as, for instance, the Fitzgibbon Greys: Mr Fitzgibbon Grey was not only head of our neighbouring jute works but was reported to own the entire firm. Mrs Fitzgibbon Grey had an *ayah*; not to look after her children – she had none – but simply to look after her clothes; in their house there was an especial bearer, an *Ooriah*, to serve drinks; a sweeper dog-boy to groom and walk the dogs.' Even in modest homes, a young boy might be employed during the monsoon rains in case his master's car got stuck in mud, in which case his job was to carry his mistress and any other women on his back over a raging river. It was customary up to the early twentieth century for a guest at a dinner party to be accompanied by a retinue of her own servants, to wait on her at table and to accompany her home. The servant in India conducted his work with a commitment that even in Britain would have been hard to command. The duties, for example, of the *khitmagar*, or bearer, might include standing behind his master's chair at mealtimes and stirring his tea, cutting his meat – everything short of actually eating the food for him. By the mid-1920s, even the most self-important pukka sahib found this kind of behaviour a little embarrassing.

Her servants were generally the first people from whom the Raj housewife, if she were curious, learned about India. There were the minutely calibrated differences in religious observance and caste to begin with. Intricate sectarian distinctions meant that each job came with its own religious significance to be carefully respected. The cook (always a man) would not touch pork if he were a Muslim or beef if he were a Hindu. The *khitmagar*, who had the task of managing the other servants, would not undertake anything but his own tasks; even moving an article of furniture would be beneath him. The work of sweeping, scrubbing or emptying chamberpots was done only by Untouchables; the work of looking after dogs by yet another caste – and often a young child. Untouchables would not handle dead animals, the disposal of which required the services of another group altogether, and the Goddens remembered that 'if a crow fell dead into our garden or one of our guinea-pigs died, Nitai, our sweeper could not pick up or touch the corpse; a boy of a special sect had to be called in from the bazaar; he put on his best shirt of marigold-coloured silk to do this grisly work'.[9]

Most servants were men, with the exception of the *ayah*, who was the household nanny, but the cook (*khansama*) would often have helping him in the kitchen a *tunny-ketch*, a woman permitted to feed the poultry, grind the spices and cook the rice, attend to the lamps and clean the master's boots, work considered beneath the dignity of the cook. A *musalchi* helped with the washing-up, a kind of scullion, described in 1890 by Flora Annie Steel: 'bearing, as his badge of office, a greasy swab of rag tied to a bit of bamboo'.[10] In most large households, a *derzi*, or tailor, endlessly stitching at clothes he was mending or copying, might be found sitting on the verandah; then there was the *dhobi*, who had the never-ending labour of the family's laundry (and most people changed at least twice a day in the heat, and then for dinner). In those places where there were no telephones, *chuprassis* were employed to send messages and acted as informal bodyguards, always on the lookout for people going in and out. And because many rural areas had no electricity and therefore no electric fans, there was also the *punkah-wallah* whose sole duty was to pull the rope that operated the fan, or *punkah*, day and night to create a cooling breeze. The night *punkah-wallah* could do it by fixing a rope to a foot and could perform the movement while almost asleep.

The 'character', the recommendation considered so sacred to employers in England, served as no reference at all when it came to servants in India. The author of *The Wife's Help to Indian Cookery* warned her readers in 1910 that 'most frequently, these characters, or "*Chitthis*", are borrowed; or they are often written for the occasion by persons who earn their bread by writing characters for any applicant who will pay them a few *annas*'. Then there was the delicate question of perquisites and the complicated web of transactions that the cook, who did the ordering of local stores, was entitled to as his cut from the local tradesmen: the system was known as *dastur* and was entirely comprehensible to those who operated within it, but impenetrable to those coming in from the outside. Certainly, many memsahibs, particularly those who did not take the trouble to learn the local language (therefore among those considered by all the advice manuals to be the most egregious examples of lax management) were convinced that their servants were out to steal from them. They would have done well to have taken the advice of the Indian writer Santha Rama Rau's Viennese aunt, married to an Indian and for many years a resident of Delhi, who understood, or at least appreciated, the nuanced relationships that the Indian domestic service industry created: 'For instance, the cook has taken on a pupil who pays him perhaps a rupee or two a month to learn his trade from him. This boy does all the marketing, peels the potatoes, shells the peas and so forth. Meanwhile, I pay the cook about twenty rupees a month and keep my eyes closed to all these backdoor transactions.'[11]

But the English newcomer, perhaps forgetting that domestic servants at home in England had a system of perks and commissions with local suppliers that was every bit as complicated as the Indian one, fell too easily into the role of uncomprehending domestic tyrant, whose relationships with her household staff were marked by constant suspicion:

> Every native servant (being more or less naturally indolent and care-less) requires strict supervision to have your work satisfactorily performed. It is better to have as few servants as possible; the more you have the less work will be done, and the more will you be cheated and robbed. Never let servants see that you are too partial to them; they immediately jump to the conclusion that they are necessary to you, and that you cannot do without them, and, native like, they will at once show their ingratitude by robbing you and becoming careless and lazy, under the impression that they will not be suspected of dishonesty, and that their negligence will be viewed leniently.[12]

Hardly surprising that the memsahib acquired a reputation in many quarters for being a shrill harridan with a fondness for drink, discreet adultery and malign gossip. This type learned to speak inadequately in the local languages, as E. M. Forster recalled, only to nag her servants with 'none of the polite forms and of the verbs only the imperative mood'.[13] Languages were important as it was judged unwise to have servants who spoke English too well lest they overhear conversations and report them back to the servants' hall – thus putting at risk the mystique of the British ruling class by exposing them to ridicule or over-familiarity. It became customary to describe a typical memsahib (particularly the junior version, the *chota-mem*), often unjustly, as spending the long, hot days in some remote outpost where the time hung heavily on her hands and whose sole interest was the agonising daily battle with sly and recalcitrant natives.

Most of the advice meted out to colonial newcomers concerned, as it did for their compatriots at home, the importance of establishing routine: the foundation stone of domestic happiness. It was the received wisdom that native servants, like children, needed the day divided into regular activities, otherwise they would run amok and all would sink into chaos. 'Too much should not be expected of them,' was the advice of a guide to housekeeping in the 1920s; 'their brains are not properly developed and they cannot be expected to see things in the same light as we do.'[14] Routine sanctified domestic life in the Raj to a series of daily rituals: early morning tea, after luncheon nap, early evening drink. The most important morning undertaking was the hygiene check: water had always to be boiled and everything scrubbed down; ants had to be kept out of the larder and snakes out of the earth closet; all vegetables had to be washed thoroughly in permanganate of potash.

Accounts of domestic life in the Raj are full of anecdotes, possibly apocryphal, of hygiene horrors: the woman who found her cook straining the soup through the sahib's (dirty) sock crops up often, as does the one about the cook who kneaded the pastry dough under his armpits. In India the heat made everything a possible breeding place for bacteria. A new set of rules about cleanliness had to be learned by heart and the terror of losing your children to tropical diseases, as so many did, sharpened the panic. And then there were the other strangenesses to contend with: the arcane religious and cultural customs that were as important as etiquette in England and just as easy to get wrong. No-one had warned Mrs Handley, wife of a forest officer in Southern India, that a man assaulted by a woman was considered unclean – until her servant charged her £12 to cover the cost of the purification ceremonies he had to undergo after he was hit accidentally by a piece of toast she tossed over the side of the verandah. One woman saw a corpse wearing her nightdress paraded through the streets on its way to cremation; it was later returned to her by the *dhobi*, laundered beautifully, and nothing more was ever said on the subject.

Maud Diver, author of a 1909 guide for the Anglo-Indian housewife, cautioned parents against allowing too close an intimacy between their children and the servants. 'Never allow your children to mix too much with the servants. Bad habits are dropped into by such close associations, and many European children have been laid in their graves or suffered considerably, through the neglect of parents in this respect.' The *ayah*, wrote Maud Diver, 'is a bone-bred gossip; her tongue is a stranger to the golden fetter of truth'.[15] Yet it is the *ayah* who occupies such an important place in the memories of children brought up in India during the Raj, and who in many instances seems to embody the melancholy heart of a sense of paradise lost. Through the *ayah*, children learned the local languages: their first words were more often than not in Hindi, Tamil or Urdu, and they learned songs, particularly lullabies. As children in England often became intimates of the servants' hall, those brought up in colonial outposts acquired an understanding of the country in which they now lived that was often closed to their parents, many of whom found very disturbing the spectacle of their children speaking the native tongue of the servants more fluently than English, sometimes till they were five or six years old.

Rumours circulated about *ayah*s and the sleep-inducing opium that they were believed to smear under their fingernails. The portrait of the young Anglo-Indian child as an indulged princeling was a common one back in England, where English nannies generally took a briskly austere line with their charges' moral upbringing. Like the spoiled, unhappy orphan, Mary Lennox, in Frances Hodgson Burnett's *The Secret Garden*, the white child in India was often regarded by her peers at home as a figure of sickly petulance, gone rotten with secret, sinister indulgence by Indian servants. Sometimes an English nurse was imported at great expense to form a barrier between the native servants and the children who had grown too intimate with them (Norland nurses were so popular that the Norland Institute designed a special lightweight uniform suitable for the tropics). The writer and broadcaster on India, Mark Tully, even in the 1930s, remembered that the chief task of his English nanny was to prevent him from mixing with the Indian servants.[16]

The key to survival seems to have been not to question anything very much – and the more enlightened memsahib surrendered to her staff and thus maintained her relationships with them. A Raj wife, Mrs Graham, recalled in 1914 an *ayah* of whom she was very fond: 'She left me three times to bury one who had never lived, and each time tucked some of my possessions into her luggage. One, packed insecurely in her draperies, fell out at my feet; neither of us evinced the least surprise, so complete was the understanding between us.'[17] Olive Douglas, however, was ticked off for not being sufficiently imperious with her servants. 'You needn't grin at them so affably, they'll only think you weak in the head,' she was told.[18] Upper-class Indians, who were accustomed to treating their own staff with complete autocracy, found the British attitude often perplexing and contradictory. Santha Rama Rau's grandmother deplored her soft dealings with her servants: 'They are not your equals, so do not treat them as such. It is not enough for the servants to be frightened of you; that fear must be founded on respect. This pandering to them is some unreasonable sentimentality you have picked up in the West.'[19]

In India, domestic British life was elevated to a degree of flamboyance and display that was not quite matched anywhere else in the Empire. Nonetheless, even in Africa, where the colonial experience was much more primitive, conditions much tougher and officers often stationed in outposts so remote that they were several days' walk from any other habitation, English formalities were maintained *ad absurdum*. In Nigeria, for example, colonial households kept the complicated rituals of the calling card well into the 1940s. In Africa, as a young colonial officer, Nigel Cook found that: 'When one got to one's station not only did you have to sign the Resident's book, but you had to leave cards in the appropriate places. I'd been told that a Resident should have a card and, furthermore, that any married couple should have two cards, but it is not obligatory to drop cards on married men who had not got their wives with them, or alternatively, bachelors without wives.'[20] There was often a special calling-card box at the end of the path to the colonial bungalow.

Everywhere the British settled they followed their rules on dressing for dinner. Despite the flies, the heat, the tinned food, the boiled water, 'in the evening everyone dressed for dinner, whether you were at home or went out; you wouldn't dream of doing otherwise'.[21] An Indian member of the Indian Civil Service during the 1920s and 1930s observed with amazement how Anglo-Indians, living in bungalows called Kenilworth, Rose Cottage or Hazeldean, stuck to routines and forms of behaviour that seemed wilfully uncomfortable: 'Left to themselves, the young officers donning dinner jackets might have preferred to be in an open-necked shirt, particularly in the hot weather . . . but personal feelings or discomforts had no place where certain discipline had to be maintained for the prestige of the Empire.'[22]

Above all, a regard for the rules of precedence infiltrated everything. Faizur Rasul, on his way to England from Bengal in search of adventure and socialism in the early 1920s, earned his passage by working as a servant to an Indian dignitary and found he had to negotiate the decks on board ship:

The lower part of the ship I reached first and stayed in all the time, was the lower deck by the stern. Presently a middle-aged Indian woman came and spoke to me. The woman said: 'I can see you are going abroad for the first time. Don't worry, son, you will get used to it. We all do. Have you seen the others?'

'Others? Who are the others?' (somewhat surprised).

The woman: 'The other servants, like you.'

'Whose servants?' I asked.

'Oh, you are new! You are a servant of a passenger aren't you?'

'Er, yes, that's right, yes I am,' was my reply.

'Well, there are other passengers, like your master, who are taking their servants abroad with them. They will all be here soon. This is the place where the servants spend their time during the day and sleep just there (pointing to the upper part of the deck, along a partition) at night, except when they have to look after their masters. There is another place inside for us women servants. Who is your master, homemade (indigenous) or a sahib?'

'He is homemade.'

'Mine is a sahib, a High Court Judge. I am the *ayah* to their children. I have been years with them. And do you know this is the eleventh time I have been to England with the family. I brooded like you the first time I left home to go abroad.'[23]

Hardly surprising then that on their return to Britain, many old colonials and their wives found the transition difficult: they were, in E. M. Forster's words, 'exiled from glory'. It was a common complaint among English servants that families recently returned from long years in the service of the Empire did not know how to treat their staff. The shabby realities of a small flat off the Cromwell Road and the grudging ministrations of a furious house-parlourmaid were disillusioning; it was a terrible come-down. Margaret Powell's despised employer Lady Gibbons – who 'peered into the old bread crock, she even counted the crusts. She looked into the flour bin and the vegetable rack and the ice box, and she ended up counting the eggs,' – had spent years in India in the heyday of the Raj and now, with her husband, retired to Kensington on a pension that could barely stretch to a cook and parlourmaid, was terrified of losing caste.[24]

Faizur Rasul's first job in Britain was as general servant to a Mr Jennings and his wife. Mrs Jennings had once been a governess in the service of a maharajah:

As time went on, the novelty of working in an English household began to wane in me. And the novelty of having an Indian servant waned in Mrs Jennings. I thought I had caught a pair of the wrong kind of English people. And Mrs Jennings thought she had caught the wrong kind of Indian. Both of us were right. She was spoiled by having been in India. I was spoiled by having been in England. She wanted to show off to her neighbours in the other flats by having an Indian servant like Queen Victoria had. I didn't come up to her expectations, either in work, or in the servility and cringing of the Indian servants she knew and liked.[25]

Vanessa Bell's housemaid Happy Sturgeon had once worked for the Governor of the Tower of London and his wife: 'They'd been in India so she was a bit, well, she'd got ideas,' she sniffed.[26] No wonder that India so often seemed to those who had lived there an Eden of leisure. In Ethel Savi's 1910 novel, *Birds of Passage*, Mrs Hurst, a memsahib of longstanding, is lost to idleness abroad – life in India having ruined her for ever for hard work. 'And, oh, it tires me to think of what a lot of housework we had to get through [in Britain] – such slavery! I am afraid I shall never want to retire there. It would be too much fag.'[27]

By 1913, Olive Douglas, born to a Raj family and still living in India, found herself wondering at the pointlessness of it all. Watching from her verandah the fleets of elaborately liveried Indian servants required to service a single household, she wrote: 'It seems to me that I go about asking "Why?" all day and no-one gives me a satisfactory answer to anything.'[28]

Chapter 10

'Bowing and Scraping'

In November 1911, *The Times* reported that 20,000 domestic servants had converged on the Albert Hall to take part in 'the most amazing meeting which has ever been held within the walls of that building . . . The Hall was packed from floor to ceiling, every place in every box and gallery being tenanted . . . thousands upon thousands of respectable girls, unable to gain admission, stand patiently in long queues outside the building, hoping in vain that by some lucky chance they might enter in and join their comrades in the great protest.'[1] Outside, a busker entertained the waiting crowds by playing *Rule Britannia* on the accordion. The issue at stake, cried the meeting's chief speaker, Lady Desart, was the 'sacred trust' between master and servant, now under threat from measures to introduce compulsory health and unemployment insurance for employees in the home.

It took two years for Lloyd George's bill of mandatory medical and unemployment insurance to become the 1911 Unemployment Insurance Act, described twenty years later by another Chancellor of the Exchequer, Philip Snowden, with its companion, the National Health Act, as 'the greatest measures of social reform ever placed on the statute book'. The proposals unleashed fury from both employers and their servants. At the first meeting of the umbrella protest organisation the 'Servants Tax Registers' Defence

Organisation', the Chancellor was likened to an agent of revolutionary terror, a 'tyrant, gagger, guillotiner, attempting to do what the worst of kings in the darkest ages of history failed to do'.[2] Lady Desart, who took up leadership of the opposition to the bill, said that both servants and their employers would protest 'every inch' of the health insurance clauses in the bill, 'on the ground that these clauses are vexatious and unsatisfactory to them and to their employers'. In *The Times*'s correspondence pages, a Mr Harold Cox criticised the bill for threatening to destroy the 'quasi-religious devotion' that underpinned the traditional sources of welfare, such as the friendly societies, as well as the delicate balance of rights and responsibilities embodied in the well-ordered home.

The social significance of the proposals far outweighed the small financial sums involved. Employers were to pay threepence a week for each employee; fourpence was then to be paid by male employees, threepence by females; twopence a week would be contributed by the state. In return, all medical attendance, medicines and maternity benefit would be available for every insured person. It was the red tape, the form filling, the paperwork (most ignominious of all, the stamps that needed licking) and the state's unwonted interference in a private relationship that irked.

Lloyd George himself retaliated to the storm of hostility by sending lecturers all over the country to address meetings and explain what the act might mean in effect: the protection of the state for workers who were all too often left unprotected. Lady Digby, on the side of the bill, pointed out that, however kind the mistress, it was impossible to keep a sick girl in the house for more than a few days or to provide nursing. Unless befriended by some society, these girls would invariably be sent to a poor home or workhouse infirmary. She believed that many servants did not entirely understand the meaning of the proposed insurance and had furthermore been prevented by their employers from learning too much about it. When a deputation of maids was invited to Downing Street to meet the Chancellor, they were all converted to the bill within minutes. Many charities concerned with the welfare of servants produced examples from their own records that put paid to the idea that the 'sacred trust' could always be relied on to act efficiently in the interests of domestic employees. At a meeting, Mrs Garnett of the Girls' Life Brigade told Lloyd George that an official of the Charity Organisation Society had told her that nearly 70 per cent of the cases of hardship and illness dealt with in her town were those of general servants who had sought aid because they were ill and had spent all their savings. She pointed out that in not one case (and some had been 'as long as fourteen years in service') had the Society received a subscription from a mistress towards the maintenance of her old servant.[3] 'They don't like ill people, you haven't got to be ill, not ever,' was how one maid remembered it.[4]

Looking back in 1944 on the events leading up to the passing of the National Insurance Act, the butler Albert Thomas regretted the ending of what he viewed as a symbiotic relationship: 'The health insurance and the children's clinics, however excellent as institutions, have killed off the personal touch between the Quality and the poor and needy.'[5] It would be another thirty years before master and servant would shake off fully the old, semi-mystical language of knowing one's 'place' in the eternal pyramid of duty and deference. But by 1915 the changes were irrevocable and the Domestic Servants Insurance Society, which had been founded to help servants manage the new Insurance Act, had a membership of 75,000.

In 1765 the judge Sir William Blackstone had called the relationship between master and servant the first of the three 'great relations of private life' (the other two being husband and wife, and parent and child).[6] It was a relationship of such complexity and operated within a scale of such minute gradations that every attempt at definition was confounded by an example of its opposite. For each instance of mistreatment or exploitation there existed another of mutual love and loyalty. Servants' relationships to authority, owing to the intimacy with which they lived with their employers, fit awkwardly into studies of labour history. E. P. Thompson's *The Making of the English Working Class* makes mention of domestic servants only three times, despite acknowledging that, next to agricultural workers, they made up the largest single group of working people during the period of the Industrial Revolution. In 1901 domestic servants still numbered more than those working in mining or agriculture.

Yet, largely excluded from the industrial unrest that rocked the first ten years of the twentieth century, servants were scorned by their working-class peers as the most despised representatives of class betrayal. 'For the most part Royalist, ultra-conservative, politically, and deeply class conscious ... these people were, by and large, the apologists and expositors of the whole class system of the time,' was Robert Roberts's opinion of the retired servants who settled in his home town of Salford at the turn of the century.[7] 'The hand-loom weaver and his wife, on the edge of starvation, still regarded their status as being superior to that of a "flunkey",' wrote Thompson.[8] Many servants, particularly those who had worked in big country houses, was deeply conservative, nostalgic even, maintaining a high respect for the social divisions of service life and of the innumerable degrees of class that underpinned it. Dolly Scannell's mother, living in poverty in London's East End, had once been a housemaid in a great house and told Dolly of the:

> enormous joints of meat and of the terrible waste of lovely food. The larders were bigger than our little house, and sometimes in the morning the huge vats of dripping would be wiped clean as though someone had washed them – rats I thought. Then the gamekeeper would organise a rat hunt and all the men would take part. I wonder if Mother thought about this waste of food when, years later, with a young family to feed, she was down to her last crust. I don't suppose so, for she always looked forward never back. She never complained about her years in service, the long hauls upstairs with buckets of coal, the petty restrictions, and she never voted 'Labour', much to Father's disgust.[9]

The charge usually levelled against the career servant was snobbery, that they had accepted without question the cap-doffing assumptions about class that kept their 'betters' at the top of the pyramid and their peers at the base. Frederick Gorst thought servants needed to be snobs for survival, because they had 'more to lose' by resistance to the status quo and much to gain by mastering the minutiae of class differences. Albert Thomas, angling for preferment after saving the life of a young aristocrat, was disappointed to find, in his first job as a liveried page in a hotel, that the residents comprised 'a rather middling crowd' from which little polish would rub off on him.[10] Servants were usually, for similar reasons, staunchly Conservative, like Charles Dean, a valet who flatly refused on principle to consider a job offer from an ex-editor of the Communist newspaper *The Daily Worker*. An acceptance of the entitlements, even the innate superiority, of the 'quality', the 'carriage trade' and the residents of the front pews, was sunk deep into the national psyche. Sidney Ford's mother was inhibited by a feeling of awe in the presence of gentry years after she had left domestic service: 'She would say, "I am as good as they are" . . . She could take a roomful of East End women and she could preside over their meeting and she could keep them in order and talk to them and hold her own, but the moment she was confronted, shall we say, by somebody with a little bit of a title or even not as high as that, she just went to bits . . . I put it down to her parlourmaid days, where she was "Yes, ma'am; no, ma'am." Curtsey when you go in a room and when you come out of the room.'[11]

It was in the best houses considered quite unnecessary (in fact poor form) for servants to knock before entering a room. This was partly because they lived in such everyday familiarity with the family that there was nothing to hide from them and partly because servants were considered so much part of the general furnishings that their presence made no difference whatsoever to whatever was being said or going on. 'Oh no, they weren't unkind for the simple reason that they took no notice of you anyway,' was the experience of Mrs A. D. 'I honestly think they took no notice of you at all. You just looked after them, you knew how to behave and if you didn't when you went you soon learned it from the others. You never raised your voice – I never heard anyone raise their voice in anger in the staff room. Everything was always very genteel. In fact there's more snobbery below stairs than ever is upstairs, much more.'[12]

Even in those establishments where they were not expected to turn their faces to the wall, servants were generally viewed as just 'there', an inevitable presence from whom simultaneously nothing was hidden and yet with whom little was really shared. In the memory of Marjorie Philpot, the servants in her Edwardian household were 'either down below or up above. And they just did what they were told.'[13]

Deference was waning, slowly, in other areas of society but in service it was still central to the underpinning of the whole engagement. Without the demarcations of class the relationship would have seemed awkward, embarrassing even: there were so many layers of expectation and status wrapped up in it; to question such a relationship was to question divine ordinance. For many servants, particularly those in urban areas, it was their first experience of the language of the lady and the gentleman. May Cosh could not remember 'having to call anyone "Sir" or "Master" until I was in service'.[14] Rural communities maintained the traditions longer, living as they so often did in the shadow of the great estate. Alfred Tinsley, a groom, had ambivalent memories of the pre-war estate where he worked:

> I've spent my life with the gentry, and that's why I don't speak broad Yorkshire: you'd get your broadness rubbed off. But to tell you the truth I think working men were a bit put upon in those days: and I'll tell you, I didn't like all that nonsense. I went into gentleman's service just as the bowing and scraping was being done away with – but it was still hard. Mrs B was a Rothschild, and she'd been brought up to servants bowing and scraping: I don't think they realised that a working man could be anything more than they thought he should be. All those times were just finishing, but when I first went into stables the older servants used to – well, I won't say they grovelled, but they stuck to the old traditions.[15]

Indoor servants saw the family at their ablutions, undressed, unhappy, ecstatic; proximity in smaller houses meant that little could be concealed from them, their employers being so often helpless in practical matters. Eveline Askwith was barely a child, a tweeny-maid, when she was asked to assist the doctor performing an emergency appendectomy on her employer – on the kitchen table. Winifred Foley, aged fourteen, shared a four-poster bed with her ancient mistress, who was afraid of sleeping alone. Jock Yorke, whose family had a large house in Yorkshire, remembered, however, the invisible line between familiarity and over-familiarity: 'And of course they were frightfully congenial. They wouldn't have "taken a liberty" with you if you know that out-of-date expression. They were always polite. Curse us if we did wrong. Joked like mad, pulled our legs. But they would never exceed, like the nice hunt servants of today, and would not more have dreamed of getting tight in our company or using filthy language, than you would.'[16] The daughter of Rosina Harrison's first employer was the same age as her and 'Rose', as lady's-maid, became her constant companion, yet she remembered that 'my opinions were never sought or given on her music, or the people we met or on anything that was personal to either of us, nor did I expect it or miss it at the time'.[17]

In 1911, the year that the 'sacred trust' was trampled by Lloyd George's Insurance Acts, a woman calling herself 'Harriet, a Householder' wrote to *The Times* warning that her butler, advertising for a new post, had been approached by an American journalist offering him payment for gossip about the celebrated guests who came to his mistress's dinner parties. *The Times* followed this up with a furious editorial, condemning such a 'disgusting invasion of the sanctities of private life' and giving voice to the fears of readers who had perhaps sometimes wondered what their servants had heard, what secrets they stored away for future use.[18] It was impossible to be absolutely sure of what leaked out, of what was talked about beyond the walls of the home. Occasionally, a little light revelation suited both parties. The valet Charles Cooper's employer Mr Wingfield kept a private menagerie and would often invite his guests to ride on the animals. Cooper purchased a Kodak box camera and on these occasions took photographs, which he sold for handsome profits to newspapers and periodicals with the full consent of their subject. Cooper wrote: 'The press of course are

only too glad to get unique and up-to-date pictures of the aristoc-
racy and pay well for them. In one issue of the *Pall Mall Magazine*,
I had ten illustrations of the various animals and a picture of Lady
Moya Brown mounted on an ostrich appeared in the *Tatler*.'[19]

The nature of the servant-master bond becomes harder to
pinpoint the more intimate it becomes. Long-standing servants
were so embedded in family life that the relationship was often
regarded by their employers in terms of friendship (though it
should be noted that servants themselves rarely use that word and
in many cases are in fact uncomfortable with it). What do we make
of the position of Alice Osbourn for example? Described by her
employer as a 'nursery governess' in one census and as a 'cook' ten
years later, it is clear from her diaries that she was a good deal more
than either of these descriptions suggest. In 1912, the year nine-
year-old Daphne Baldwin started at Roedean, Alice accompanied
Mr and Mrs Baldwin to Brighton, where all three of them stayed
for several worried weeks to see Daphne settled in at school.
Daphne's emotional welfare, however, seems also to have been
Alice's charge: concerned by a tearful telephone call, it was she who
was summoned to talk to the school's headmistress. 'I went to tea
with Miss Walton and talked Daphne over,' was characteristically
all that she wrote about the meeting.

Alice's social position is as hard to gauge precisely as are her age
and her origins; but it is clear from the diaries that she formed an
indispensable part of family life at Rectory Farm House. She seems
to have inhabited the same slightly ambiguous social region as the
governess: in any case we can sense great affection between the
family and Alice; the Baldwin boys rag her and she sighs at their
boisterousness; it is to Alice that Daphne goes when she is afraid or
unhappy. Quite often her journals record that she accompanied the
boys as they grew older to the theatre. She is known affectionately
in the family as 'Obbs'. Mr Baldwin himself seems to have taken
charge of Alice's personal finances to great effect. In 1912 she noted
that she received a very handsome income of £121 for that year,
most of it from investments, her own modest earnings as a servant
constituting only £25 of the full amount. Mrs Baldwin seems

constantly to have been bed-bound by undefined, vapourish malaises, and so the management of the home was left entirely to Alice. She had given her life to the Baldwins and they in turn took care of her. Slipped inside the cover of one of Alice's diaries is a letter from Mrs Baldwin to a domestic employment agency, applying to hire a new maid: it stated that there were two other servants at Rectory Farm House: one a 'lady-housekeeper' who 'dines with the family'.[20]

Certainly deep affection was not uncommon, and in fact was held to be one of the factors that redeemed Sir William Blackstone's 'first relationship' from the grubby taint of more commercial employment transactions. But the chain of domestic dependency also nourished rivalries and jealousy in a closely controlled atmosphere. The subject of money or wages was actively discouraged in conversation: when Dolly Davey went to work in a household in Chelsea, 'we all got different levels of wages, but we never knew what each got'. On pay day, the butler would bring the envelopes in on a tray and hand them out to Dolly and the other servants in complete silence.[21] At Cliveden, that model of the lavish and well-run country estate, an employee remembered how the servants behaved towards each other in the 1920s: 'I think they needed to watch each other more than I'd realised at first. It was when I'd been here a while I began to see that they were all watching one another ... In one way, it wasn't a bad job and on the other hand – I never liked ... I tell you what I've always thought, and I've viewed it in other places, it's just the same, people watch each other too much, they're frightened you might get more than he does, you see what I mean.'[22]

Even the most liberal employers took the view that the central dynamic of dominance and subordination needed to be upheld for the sake of domestic order. Most attempts to blur the distinctions between served and server were viewed as self-indulgent humbug in the manner of J. M. Barrie's foolish Lord Loam. The hierarchy of the big estate continued to be seen as the spiritual source of a working relationship: its delicate ecology as mysterious and sustaining as the laws of nature. Violet Markham, all her adult life a public servant and vigorous campaigner on behalf of domestic servants, described her housekeeper, Mildred Brown, as 'for forty-one years my most beloved and trusted friend'. Yet, Violet, both the child of Tapton House and a new woman of the suffragette age, still considered that the wellspring of Miss Brown's distinction, her 'flawless loyalty and integrity', was her upbringing on a large estate where her father was a forester: from that deep engagement with the aristocracy she had 'absorbed the spirit of her surroundings'.[23]

Discussions of the master-servant relationship are often couched in a hazy, quasi-mystical language: nonetheless, it is impossible not to be moved by accounts in which patronage and subservience were transformed into something else, a mutual dependence that became deep affection, even love. In the Bodleian Library in Oxford there is a small collection of letters written by Gwendoline (Lina) Rush to her employer Mrs Wansbrough; they include an anxious little note about whether dogs go to heaven (the Pope having recently ruled out the possibility) that the dog-loving Lina slipped under Mrs Wansbrough's door one night. 'It is the Pope madam who is making me so restless although he does not know it and would not care if he knew I don't suppose. I'm not being disrespectful to the Pope because he does not know the joy he could bring to us all, anyway we live in hope if we die in despair. Goodnight Madam.'[24]

There are countless stories of such devotion: relationships that were on the surface formal but which time and proximity had endowed with many layers of reciprocal understanding. 'Take me in your arms, Margery,' were the last words of William Lanceley's employer to her beloved maid. Mary Gladstone, daughter of the Prime Minister, wrote to her German maid Auguste Schlüter in the late 1880s when Schlüter went home to visit her mother: 'It feels very desolate without you, but I must get used to it and meanwhile I delight in thinking of you and your mother's happiness now you are together, after all, it is not far off; I shall imagine you tomorrow evening arriving there.'[25]

Despite the elaborate architecture of 'bowing and scraping', the *de haut en bas* attitude of the aristocracy towards their servants was often marked by an appearance of informality, as if the preceding century of green baize doors and tradesman's entrances had left no real imprint on a feudal relationship. The Sitwell siblings – Osbert, Edith and Sacheverell – at Renishaw Hall in Derbyshire were entirely reliant on their childhood servants into middle age, depending on them for an easy everyday affection that had been markedly missing from their parents. When Evelyn Waugh visited Renishaw in 1930, he found 'the servants very curious. They live on terms of feudal familiarity. E.g. a message brought by footman to assembled family that her ladyship wanted to see Miss Edith upstairs. "I can't go. I've been with her all day. Osbert, you go." "Sachie, you go." "Georgia you go," etc. Footman: "Well, come on. One of you's got to go."'[26]

At Erddig, in rural Wales, six generations of the Yorke family lived in cranky familiarity with troops of servants and estate workers whom they celebrated in verse and with portraits that hung alongside those of their employers. When the last Yorke died in the 1970s, the house was a dimly lit (electricity was installed only in 1966) mausoleum of family history, peppered with leaking holes and with an accumulation of maundering treasures. In the servants' hall, the portraits of servants past were flaking and peeling, and in one case had been used as a dartboard. Examples of the Yorkes' annual tradition of writing poems in honour of their servants were stuffed into overflowing drawers or glued to the walls of the kitchen-corridor-like wallpaper. Always in rhyming couplets, the poems, unself-conscious doggerel though they are, give us a vivid picture of the often eccentric relationships formed around domestic life. Here are a couple of lines from one, written to the housemaid Betty Jones: 'To Betty Jones, I am as much in debt/I daub her hearths and give her many a sweat.'

The Yorkes of Erddig saw the estate as a self-sufficient community needing little intervention from the outside world: they paid their employees rather less than the average wages for domestic service but they offered them protection, accommodation, a share of the bounty of the estate. Many of the Erddig servants stayed for fifty years and married within the estate, bringing a new generation to employment there. In 1911 the Yorke children's nursemaid married the groom and the family, as per tradition, penned a verse to celebrate the nuptials: 'We trust th'attachment here begun/May last while life its course shall run/And love, to ours so freely shown/Be spent on children of their own.'[27]

The household at Erddig was an old-fashioned one, family and retainers jostling together. The paternalism of richer landowners sometimes took a whimsical turn, creating, for example, elaborate model cottages, even villages, for their estate workers, or in the case of the late-nineteenth-century Duke of Portland (who drove through his estate in a closed carriage throwing silver coins out of the window), an ice rink on which he insisted the servants disport themselves for their own benefit.

The charity extended by the gentry in their dealings with the poor was rewarded, in principle, by loyalty. The bestowing by the big house of traditional gifts of logs, coals, Christmas hams, clothing and soup for the sick was often accompanied by a chat. The gifts themselves often simply reinforced the humble position of the recipient: the customary Christmas presentation of a length of printed cotton to be used for making a new uniform was particularly resented by women servants. The voluntary nature of the relationship in many people's eyes sanctified it as a Christian duty but the Countess of Warwick remembered that 'blankets, soups, coals, rabbits and the rest were all paid for . . . in subservience, in the surrender of all personality'.[28] The emotional detachment of this engagement was sometimes painfully acute; there was a chasm dividing the experience of the rich from their dependants. During one particularly cold winter in the 1890s, Kate Taylor's mother received some sheets of brown paper from the big house, delivered by a groom, with the message that 'these will keep the children warm and when the warm weather comes they won't need washing but can be burned'.[29] On first arriving at Blenheim Palace, Consuelo Vanderbilt noted how the butler poured all the leftover food from meals into a single huge bowl, regardless of whether it was pudding, bones or soup. When she asked where these slops were to go, the butler replied: 'the Poor'.

A well-run country estate in its glory operated by maintaining, unarticulated, a delicate mutual understanding between all parties.

Indeed, everyone on the estate depended on each other for their very existence. An astonishing number of people were employed on even small estates in specialist but necessary tasks of continual maintenance and repair. There were fencers, hedgers, pig boys, slaters and spider brushers. Estates supported innumerable niche skills for which the pay was minimal but over which the arc of the estate's patronage was extended to their practitioners. 'Letter Betty', for example, for fifty years did nothing but sort the mail on a Scottish estate.[30] At Longleat before the First World War, which was not untypical of the largest country houses, they employed not only at least two coachmen, recognisable by their cockaded three-cornered hats and silver-buttoned capes, but also several under-coachmen and grooms, a steel boy (whose job was to burnish the metal parts of the horses' harnesses) and a 'tiger', a small boy dressed in miniature livery employed to sit on the box of the carriage with his arms folded across his chest like a decorative ornament. At Heythrop in Oxfordshire at the turn of the century, Jack Claridge was 'official vermin-catcher, earth stopper and walnut basher'. Jack's job was to beat the trees to raise their sap, as his father had done before him, before they were felled to meet the demand for walnut veneer on radiograms and car dashboards.[31]

The traditional endowments of housing, almshouses, charitable institutions and hospitals could offer a cradle-to-grave security for the estate's employees. The Lady Bountiful figure, who became such a crucial component of big house mythology, reached her apotheosis in the mid-nineteenth century, in part owing to the influence of evangelical Christianity on the upper classes and in part as a response to an increasingly riotous and politicised urban working class. Much was made by the proponents of the ideal village of the mistily antiquated traditions from which this patronage emerged and its origins in a chivalric past. 'As far back as Anglo-Saxon days,' wrote Mrs Macrae in 1901, on the subject of servants in *Cassell's Household Magazine*, 'a code of manners existed.' Yet this kind of distant patronage, or the 'extreme condescension' described by Lady Warwick, locked those who received it onto a wheel of loyalty and gratitude, usefully adding to the impression that the hierarchy of the estate, the patrimony of land, was divinely ordained. 'Church of England Preferred' was the typical stipulation on an advertisement for service in all sizes of household. The church being central to the village, the servants must be part of the church. 'I always had plenty of food, and I was expected to go to church Sunday nights, and I remember quite well I didn't go one Sunday evening and Mr D ... before he had his breakfast came to the kitchen and said "Annie, you weren't at church last night."'[32] As the 1853 *Common Sense for Housemaids* put it, the good servant was one for whom the sound of the church bell 'comes as music to her ear'.

The teachings of Christianity could be selectively plundered to support the idea that domestic service constituted in itself a claim to virtue. 'He is most godlike who lives not to be ministered unto but to minister,' readers were reminded in an article on the 'Servant Problem' of the 1890s. The *Servants Magazine* even printed a slogan to be hung in the Victorian kitchen: 'Never change your place unless the Lord shows it will be for your own good.' Some households did not approve of working on Sundays, so domestic work had to be carefully weighed as to whether it came within the rules, as Bronwen Morris found when working as a maid-of-all-work for a Mrs Budd in Acton, who wondered if it would be correct to change the curtains on the Sabbath: 'Mother Budd placed her hands together and quoted: "The Lord is not extreme to mark what is done amiss." So it was that I climbed the ladder and changed the curtains.'*[33]

Daily prayers were a feature of households of all classes, led by the master of the house, and in his absence a butler. One twelve-year-old tweeny, awake since five making up the fires, on her first day at work was handed a piece of paper during prayers on which she read the biblical injunction: 'Come unto me all ye who are weary, and I will give you rest.'[34] On most estates church services on Sunday

---

* In 1911, when Bronwen Morris left rural Wales to be a kitchen-maid, her parents presented her with a Bible inscribed in Welsh, which read: 'To Bronwen Morris on her departure from Carnarvon to London. Hoping that she will be a good girl, obedient to master and mistress, also to read this book, as it will be a guide to life and a light to her path, that is the wish of her father and mother.'

were obligatory (except for the kitchen staff who were permitted to go to Evensong later in the day as they had to prepare lunch). Even the higher-up employees had to turn out for morning service, ranked in the pews, of course, in order of superiority. Marjorie Philpot married a land agent on an estate in Suffolk and found they had to go to church because their employers insisted on it: 'my husband complained because he said he worked all week in the office, and then on Sundays he had to go to church, he'd no free day at all'.[35] As a young footman, James Hughes refused to sit, as instructed by his employer, in the servants' pew: 'Well, I'm not sitting in a servants' seat while I've got blood in my body ... He nearly gave me the sack.'[36]

Catholic servants were regarded with particular suspicion (Lady Astor was among many who absolutely refused to employ them) often because they were regarded as having divided loyalties. Furthermore their insistence on going to a different church on Sunday upset the delicate equilibrium of social patronage of which the Church of England formed such an integral part. Charles Cooper's Mr Wingfield insisted that all those of his employees who were not confirmed into the Church of England immediately be so.

For resident servants, many employers viewed themselves *in loco parentis*; indeed, their servants were very often pre-pubescent. Mrs Praga took her two servant girls with her on holiday simply because she thought they were too young to be left in the house on their own. But the assumption of a parental role also justified the imposition of curfews, the laying down of rules about 'followers' or the wearing of make-up. There was an infantilising degree of control over their every action, mode of dress or behaviour. 'Independence has many dangers,' wrote the head of a local branch of the Girls' Friendly Society in 1913. Mrs Dence of Leatherhead told the historian Pamela Horn that when she was in service in 1906, 'one must ask to post a letter although the post office was just outside one of the entrances. If you had shopping to do you must ask and say where and what for. We were not allowed to speak in the corridors or to the menservants, although we were often working in the same room.'[37] At Cliveden the strictly teetotal Lady Astor discouraged pub-going by providing her staff with their own social club serving only non-alcoholic drinks.

As representatives of what was viewed as a feral and unformed class, servants had to be set boundaries for their own good. Advice books for housewives often likened servants to children who should be treated kindly and indulged occasionally but required the imposition of rules in order successfully to flourish as happy workers. 'We are no advocates for spoiling servants any more than we should be for spoiling children, but we want them to be happy,' wrote Mrs Panton who exhorted her readers to 'do all in your power to raise them to your station'.[38] The station in which they would be happiest of course remained some way below Mrs Panton's own station. Servants' quarters were to this end as austerely functional and morally bracing as this Edwardian nursery: 'We had no whimsical pictures on the walls of rabbits or squirrels, and no chairs and tables adapted to our smallness of stature. We knocked up against hard surfaces and uncompromising corners, thus being prepared for some of the harshnesses of adult life.'[39]

Like children's food, servants' meals in the middle-class household tended towards the plain and wholesome. 'Mrs Clydesdale thought only of our nourishment, so we used to have things like herring and cod and stews and milk puddings. But none of these nourishing foods found their way upstairs,' remembered Margaret Powell.[40] Cheap foodstuffs like herring, bread and margarine featured prominently on servants' menus. Viewed as childlike, dependent, their lives entirely absorbed, by necessity, by the families they lived with, the limits and means of servants' contentment was often completely bound by the behaviour and character of those who employed them and in whose houses they lived. There was often kindness in the relationship, often affection, even intimacy; yet a haunting distance frequently loomed between servant and master in which much remained unspoken. Mistresses were often surprised to discover the unhappiness of those in their employ – Vanessa Bell (whose daughter Angelica Garnett recollected her mother addressing her servants as though hailing them from a fast-moving train) found a half-finished novel about life with the Bells that was left behind by a departing governess and was 'amazed by its bitterness'.[41]

Some servants recall being encouraged to read and to borrow books from their employers. A woman who went into service in the late nineteenth century told Margaret Llewelyn-Davies in 1931 that she had worked in one household 'where reading was not considered a waste of time and books were supplied to me to read which were suitable for a young, impressionable girl, far different from the trash I had read before'.[42] Although many larger houses boasted 'servants' libraries' (stocked with carefully selected uncontroversial, non-political and generally improving reading), servants who enjoyed books or study were usually viewed with bemusement and often hostility. It was generally assumed that female members of the working class were easily seduced by penny papers and trashy romances which led inexorably to indolence, degeneracy and even socialism. 'All ordinary housekeepers are at the mercy of the filth and insolence of a draggle-tailed novelette-reading feminine democracy,' says Harvey Rolfe in George Gissing's *The Whirlpool*. It was important therefore to oversee all reading matter that might find its way downstairs. Mrs Panton suggested magnanimously: 'Let your maids have good books to read, and let them see newspapers, but do not keep a kitchen bookshelf ... and look out for their own literature which is generally pernicious.'[43] In 1909 the lighting engineer Borlase Matthews even recommended a centralised lights-out mechanism to deter too much reading below stairs: 'The lighting of servants' bedrooms is a debatable point, as it encourages reading and consequent long hour-burning ... in some houses, the lights in the servants' bedrooms are so wired that they can be controlled by a switch in the dressing room or similar place, so that the consumer can extinguish their lights when he goes to bed himself.'[44]

The one thing worse than low culture in the servants' hall was high culture: this positively went against nature. There was often uneasiness when good books for servants spilled over into the books that might also be considered good for their employers: when Thomas Carlyle came downstairs to find the Carlyles' maid Jane Ireland sitting beside a half-scoured grate reading Goethe's

Wilhelm Meister, he found the girl's literary taste 'strange and even touching in the poor soul'. Other pursuits that bordered on the cultural were also generally discouraged. Grace Fulford's mother once discovered her newly engaged maids practising music in their room. 'The strains of a violin came downstairs. She said "Where on earth is that coming from?" – Waiting for afternoon tea you see. Goes upstairs, there's one of them – it's an easel up in the bedroom with music up on it and there she was playing away and the other one sitting back in her chair with her feet on an ottoman cushion. Oh, they went faster than they came in.'[45] *Her feet on an ottoman cushion*: what decadent disorder is suggested by that phrase! Mrs Miles, author of *The Ideal Home*, encountered her housemaid blacking a grate without enthusiasm and asked wonderingly why it was the maid did not seem to enjoy her ennobling manual labour. The maid responded that not only did she hate her work but she would actually prefer to write books, like Mrs Miles, adding furthermore that she was always writing and could not wait to get back to her pen and paper. 'So I tried to show her that it would make her life much happier and easier if she would really excel in the work she had to do, and if she would strive to do it better than anyone else could do it, instead of thinking of a life she was not educated for and in which she would probably fail.'[46]

In such an atmosphere, it seems natural that children and servants were thrown together in an intimacy and, often, a playfulness that was difficult to recapture in later life. The dropped 'g' that marked the 'huntin', shootin', fishin'' accent of the fashionable sporting upper-class Englishman was an indication of formative years spent hanging around the stables with the estate workers. Lord Willoughby de Broke was constantly in the company of his father's gamekeeper: 'It was with him that I saw my first fox killed; it was with him that I killed my first pheasant, partridge, duck, hare, rabbit and rook; also my first fish. He showed me my first rat hunt and escorted me on my first expedition in quest of birds' nests . . . No wonder I was attached to him.'[47] Lady Violet Brandon and her siblings were typical of children of their class in that they ate their meals in the nursery wing with their nurse and their governess, waited on by the most junior under-footman. 'So one knew the under-footman, he was a friend, one knew him to talk to and run about, he'd do kind things and play with one, carry one upstairs when one's legs ached, that sort of thing.'[48] One of the footmen in Pilgrims Hall was remembered as 'a terrible tease'.[49]

As children grew to adulthood, eventually progressing down-stairs to join the grown-ups, the relationship with servants became different, the balance often reversed, with the servant being the recipient of kindly but distant affection where once they had been intimates. For many, servants were their first and only encounter with people who came from poorer backgrounds than themselves. 'With a child's open-eyed curiosity,' remembered Viola Bankes of her Edwardian childhood at Kingston Lacy in Dorset, 'I used to question Bessie about her deeply ribbed fingernails. "Bessie, why are your nails like that?" "I'm sure I don't know, Miss," Bessie would say and hurry about her work. No-one ever thought in terms of vitamins, proteins or calories.'[50]

Servants, once friends and allies, are often consigned in the adult memory of their former charges to be 'characters'. Among the prevailing characteristics of memoirs of nannies, for example, is that they smell of castor oil and cabbage. They are, like Frances Partridge's recollections of her 'faithful Nan' Lizzie Croucher, often given to 'runic sayings' such as: 'If you want your hair to curl you must eat fried bread behind the door'. Beloved at the time, in adult memory Lizzie became a comically child-like figure, a 'benevolent and reas-suring little being' in flannel petticoats, 'a pointed bonnet like a gnome's hat, trimmed with jet and artificial flowers'.[51] Women serv-ants were often remembered as being of a mordant cast of mind nourished on penny-dreadfuls: their conversation was thrilling at the time and hilariously quaint in recollection. Two virginal elderly maids of her youth were remembered by Susan Tweedsmuir thus: 'like two sombre ravens the talk always ran on gloomy topics and the seamy side of things. I remember sitting unobserved and trembling, while Blackie related to Soey a story that culminated in the words: "And he threw an orange at her, and he hit her there (touching her ample bust) and she died at once." The story haunted me for years.'[52]

Yet time and again, the memories of the Victorian and Edwardian nursery servant are riven with the melancholy of parting from their charges. The work, intense, often isolated, too often became analogous to religious calling, and they were left bereft when the object of their devotion abandoned them. (A survey in 1935 showed that only 25 per cent of Norland nannies had themselves married.) As upper-class children sailed forth into the world, their servants were left behind in a kind of nursery no man's land, often staying on in the house until their death, taking a keen and poignantly loving interest in the lives of their former charges and their new families. Being a female career servant had few prospects except for marriage (or possibly running a boarding house) and if neither of these options were available to you then the role of the faithful retainer beckoned. As the children in one's charge grew up, the gulf of opportunities that divided servant and child became wider and more pronounced.

Poor Auguste Schlüter, the German lady's-maid of the Gladstones, was heartbroken when Mary Gladstone announced, at the age of thirty-eight, that she was to marry the Reverend Harry Drew, a curate ten years her junior. 'She tried all day to make me believe it,' wrote Auguste, 'and although my heart refused, a cold fear crept over me ... When I saw Mr Drew, I felt like a tigress wishing to throw herself upon the enemy.' Auguste wrote to Mary's betrothed, pathetically: 'I must learn to love you as much as I love her,' and reported later that: 'No letter could have been more gentle and kind than his reply.' At the wedding, however, a guest, Mrs Alfred Lyttelton, 'came across poor Schlüter in the aisle, in great disorder, and comforted her as best I could'. Auguste later returned to her family home in Hamburg where she struggled to fit in, being as she put it 'a fish out of water'.[53]

Courtesy and consideration on the part of the employer was counselled, quite rightly, as one solution to the problem of girls reluctant to go into service, but respect for servants tended to come with its own inbuilt limitations. Grace Fulford (she whose mother had dismissed her servants for playing the violin) was told by her father: '"Courtesy costs nothing, but it opens the door to

many opportunities." And he was right. If we were heard talking
to the servants as if they were dirt like sometimes you do if you're
a bit young, we were very quickly reprimanded. Treat them with
proper respect.'[54] It was an orthodoxy among the working and
upper classes that the middle classes, pinched on both sides, were
the worst offenders when it came to the treatment of servants. 'Do
the middle classes good to lose their cooks,' wrote the Marquess
of Salisbury's sister Nelly Cecil at the outbreak of the First World
War: 'They treat them like dogs when they've got them.'[55] What
were loftily viewed as middle-class pretensions were regarded by
the upper classes rather as they might have viewed tinned food or
gas lighting: inauthentic, pretending to a confidence about the
relationship to which they had no right of birth or breeding.
Giving oneself 'airs' was particularly despised. 'The way they
went about you'd think they were the be-all and end-all of aristocracy,' was cook Margaret Flockhart's opinion of her employers
in the 1930s.[56]

Although the truth is that there are instances of aristocratic
employers behaving badly as often as there are in the much-derided
middles, servants tended to the sentimental view, ascribing courteous behaviour and consideration to 'real' gentry, the authentic article, initiates by breeding of the 'sacred trust'. Albert Thomas, working as a butler in a block of service flats just before the First World
War, developed a great affection for a barrister's wife he refers to as
'Mrs Lovely' and 'a daughter of the old school'. 'She was no trouble
at all,' he writes, and 'her husband too was a perfect gentleman, and
we were often invited to their flat of a night, much to the disgust of
the old maids in the flat next door.'[57] When the Oxford social
worker Violet (C. V.) Butler undertook a survey of servant girls in
1913, she found the theme of 'real' gentry recurring: 'The better-
bred people, the real gentlefolk, do treat their employees as flesh
and blood, the jumped-up rich middle classes as cattle,' wrote one
of her participants. 'Rudeness,' Violet Butler found, 'was complained
of as a fault particularly with self-made employers leading to the
opinion among maids that you should not take a place with people
"no better than yourself".'[58] Less grand employers who were good

to their servants are generally described, if not as gentry, as being blessed with an aristocracy of nature.

There was one new type of servant, the only new type of servant, to emerge in the early twentieth century, who brought with him a breezy un-stuffiness that seemed to herald a new age. With the rapid increase in the number of motor cars in private ownership, the chauffeur was fast taking over from the traditional coachman in private service. Many of the new car owners found it difficult to dispense entirely with the trappings of the coach and four: Charles Dean, as a young footman, was dressed up in full livery to sit next to the chauffeur (whose livery matched), as if he were on 'box work' (the role of the young boy who used to sit next to the coachman). According to the census of 1911, the number of chauffeurs and coachmen was almost equal, yet by 1921 the coachman was almost redundant and chauffeurs in private service numbered 5,200. As they did not emerge from a tradition of service but very likely from a background in mechanics or engineering, chauffeurs acquired a reputation for being cavalier with servants' rulebooks that had been written for an age long before the democratising energy of the motor car.

Before the advent of the closed-in saloon car, a chauffeur was able to overhear intimate conversations between passengers in the back seat. Later, cars were designed with a glass screen between the driver and his charges – often with a speaking tube that had to be turned on. But in the years preceding these modifications, the confined space made the requisite formality difficult. 'Made for weasels, my dear, for weasels,' the Countess of Lovelace complained when she attempted to ease herself into a pre-First World War motor.[59] 'Four-Inch Driver' – the anonymous author of the chauffeurs' handbook – warned in 1909 that: 'More chauffeurs lose their places through rudeness, in many cases quite unintentional, than through neglect of their car or bad driving.' Often finding himself on a long drive with his employer, the chauffeur was reminded that 'sulkiness and bad temper should not be among the chauffeur's qualifications; the owner may be able to supply these himself, and, if so, the chauffeur should make allowances for him; he doubtless has worries of his own, and the chauffeur should efface himself as much as possible if he sees a storm brewing'.[60]

In addition to handsome liveries of peaked cap, gauntlets, goggles, gaiters and brass-buttoned uniform, chauffeurs had a reputation for freedom and ease of manner. They often travelled widely with their employers and some of them had foreign languages, gained while doing lucrative work ferrying overseas tourists around the country. In contrast to other menservants, the image of the chauffeur has impudence and glamour without servility. When the Lawrence family's chauffeur went on holiday to France, he sent the teenage Lesley Lawrence a thrilling postcard with the words: 'My love is for you.'[61] Margaret Powell described the 'fluttering in the hen coop' when a visiting chauffeur would deign to have a cup of tea in the kitchens of the houses where she worked in the twenties; and Edith Hall left this account of a charged encounter in the kitchen:

One day, a handsome young man wearing a chauffeur's uniform came down the basement steps and addressed himself to the cook: 'I've been sent down to get myself lunch,' he said. 'My boss is the doctor and he's having his upstairs. He's attending a patient there.' Cook served him a substantial meal of what there was and, watching him eat, I could hardly take my eyes off him. I don't know why it should be but thin men always look pathetic when they're eating, particularly if good-looking like this one was. After a while the mistress came down to the kitchen; 'And whose follower might this be?' she asked, eyeing the young man. Did she suppose that fat old cook, or gauche me, could have enticed such a creature down our area? Then it was revealed; the chauffeur's mistake was accepted; he had come down the wrong steps; his boss was having lunch next door. He finished his meal and we watched him go up the steps and down those next door where, according to their maids, he had another meal.[62]

By 1913, Violet Butler found to her surprise that, despite being the butt of scorn from their contemporaries, many servants, particularly those working grindingly long hours as maids-of-all-work, 'were not immune to the social unrest that is sweeping the rest of the working class'. Butler had received hundreds of responses from both employers and servants to the questionnaires she sent out; these suggested that the gulf between the two sides had widened further since the turn of the century. Servant girls worked in conditions that seemed unnaturally dependent and old-fashioned to their peers working in shops and factories. In Violet Butler's respondents we hear the voices of the lonely maid-of-all-work and the discontented middle-class mistress glaring at each other over an unbridgeable divide.

Servants felt trapped, unable to leave the house except on their one, strictly curfewed, weekly afternoon off. The nature of the work made them feel they were never off duty. The uniform cap, so beloved of the status-conscious mistress, was particularly resented, being seen as 'the badge of servitude'. They objected to having to address the baby of the house as 'Master' or 'Miss'. There was a general bitterness about the assumption that servants could not appreciate culture. 'I think that if a mistress would only realise,' wrote a London general maid, 'that a maid is quite capable of appreciating a good concert or a library and would arrange a little time to be allowed to develop a hobby, it would tend to a much happier state of things.' Butler learned of the terrible isolation both of the unmarried general domestic aged between fifty and sixty and facing the prospect of a pensionless retirement, and of the very young between-maid, her every minute strictly monitored in a household of middle-aged servants. But most of all it was the ignominy that hurt, the loss of caste faced by servants not only among the classes that employed them but outside the home, on the streets where they had to undergo cat-calls of 'skivvy'. The maid found herself viewed as an embarrassment on all sides: 'She is always spoken of slightingly and with contempt.' A cook wrote that she used to take her holidays in a seaside hotel where there were a number of 'business girls', but she felt she could never reveal to them what she did for a living: 'Once a servant you are treated as belonging to quite an inferior race to all other workers; it's as if the lowest point had been reached.'[63]

As the Edwardian era drew to a close, the long political and cultural hegemony of the aristocracy began its final descent. For those who had lived under its wing, it seemed impossible that it could ever end. 'When my Lord came in to have his hat ironed on those spring mornings of the springtime of this century I firmly believed that this kind of life was to continue forever,' said hatter Fred Willis.[64] Many of the 20,000 servants who marched in support of the 'sacred trust' in 1911 would soon be working in national munitions factories or as bus conductors and drivers. By 1914, all that had once seemed so certain was in flux: not only was the working class flexing its political muscles but also women were mobilising themselves into a formidable force for change. The liberal politician and historian George Dangerfield saw in the suffragette movement the embodiment of 'the cloudy desires of hundreds of thousands of unmarried women condemned to do nothing. In this atmosphere of the unlived female life, which invaded – unasked and irresistible – the remotest rooms of her being, she was restless and irritable.'[65] While freedoms for other women were expanding through education, for their domestic servants, choices had over the last century actually narrowed: 'Fifty years ago the servant girl had much more liberty than the employer's daughter, but now the reverse is the case,' Violet Butler was told.

In such a tense atmosphere, the announcement of war in 1914 brought a brief unity to two hostile camps. Ernest Squire, who was a footman in Herefordshire, joined up almost immediately. At the recruiting office in Wrexham he found: 'Thousands there, men of every description, miners in the working clothes straight from the pits, some in smart suits from offices, a few in oddments of uniform and one man actually in morning dress and top hat.'[66] Frank Lovett, once the butler at Erddig, joined the army in the first few months of the conflict. 'No doubt you will be very surprised to hear from me, but being one of your old servants I thought I would let you know my whereabouts,' he wrote to his former employer, Philip Yorke: 'As you will see, I have donned khaki and doing my little bit for King and Country . . . It is a terrible war is it not, but I shall go with a light heart trusting to God's providence for a safe return.'[67]

PART III

The Age of Ambivalence

Chapter 11

'Out of a Cage'

Shortly after war was declared in 1914, Hannah Clark went to work in the gardens at Clyro Court, near Hay-on-Wye, where her father was employed as head gardener. 'I couldn't go from home because my mother was a good bit of an invalid by then – and couldn't be left a lot,' she remembered. 'So I couldn't join the forces, I had exemption. Now I think there were five gardeners by that time, but they gradually had to go into the army: and we were left with my father, and one old man and myself!'[1]

Large households tried to hang on to their menservants for as long as they could after the outbreak of war, often citing increasing unemployment as a reason for not letting them go. Mrs Peel reported a conversation that took place during this period: 'One of our number begged us not to dismiss our servants. There would be much distress, because people would not be entertaining and so would not need such large staffs. She feared that there would be great suffering all over the country by reason of increasing unemployment.'[2] Queues of men signed up for active service in the first months of the war. By 1916, when the enlistment of unmarried men between the ages of eighteen and forty-one became compulsory, the idea that it was a duty not to sack one's servants seemed ludicrous: the problem was *finding* servants. 'If things go on as they are going now, the domestic servant will soon be as rare as breakfast bacon in Germany,' wrote *The Times*.[3] At

Rectory Farm House, Taplow, Alice Osbourn found servants were as difficult to secure as they were elsewhere in the country. The Baldwins had become accustomed to the difficulty of finding (and keeping) staff before the war; during wartime it became almost impossible. We do not have Alice's diary for 1914, but by 1915 she seems to have become the housekeeper, cook and cleaner. Although domestic servants' wages were inflationary during the war years, reflecting the shortage of domestic labour, in 1918 Alice's earnings remained at a very modest £25 a year – those of a nursery governess at the turn of the century. Mr Baldwin continued to invest her savings for her, however, and by the final year of the war the interest she had received on a war loan came to £66, and the interest on her two mortgages in Birmingham was a handsome £58. But her worth in terms of work was now considerably more than her meagre wages. Mrs Baldwin, to say nothing of Daphne and Mr Baldwin, seems to have been almost constantly ill – with headaches, liver problems and colds. Alice was no longer simply running the house, she was running the family and their affairs too, in addition to looking after Daphne who, despite boarding at Roedean, was at home a great deal.

In 1916, Talbot, the Baldwins' gardener and chauffeur, was called up and Alice makes many references in her diaries to the problem of finding people to help with the garden. Daphne, between her bouts of ill-health, was showing an interest in gardening which proved useful as the war dragged on. Alice does not mention food shortages but, according to her weekly orderings for the store cupboard, the family consumed startlingly large quantities of cream crackers. The weather was still detailed in Alice's daily bulletins, described variously as 'boisterous', 'glorious' or 'miserable', but her wartime diary entries began to include more personal details than in earlier years. She reported regularly after 1915, for example, on news that the Baldwins' younger son, Harold, who had joined the army, had en route to the Dardanelles been taken seriously ill. After returning home to convalesce, he was posted again, to Egypt. Alice recorded the anxious periods at Rectory Farm House of waiting, endlessly, for news from Harold: either 'no news from Harold', or the thankful arrival of one of his thrifty telegrams, containing just the word: 'WELL'. In 1915, on 23 May, Julian Grenfell, poet son of the Desboroughs at Taplow Court, was killed in action. Alice noted five days later that, as Julian was buried at half past three that afternoon, the church bells rang out in Taplow. The Desboroughs' younger son Billy Grenfell was killed less than three months later on 5 August.

In November 1915, Alice carefully copied out a letter sent to the twelve-year-old Daphne from a young swain who had recently left to join the sea cadets. 'You mustn't be angry with me or I shall go away and die of lonely living,' wrote Guy Eardley Wilmot, signing off with 'simply tons and heaps of love'. Alice folded her copy carefully and put it in the back of her diary.[4]

After a year of war, thousands of women had been mobilised into work as agricultural labourers, munitions and factory workers, bus conductors, drivers, canteen organisers and nurses. The number of male estate workers and servants such as footmen was now vastly reduced as they joined either the services or necessary occupations at home. Big houses were forced to shut up wings or, as a last resort, use women in the traditional manservant roles. In many cases footmen were replaced by women, known racily as 'footgirls', all of whom generally had to be the same height. Uniforms were designed for them that resembled as much as possible a footman's livery: pink dresses in the morning, for example, changing into wine-coloured dresses with stripes or buttons for afternoon and evening wear, with black shoes and silver buckles. Eric Horne of course disapproved: 'Gentry don't really like female butlers, a war product; a topsy-turvy affair. Fancy a young gent having a female valet. Fancy a lady having a man as a lady's-maid.'[5]

During the First World War, the advent of the female driver, the chauffeuse, added yet another frisson to a relationship already thought to be dangerously free and easy. In 1917 an article in *Punch* suggested that in the confined space of a car, the chauffeuse might constitute a dangerous allurement to a wealthy heir. 'In threatening the single lives of people's eldest sons, the chauffeuse is leaving the eternal chorus girl down the course, and in releasing *one* man for the Front, she's quite likely to capture *another who counts consider-ably more*.'[6]

The 'general' maid-of-all-work all but disappeared during the war – there were simply too many alternatives for the girls who once worked and slept in the kitchens of thousands of small houses. Where a general could still be secured, relations in small households that had been fraught before the war often became strained to breaking point. In 1917 the Women's Section of the National War Savings Committee held a meeting of domestic servants in a London theatre at which the maids aired their grievances, particularly about the meanness of mistresses who were niggardly with food. 'It was generally found that when employer and employed shared alike, rationing difficulties ceased, but in cases which did occur when the mistress frankly owned that she and her family intended to eat what butter could be procured, leaving the margarine for the maids, feeling was apt to become strained.'[7]

The years of war fixed for ever the supremacy of margarine in the larders of the ordinary house: 8,000 pounds of margarine was manufactured every week in 1918 – eight times the amount consumed before the war. Budgets were tightened still further by shortages of basic foodstuffs. Though compulsory rationing was not introduced until the end of 1918, a clergyman's wife wrote piteously to Mrs Peel: 'we make efforts to achieve palatable cakes with cocoa butter and make jams with glucose. The long and losing battle with "substitutes" almost wears me out.'[8]

'A good chef can do a great deal by illusion,' wrote Gabriel Tschumi, King George V's head chef, struggling with the meagre allowances of those basics such as butter and sugar on which so many pre-war recipes had relied.[9] The Royal Family continued, despite these deprivations, to maintain a vast staff to facilitate the routines by which the King set so much store. In 1918, Lord Esher visited Buckingham Palace and found 'a Rip Van Winkle appearance upon the scene. Either the world has stopped still or Buckingham Palace remains unchanged. The same routine. A life made up of nothings – yet a busy scene. Constant telephone messages about trivialities.'[10]

The numbers in domestic service during the Great War did not fall as dramatically as one might expect – there were 1.6 million in service in 1914 and 1.2 million in 1918, a drop of 400,000.[11] Nonetheless, by 1917, more than half the total number (about 2,500) of bus conductresses were former domestic servants. At the Gretna National Cordite Factory, of the 80 per cent of women workers who had been previously employed, 20 per cent had been in domestic service. In a gloomy 1915 article that wondered if it would ever be possible to persuade girls to go back to service, *The Times* remarked that 'the conditions of war have opened up to women a hundred new avenues of work, nearly all of which offer free evenings, much intercourse with the world, and good wages. The chief of these is, perhaps, munitions work; but women are now acting as chauffeurs, conductors of tramcars, messengers, door-keepers, pages, waiters in clubs and restaurants, and in a number of other capacities usually confined to men and boys.'[12] The war brought women of all types and classes opportunities in work that would have been unimaginable a decade before. In 1916, *Common Cause*, the suffrage magazine, described an examination branch for the recruitment of women into war work:

The examination branch is completely filled by women from the trained industrial classes, the domestic servant class, and a great deal by married women. Let me tell you of those I personally know. I can think of three fever nurses, two dressmakers trained at Debenham and Freebody's, a showroom woman from a very high-class milli-nery shop, two cooks, a lady's-maid – all in good situations – a parlourmaid from a house in Cavendish Square, two sisters who kept a boarding house with their mother but find it more lucrative to be at the Arsenal, a waitress, a laundry-maid who has been at one place for fifteen years, several clerks, two or three married women with no children and several more with children of school age.[13]

Lily Truphet, a housemaid who had once been paid five shillings a week to work for a woman who weighed the contents of her vacuum cleaner (a cup and a half of dirt was considered a job well done), went to work in a munitions factory. Years later, she remembered that it was 'like being let out of a cage'.[14]

Because of the shortage of staff, many houses were shut up, their owners living in hotels or boarding houses, or the family reduced to camping in a few rooms. Some tried, on the whole unsuccessfully, to argue that domestic help constituted vital war work. The letters pages of *The Times* raged with suggestions on how to relieve the burdens of the servantless housewife. In 1915 a correspondent wondered if dressmakers who complained that straitened times had reduced their work might consider 'swallowing an old prejudice' and going into service.[15] Another thought that those servants who were still in service might actually be persuaded to take a patriotic 25 per cent cut in their wages – for the war effort. Yet another mused that 'ladies of gentler birth' might be persuaded to go into domestic service but on reflection decided that they would 'expect an impossible amount of consideration and . . . insist too much upon their social status'.[16]

In these conditions, the Baldwins, like so many others, found it almost impossible to find anyone to help Alice Osbourn at Rectory Farm House. 'Frightfully rushed', was Alice's only comment on the situation, though her wartime diaries contain letters from prospective servants, and advertisements were regularly placed for new ones. A parlourmaid, the inaptly named Jane Perfect, arrived with great fanfare in 1915, then walked out one month later. The same year, a letter to Alice from a Miss Turner reveals that Mrs Baldwin had offered her the job of cook-general but that Miss Turner did not think she could take on the work 'when there is only two servants' to help her. In April 1918, Elsie Pinchin, the cook, gave notice ('so I am entirely without anyone. Cannot hear of even a maid,' wrote Alice) and her replacement, Anne Belson, left just before Christmas, summoned home by her mother. At about the same time, Elsie Pinchin, ensconced in a new job not far away, wrote to Alice recommending her sister, an experienced 'house-parlour', who was between jobs and might have time to help out if required. Pre-war standards had to be compromised and servants could lay down terms when there was so much demand. Elsie's sister, she wrote, 'cannot cook but she would do vegetables'. It seems from her correspondence that Alice tried to woo Elsie back to Taplow to no avail; a letter from the cook suggests that she has been courted by another: 'A lady called yesterday to see Mrs Wilder and she was in want of a cook so saw me, and I decided to go to her if my referance [sic] is satisfactory.' Even Mrs Pollard, the charwoman who came to do the rough work and help with the ironing, could not, by 1918, consider any extra hours: 'my husband's leg is very bad and Edie is not much better'.[17]

By the end of the war, the idea of returning to a domestic world run in deferential silence by the starched and obedient retainers of the past seemed impossibly optimistic. Jack Leech, who lived near the Lyme Estate in Cheshire, found, like so many others, that the experience of war changed everything about coming home: 'You had a different outlook on life when you came back. It's surprising what war does to a man. There's more of a comradeship amongst men. There was an element got into things that the men who were doing the fighting should be classed with the instructing men. It developed – definitely – into what today is the Labour movement.' Leech recalled returning from the pub while on leave with a friend, Tommy, who had been wounded in the Dardanelles. The two men walked down a country road together and when a motor car appeared, in those days honking and fuming down the middle of the road with all the arrogance of its wealthy owner, Tommy refused to get out of the way. 'He thought he had as much right to be there as that motor car. That was the attitude that came from the war.'[18]

The upper classes began to prepare themselves for a different world. 'Old England is cracking up,' was the prognosis of the former butler Eric Horne, looking back on the advent of war in his 1923 autobiography. Manpower on the estates was in desperately short supply and would not be replenished as so many thousands of labourers, farmers and landowners had lost their sons in the war. Furthermore, the post-war agricultural depression and increases in both taxation and death duties introduced by the budget of 1919 forced large landowners all over the country to sell up: between 1918 and 1922 a quarter of the land area of England and Wales changed hands. The 'nobility,' Horne wrote, 'are selling their estates and large houses, which are being turned into schools, museums, hospitals, homes for the weak-minded. It seems a pity that the old usages and traditions of gentlemen's service should die with the old places, where so many high-jinks and junketings have carried on.'[19]In 1919, in a valiant attempt to show that society was back to normal, the Season returned. 'It was a wonderful Season – gay and bright, with all the men in uniform throwing their money about any old how, they were so glad to be alive,' was how Lady Phyllis Macrae, a 1919 debutante, remembered it.[20] But just a year later, everything had changed. There were strikes and hunger marches and the atmosphere was tense with resentment and desperation. Even the most conservative career servants looked back on the war years as a time when social structures seemed to be cracking at the edges. *Punch* published a cartoon in 1920 of a fashionable couple discussing a country house party to which invitations would have to depend on the guests' skills at washing-up or cleaning shoes. In the *Daily Mail* in 1918, the writer Ward Muir thought the war had marked the end of domestic service for ever: 'I have seen Mary's bedroom, furnished with a "servants' set". I have seen the bare little kitchen in which Mary wasn't allowed to receive admirers (not even the jolly young motorbicycle repairer), but in which she was supposed to sit very contentedly for six evenings a week. And I don't think that Mary will come rushing back to these havens of luxury.'[21]

Chapter 12

'Don't Think Your Life Will Be
Any Different to Mine'

Disappointment, disillusion and the dole queue formed the undercurrent to the 1920s, while on the surface, a racket of flappers, pyjama parties, daring shingled haircuts, jazz, nightclubs, cocktails ('sherry and cocktails seem to have put an end to tea-drinking', noted the manservant Charles Cooper in 1930), sunbathing and other celebrations of the body beautiful attempted to suppress the awkwardness and guilt aroused by the sight of crippled veterans hawking chocolates or busking for pennies on street corners. Former footman Ernest Squire received a disability pension after the war – but work was very hard to find. 'The disabled man was exploited from the time he was discharged from the forces,' he remembered. Government-issue suits handed out to servicemen returning to civilian life were so notoriously thin and badly made that they became known as the great 'reach me down' scandal. In Ernest Squire's experience, 'by the time I reached home after my discharge most of the buttons had parted from the suit and taken a piece of cloth with them. The quality was so poor I was never able to wear it again.'[1] Footman Gordon Grimmett in the mid-1920s found an old acquaintance from his country house days, a travelling entertainer, selling matches from a tray marked 'Blinded in Action'. Grimmett asked him why he was pretending to be blind. 'It's the only thing that works now, there's too many of us, it pays to be blind,' was his reply. 'Bitches, bitches,' Grimmett heard him murmur as two well-dressed women walked past.[2]

The contrast between the two worlds, the public face of the 'Roaring Twenties' and its dark and fearful shadow, was devastating. Entire regional populations, particularly those dependent on a single industry, were blighted by poverty and unemployment. 'The atmosphere in industrial areas,' remembered the journalist Leslie Baily, was 'heavy with hatred and foreboding.'[3] Disappointed women and girls, their hopes raised by war work and independence, grudgingly returned to service in part because in a post-war economic depression there was simply no other work available to them, and in part because of a powerful resurgence of the traditional domestic ideal of femininity. Stung by guilt and pity at the sight of the lines of war-shattered men returning from the front, women of all classes were encouraged to give back their jobs to former servicemen and concentrate instead on creating the nurturing, comforting home that had made the war worth fighting.

In the press and in government, the wartime woman worker came to be perceived as an aberration, the return to the roles of wife and mother personifying the return to peacetime normality. Herbert Asquith, the Prime Minister, had reluctantly conceded in 1916 that women's wartime contribution had earned them the right to a vote, but the Parliament Act of 1918 was a rushed-through compromise, enfranchising only female householders and the wives of householders who were aged over thirty-five (roughly six million of the thirteen million adult women in the country). 'My butler votes, why can't I?' had been a burning question for the upper-class campaigner; but for the suffragette Sylvia Pankhurst, the act excluded those women most in need of voice and representation, and crucially, 'still upholds the old class prejudices, the old checks and balances designed to prevent the will of the majority, who are the workers, from being registered without handicap'.[4]

Many of the militants who had galvanised factory workers and suffragettes before the war fell suddenly silent in the face of a new kind of feminism: the kind that believed the battle won and that promoted the ideology of 'separate spheres', of men and women being biologically determined by innate and natural differences. Eleanor Rathbone, in a 1917 article in *Economic Journal*, argued for the latter view as being in the best interests of women: 'the majority of women workers are only birds of passage in their trades. Marriage and the bearing and rearing of children are their permanent occupation.' In the official discourse of the twenties, as a new world emerged from the dislocating wreckage of a terrible war, the home was the only place of safety – and its presiding spirit was the mother, the wife and the housekeeper. In 1922 the first British edition of the magazine *Good Housekeeping* told its readers that they were poised on 'the threshold of a great feminine awakening. Apathy and levity are alike giving place to a wholesome and intelligent interest in the affairs of life . . . and above all, in the home.'[5]

During the war, women had been lavishly praised for their stoicism, their spirit, courage and unstinting efforts at the coalface and in the factory. Now the war was over, a woman in overalls or at a steering wheel began to look dangerously transgressive. The mood changed dramatically. A correspondent for the *Leeds Mercury* wrote in 1919 that women's 'shrewish behaviour will remain one of the unpleasant memories of the war's vicissitudes'.[6] Women workers, freewheeling about in shameless displays of independence had long generated hostility. The *Daily Mail*, always a reliable chronicle of public indignation, in 1915 crossly reported on the number of women seen brazenly eating in restaurants, even smoking in public. 'The wartime business girl is to be seen any night dining out alone or with a friend in the moderate-priced restaurants in London. Formerly she would never have had her evening meal in town unless in the company of a man friend. But now with money and without men she is more and more beginning to dine out.'[7] By the end of the war, alarmists saw signs of female moral turpitude everywhere. Munitions factory workers, known as 'Munitionettes', had acquired a reputation during the war for promiscuity; contraceptives, almost unknown before the war, could by 1919 be purchased in every village chemist. 'Morality mongers,' wrote Sylvia Pankhurst after the war, 'conceived most monstrous visions of girls and

women, freed from the control of fathers and husbands who had
hitherto compelled them to industry, chastity and sobriety, now
neglecting their homes, plunging into excesses, and burdening the
country with swarms of illegitimate children.'

As always, the revival of domestic service was seen as an answer to
the problem of social chaos; but now it was also viewed as a reward
for the hard-pressed middle-class housewife who had battled so
stoically on the home front. Domestic servants were excluded from
those women war workers entitled to post-war unemployment
benefit, yet in the public imagination the 'dole' was routinely
condemned because it was thought to deter girls from entering service (quite wrongly, as the 1923 Commission on Women's
Employment discovered). For readers of the *Daily Mail* and many
others, the 'servant problem' boiled down to stubborn insubordina-
tion on the part of welfare scroungers. 'It is almost impossible to get
a domestic servant in this town, and it is certainly high time this dole
business ceased. The streets are full of girls dressed to death, who,
frankly, say that as long as they are paid to do nothing they will
continue just as they are,' wrote a correspondent.[8] Girls known to
have been in service before the war were reported for drawing the
dole and in 1921, the National Insurance Act was expanded to
include a clause requiring applications for social security to prove
they were 'genuinely seeking work'. Those unwilling to take jobs in
service were often refused benefits.

It became regarded as unpatriotic and unwomanly to hold on to
a job that might be taken by a man. Pam Taylor, for example, writes
that her mother worked as a commercial traveller during the war
but regarded it as 'keeping a man's job open for him'.[9] 'The year
1922 was not a good time to be setting out on one's career,' reflected
Lavinia Swainbank, who was forced back to work as a housemaid.
'For those were the days of depression on the Tyne, when the ship-
yards were idle and the pits closed down and every day the queue
of sad-eyed men signed on for dole grew longer and hope of finding
work grew more remote.'[10] Dolly Davey, who came to London
from Stockton-on-Tees in search of 'adventure' in 1924, thought
that of the choice of domestic service or factory work, service held

the chance of 'bettering' herself. Her mother at first would not hear of it 'but mostly, you see, the only jobs available at that time were farm jobs'.[11]

At Rectory Farm House in 1920, Alice Osbourn received a letter from the former cook Elsie Pinchin. In a letter headed 'The Empress Club, Berkeley Street, London', Elsie (who in the last years of the war had called the shots for perhaps the first time in her working life) wrote: 'I am just writing to ask you if you are suited. If not I would like to come to you as I am leaving here in a fortnight's time. I cannot stay here as the food is so bad and so hard, that is if you would wait a fortnight for me.'[12] By that time Alice had employed a new cook called Mary Marshall and we never read again about Elsie Pinchin in her diaries; but we do know that the economic depression was closing employment opportunities and returning the balance of power to the employers. The wives of disabled ex-servicemen, for example, were often forced back to work as daily charwomen because, looking after their husbands, residential service was impossible for them. In *Good Housekeeping* in 1923, Margery Benn put her readers' minds at rest as to this new, hitherto inferior, form of service. Although, she wrote, 'a vista of inconvenience opens up and to the mind's eye, the daily maid appears as slovenly, unpunctual, perhaps actually dishonest, introducing burglars and herself vanishing from sight', this new type of non-residential daily woman was altogether more 'competent and superior'.[13]

Many of those working-class women for whom the war had promised a new beginning were destined for crushing disappointment. In 1911, according to the census, 32.3 per cent of British women described themselves as 'gainfully employed', but by 1921 the figure had fallen to 30.8 per cent. In areas hard hit by unemployment, domestic service was, yet again, the only work available. Joyce Storey and Jean Rennie were both forced into service in the 1920s, and both saw their mothers' hopes for their futures dashed. 'I saw myself like a floating piece of seaweed half submerged,' recollected Joyce. 'Against the quickened thumping of my heartbeat, and the desire to escape, I saw my mother's eyes burn into mine. "Don't think your life will be any different to mine".'[14]

Joyce's stint as a general maid in a grocer's household was cut short only when the grocer's wife asked her to clean the coal cellar on her afternoon off. 'It was only when I came to the final patch that I looked up and swore a terrible oath. "This is the last time in my entire bloody life I will ever be on my knees with my nose to the ground, for I belong up there with my eyes to the light, and walking upright and tall".'[15] Jean Rennie's mother had hoped for much more for her daughter: 'I can only vaguely imagine what my mother must have felt. All that time and all those books, and all my education – I know she was inarticulate but I can see now the hurt in her eyes, that after all that, her daughter, her eldest, gawky, clever, talented daughter, was going "into service" as she herself had done at the age of twelve.'[16]

Jean's father was a riveter with a beautiful tenor voice whose heavy drinking had left the family desperately hard up; but Jean passed the qualifying examination for secondary school and at fourteen took the higher leaving certificate, passing with honours (her father drank the £5 bursary she was awarded). She attended evening classes in shorthand, typing and bookkeeping and finally secured a job at a mill which lasted less than a year. Every day Jean went to the library, searching for jobs and opportunities that never materialised. From 1922, benefits were only available to those prepared to do any work available and, finally, in a last resort that would lead to sixteen years in service, she applied to be a housemaid in a large country house – and got the job. 'Obedience was deeply rooted in my character,' she reflected later. It was her first experience of the strange and sealed world of the landed estate and the very first evening she listened to her fellow servants' snobbish gossip and watched them tuck into a vast tea, laden with butter, jam and fruit cake, then toss the leftovers into a bin for the pigs. 'I nearly choked with anger at the wanton waste. I could remember so many hungry children – and here was good food being contemptuously pushed aside.'[17]

Damaged ex-soldiers sometimes filled the gap opened in the domestic service market: a training in the armed services equipped one well for many of the duties and disciplines of, say, valeting, cleaning silver or managing menial staff. 'Temporary gentlemen' – former officers who had gained commissions on the basis of merit rather than background – were particularly popular, their military bearing and efficiency being seen as an asset. The socialist author Naomi Mitchison's husband was approached for work by an ex-serviceman called Levinson whom the Mitchisons employed to wait at table; his wife became the cook. But Levinson drank, and Naomi found him unnerving and unpredictable. The spectre of the horrors of war cast such a shadow over veterans that they were often awkward and alienating presences in a bright social world. 'All was not right with the spirit of the men who came back,' wrote the journalist Philip Gibbs in 1920. 'They were subject to queer moods, queer tempers, fits of profound depression alternating with a restless desire for pleasure ... Many were bitter in their speech, violent in opinion, frightening.'[18]

The post-war sale of landed estates drove another blow into the 'sacred trust' that had underpinned the pre-war patriarchy. Successful businessmen or war profiteers who bought country houses from impoverished gentry were often regarded with hostility and confusion by those retainers who went with the house. It was the corporate, bureaucratic officialdom of the new order that grated, 'the impersonal touch, the reluctance for a long chat, the circular letters, the raising of rents to an economic level, and especially the private investigations by secretaries and agents, which they regarded as ungentlemanly spying'.[19] Eric 'George' Washington had a deformed foot which made it impossible for him in the early 1920s to train for any work but domestic service. Reluctantly, in the teeth of his parents' opposition (they thought service 'the lowest of the low'), at fourteen he became a hall boy at Little Missenden Abbey, the new owner of which was an Australian wool tycoon. Washington, with the snobbery that only a country house servant can muster, disliked it there: Mrs Ronald, he considered, was a middle-class wife 'trying her utmost to ape her betters', but lacking the natural warmth of the gentry's genuine article.[20]

As early as 1913, Lily Frazer, the wife of James Frazer (author of *The Golden Bough*), had imagined a world in which the average

English home would have to do without servants entirely. In *First Aid to the Servantless*, the German-born Mrs Frazer was a bracing champion of the beleaguered middle classes. The English aristocracy she regarded as idle and corrupt, and the working classes as incorrigibly venal and lazy. Deploring the ignorance and ineptitude of British housewives enslaved to standards they could not afford to maintain, in Mrs Frazer's vision of the future, servants would no longer indicate status; she even questioned the point of 'the ritual of the front door'.[21] Instead, she pointed out that a maid was a daily reminder of a resentful relationship that was increasingly unsettling and difficult to navigate.

A decade later, the artist and suffragette Ernestine Mills, author of *The Domestic Problem, Past, Present and Future*, picked up Mrs Frazer's theme and radicalised it further. She detected double standards in the treatment of men and household work, pointing out that when it was suggested that domestic work might be usefully undertaken by one of the many men unemployed by the war – as 'houseparlourmen' or cooks – there was 'uproar'. 'Why cleaning a house should be considered more "unproductive" than cleaning a motor car or a golf course has never been explained, or why it should be shocking to employ a man as a general servant, but rather distinguished to have one as a powdered footman. Or again, why a man ought not to be a "plain" cook but is universally admired as an overpaid chef.'[22] But Ernestine Mills's proposals did not fit the cautious mood of the age: men had fought a war; it was for women to create a peacetime home for them. By 1929, that prolific journalist Mrs Peel, whose many publications form a useful barometer of social trends, dashed off *Waiting at Table*, a handbook of instruction for the servant and his employer. It included directions for mixing cocktails, a popular import from the United States, but otherwise reinforced all the old and hated regulations of the old days: 'do not breathe heavily'; 'do not rattle knives and forks'; 'do not speak unless necessary. If a direction must be given to an underservant it should be in the lowest possible tones.'[23]

A report in 1923 by the Central Committee for Women's Employment on the supply of female domestic servants recommended, as well-meaning reports of this kind generally did, that pensions for domestics be regularised; that a maid should have a statutory two hours off *every day* and two weeks' holiday a year; that efforts should be made to give servants comfortable rooms 'adequately ventilated and lighted'; and that wages should be regularised. If women were to be enticed back into service, then service itself must be regulated, and its practitioners given a professional-sounding new title like domestic houseworker, and endowed with training, qualifications, diplomas and certificates. It was not the first time that attempts had been made to safeguard domestic service with regulations, and it would not be the last. But service relied on a relationship that, by its very nature, its place in the home, was impossible fully to regulate.

In 1921 the suffragette magazine *Time and Tide* invited an *actual housemaid* to write her answer to the great and baffled public question of why girls did not want to return to the lonely basement of the maid-of-all-work. Her article encapsulated the problems at the heart of the matter, those that no regulatory body could fix: she wrote of the indignities of never being thanked, or addressed, or acknowledged at all; of returning from a day off to find washing-up that took more than an hour to finish; of mistresses who would prefer food to be burnt or thrown away than given to the odd-job man. 'For one thing the whole atmosphere is so awful; the way one is spoken to is so insulting, and so often what one says is disbelieved. Surely, a servant coming from a good home, brought up to be truthful and honest, would find it very difficult to remain so under these circumstances.'[24]

The loneliness and ignominy of it was indeed often hard to bear, especially for girls away from home for the first time. When Jessie Cox arrived in Paddington to be met by a parlourmaid for her first job: 'I was recognised by a mop of fair curly hair, a navy coat and a buttonhole of parsley. I felt like a lost dog and the indignity remains with me seventy-one years on.'[25] In the 1920s, skivvydom felt again like a life sentence; it defined who you were for ever. When Jean Rennie tried to leave service and get a job as a waitress, or 'nippy', in a Lyons Corner House, she overheard a customer saying: 'Bloody skivvy with ideas.'[26] A few years later, the novelist Patrick Hamilton's fictional maid Jenny wonders 'if there is something mean and debasing in being "in service", in being a "skivvy"?' Her conclusion would echo those of a maidservant one hundred years before; it was service or the streets: 'Well, there was in a way: she knew that. But she was "born to that class" and that was that.' As an editorial in *Time and Tide* concluded, only financial desperation could force girls back into domestic service; it certainly would not be the moral outrage of newspaper commentators trying to persuade them 'that [their] only hope of virtue lies in self-sacrifice'.[27]

In 1920, the Central Committee on Women's Training and Employment established a wide range of courses offering training and diplomas not only in 'domestic work' but in other subjects such as midwifery, clerical duties, hairdressing, massage, teaching and music. The committee was charged with finding employment for women that did not 'trespass upon occupations especially suited to disabled men'.[28] Nearly 4,000 women took part in the courses, but two years later the scheme was wound up, funds having run out. Increasingly thereafter, other opportunities slipped away, leaving the emphasis on training for domestic work only, using the newly established Homecraft Centres or membership of the League of Skilled Housecraft. Those students who could not afford the uniforms they needed to take up jobs were given them by a charitable fund (but had to return them if they left the job before three months). Students included former clerical workers, shop assistants and clerks and, inexorably, work for women moved again towards domesticity. As the depression bit harder, vocational courses in office work or other skills were further cut to maximise funding for domestic ones. In 1924 over 23,000 girls matriculated from a Home Crafts course and only 145 completed a vocational one. The numbers reached their height in the unemployment crisis of the mid-1930s – courses in domestic work rising steadily until they peaked in 1938 at 82,937 students and were interrupted by the advent of another war. By 1931, domestic service was yet again the largest single employer of female labour, absorbing nearly 24 per cent of all women workers.[29]

The Ministry of Labour's original ambition of finding gainful employment for former war workers had metamorphosed stealthily into a mission to train them to be domestics. In areas of high industrial unemployment, young girls were often the only members of a family whose skills could productively be redeployed. From 1929 the government's Juvenile Transference Scheme took girls from Britain's most depressed areas, particularly Welsh mining regions devastated by unemployment, and resettled them in domestic service, particularly in the south-east and London. For many girls it was a terrible, dislocating experience. Thomas Jones, the Welsh civil servant and liberal protégé of Lloyd George, wrote in his diary: 'What we have found in some of the more remote mining villages is this: girls of 17–20 who have never slept alone in a room, who have never known what it is to have ordinary bedclothes, and some who are unfamiliar with knives and forks – all of which seems incredible today. You can imagine the bewilderment of one of these girls when transferred to a strange house in London.'[30]

First, the girls, most of whom had never left home before, were sent to domestic service centres to learn laundry work, infant care, hygiene, cleaning and needlework. Much was made of the usefulness of these skills in some rosy future experience of 'married life', perhaps to give the courses a gloss of uplifting self-determination. At the end of the 1920s, however, the London School of Economics researcher Frances Livingston concluded that most domestic servants did not find their job a useful training in household economy, or certainly not for the kind of households that a young maid might expect to have if she was to marry in the future. It was, Miss Livingston wrote, 'rather a disadvantage', according to one of her interviewees, 'as orders given on the phone, at the door, etc., give no comparison of prices, and in large houses cost is often a minor consideration, in marriage cost is generally of vital importance'. Another woman said that service set up unrealistic expectations: 'My experience of girls in service is that they lose all ambition of home life. Their aim is to get out and when they marry they cannot make a home on a small scale; as regards cooking, unless a girl has absolutely been with the cook in a kitchen of a big house she knows no more about cooking than the business girl and does not seem as keen.'[31]

The new femininity therefore looked remarkably like the old femininity: and one's view on that would rather depend on where one stood in the social scheme. In the affluent classes, after all, there was a relief that after the horrors of the war, domestic life seemed to be back to normal. Rose Luttrell, wife of a banker in the 1920s, had a full staff: 'I had a cook and a kitchenmaid, a housemaid and a parlourmaid, and a nanny and a nurserymaid. I had six servants you see. I never did any housework or any domestic work at all. I saw the cook in the morning and ordered the meals for the day and I never went near the kitchen. You didn't go interfering.'[32] Many families struggled on, as Mrs Praga's had before them, maintaining appearances on limited incomes. Happy Sturgeon's first job, in Bungay, Suffolk, was as 'one of two maids pretending to be an entire household'. The child first of an orphanage and then of a training scheme, Happy was powerless to change her situation, but she could take some wry pleasure at the ridiculous sight of 'Madam, tripping down in her little heels', with rubber gloves, hair tied back and spotless overalls, to show her new fourteen-year-old maid how things were done.'[33]

Chapter 13

'It Was Exploitation But It Worked'

The clothing and general appearance of women changed so thoroughly in the 1920s that it seems hardly credible that the war lasted only four years. The unyielding buttresses of Edwardian costumes gave way to lightweight, sporting lingerie for fashionably boyish bodies. By 1927 hemlines had shot up above the knee and the sought-after silhouette was 'sexless, bosomless, hipless, thighless'.[1] The clothing revolution affected women of all classes. Off-the-peg clothes in new, factory-made fabrics such as rayon and artificial silk were now so convincing that they resembled the tailor-made version until you got up close. On her day off, a servant need no longer always look like a servant. She might even look as if she were in the movies, one of the new stars of popular culture's most exciting innovation. It was not uncommon, among all classes, to go to the pictures every night of the week. Celluloid dreams were a social leveller; there were no class distinctions among the seats in the cinema.

In 1924, when fourteen-year-old Winifred Foley arrived from the Forest of Dean to take up her first job in London, she was met at the station by Blodwen, a maid from the household in Stoke Newington where she was to work. 'She didn't look like my idea of a maid at all. Her good looks were hidden, rather than accentuated, by an overdose of lipstick, rouge, powder and mascara. She had the first cropped hair I'd seen, and she wore a flapper-length black satin coat fastened with big fancy buttons. She was in high-heeled black court shoes and pink silk stockings. I was very impressed.' The railway porter was less impressed: '"She come up to skivvy in the same place as you, then?" he asked her. Like me, he was ignorant of the fact that she really longed to be taken for an actress, so she was stung to the quick that he saw through her.'[2]

A revitalising new spirit seemed to have blown through the relationships in Rectory Farm House too. Mr Baldwin had died in 1919, a few months after the Armistice, and Mrs Baldwin in 1925. By the middle of the decade, therefore, Daphne, then in her early twenties, found herself living alone (her brothers having both married and moved away) in a large house with Alice Osbourn as housekeeper, and as post-war unemployment drove more servants on to the market, with a cook and a house-parlourmaid, and Talbot, the gardener, who had survived the war. In 1926, Alice's accounts tell us that her wages had been doubled to £50, the first time they had been increased at all since she noted them down in her diary of 1906. During this period, the diary begins to refer to Daphne as 'Daph' or, quite often, 'Old Daph'. Daphne learned to drive and bought a car, a Morris Bedford and later a Morris Cabriolet.[3] Car ownership had more than doubled after the war: in 1914 only 132,000 cars were in private possession but by 1922 there were 315,000; by 1930 there were over one million. Eric Horne disapproved. Looking back at his butlering glory days in the late nineteenth century, he missed the 'gaily caparisoned horses' of the past and found the people of the 1920s worn down by speed and 'hurry and scurry'; he even speculated that marriages were breaking down, the old order of discretion rotting from within, now that a chauffeur could be kept waiting for hours while his master or mistress conducted assignations.[4]

But at Rectory Farm House, the new automobile was a great source of enjoyment to Alice and Daphne. Alice's entries are full of details about the car, its 'de-carbonisation' problems and its too-long spells spent in the garage for repairs. Most pleasurably of all, she records the two of them, Daph and Obbs, motoring all over the country visiting friends, shopping in Maidenhead, collecting weekend visitors from the station, driving to Brighton. Daphne plays tennis, goes to house parties and to London (unchaperoned), and takes part in charity theatricals put on by her friend Imogen Grenfell at Taplow Court. 'Dear old Onion!' begins a letter to Daphne from Imogen, a reply to a party invitation. Like many of Daphne's letters it was folded in the back of Alice's 1925 diary and nearly ninety years later, suggests that Daphne is having a high time, that her life has opened up – and that Alice's life has opened up too.

In the manner of the official recorder, Alice's diary entries tell us that she and Daph go to the pictures in the Cinematograph Alhambra in Maidenhead at least twice a week; in 1928, Daph had a permanent wave; and in 1929, Daphne (surely one of the lucky ones, in those days when unmarried women so outnumbered men) became engaged and then broke off the engagement six months later: the unlucky lover was 'too persistent' is Alice's only, cryptic, comment. There are far fewer references to her charge languishing in bed all morning and, though Daphne's liver and headaches still feature quite prominently in Alice's everyday concerns, the debilitating and mysterious ailments that took up so much of her youth are less in evidence. It seems as though the twenties were a tonic for both Daph and Obbs.[5]

Alice's diary tells us nothing about Daphne Baldwin's politics, if indeed she had any interest in politics at all. But the 1920s were a decade of disappointment and contradictions for women who had been politicised by the suffrage movement. Nancy Astor, Conservative MP for Plymouth and the first woman to sit in the House of Commons after the 1919 Suffrage Act, was hardly representative of either the hard-pressed housewife or the career woman. Immensely wealthy and a domestic autocrat with a huge staff at her disposal, the witty, sometimes abhorrently rude, formidably energetic, bossy, elegant and eccentric Lady Astor was, according to the *Evening Standard*, 'laughing her way into Parliament'.[6] A Virginian, born into the feudal aristocracy of the American South, and a Christian Scientist teetotaller 'who had no time for illness or feminine weakness', Nancy Astor was accustomed to complete reliance on servants for the smallest task.

It is significant that among the most vivid pictures that have been left to us of Nancy Astor was the one painted in the 1970s by her lady's-maid, Rose Harrison, who arrived at Cliveden in 1928. Rose and her employer lived together for thirty years in rancorous, bickering intimacy. Charles Dean, a footman at Cliveden in the late twenties, remembered the 'glorious' slanging matches; how 'Rose came running in with her hackles up' if Lady Astor threatened mutiny and how she secretly doctored her teetotal employer's favourite Ribena tipple with Dubonnet if she looked 'down in the dumps'.[7] Nancy Astor was entirely dependent on Rose for every last detail of her public and private appearance. The lady's-maid even had to remember that her ladyship always needed to have a pair of false teeth in her handbag in case she should be called upon to do her celebrated impersonation of Margot Asquith. At Cliveden in the inter-war period, the Astors exacted Edwardian standards of luxury and discipline from all their employees. Lady Astor's suede gloves were worn once only before they were cleaned; the signature gardenia always in her buttonhole was picked fresh for her every day by Cliveden's head gardener (and when she was in London was sent by early morning train to her house in St James's). She got through five sets of clothes a day and all collars and cuffs, worn once, had to be laundered and ironed individually.

The First World War, Rose Harrison wrote poignantly, had been 'very much a time of women's lib' below stairs'; but by the early twenties servants like Rose had again slipped back below the radar of progressive politics and of feminism. They were just too useful: in many cases they made the new freedoms for women possible. 'We took [service] for granted,' wrote Naomi Mitchison, who had married just after the war. Comfortably off rather than wealthy, the Mitchisons had two maids and a cook: 'For me the servant basis meant that I could have parties, without having to think about the washing-up.'[8]

Ethel Mannin, the daughter of a postal sorter in Clapham, was a socialist, a feminist, a pacifist, and a leading supporter of progressive theories of education, family and sexuality. In 1920 she was just setting out in life, aged nineteen and married to John Porteous, an advertising copywriter. The couple had set up home in a small semi-detached house in the London suburb of Strawberry Hill. Ethel had a new baby and was a busy writer, at large in the first years of Modernism: 'Living My Life', was how she described it in her energetic capitals. A steady stream of romantic novelettes, churned out at a guinea per thousand words, provided Ethel's income. The household kept a cook-general at thirty shillings a week, a sum Ethel considered generous (the going rate being twenty-five shillings). 'Cap and apron, of course; blue cotton dress in the mornings; black cloth in the afternoons – and coffee-coloured caps and aprons were just that much smarter than plain white ones.'[9] Her socialist principles were apparently untroubled by the maid, who called her 'Madam' and who referred to her husband as 'the Master'. As Mannin saw it, domestic help was a necessary component of her freedom. 'It was snobbish; it was class distinction; it was exploitation but it worked,' she wrote fifty years later. Educated, perceptive, imaginative, free-thinking, questioning, below the frenetic glitter of 'the amoral decade, the Sweet and Twenties, the Bitter-Sweet Twenties, the gay Twenties, the Bright Twenties, the Roaring Twenties', Ethel was more conventional than she had imagined herself at the time: 'I probably gave [the maid] ten bob at Christmas and the occasional dress I was tired of. Quite intensely I dislike the memory of myself when young; but it's the way I was. I was of my times; quintessentially.'[10]

Though Ethel Mannin was later to write that 'the war dealt a great blow to snobbishness', the old awkwardness, the looming divide between women living under the same roof continued to be considered not just normal but necessary. When Rose Harrison first went to work as a lady's-maid in the mid-twenties, her charge was Patricia Tufton, who was eighteen, the same age as Rose. 'My relationship with Miss Patricia isn't easy for me to describe. We weren't friends, though if she were asked today she might deny this. We weren't even acquaintances. We never exchanged confidences, never discussed people, nothing we said brought us closer; my advice might be asked about clothes or bits of shopping, but my opinions were never sought or given on her music, or the people we met or on anything that was personal to either of us, nor did I expect it or miss it at the time.'[11]

Old retainers like Alice Osbourn, with the flexible and some-times irreverent intimacy that came from years of living with a family, usually made for less fractious and exacting relationships. It is difficult to imagine what Winifred Holtby and Vera Brittain would have done without the contribution of Winifred's old nanny 'Nursie', who came down from Yorkshire to live with and look after them. Socialists, pacifists, passionate fighters for the cause of women, Brittain and Holtby shared a home, on and off, for nearly fifteen years. 'Throughout history,' wrote Winifred in 1934, 'when-ever society had tried to curtail the opportunities, interests and powers of women, it has done so in the sacred names of marriage and maternity.'[12] While Holtby herself eschewed both marriage and maternity, she also had the great good fortune of rarely having to trouble herself about domestic responsibilities. She and Vera lived first in a London studio, where they delighted in the shabbiness that was such a contrast with their own prosperous, provincial backgrounds – 'skylights, the penny-in-the-slot gas fires'; and eating 'egg and cheese suppers cooked on a gas-ring'. In those days, they had a charlady who came in every day to do the cleaning. By the time 'Nursie' was summoned to be their housekeeper, the two women were living in Maida Vale, and the former nanny, thought Winifred, had herself been brushed by the gold dust of female inde-pendence that they enjoyed. Winifred wrote to Vera with the good news that Nursie was 'over the moon at the idea of London and Life. She says she's never been really on her own. Now she's going to live . . . she says that you shall have breakfast in bed every day if you like.'[13]

Intellectual life, its thriving so dependent on domestic help, seems often to have emphasised in its participants an embarrassed distance from the reality of the shadowy figure in the kitchen. Bohemians, keen to burst the bounds of bourgeois conformities, seem to have been remarkably ill at ease with their own servants, perhaps because the servants themselves, being human, rarely conformed to the amusing stereotype (faithful, respectable, a fount of old saws of working-class wisdom) that the novelist often required of them. Katherine Mansfield was thrown into vapours by the behaviour of one member of staff, as she confided to her diary in 1919: 'The cook is evil. After lunch I trembled so that I had to lie down on the *sommier* – thinking about her. I meant – when she came up to see me – to say so much that she'd have to go. I waited, playing with the wild kitten. When she came, I said it all, and more, and she said how sorry she was and agreed and apologised and quite understood.' Later, in a letter, Mansfield wrote: 'How blessed! It is dreadful enough to be without servants but to be with them – is far more dreadful. I cannot forget the dishonest hateful old creature down in the kitchen. Now she will go & I shall throw her bits to the dustman & fumigate her room & start fair again.'[14]

The author Ronald Blythe has suggested that in the years after the end of the First World War, a terrible shame and guilt crept over people at the sight of 'unemployed ex-servicemen and their families, these hordes of shabby young men and women made spiritless, drab and ugly by broken promises, malnutrition and loss of hope'. It produced, Blythe went on, in the middle classes, a 'contempt for working-class people of a kind quite unknown before the war began'.[15] Grace Fulford's account of an encounter with her recalcitrant cook, who had been found feeding the baby his food on the floor, in its physicality, its appalled distance, its fastidious horror, illumines a chasm of distrust and fear. One might have thought that Mrs Fulford, in her own eyes a delicate flower, was in the presence of an axe-wielding murderess: 'And I remember her coming in, coming in to me in the morning, standing over me just like a Grenadier guardsman. I was so small and she was so big.'[16]

Helen Campbell, American author of *Household Economics*, in 1907 defined one of the central paradoxes of the servant-master relationship, certainly as it was played out in the small home: 'The condition of domestic servitude allows only the development of a certain degree of ability, not sufficient to perform our complex domestic industries. So there we are. When we find a person able to carry on modern household industries, that person will not be our servant. And when we find a person willing to be our servant, that person is unable to carry on modern household industries.'[17] Most people preferred not to look closely at the relationship, with its awkwardness and its responsibilities. One woman writer in the early twenties, however, was brave enough to address it full on, and with a refreshing determination to look its contradictions straight in the eye. Under the pseudonym Dion Fortune, Violet Firth went on to became a theosophist, occultist, psychic, a founder of the esoteric society, 'The Fraternity of the Inner Light', and the author of now long-forgotten works such as *The Goat-Foot God* and *The Cosmic Doctrine*. In the years immediately after the war, however, Firth was also a student of psychoanalysis, practising (under her own name) as a lay psychotherapist in London.

In 1925, she published a remarkable short polemic entitled *The Psychology of the Servant Problem*, which would be a work of radicalism in any age. Drawing on her years of war work as a gardener for a big country house, Firth examined what lay behind the intractable and inexplicable problem of what domestic service meant to those who had to perform it. She recognised, crucially, that what made service so difficult to define, and therefore to legislate for, was the hazy nature of the relationships in the home. 'Because I was also a servant and had to come in at the back door, I got to know the minds and feelings of those girls I met during those three years,' wrote Firth, pointing out that the disinclination of girls to become maids was not a matter only of wages but of something deeper: 'being a servant is very painful to one's self-respect and no amount of money will compensate that injury to anyone who has independence of spirit'.

Being a servant was an 'identity', not just a job. *The Psychology of the Servant Problem* was a call to the renewal of education for all women, of all classes, for domestic work to be regarded without sentimentality but with the same respect accorded to any other form of work. Firth actually looked forward to a time 'when the home-help might freely be able to choose a husband from the family she serves'.[18] The 'servant problem', as Firth saw it, was not one simply of demand outstripping supply, or of a failure in the 'quality' of the servants available, but of deeply held attitudes, of unexamined habits masquerading as unbreachable social certainties.

Violet Firth was far ahead of her time, grasping the knotty contradictions of domestic labour that were to characterise the theme during the rest of the century. How are women to enjoy the fruits of education and liberation if they are not relieved of the burden of domestic work in the person of another woman? When Frances Marshall, intellectual and Bloomsbury set member, set up home with Ralph Partridge in their first flat in Bloomsbury in the late 1920s, she employed a maid, a 'frightened, middle-aged spinster', who came to 'do for us': poor shadowy Mabel, one of the lonely civilian casualties of war. Frances took care not to tell her that she and Ralph were unmarried lest her respectable sensibilities be shocked. 'Who bought the bacon, the butter, the fish? I suspect it was our faithful Mabel. I've no recollection of doing it myself.'[19]

Chapter 14

'Tall, Strong, Healthy and Keen to Work'

Of indeterminate status, perching genteelly somewhere between the servant and the unmarried daughter of the house, was the lady-help. As her name suggests, the lady-help was a form of domestic servant whose background prevented her being called upon to perform menial duties; generally an impecunious middle-class woman who, for want of means or opportunities, had been forced to throw in her lot with another family and hope for their protection. This category, whose members are sometimes difficult to define but nonetheless easily recognisable, included the paid companion, or a general factotum whose duties were never quite specified: a little light governessing or nursing; domestic work that did not include anything rough or unduly physical; reading out loud; some secretarial and administrative duties. In her appearances in fiction, the lady-help is often a poor creature: dependent, lonely, necessarily fearful of the future and despised by those both below and above stairs.

The lady-help had been sitting on the domestic sidelines since the early nineteenth century; sometimes she was a poor relation, sometimes a refined person who received low wages and some protection in return for a little light domestic work. In 1848 a correspondent to *Graham's Magazine* described the usual incumbent of the role as a 'nondescript kind of creature'. But the duties of the lady-help rarely permitted a character to shine; being nondescript was often the safest option. Mrs Rose Mary Crawshay in her 1876 handbook on *Domestic Service for Gentlewomen* called for the increased employment of respectable, well-brought-up ladies who had fallen through the slats of life. She also wondered if such women might on occasion even be given the title 'hand-maiden', which suggests that the work might have the lustre of a vocation, like that of a vestal virgin. Mrs Crawshay had found that as standards of education went up, women who might once have been engaged as nursery governesses no longer had sufficient qualifications even for that job. She was adamant that lady-helps were not there to do 'the rough': 'I will be no party to any lady engaging herself to scour floors, black-lead grates, clean "pots and pans" nor to varnish any shoes but her own; neither to carry pails, water nor coal.' These, said Mrs Crawshay, were duties no 'lady should undertake'.[1] They would, instead, help with waiting at table and administering the other servants, but they certainly should not be expected to eat in the servants' hall.

Seen in this light, the role of the lady-help begins to look something like the older form of dependant that one might have found in the seventeenth-century household: the relative, widowed perhaps or unmarried, who occupied a place in the house, however devoted the family surrounding her, which was ambiguous; whose duties were those of someone in a position of emotional as well as financial dependency, rather than the straightforward subservience of the paid underling. Someone rather, in fact, like Alice Osbourn.

But for many householders in the twenties and early thirties, the idea of a domestic lady-help was a winning solution to the problem of recalcitrant servant girls and the lure of factory work. *The Dictionary of Employments Open to Women*, published in 1898, had pointed out that 'the very restrictions which are causing a host of workers to prefer the factory or the workshop to domestic service may not be so irksome to women whose lives have been spent in strictly ordered homes, and might value comfort and security above the freedom of more precarious employments'. By the turn of the century, lady-helps were absorbed into the move to give domestic

service the status of a profession. Groups devoted entirely to the
training of impecunious ladies in household skills included the
Guild of Household Dames and the Guild in Aid of Home Duties.
The *Dictionary* went on, 'the thought now was that domestic service as a career for gentlewomen should not be the last resort for the
untrained but a recognised profession for which a thorough practical and scientific training will be required'. Three establishments
ran courses exclusively for training lady-helps as cooks, parlourmaids and housemaids. They also trained ladies in domestic duties
to prepare them for emigration to the colonies and, as we have seen,
the hopes, often dashed, of a better life.

Yet the most visible manifestation of the idea of the lady-help is
not the domestic but the paid companion, for whom too often the
price of comfort and security was the terrible dullness of a companionship which could rarely be about real friendship, and in which
small humiliations and social differences were often emphasised
rather than obscured. Efforts continued to use the superior training
in thrift and orderliness that the impecunious lady had had to
absorb through bitter experience. Mrs Frazer thought the impoverished daughters of clergymen might be employed in anxious
middle-class households to teach the struggling housewife how to
manage her budget. The idea of a ladylike domestic was under-
standably popular with employers, but the ambivalence of her
social status meant that it never really caught on with those ladies
who might have been its recruits. The lady-help could only continue
to be called a lady-help if her ladylikeness was maintained – and
domestic work of the kind that many households required was not
work that a woman who had no experience of heavy lifting or long
hours felt able or willing to give. The lady-help therefore only
salvaged her dignity by maintaining her separation from the other
servants by small indications of her position.

Living on a social mezzanine floor, between one world and
another, could be isolating and lonely. In 'Mary Postgate', Rudyard
Kipling's horribly disturbing short story of 1915, the repressed
emotions of a colourless, middle-aged paid companion, Miss
Postgate, find their only outlet in her maternal devotion to her

employer's nephew, who rags her mercilessly. When he is killed, she turns the pain of her loss into hatred for the German enemy. In a ghastly denouement, when she encounters a fallen German airman, she finds sensual pleasure, the only such pleasure she has had, in an act of dreadful and sadistic cruelty.

Lady-helps who were cast adrift without legacies or pensions could expect a similar fate to the governess in the same predicament. By the 1920s, the governesses of young Edwardians or Victorians were mainly retired. The Governesses' Benevolent Institution, set up in 1843, was in 1934 still providing financial relief for former governesses who were over fifty-five. Until 1937 the Institution ran a seaside guesthouse at Shanklin on the Isle of Wight, and retirement homes in Chislehurst and Beckenham. In order to qualify for a place, the women had to suffer the ignominy of making their case before an adjudicating panel. In 1930, 2,999 governesses benefited from funds, shelter in one of the homes and paid holidays in Shanklin. Ninety-seven of them were so badly off that they received parcels of clothing from a special fund.[2]

During the 1920s, however, the idea of the lady-help underwent something of a transformation. The pathetic dependant was reincarnated as a domestic amazon who made a positive virtue out of the spinster's lot. The refined and adenoidal lady-help, described with stinging accuracy in Katherine Mansfield's 1923 short story 'At the Bay', who must gamely make herself useful on a boisterous family holiday, would soon be a figment of the past. The experience of war had unlocked for many women skills and spirit that were to prove useful in a variety of un-looked-for situations. A new kind of classified advertisement could be found slotted into the 'offered' columns of the Sits Vac, between the paid companions and private secretaries and the upper-servants, lady's-maids and housekeepers. Often the advertisers flagged up nursing experience accumulated during the war, or perhaps some light childcare. Behind many of these women were histories of respectable poverty and, very often, bereavement. 'Board and Residence in comfortable, luxurious home for lady companion and nurse, lately recovering from mental trouble result of war strain', read one advertisement in *The Times* in

1920.[3] Women who wanted to return home to families abroad, or simply to try a new life in the colonies, offered companionship or nursing on board ship in exchange for the price of their passage. 'Tall, strong, healthy and keen to work', is how one woman hoping to get to South Africa in 1920 described herself; another trying to work her fare home to Vancouver just after the war offered to 'take charge of children or act as maid companion'.

Increasing numbers of employers advertised for lady-helps hoping for a superior domestic for the lowest possible wages. Like many other Welsh girls, forced to leave home during the depression of the late twenties, Doris Grayson left South Wales in 1929, for service in London: 'I really can't imagine what I expected. I only knew that my first place was a dreadful shock to me. The advert said "lady's help". My mother, who'd been a lady's-maid before her marriage was under the impression I would be trained in that kind of work and would travel with the family. We were completely misled as I was the only servant kept. I was paid six shillings a week, I felt as though I were in prison.' Another Welsh girl, Gladys Evans, was promised when she took her job that 'a woman would be in to do the washing'. The washerwoman never materialised.

Many newspapers tried to counter the trend by running disapproving features about sad women living alone in bedsits with one-ring cookers and their underwear drying over the bath. 'Sally lives very uncomfortably in a bed-sitting room near Victoria rather than in a comfortable home with her family in Knightsbridge,' began one such article in 1937.[4] With her cropped hair, her knee-length skirts, her freedom to smoke, to drink, to work, Sally was certainly not returning home to Knightsbridge to wait for the husband who now would almost certainly never come. Gradually, employers were meeting the challenge of the needs and ambitions of the spinster. The rules, for example, that prevented married women from continuing their employment in the Civil Service, worked to the advantage of the unmarried, who could rise through the ranks.

The lady-help, once thought of as a pathetic, eager-to-please old maid, was now epitomised by a new kind of woman, one who turned to her advantage not only social anxiety and the servant shortage but a wartime training in practical action and a taste for independence. Earning one's living was not always an adventure for the middle-class woman cast adrift in the 1920s, but there was at least the consolation of knowing that she was not alone in her endeavours. Cheerful practical competence was more valuable than drawing or elocution and there was a healthy employment market to use it. On leaving school in the mid-1920s, the diarist James Lees-Milne learned to type at a London agency whose name encapsulated the spirit of the age: it was called Useful Women.

The establishment of another agency, Universal Aunts, embodied the new amazon. At the end of the war, its founder, Gertrude 'Gertie' Maclean, was in her thirties, unmarried and, though from a family of impeccable upper-class credentials, not in possession of a private income. She had witnessed during wartime the resourcefulness and confidence that had been released in so many women of her type and generation. Being a busy and conscientious aunt to the many children of her six siblings, she decided to capitalise on her talent for being thoroughly useful and open an employment agency for like-minded women. 'I plan a venture,' Gertie wrote to her family's solicitor Joshua Owen Steed, 'which will, I hope, fulfil my search for an opportunity to use my time and intelligence. I would hope too, that other like-minded ladies can become involved. Since the war forced open the drawing-room doors, so many women with the advantage of background, commonsense and family experience have found it difficult to return therein.'[5]

Universal Aunts, 'Britain's first personal service bureau', opened in 1921 in a small room behind a bootmaker's shop in Sloane Street, rented for ten shillings a week. Gertie Maclean advertised for an assistant who could bring the enterprise 'refinement and common sense, tact and discretion'. Then she placed an advertisement in *The Times* for 'ladies of "irreproachable background" to take care of children, chaperonage, home furnishings, shopping for the colonies and research work'. No job would be too peculiar to be beyond consideration (though the task of supplying regular top-ups of ice for an American party on a Thames river cruiser proved almost insurmountable). It was the lighter end of service: no-one, least of all Gertie Maclean, thought that Universal Aunts would supply doorstep cleaners or housemaids. But it nonetheless reflected a new busyness, a purpose both social and financial, and a light loosening up of the brittle social boundaries that had once ruled the lives of women such as Gertie and her friends and colleagues. Violet Firth had hoped that one day the domestic help might see herself as absolutely the social equal of the family she served: Universal Aunts went a little way towards making that a possibility.

The brutal fact was that the employing classes, now struggling with taxation, death duties and economic depression, needed to regain control over their domestic finances. It was no longer impossible to imagine that a middle-class daughter might need to work as a contribution to the family pot. It was important that such an arrangement did not threaten the delicate relationship of servant and master but might in fact be to their mutual benefit. 'At most levels,' wrote Joshua Steed in a letter to Gertie Maclean, 'finances are strained. A daughter's allowance, for instance; an income earned by her would surely be encouraged. Stringencies are practised above stairs; below stairs, the staff and tradesmen continue their usual arrangements, so that no benefit is being felt by the master. Your proposed service might do well to include a discreet household management course, ladies who could act as short-term stewardesses. A sorting out on a professional basis, preventing loss of face downstairs.'[6] (Servants were the first to see that their employers were struggling. Winifred Foley, seeing that her elderly mistress, living in a large house, had very little money, pretended to be happy with the evening meal they shared of 'a plate o' taters wi a knob o' marge', because she understood that meat was too expensive.)[7]

Gertie box-indexed her 'Aunts' with thumbnail sketches in order to remind her of their individual assets. They were no longer ladies with vaguely refined accomplishments but robust, curious women, game for fun and new experiences: the sort who were as likely to ride a motorcycle as crochet a pen-wiper. Mrs Violet Rumpton, for example, aged forty, was 'fully informed on circuses, pantomime and *Toad of Toad Hall*'; Miss Charlotte Hedgecome, fifty-five, was 'hefty, stern, stood for no nonsense, a stickler for etiquette and deportment. On borstal board of governors, Zoological Society's certificate. Cope older boys, any number.' Elizabeth Pratt-Steed was a 'Disciplinarian. Firm without being brutal. Can converse on physics, spiritualism or foreign missions.' Miss Phyllis Beckett 'knows all about footer and white mice. Guaranteed not to nag. Can slide down banisters at a push.' In her late thirties, Miss Hyacinth Plummer was a dab hand at 'Snakes and Ladders and Halma', but her necklines were too low and she might need to be pointed in the direction of 'a modesty vest'. Thirty-two-year-old Miss Pansy Trubshawe understood cricket and foreign stamps, 'but not much else'.[8]

The Aunts were often women getting on a bit, too late for marriage and certainly unlikely to find a spouse in male-bereft 1920s Britain. Perhaps they were widowed or had lost fiancés or lovers in the war; perhaps they had never had the chance to find one before the war broke out. Most were genuinely in need of money, some more than others, and some signed up for the adventure of it. If an Aunt were too ostentatiously looking for a man, she was marked up by Gertie as a 'husband-seeker' though sometimes qualified with 'but not dangerous'. Aunts picked up children from trains, walked dogs, did the shopping, advised on interior design. Catching, as Daph and Obbs had done, the excitement and popularity of car ownership, the new excitement about flying, the fashion for female aviatrixes, Gertie's friend Mildred 'Bay' Leith, a qualified mechanic, set up the 'Universal Aunts Car and Air Department', which supplied cars for sale and hire, flying tuition and motor boats ('all makes supplied').

The ingenuity of Universal Aunts was extraordinary, in the spirit of the best of the practical lady philanthropists of the nineteenth century, but without their suffocating moral high-mindedness. It was Universal Aunts that instituted the service that transported hot food to housebound elderly people; the practical machinery for Meals on Wheels, which was founded in Hemel Hempstead in 1947, was inspired, characteristically, by the metal dishes kept warm in hollow casings that Gertie remembered from her grandfather's shooting lunches (although in fact a correspondent to *The Lady* had, as early as 1902, suggested that, in the absence of live-in cooks, 'electric vans could take round meals each day and each morning could call for orders'[9]).

Universal Aunts provided another useful service: instruction in the arts of winning social acceptance, a course in subtlety that upper-servants had been discreetly providing to nouveau riche employers for a century. A career servant knew to his fingertips what marked old money from new. An experienced butler could be the most powerful weapon in the armoury of the social climber. Rolfe, butler to the fabulously wealthy American Mrs Laura Corrigan, helped engineer her entry into London society by standing on the doorstep of her house in Grosvenor Square and accosting passing members of the fashionable set with the words: 'Good morning, I'm sure Madam would like you to come in for a drink.'[10]

One of Gertie Maclean's correspondents spotted this lucrative seam, writing to her: 'There is too, the new money. Are those newly rich not likely to see you as an answer to their prayers for guidance through the minefields of society, more hazardous to them than those they faced in the war?'[11] It was a good wheeze. The new-rich industrialists and war profiteers had bought up the country's great houses and estates, so why couldn't the impecunious upper classes make some more money by selling them tips on behaviour and style, giving them a leg-up into fashionable society? Universal Aunts offered chaperonage for the debutante or the wealthy American visitor who could only secure a presentation at court if they were presented by a former debutante. For £1,000 a well-connected chaperone could be hired from the Aunts, along with some lessons from an expert on how to make the required deep curtsey. E. V. Lucas's 1923 novel *Advisory Ben*, based on the Aunts and featuring an agency called 'The Beck and Call', even introduced the idea of an elegant young woman whose father has recently made a lot of money who seeks work as a parlourmaid. Her intention, she tells the agency, is to pick up tips from a good family on how to behave: her own family is wilting under the open contempt of their chauffeur. 'Mother and Dad of course will never be able to deal with servants, but I feel that after a little while I shall know enough to keep them in their place.'[12]

The Beck and Call agency has a problem placing the would-be parlourmaid because so few aristocratic families, writes Lucas, can afford help. Yet the new poor themselves formed another fruitful area where in real life the Aunts could assist. They often had simply no idea how to live within their means and their homes crumbled about them, while fleets of retainers grew old with employers who could only just afford to pay their wages. Middle- or upper-middle-class war widows had to make a life of grinding frugality resemble a state that was both morally uplifting and even rather tasteful. 'Most of them lived in poverty and, what is more gracious, hidden poverty,' remembered one observer. 'It is really extraordinary that keeping up appearances might involve having two maids, and paying them nothing.'[13]

Brought up with Edwardian ideas of extravagance and luxury, with servants for every household task, they were hopelessly ill-equipped (as Mrs Frazer had noted so derisively fifteen years earlier) to gain any practical control over their finances. The journalist Charles Graves, in an article on Universal Aunts, noted that the new-rich may have provided the 'comedy' of the agency's work but the tragedy was provided by the new poor, 'who suddenly find that they can no longer afford a housekeeper-secretary (not to mention other luxuries) to protect them from the worries of looking after such mundane affairs as housekeeping books. In many cases their efforts to run their homes themselves are positively pitiable. They are robbed left and right. The extravagances, though curtailed, continue to be absurd.'[14]

Chapter 15

The Mechanical Maid

In 1929, Ethel Mannin left Strawberry Hill, and her husband, and bought herself a small house in Wimbledon – Oak Cottage. Inside, it was not in the least cottagey. A riot of shiny, lacquered blue, black and orange with Egyptian runners on the wall, a print of Van Gogh's *Sunflowers* over the fireplace and the cabinet gramophone painted in bright zigzags, Oak Cottage exemplified the new aesthetic of the twenties. 'Modernity,' wrote Mannin, 'was cube-shaped and jazz-patterned.'[1]

Imported from the Continent, the modern form was sleek, tubular and technological. For the first time designers and architects began seriously to contemplate homes in which machinery might take the human drudgery out of housework. The authors of *The English Home* had argued in 1910 that, 'Tradition in art should be adhered to, but antiquity should not be worshipped for its own sake,' though the allure of 'costly, discrepant old things' was still difficult for the English to relinquish.

The newness of the new house was about more than electrical sockets and washable curtains; it was about liberation from the messy and uneasy relationships of mistress and servant. It was concerned with freeing up time that would be better spent on the contemplation of higher subjects than housework. 'We are all busy now making the world anew,' wrote the architect Randal Phillips in

1924. As editor of a new magazine, *Homes and Gardens,* Phillips was a vigorous champion of the small house; a Phillips home was an efficient, sleek living-machine, designed to be run with maximum efficiency and a minimum of labour. The evangelists of the new jettisoned for ever kitchen ranges that needed blackleading, the fringed, stuffed, frilled furnishings, the knick-knacks that gathered dust on whatnots, and the picture rails in rarely used, shuttered and fusty parlours. Gone too would be the maze of tiny rooms that sealed the labour of the house in its own compartments; the whole space would be opened up, air circulating freely around a modern community whose relationships were reanimated by a new informality.

In *The Servantless House*, Phillips suggested that drawing rooms, hitherto used merely for display or for receiving visitors – 'some rather artificial place for special occasions only, where everyone is supposed to be on their best behaviour' – were henceforth to become 'living' or 'sitting' rooms where furniture was encouragingly comfortable in contrast to the spindly chairs and pointless 'occasional' tables of the calling-card generation. Phillips also suggested the use of linoleum, formerly the preserve of basement kitchens, rather than parquet or carpets; and all-purpose kitchen cabinets on the American model with utilitarian surfaces in wipe-easy enamel.[2]

Phillips's low-maintenance ideal is echoed in the stripped white interior designs of the influential interior designer Syrie Maugham, most of whose clients hardly needed to worry about a shortage of servants. The daughter of Dr Thomas Barnardo, Syrie opened her first shop in 1922 and by the end of the decade, according to Cecil Beaton, had 'bleached, pickled or scraped every piece of furniture in sight', the houses of her wealthy clients becoming a luxurious melange of off-white shades and sheepskin.[3] Maugham-influenced limed oak became a particular favourite of the middle-class home as it required no polishing; her 'scumbling' of paintwork was a handy trick for front doors as it helped them keep their appearance without washing. In an assault on the most sacred precinct of the English home, Randal Phillips recommended that the daily grind of brass polishing might be bypassed by painting the brass door knocker and letterbox in a dull 'Japan' black. He even suggested letting your doorstep weather naturally to actually add to its attractions, obviating the need for the polishing stone that had been one of the drudgeries of the dawn-rising housemaid.

Ernestine Mills was another who faced squarely the call that freedom for women was freedom from servants, as well as freedom for servants. For Mills, the dismantling of the old home, with its fussy decorations, its cumbersome furniture and the great profusion of 'stuff', under which its shelves and cupboards sagged, would be a call to a new balancing in the relations between men and women of all classes: 'In the artisans' homes, as women become more interested in their newly acquired citizenship, and in various social problems, and as through better education they acquire wider interests, they will demand more leisure. And as the hours of their husbands' work are reduced to eight, or even five or six hours a day, they will be called upon to relieve their wives, and to take some share in the work of the home.'[4] In 1925, in *The Domestic Problem, Past, Present and Future*, Mills observed that women like her should become the standard-bearers of the new way of living: 'We find that when educated women have to do their own housework there is a tendency to simplify the household arrangements, to abolish useless, dust-attracting ornaments, and to make use of all modern prepared foods and even of the public restaurant.'[5]

The 1920s saw a post-war building boom and a corresponding fever of labour-saving housework advice from the many women's magazines that sprang into existence almost for that very purpose. London alone, wrote one commentator, 'witnessed the greatest amount of rebuilding all over the metropolis that has ever taken place within so short a period of time since the Great Fire of London'.[6] Freeholds for newly built small houses sold for around £250–£450. Larger semi-detached villas, with four or five bedrooms, sold for up to £2,500. It was the era of suburban ascendancy, when the suburban aesthetic established itself fully in the national psyche. Designed by a happy lucky-dip of architectural elements taken from all periods – a bit of Queen Anne, some Tudor beams, a stained-glass window over the door, a lych gate, a novelty turret or a barley-sugar chimney – suburban houses still represented the oldest English ideal of all: the image of the cottage, nestling secure within its own small piece of land. In 1920, the *Daily Mail*, which had been running its Ideal Home Exhibitions since 1908, offered £300 as first prize in a competition to design a one-servant, coal-less house costing no more than £2,500. The winning entry was a substantial five-bedroom house which included a maid's room but which also had electric plugs on the landing for vacuum cleaners and polishers. The house had no polished surfaces or hard angles to attract dust; there were sleek fitted radiators and smut-free electric fires. There was also an early version of a dishwasher – a wooden rack above the sink in which the dishes and plates were placed and then sprayed messily with a rubber hose and shower head.

The tone of the post-First World War exhibitions reinforced the new sense that domestic life had to be pared down, to be streamlined in tune with a new world. The idea of dispensing with residential domestics altogether was a step too far for the larger homes but, nonetheless, ingenious ways were found to use space in a small house and to minimise dusting, for example, by combining the uses of household objects: the 1923 Ideal Home Exhibition featured a crafty table lamp with a gramophone concealed in its base. The minutiae of daily life were examined in every detail for their ergonomic efficiency: the 1919 Exhibition even demonstrated by elaborate diagrams how a well-planned kitchen might reduce the number of steps required to make afternoon tea from 350 to 50.

Central heating was no longer uncommon in large houses (though owners of stately homes still tended to prefer the long, cold corridor and the hand-laid fire), and indoor bathrooms were almost universal in all middle-class houses built after 1900. Although many of the new houses still advertised pantries, sculleries and maids' sitting rooms – and most of them included electric bell call systems – there was a move towards houses that had been reshaped to accommodate a new way of living. The eat-in kitchen was a tentative innovation, followed in due course by the introduction of service hatches, hostess trolleys and hotplates (all of which came to be regarded as undesirable by the fashionable classes because they suggested pretensions to entertaining without the staff to sustain the enterprise). The dining room (or breakfast room even) was often now designed to be next to a kitchen that was no longer hidden away in the basement.

Small houses became fashionable in cash-strapped quarters, and cramped was re-christened *bijou*. It was the beginning of the conversion, in London particularly, of those mews houses no longer required for horses or chauffeurs, into smart little pieds-à-terre: 'perverted coachmens' homes at a quite aristocratic rent', was how H. G. Wells described them. The decade also saw the increased popularity of service flats, popular among unmarried men, professional women and retired couples on modest annuities. Much of eighteenth-century Mayfair was demolished in the 1920s to make way for flats. Ivy Provine's parents worked as the live-in servants for a block of residential service flats in Mayfair: 'Mother cooked traditional plain food, producing a set menu every day for the residents. Father washed all the china (that came down from the flats by lift) and cleaned all the shoes and suits. They had the help of a kitchenmaid and two housemaids.' Ivy attended St George's Primary School, Hanover Square, for the 'working class of Mayfair', the children of domestic servants.[7]

There was a degree of fraternisation in this more regularised arrangement than in 'digs' or lodgings. The butler Albert Thomas worked for a time as a steward in newly built service flats in London, before the First World War. The flats were a comfortable compromise between a hotel and a well-staffed private house, but at a lower cost with less responsibility than either of these. Thomas remembered the flats as:

> nicely furnished and the rents included service. The maids used to
> attend to the cleaning of them, and also took the orders for meals
> every morning and brought them to me, but no meals were served
> before eight in the morning, or later than 8.30 at night, because all
> the maids slept out. By the conduct of some of the tenants there I
> could see that the reason that they chose to live in flats of that kind

was because they were incapable of running a home properly, and as a result could not keep their servants. This applied to both men and women, for all the men were bachelors and the women were either widows – or had left their husbands – or were old maids.[8]

A faint whiff of moral disorder hung over blocks of this kind: they fell somewhat outside the usual domestic sphere. In Evelyn Waugh's *A Handful of Dust*, Lady Brenda Last's decision to take a room in a London service block, apparently for occasional shopping and cultural excursions, is a cover for her clandestine affair with the cad John Beaver. Ivy Provine thought her father had been led into alcoholism because of his fraternisation with the residents of their block: 'Unfortunately, my father was an intelligent man and he mixed with all these lords and ladies and he became a very heavy drinker.'[9]

Other alternative residential set-ups included hostels, such as the one where young Bronwen Morris worked as a kitchen-maid, helping to produce three daily meals for 'young businesswomen', just off Sloane Square, London. Bronwen was kept busy cleaning the kitchen and peeling vegetables and was later upgraded to the post of cook, producing three large hot meals a day for seventy-two young women who came back for lunch: 'bacon, bloaters or kippers and boiled eggs for breakfast, rabbit stew or rabbit pie for lunch and dinner, or pork, beef with vegetables – also always steam or rice puddings and suet puds'.[10] By the 1920s there was a proliferation of these residences for girls working as stenographers, typists or clerks or generally what E. M. Forster's anxious Mrs Honeychurch called 'messing with typewriters and latchkeys'.

Manufacturers were quick to seize the opportunity of capitalising on 'the servant problem'. The British Commercial Gas Association in 1918 ran an advertisement: 'The ideal servantless home is the all-gas house, which is becoming a distinctive feature of modern building schemes. In the all-gas house, convenience, cleanliness, economy, efficiency and comfort, without unnecessary labour, are signs of progress which no woman can afford to disregard. Dirt and drudgery disappear with the disappearance of smoky fuel.'

Electricity was the fuel of the future, however, and even in 1914, Magnet were advertising products including an electric fire, a radiator and hotplate, an electric kettle, an iron, a toaster and a milk steriliser. In the inter-war years, the pace at which home technologies were adopted suddenly accelerated. In 1910, only 2 per cent of houses were wired for electricity; nearly thirty years later, in 1939, almost 75 per cent were plugged into the mains; and in the same year, 30 per cent of households had a vacuum cleaner and 80 per cent owned an electric iron.[11] 'To develop the personality', was Caroline Haslett's brave new prediction for the uses of electricity (Mrs Haslett became Director of the Women's Electrical Association in 1924). 'Upon nothing has the attitude of the general public changed so completely as on this question of domestic work and how it should be performed,' she wrote. 'At one time the housewife who said, "I work in the house from morning to night," thought she exhibited a high degree of domestic virtue, but the woman who says this today stands self-condemned as a being lacking in imagination and backward in her ideas.'[12]

There was certainly no shortage of imagination in the ingenious articles of electrical apparatus that began appearing in the 1920s and 1930s: dryer cupboards ('in appearance resembling the steel cabinets found in modern offices') and egg cookers, footwarmers, electric gongs and parquet floor polishers. There was an electric 'tie-iron' not unlike the old-fashioned goffering irons around which the traditional laundrymaid would press yard after yard of silk ribbon. Mrs Haslett's book, *Household Electricity*, is illustrated by a man triumphantly and unaided removing his own neatly creased trousers from an electric press. A *Daily Express* publication of 1935, *The Home of Today*, confidently told its readers: 'Each year – almost every month – science brings some new discovery to the home. Ether waves are used for the preservation of food; wireless waves are made to boil water for the household; invisible rays protect the home from unwelcome intruders; and many other such wonders are rapidly being included in everyday household services.'[13]

Expectations of cleanliness were often actually raised by

labour-saving machines and the new home and all its accoutrements
became the visible sign of finances being stretched to the limit.
Servant and mistress lived often in an agony of fear about dirt and
its costliness. In Forest Hill, where Happy Sturgeon once worked,
'it was a terrible thing to put your foot on the front stairs because
the master paid so much for the carpet'.[14] In *First Aid to the
Servantless*, Mrs Frazer had suggested that the housewife needed to
shed for ever the image of a careworn household despot, exhausted
by bossing her slatternly servants and making ends meet. She advocated a modern villa for a model new couple, a 'Mr and Mrs Smith',
which would have 'electric lift and other modern appliances'. Mrs
Smith would do the washing-up herself with the 'Dreadnought'
dishwasher 'saving labour, breakages, time, space and temper',
while the household might also employ a Semco boot polisher,
washable mattress covers and rubber gloves 'as worn by surgeons'.
The pretty hostess with her electric cooker would therefore be
ready with a time-efficient meal for her husband's return from
work: 'oatmeal soup, steamed whitings, meat pudding, baked tomatoes, potato snow and fruit salad'. The vigorous exercise afforded
by a daily round of housework, opined Mrs Frazer, was good for
the figure and servantless Mrs Smith need not worry about a slen-
der maid distracting her husband's attention.[15]

By the 1920s, despite the best efforts of Mrs Frazer and the media,
the bustling little housewife prettily going about her duties was far
from the reality for most women. The servant, the retainer, the
shadowy, silent figure in the kitchen proved hard to shift from the
national image of domesticity and few middle-class women could
imagine doing without servants altogether. Labour-saving appliances were often given servant-like names (the 'Betty Anne' and the
'Daisy' were two brands of vacuum cleaner) to distance their owner
from the labour of using them. But in fact most of those who could
afford to buy the new appliances could also afford a servant of some
variety to operate them. 'Splendid, Mrs Rawlins' is the strapline on
a 1925 advertisement for Robin Starch which pictured an elegant
modern mistress and a dumpy, aproned cook-general folding sheets
together. 'Well Mum, I'm glad you like them,' says Mrs Rawlins,

'but I always say the credit's due as much to Robin Starch as to me.
And it's that easy. The iron glides over the things like one o' clock.'[16]
A multi-purpose clothes washer, rinser, wringer, drier, ironer and
vacuum cleaner called Atmos was advertised as 'The Mechanical
Housemaid'. Even the huge increase in car ownership had not
dented the allure of a driver; in 1924 a petroleum advertisement
maintained: 'Your chauffeur will drive better on BP.'

But the fact remained that in the years between the wars, despite
the best efforts of the manufacturers of irons and vacuums and
washing machines, most houses in Britain were still as labour-
intensive as they had been a century before. The British overall
simply had a resistance to labour-saving devices that was not found
on the Continent or in the United States. Sometimes it was simply
because the new machines were so cumbersome to operate that it
was quicker to use the old method. Dolly Scannell's father, a poor
man in the East End, bought a washing machine for his wife who
took in laundry. It consisted, remembered Dolly:

> of a broom handle at the end of which was a copper trumpet. In the
> trumpet where it joined the handle were circular holes and through
> the holes one could glimpse glass marbles. This machine had to be
> pumped vigorously up and down in the bath of hot soapy clothes, it
> needed a strong navvy to work it, or a tall amazon. Mother treated it
> with disgust after Father gave the first demonstration of this wonder
> invention. Watched by an eager family, rolling about in hysterics,
> Father tottered out of the scullery wet, red, hot and exhausted and
> breathing heavily . . . 'That's the last thing I do for your mother,'
> Father shouted: 'She's an obstinate woman in every respect, against
> progress, we *must* move with the times,' he yelled.[17]

So long as there was a supply of servants available to light fires,
most householders saw no need of going to the bother of putting in
central heating or electricity. When Daisy England found a job in a
middle-class house, aged fourteen, in the mid-1920s, she reported
that: 'candles lit our way to bed and gaslight illuminated downstairs
activities'.[18] Mrs Bunce worked in a London house where there

were twelve bedrooms and only two bathrooms; if she wanted a bath herself, there was only a small hip bath and water had to be carried in buckets from several floors below. A small gas cooking stove standing in the corner of the kitchen was the only gadget giving instant effortless service in the house.[19]

The introduction of technology in most British homes was therefore precipitated by the servant shortage, not by the usefulness in itself of labour-saving gadgetry. Working-class girls were themselves often nonplussed in the presence of newfangled plumbing. Winifred Foley, arriving in London in 1924 from the Forest of Dean, was astonished to see a flush lavatory in the house where she was employed as a general. One maid was found sobbing in the pantry with water flooding out of the butler's sink because she didn't know how to turn off the tap. She had never seen a tap before in her life.[20] There were prejudices against household technology across the classes: many of them for the reason that machines were not real 'labour' and that girls not properly engaged in heavy-duty work would become idle or 'flighty'. As Edith Hall remembered: 'The greatest stigma against a woman was to be considered lazy. Many men were opposed to any kind of labour-saving device in case it made them so.'[21] In 1925 an article in *Good Housekeeping* gave voice to the widespread but apparently paradoxical suspicion that the more maids were supplied with labour-saving devices, the less work they did. 'Until 1916,' wrote the anonymous author, 'I experienced few housekeeping difficulties, always having had one good maid to depend upon even if the second one was indifferent. Since then, I have gone in for labour-saving appliances such as washing machine, electric iron, vacuum cleaner, stainless knives and central heating, but find that the more I consider the maids the less work they do.'[22]

The French writer Odette Keun found the dinginess of the average living conditions in England quite insupportable: 'I came to London and I searched wildly for the beautiful, noble, spacious and ultra-modern dwellings in which every man-jack of the English lived. What is there are millions of old, dark dingy, huddled, dreary, uniform houses – entire quarters of them – looking like particularly mean barracks.' She went on: 'Here is the list of the "Comforts of the English Home". Total Absence of Central Heating. Coal fires that warm about a square inch of space immediately in front of them. Smoke from the Coals until they are really lit. Suffocation from that smoke. Windows that must be left open whatever the weather may be, to counteract by freezing the asphyxiation induced by the smoke of the coal fires or the fumes of the gas fires . . . It is true that the English windows, whether they are open or closed, all let in the air anyway; they all rattle; and their panes are all opaquely grey.'[23]

One of the reasons that there was such a cautious adoption of household technologies was that they were simply anathema to the English romantic imagination. The middle classes may have their knocked-through living spaces and their vacuum cleaners, but the mechanical maid was a poor substitute for the human version with all the layers of traditional social interactions she represented. A profound nostalgia for the past was to harden in the upcoming decade, as social change gathered pace and the suburbs sprawled further into rural England.

In Lettice Cooper's novel of 1936, *The New House*, an elderly woman, Mrs Powell, prepares to move with her daughter from her husband's family home of Stone Hall, a large Victorian house, built in the 1840s on the edge of a once prosperous northern manufacturing city, to the eponymous new house, a well-appointed modern box with bathrooms, electricity and all modern conveniences. Mrs Powell sees her residential servants reduced from five in number to a solitary cook-general-maid-of-all-work named Ivy. It is the end of the age of display for Mrs Powell: as the removals van comes to take her furniture to her new home, she looks back in panic at Stone Hall, shortly to be turned into a convalescent home: 'The things of her old world seemed like a row of sandcastles beset by an incoming tide of the ugly and utilitarian.'[24]

PART IV

Outer Show and Inner Life

Chapter 16

'A Vast Machine That Has Forgotten How to Stop Working'

'The large-scale private paradise is already obsolescent,' was the opinion of the architect Clough Williams-Ellis in 1928.[1] Yet a closer look at those country houses still in private hands shows this to have been far from the case. The 1930s may have seen the final flowering of the great house but it bloomed with a spectacular show of traditional colour in those final years. 'World War One didn't make an awful lot of difference to life,' reported the Duke of Richmond and Gordon, whose country seat was Goodwood in Sussex, 'except that people started disappearing. For instance, my chauffeur, Charles Tilbury, whose home was in the Hatfield Cottages, he disappeared.'[2]

At Chatsworth, where thirty indoor staff were employed throughout the 1930s, the only real change in the running of the house after the war was the jettisoning of the ancient role of Groom of Chambers, whose job of looking after drawing rooms and writing tables was taken over by footmen. Lady Hambleden, born into the Herbert family and brought up at Wilton House before her marriage in 1928, remained almost untouched by the shift, so noticeable in most large houses, from male to female front-of-house staff, from butler to parlourmaid: 'We did have quite a lot of staff: there was a butler – I think most people had butlers. I can only think of one person who had parlourmaids and everybody rather noticed it.'[3]

On the Rothschilds' estate, at Waddesdon in Buckinghamshire, the gardeners still sent the vegetables to the kitchen door every day in a specially constructed pony cart painted in the Rothschild racing colours of yellow and blue, the coachman who drove it dressed in a matching livery and cockade. At Woburn Abbey, the eleventh Duke of Bedford maintained until his death in 1940 not only a household of at least sixty indoor servants to attend solely to his wife and himself, but two separate, fully staffed residences in Belgrave Square, including four cars and eight chauffeurs; the Woburn parlourmaids were all amazonian at over five foot ten, as had always been the Bedfords' stipulation.

Vast, labyrinthine holding areas of tradition and ritualistic routine, these estates continued to function as if the social changes of the inter-war years were remote. When James Lees-Milne travelled round the country in the 1930s and 1940s in his role as secretary of the National Trust, he found many houses where a touching loyalty to the old forms of behaviour, however spectral and superfluous, still clung on. During a visit to the Marquess of Bath in 1936, a row of liveried footman gathered in ranks on either side of the steps to see Lees-Milne bicycle away down the drive; one of them solemnly carried his bicycle to the front of the steps while his host stood at the top watching until he had vanished.

In 1959 the Duke of Bedford's grandson, the thirteenth Duke, looked back on his grandparents' chilly and absolute adherence to the rules of lavish and formal hospitality: guests 'never travelled with your suitcase, that was not considered the thing to do. It had to come in another car, so you had a chauffeur and a footman with yourself, and a chauffeur and a footman with the suitcase, with another four to meet you. Eight people involved in moving one person from London to Woburn.'[4] The Duke and Duchess rarely entertained and, by the outbreak of the Second World War, the Woburn regime was centred round the couple alone, who stuck rigidly to habits that had remained unaltered for fifty years: the Duke always started meals with his own cup of beef consommé and a plate of raw vegetables served to him on a three-tiered dumbwaiter. The Duchess's secretary-companion had her own quarters that included a cook and maid; as did the Duke's mistress, who lived in rooms of her own with her own staff. Enid Field, a house-maid at Woburn in the thirties for two years, only met the Duchess once – when she was surprised by her while sweeping the grate in the Duchess's bedroom. She was perfectly pleasant, remembered Enid, but 'I was terrified'.[5]

In grand country houses there were still nightingale-listening expeditions and elaborate picnics, dressing-up, party games and sporting weekends. Standards of luxurious hospitality remained high. Newspapers and shoelaces were still ironed every morning in well-staffed homes (flat irons 'had to be heated in front of the fire and that alone took nearly quarter of an hour. Never in all my life have I seen such a footling procedure,' snorted Margaret Powell[6]). House-party guests were woken with tea and thinly sliced bread and butter in the morning and in each bedroom would be a tin of biscuits and a writing desk with blotter, headed writing paper, pen and ink, and a selection of books. Lady Richard Cavendish at Holker was a particularly meticulous hostess with Edwardian standards of attention to detail, every meal, entertainment and travel arrangement seen to with military precision. A visitor remem-bered: 'When guests left Holker they were given a little papier-mâché attaché case, with the most delicious things in it. For each guest there were made-that-minute, feather light scones stuffed with Morecambe Bay shrimps. All the things were wrapped indi-vidually, and labelled. And then inside the attaché case used to be put a label with stamps, so all you had to do was to shove the empty case into the nearest post office and post it back.'[7]

Social mores, however, even on the big estates began gradually to change and the rules that governed social life were loosened up: men and women socialised more freely together, in all classes. Concessions were made towards slightly smaller numbers of house-hold staff but also to a generation that had begun to enjoy some independence and was not quite as deficient in practical skills as its parents' generation had been. Breakfasts in grand houses, for exam-ple, became increasingly self-service, the dishes arranged on the sideboard. Margaret Flockhart remembered that in the late 1920s, when she worked as a cook, cold hors d'oeuvre such as sardines, beetroot, cucumber, mushrooms and silverskin onions became increasingly popular, especially in less voluminously peopled establishments. Though dinner was still sacrosanct, the less formal black tie was now more popular than white tie for evening wear, though at Belvoir the Duke of Rutland made it a rule right up to the Second World War that white tie, with white waistcoat and dress coat, should still be worn for dinner if a woman or a clergyman was present. It became less common to maintain the separation of the house into constituent areas of labour or leisure; smoking rooms were no longer fashionable and men and women now smoked together in the drawing room. Small infringements of what had once been hard and fast rules crept in. Make-up may have been considered dangerously flighty for a servant but it was more than acceptable for the upper-class fashion plate: in the 1920s, Lady Curzon, staying for the weekend in a large country house in Somerset, flatly refused to come down to dinner because her make-up box had been lost on the train to Taunton.

For a younger generation of house-party guests, these weekends could now be a strain, especially for the newly cash-strapped. For one thing, there was the business of tipping – a minefield for those who enjoyed only a modest allowance. Because it was never done to talk about money, at the less well-off end of the upper class, where young men might even have to consider getting jobs, it was not uncommon to borrow from one servant enough to tip another. Lesley Lawrence dreaded the totting-up of substantial tips on Sunday evening. 'The men's would run into pounds and except for a long stay of a week or more, ten shillings was probably usual for women to give to female servants. Single girls could get away with five shillings, and as few of us worked and most were kept pretty short by their parents, in cash though not in kind, it was sometimes difficult albeit absolutely essential, to reserve these sums. Porters and taxis might prove unexpectedly expensive, a loss at games in stakes reckoned in threepences would be disastrous, and a chauffeur instead of your host driving you to the station probably cost you your lunch on the train.'[8] According to Mrs J. E. Bratton, her uncle, who was a chauffeur in the 1920s, once lent Winston Churchill half a crown for a taxi to Blenheim Palace: 'Still not repaid!'[9]

For many women of Lesley Lawrence's generation (she was nineteen in 1930), these silent swarms of servants were style-cramping and faintly uncomfortable – 'a cloud of witnesses around one'. There were many attendant anxieties for the guest, such as bringing enough clothes to ensure you would have something to wear for every occasion without having them laundered and incurring the cost of a tip. If the housemaid (acting as a lady's-maid if the guest had not brought her own) laid a dress out on the bed, would her feelings be hurt if you chose another one? Would one's underwear, unpacked by a servant, be too shabby? What if a maid had removed your shoes to have them cleaned and they had not arrived before dinner. Would it be correct to ring for them?[10]

Meals still tended to the gargantuan: vast quantities of cheese, butter and cream from the home farm, vegetables and fruit from the kitchen garden and meat from the estate. While the struggling classes began to give in to newfangled processed foods such as breakfast cereals, custard powder and cake mixes, the big country house continued to rely on the still incredible bounty of its own estate. When housemaid Doris Hazell, brought up in a poor family on margarine, marvelled at the butter in the servants' hall she was informed: 'That's real gentry.'[11] For Helen Mildmay White, whose family lived at Flete House, breakfast was, without fail, 'bacon and eggs and when there were visitors, four different kinds of eggs and bacon, sausages, kidneys and always a kedgeree, cold ham and cold tongue and scones with butter and Devonshire cream'.[12] Miss Ellery, who worked as a cook in country houses throughout the thirties, recalled the fashion for fiddly gastronomic miniaturism: baby rabbits' legs fried in batter; tiny quails served on coloured beds of rice; miniature pimentos with peas; and oval-shaped fish and chicken creams floated on a bowl of consommé. The art historian Kenneth Clark wrote of an occasion when, dining at Mrs Ronnie Greville's, he noticed Bacon, his hostess's eccentric and often drunk butler, so overcome with 'insuperable longing' at the sight of a dish of baby lambs' tongues that he could hold out no longer and stuffed them into his mouth before the astonished gaze of Clark, who saw 'the sauce running down his shirt front, his jaws working furiously'.[13]

There was still a great deal of sieving and pureeing; soups and stocks strained through sieves made with fine haircloth of horse or camel hair until they were velvet smooth, for example. 'Washing hair sieves was terrible! We couldn't use hot water because it would cook the bits of chicken and fish trapped in it!'[14] For grand dinners, it was popular to break down raw ingredients completely, then recreate them. Miss Ellery learned that the Christmas turkey was customarily boned completely, then reassembled stuffed with turkey liver pâté or foie gras which made it look as if the bone were still in place. When Mrs Emmitt worked, as one of six kitchen staff, for a small estate in Surrey from 1932, the stores were sent down from London in industrial quantities every week: 'They used to have seven pounds of currants or any of the pulses, rice tapioca and barley. And what we used to call a keg of mustard ... I should say about seven pounds of mustard powder.'[15]

It is hardly surprising then that even in poor families where domestic service was held in contempt, the prospect of life in employment with a great estate still had appeal. Jean Rennie, who had gone into service so reluctantly in 1923, remembered of her time as a kitchen-maid in Ballimore, a castle on Loch Fyne: 'We ate masses of the very best food, with butter, homemade jam, cakes and scones; meat, vegetables and puddings.'[16] Servants' food still tended to be institutional and hearty: 'boiled bacon and pease pudding, banana jelly you could have bounced, and bread and butter pud', was how the former kitchen-maid K. M. Hayles remembered mealtimes at Osborne House on the Isle of Wight in the mid-thirties.[17] It made a sharp contrast to the acute poverty of both the rural and urban working classes. In the early years of the Second World War, a report following a survey of East London evacuees found that malnourishment was common and 'bread and lard, broken biscuits and chips were the usual meals'.[18] Lucy Holmes's father was an unemployed farm labourer when she went into service as a kitchen-maid: 'Food was pretty grim looking back. I can see Mum now, cutting a boiled egg in half with a sharp knife and putting half in each egg cup without wasting a bit . . . we had half each. Dad had a whole one and Mum said she didn't like boiled eggs.'[19]

If you had to go into service, then the big country house was still the best place to get your feet under the table. In the house where Doris Winchester worked, the servants were so numerous that they ate more than twice the daily quantity of their two elderly employers: 'If they had roast pheasant in the dining room and there was just the two of them they had one pheasant and I had to do five pheasants for the servants' hall.'[20] Furthermore, the lower wages often paid for service on rural estates were more than compensated for, in financial terms, by the food, accommodation and other perks: country house servants had their laundry taken care of and their meals provided. Eva Walton, one of a team of laundresses still working at the steam laundry at Lyme Park in the 1930s, recalled a pint of milk delivered every day for each laundress, and 'vegetables of course were allowed from the gardens, of course there was always the coal, everything was supplied, it was luxury!'[21]

Country house service for these reasons was still considered a career in a way that domestic service in the hard-pressed middle-class home was not. According to Eileen Balderson, a country house servant, 'girls had to move from house to house to progress', using the most reputable agencies and always asking for a higher wage than they hoped for. The reasons they gave for moving on were varied; black beetles in the kitchen disgusted one so much that she left the day after she arrived, and Eileen herself left one house because she 'found the change of staff unsettling'.[22] When Rose Harrison resigned from her first job, her employer, Lady Cranborne, who wanted her to stay, refused to give her a reference – but Rose applied for a new job anyway, and got it: 'I'd struck a blow for freedom, my freedom of choice at any rate. The next day I gave in my notice.'[23]

By the 1930s, despite their continuing influence over the cultural imagination, the political influence of the aristocracy and with it the influence of land was waning. In 1913, the writer Sir Philip Gibson had deplored the low level of intellectual enquiry, the aggressive philistinism he found in the Edwardian aristocracy: 'They hate the truth and go across the way to the great music halls where the ragtime reviews dispense with all need of thought and laugh at truth.' Gibson excoriated the ruling classes for laziness, for wasting their time reading rubbishy novels and romances. Even their servants, he wrote, displayed more interest in current affairs, and the smartest household will 'take in *The Times* for the sake of the family butler, and the *Daily Mail* for its own use'.[24] But after the First World War, such privileged revelling in low culture became viewed as poor form and aristocratic families in straitened circumstances felt forced to plead their cause by drawing attention to their value as custodians of the nation's treasures, and to their role in maintaining the traditional bond that existed between servant and master, the proletariat and the ruling class.

The estate gradually assumed an elegiac countenance in the public mind and the family retainer became bathed in the nostalgic glow that illumined the English home in a happier historical past. The columns of *The Times* during the twenties and thirties were filled with touching death notices and tributes to servants of the old school. In 1920, for example, we read of the passing of Hannah Ordish 'for 45 years the faithful servant and friend of the Buccleuch family'. In 1925: 'Our dear Pike', who died at Ormesby Hall in 1925, was 'the faithful servant and friend of the Pennyman family for forty four years'.[25] The death of Jane Firth, 'the nurse and faithful friend' of the dowager Lady Mowbray and Stourton was recorded the same year.[26] These retainers represented devotion and faithfulness in a time of flux and insecurity. The old-fashioned employer could no longer always repay loyalty with job security but to make every effort to hold on to servants when unemployment was rife was considered a moral obligation – and a public service that should be rewarded by the government. In 1930 a correspondent wrote to *The Times*: 'The result of any increased taxation in my individual case is that I shall have to reduce my servants by half. I now have eight dependent upon me and in order to requite good and faithful servants I have made large inroads on capital.

Alas! I have passed the margin of safety, and the moment that my income is further taxed I shall have no alternative but to reduce my establishment of servants . . . domestic servants, gardeners, grooms and chauffeurs, the majority faithful servants, must go to swell the total of unemployed.'[27]

Country house servants themselves seem often to have realised that their working experiences, however magnificent their manifestation, were merely the embers of another world. George Washington followed his stint with the Australian wool millionaire by taking a job as a hall boy at Holland House in London, the seventeenth-century mansion that still stood, a ghost of rural Kensington, in the private parkland of what is now Holland Park. The only occupant of the house was the dowager Lady Ilchester, an invalid confined to a bath chair.

Holland House was so vast that when George first arrived he was instructed to go to the front door as people had been known to spend 'days' searching for the servants' entrance in the maze of courtyards and passages behind. Waiting on Lady Ilchester was a butler, footman, odd man and second footman, housekeeper and four-maids, a stillroom maid, a cook, two kitchen-maids and two scullery-maids, a chauffeur, nine gardeners, a lady's-maid, a night nurse and a day nurse. The odd man was so old that he was unable to do any heavy work. 'When I look back over my three and a half years at Holland House,' wrote Washington, 'I can see now there was something particularly sad, almost unreal, about them. We were propping up something that belonged to another age, trying to pretend that what had passed still existed or even if it didn't that if we tried hard enough to keep the old order of things going, it might come back.'[28]

Households peopled by ancient retainers looking after (or being looked after by) impoverished gentry had been a theme in gothic fiction since the nineteenth century; now they were reworked by a new generation of novelists. Locked together in dark dependency, the power struggles of master and servant were hilarious rather than eerily unnatural. The cumbersome social machinery of pre-war England had begun to look ridiculous. In Evelyn Waugh's

Scoop, the Boot family of Boot Hall in Boot Magna support an unwieldy household of ageing, cobwebbed nannies, footmen and governesses, all of whom wait upon each other and upon a family now considerably poorer than their own servants.

For many, the grandeur was indeed moth-eaten. Many houses were run with a combination of public profligacy and private thrift that reflected straitened times. Jean Rennie worked for a bachelor baronet, living alone, who kept an indoor staff of ten and subjected them to a level of domestic micro-management that could be considered almost deranged – except when you think of the cost in the late 1920s of maintaining a house and estate in its full pre-war levels of display. Sir James had sardines served in tins so that he could count them; when the footman found the sixpence in the servants' Christmas pudding, he had to return it to his employer to be used again the next year. Standards of luxury in country houses remained unstinting, yet behind the scenes the servants toiled to make things last. As Jean Rennie remembered: 'Between evening duties we had all the household linen to repair . . . When the laundry came back we had to open out every article – sheets, tablecloths, pillowcases – to see what required mending. Nothing was ever put away without being mended. Sheets were turned sides to middle. If the sheet was thin down the middle, it was cut down the centre and the thinnest part taken out then pinned together with outer edges. All by hand. Holes in pillowcases, towels, dinner napkins were darned with a flax thread; fine flax for linen, coarser for towels. When they were too worn to be darned, they were patched.'[29]

Not all country houses were resistant to technological change and a few new ones positively embraced it. Middleton Park in Oxfordshire, built by Edwin Lutyens at the end of the 1930s for the Earl of Jersey, had fourteen bathrooms, electric lighting that did not require a vast outside generator, and refrigeration. Furthermore, in a more radical move, the kitchen was linked directly to the dining room so that dishes no longer had to be carted miles along freezing corridors – thus averting the situation Lady Violet Brandon remembered from her Edwardian childhood when in her father's house the distances were so great that the lamp man 'dragged a sort of truck with the food because it was a long way from the dining room to the kitchen'.[30]

'Rooms, rooms, rooms!' remembered Eileen Balderson.[31] At Rise Park in Yorkshire, where Eileen first went into service as a scullery-maid, there was the usual old-fashioned huddle of small compartments, each devoted to its constituent area of expertise, among them a flower-arranging room, and a linen room where the hampers that were to be sent to the laundry were kept, together with careful inventories of each item. The brushing rooms, stillrooms, lamp rooms and pantries of the past were still in evidence in large houses, even though in designs for new country houses they were rationalised into larger work spaces.

On the whole country house owners tended to prefer new technologies, if they succumbed to them, to be cunningly disguised. Many clung to the belief that the installation of electricity was a greater fire risk than continuing with candles or oil lamps. There was still a deep-rooted resistance, on grounds both moral and practical, to the introduction of labour-saving technologies. They found their way slowly into the big houses only in a piecemeal fashion. At Cliveden, central heating was installed in 1928, but there were no vacuum cleaners until 1940. Concessions to labour-saving were furthermore often somewhat eccentric in their reasoning: Miss Ellery worked in a house in London where the maids had no vacuum cleaners but sped around the rooms upstairs on motorised coal shuttles. Moreover, if the great house, the last legacy of the landed tradition, had to be defiled by new apparatus, then it had to be as unobtrusive as possible, or at least constructed to emulate a more pleasing pre-industrial model. Radiators were generally concealed by complicated lattice-work covers, electric bulbs were shaped like candles and bulb-holders moulded with artificial wax drips. This taste for concealing new technology trickled down into the new houses of the middle classes, where the wireless, for example, was often hidden inside an especially constructed cabinet.

Sometimes the staff were themselves part of the pretence, maintaining an illusion of elaborate labour where technology had in reality made it redundant. At Flete House in Devon, the footmen had to remove all the electric table lamps every morning and bring them back in as soon as it grew dark. 'I can see them now, groping about under the big table in the library on their hands and knees, plugging in those lamps. It must have been a relic of the old days when oil lamps were always taken out to be filled and trimmed.'[32] When electricity was finally installed at Woburn in the late 1920s, the Duke of Bedford believed his guests would be so unaccustomed to this new form of illumination that he had black and white plaques made especially to go above all the switches, inscribed with the explanatory words 'Electric Light'.

The aristocracy maintained their cheerfully ambivalent attitude towards cleanliness, and the idea of sharing a bathroom with others, quite possibly strangers, was anathema to people whose most intimate secrets, paradoxically, had long been shared with the valet or the lady's-maid who undressed and bathed them. The old-fashioned ablutions remained popular: the round bath tub placed in front of the fire with all the accompanying impedimenta of hot and cold water jugs, soaps and sponge bowls, towels and mats; the water carried in jugs from a distant source in the servants' quarters. Guests in houses that had no hot running water could wallow in the early morning ritual of being 'watered' by a maid or a manservant carrying a steaming hot jugful and a clean towel. As for lavatories, newly built houses in England now always contained a flush loo, chamberpots mostly being reserved for the incontinent, the very old and the very young. Yet, as Jean Rennie remembered: 'The gentry were not altogether fussy in their habits ... I've known them go past a lavatory to get to their bedrooms to use one of those things.'[33] Those lavatories made with the country house market in mind had grandiose names hinting at sublime natural forces, such as Deluge or Niagara. They were often lavishly decorated with dolphins, lions or moulded foliage.

In regions of rural England, the old social order still seemed unbreachable, apparently quite out of reach of the changes sweeping urban society. When Miss Ellery worked in the kitchens of a great house in Leicestershire, a passenger train was held at Market Harborough station while the footman who had forgotten the silver he was supposed to be bringing up to London went back to the house to fetch it. The curious, unspoken intimacy that, at its best, had characterised the master and servant on the landed estate, became increasingly precious to those who lived within the world of the estate because it was perceived to be in retreat, under threat from forces on the outside. Servants often behaved like the keepers of an arcane flame that a new generation of employers had long forgotten. Twenty years after the First World War, and on the brink of the Second, Helen Mildmay White, then thirty-two and newly married, wandered into her garden and picked a peach. The next week the head gardener came to see her: '"Miss . . . I'd like to speak to you," he said. "You've been to the greenhouse and you picked a peach." I said "Yes I did, I picked it for a friend of mine." And he said: "That's not the sort of thing that happens in this kind of house. It might happen in a doctor's household or a parson's household but it does not happen in a household like this."'[34]

The country house may have been slow to take up the new, but its mystique was nonetheless exploited by the manufacturers of new chemical cleaning liquids and domestic machinery. The scent of the old English house that Jean Rennie remembered, 'a smell I've never forgotten – a combination of rich carpets, velvet hangings, polished floors and furniture, especially when it's polished with bees wax and turpentine, instead of manufactured polishes',[35] was replicated in lavender-scented furniture creams with names such as 'Mansion House' and cleaning fluids that smelt of lemon or vinegar or pine oil, or any of the traditional cleaning methods redolent of the past.

That even a few country estates survived in this style into the thirties seems at least partly because of the silent agreement extant among those who owned the land and those who worked on it, that the old patriarchy still wielded power over all aspects of life. Bill Denby, a farmer on the Heslington estate near York, found on his arrival there in 1930 that, 'you had to behave yourself – it was a known thing. You were supposed to go to church on Sunday, and you hadn't to cut the ivy off your house, because his Lordship liked to see it . . . Then you hadn't to chop branches off trees, and you'd to leave a good big wide hedge bottom for game purposes.'[36] The new-rich held the moneybags but they were made on all sides to feel the absence of that secret understanding that no money could buy. Margaret Powell – clear-eyed, intelligent, furiously socialist, a servant against her will – nonetheless was typical in ascribing the thoughtful and considerate behaviour of her employers Lord and Lady Downall to the fact that they were old-school gentry, raised in the courtly mysteries of proper behaviour. 'They were so pleasant and unassuming in their contact with us that I think for the first time since I started work, I lost the feeling that we were a race apart, and that the gap between us was unbridgeable. They spoke to us in exactly the same way that they would speak to people of their own society. For instance, we were all called by our Christian names. And it was the first place that I'd been in where the people above "them" called you by your Christian name.'[37]

Nonetheless, though they enjoyed their final flourishing, the ways of life on the great estates of the thirties were doomed to end with the decade. A new generation of young aristocrats no longer always wanted their parents' commitment to the imperatives of duty; for them an enormous country house looked less like an ancient privilege and more like a burdensome white elephant. Even in 1930, when fourteen-year-old Barbara Woman cycled to her first job as a kitchen-maid in a large house, the dust-sheet-shrouded rooms of the one elderly maiden lady who employed her were testament to a way of living that would gradually be shut down.[38] When Gretta Guy arrived aged eighteen from County Galway 'with no trade of any description', she went into service as a house-maid paid £1 a month: 'I knew enough to know that everything was changing.'[39]

A new breed looked at the ways of the past as wasteful, a burlesque theatre of the absurd. In 1939, Celia Fremlin, employed by the new social research group Mass Observation, embarked on a job (for investigative purposes) as scullery-maid for an elderly woman living, bed-bound, in a huge London house. Fremlin's first evening was a surreal experience:

That night her aged ladyship had decided to sup on a cup of Benger's food [a malted milk drink, rather like Ovaltine] and a digestive biscuit. So like a vast machine set in motion, the eight members of the staff were mobilised as if for a full-time dinner party. First the housekeeper (1) came down to the kitchen to tell the cook that this was to be the menu tonight. Then I, the scullery maid (2) was dispatched to fetch the new tin of Benger's from the store-room, and the special enamel saucepan. I handed them to the kitchen-maid (3) who took the lid off and handed the tin to the cook, together with the other necessary apparatus. The cook (4) then set to work making the Benger's. Now the footman (5) came into action. He went to the butler (6) for the key to the cupboard which contained her ladyship's silver tray. The butler gave him the key and waited while he took out the tray. Then the footman put the tray on his trolley and wheeled it to the kitchen, where the Benger's and digestive biscuit were now standing in state awaiting him. He put them on the tray and wheeled it off to the hall. Here the tray was taken by the head-housemaid (7). She took it up to her ladyship's landing and knocked in her lady-ship's door. It was opened by the lady's-maid (8) who took the tray and disappeared.

Fremlin, a professional middle-class woman for a new age, for whom this operation was as distant as the rites of a remote tribe, watched in awe as this performance got under way. 'It was like watching a hundred-ton crane picking up a safety-pin; like watching a huge sweet factory producing one peppermint bulls-eye; a vast machine that has forgotten how to stop working.'[40]

Chapter 17

'Bachelor Establishments Are Notoriously Comfortable'

Shortly after the First World War, a cartoon in *Punch* featured a cigar-smoking industrialist telling his young son: 'Well, Sonny, we've decided to give you the best education that money can buy. After all, you won't have to do anything except be a gentleman.' Trying to work out what precisely constitutes that mysterious entity, the gentleman, runs as a theme through the history of English national life; but in the 1920s most people would have hazarded a guess that a gentleman had leisure at his disposal: he did not have to *do* a great deal. The ancient definition of the gentleman as characterised by chivalric virtues of meekness, humility and service had become obscured over the Victorian and Edwardian periods by an obsession with form, costume and sportsmanship. Appearances, as defined by strict and exclusive sartorial codes, had increasingly become short-hand for gentlemanliness. It was a language of class and culture more socially manageable than the Christian virtuous ideal, and the notion of gentlemanly discretion had 'come to mean little more than the avoidance of discussion about uncomfortable subjects'.[1]

The silly-ass gentleman of the 1890s and the early twentieth-century idle, over-bred, impractical and foolish gentleman was given fictional life in the likeable but absurd figure of P. G. Wodehouse's Bertie Wooster, who made his first appearance in 1915. Yet it is

Bertie's Spinoza-reading manservant Reginald Jeeves who more fully embodies the gentlemanly ideal as a man of both service and worldly shrewdness. Jeeves is the perfect 'gentleman's gentleman', an amalgam of the new concentration on form and the old tradition of duty. Not only does he to perfection and without resentment perform his work of ironing, cooking, opening the door and advising Bertie on his choice of tie, but his superior diplomatic intelligence prevents Bertie from the social embarrassment into which he would otherwise collapse at every opportunity.

Retaining the services of a valet was a means of preserving the gentleman's image from despoilment. In 1929 it was the opinion of Mrs Peel that society had 'begun to see the end of the male servant as the most important male figure in the ordinary upper- and upper-middle-class house'. She put this down to 'the haughtiness of menservants' and their objection to performing 'menial duties which they considered to be women's work (but which Continental menservants perform without loss of dignity) and also their liking for too much beer'.[2] Yet, if they were no longer as popular in families, the manservant was still a common feature of the domestic life of the bachelor about town. After the Great War, there were many service veterans and former batmen whose discipline, attention to detail and maintenance of correct appearances made them ideal for the work. Indeed, bachelor establishments were often run with a military precision envied by housewives. In 1929, Mrs Alfred Sidgewick, in a spirited article to champion the working woman, pointed out how invidious it was to criticise women for poor budgeting when, unlike men, they had so few opportunities to earn their own money and apply those principles to the household: 'Bachelor establishments are notoriously comfortable and do not have stair carpets in holes . . . but no-one tells stories about their extravagance because they are spending their own money.'[3]

Researchers for the London School of Economics' *New Survey of London Life and Labour* found in 1930 that a post with a 'man about town' was considered particularly desirable among male servants. Even in 1911, when the Greek manservant George Criticos arrived in London, he realised quickly that his job as a gentleman's gentleman for a bachelor in Piccadilly was for the most part to be a 'companion in crime'.[4] Not every manservant would have George's merry experience of 'rip-roaring days and nights', but for many there was the appealing fraternity of the boarding school or the officers' mess about bachelor living. In the early 1930s, Allen Lane, the publisher and founder of Penguin books, lived with his two brothers Dick and John in a London house that had recently been renovated in tune with latest standards of cruise-liner elegance – with parquet floors, a bar with glass shelves, a gas-powered fridge and an up-to-the-moment bathroom. The brothers employed an ex-marine called Knight who lived out but arrived first thing every day to make early morning tea and cook breakfasts and evening meals – when the young men weren't out – specialising in steak and kidney pies. The three brothers shared the same bathwater but it was Knight who ran the all-important daily bath.[5]

For the most part the job of the valet was in the detail. The mysteries of masculine grooming, particularly shaving, were attended to with rigorous precision. 'Fill the tumbler half full with cold water on the washstand, placing the toothbrush across the top of the glass,' were the instructions in Mrs Leverton's *Servants and their Duties.* Eileen Balderson's employer, Captain Bethell, insisted that his valet took his shaving water daily from a rain butt positioned outside his dressing-room window because he found it softer. *Servants and their Duties* laid down the valet's instructions:

> To brush his master's clothes, to clean his top-boots, shooting, walking and dress boots; and to carry up the water for his master's bath, to put out his things for dressing; to shave him, if necessary; to assist him in dressing; to pack and unpack his clothes when travelling; to put out his master's things for dinner; to carry up the hot water to his dressing room, to load for him when out shooting; to stand behind his master's chair at dinner; and more especially to wait upon his master and the lady taken down to dinner by him. When at home he is expected to wait at his master's breakfast, and at the family luncheon and dinner; he attends to his master's wardrobe, and sees that everything is in repair and in order.[6]

A knowledge of the arcane rules of dress by which a gentleman was defined was, therefore, crucial. Clothes had become the first indication to the outsider of where one stood in the social scale. The list of rules compiled by 'The Major', an Edwardian pundit on the sartorial arts, demonstrates how difficult they were to master; it was like becoming the initiate of a secret rite. 'When you are in town you mustn't appear in a lounge suit and a bowler after lunch; and of course, if you have any business appointments in the morning, you would wear a frock or morning coat with a silk hat'; 'Don't wear tan boots or shoes with a black coat of any kind. Don't wear a bowler hat with a black morning coat. Don't wear a silk hat when you are wearing a navy blue jacket'; and 'of course, no gentleman ever wears a made-up tie'.[7]

Even in the hottest reaches of the Empire, it was important to get the clothes right. 'Did one wear a uniform? Did one wear short or long stockings? Did one wear very long shorts? Could you wear an open-necked shirt? Did you have a tie?' were among the anxieties of Anthony Kirk-Greene when he was posted to Africa in the early thirties.[8] The answer to the question 'why' to any of the rules would be met simply with the response that non-compliance was 'bad form'.

The sartorial gentleman took his lead from the monarch. Edward VII showed a keen eye for correct male attire but his more whimsical personal preferences went on to become cast-iron standards of gentleman's style. It was entirely due to the portly King, for example, that Edwardian gentlemen felt it necessary to leave the bottom button of their waistcoats undone, and to have their trousers pressed with a crease down the middle. His son, George V, conferred upon these dress codes an almost totemic significance. He was as meticulous in the correct observance of both military uniform and civilian dress as he was on etiquette, orders of precedence and forms of address. As a rule, wrote his biographer Harold Nicolson, George V 'favoured the fashion before the last and was inclined to regard any deviation from the norm of the previous decade as indicating affectation, effeminacy, or potential decadence'.[9] The King's trousers, like his father's, were therefore ironed down the middle, his ties were pulled through a ring, rather than knotted, and then fastened with a pin; his spats always had eight buttons. It was frock coats for formal occasions, dark suits and bowlers for occasions less formal. In Scotland he wore a kilt and feathered bonnet; while sailing he sported white flannels; for shooting, tweeds. On one occasion, he spied Sir Derek Keppel, a senior member of the royal household, entering the palace wearing a bowler hat and accused him of looking like a 'rat-catcher'. The King's trenchancy on the subject of dress was matched by the minute attention that he paid to grooming details: he wore lavender water on his beard and his hands were always beautifully manicured.

Valets were therefore a necessity for the single man with a private income who aspired to the life of a gentleman. Away from home, they were also an indispensable guide to the intricate workings of the sporting house party. The Major considered that any man 'who pays rounds of visits to country houses cannot easily dispense with a valet. Sports men and men given to hunting and shooting find one invaluable.' Up until the Second World War, wrote the former valet Stanley Ager, 'any gentleman of any consequence' had a manservant. The ideal, facilitated by a valet, was to achieve an appearance arrived at by infinite pains but which affected a modest indifference to outward show. Cleanliness was a key component of the day and the daily bath a ritual. The accoutrements designed specifically to help the fashionable gentleman arrive at perfection were legion. There were silver holders for the fresh flower in the buttonhole, for example, and numerous different styles of dress studs and cravat pins, depending on the occasion. The gentleman's dressing room was a shrine to grooming: sticks of petroleum pomade for chapped hands; unguent of some kind for taming unruly hair (in the early nineteenth century, it was bears' grease); silver or ivory hairbrushes, in pairs of course and initialled; shoehorns, toothpicks, glove stretchers, buttonhooks and clothes' brushes. For travelling there were ingenious devices such as collapsible buttonhooks, toothpicks in retractable containers and extravagant manicure cases.

By the 1920s, gentlemen's fashions reluctantly began to accommodate new social mores. The German writer Wilhelm Dibelius,

The household servants of Erddig in Wales in 1912, each holding
a tool representing their particular work. The housekeeper holds
a large bunch of keys; the footman (*front left*) a silver salver for
conveying visitors' calling cards.

A housekeeping book from 1900 in
which the mistress has kept a record of
the wages and duties of her servants.

130

Servants' Agreements

*Grace Clements of South Pool, Kingsbridge
from Oct. 26/96, £23 to be raised to £25.*

*Lucy Miller, 66 Paris St. Exeter. £18 a year, from
Oct 28/96 — (now raised to £20)*

Alice Pearce, from Oct. 24/96, £20 a year.

E. A. Smith from May 26/97 £18 a year

Emily Worthy from ? £25 a year.

Margaret Oakley from Oct 11 97 at £8 a year

Ethel Harris from Nov 15 — £18 to be raised to £20

Sarah Hawke, to be raised to £25 from Nov 15/97

Annie Wake (£25 per annum) from Jan 10?/98

Annie Harris (£20, to be increased) from July 27, 1903

A housemaid scrubs a doorstep until it shines. The daily cleaning of the front step, whitening it with a 'donkey stone', was a dawn chore from the terraced one-up one-down to the London mansion.

Edwardian parlourmaids wearing the dark dresses with lace caps and aprons that were required for serving lunch and for opening the door to afternoon callers.

A row of young girls in Dr Barnardo's Barkingside Village line up for inspection by Queen Mary before the First World War. 'The Village', as it was known, was designed to be a wholesome pre-industrial idyll in which destitute children were trained to be domestics.

The role of the manservant lost status during the nineteenth century – when domestic service became overwhelmingly a female occupation. In 1890, the butler John Robinson described the humiliation of being mocked as a 'flunkey': 'The paralysing influence of the servants' environment has prevented his calling very loudly for more freedom'.

The women of Universal Aunts advertise their services. Founded by Gertie Maclean 1923, the agency's Aunts were 'ladies of irreproachable background'.

A Punch cartoon by George Belcher, 1926. There was a widespread view among the middle-classes that the availability of post-war unemployment benefit had encouraged girls to turn up their noses at life in service. In fact, economic depression was forcing them back in huge numbers and by 1931, domestic service was again the largest single employer of all women workers.

Mistress. "TELL ME, GREY—YOU'VE BEEN IN SERVICE A LONG WHILE—WHAT IS THE CAUSE OF THIS DIFFICULT SERVANT PROBLEM?"

Grey. "WELL, MADAM, SINCE YOU ASK ME, IT'S LIKE THIS: YOU'RE GOING DOWN, AND WE'RE COMING UP."

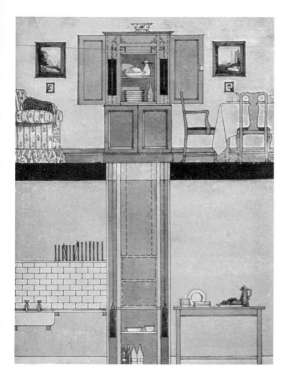

From *The Servantless House* by Randal Phillips, editor of *Home and Garden* (1920). 'We are all busy now making the world anew', Phillips wrote – though most British households were to prove resistant for many years to the idea of ergonomic efficiency in place of human labour.

Advertisements for new cleaning technologies often drew on nostalgia for a golden age of well-run country houses and a plentiful supply of cheery staff. Early vacuum cleaners, for example, often had comforting maid-like names such as the 'Mary Anne' or the 'Daisy'.

Floors & Furniture reflect the brilliance of
MANSION POLISH
which is equally good for Linoleum
In Tins 6d., 10½d. & 1/9. Large family tin 3/- contains 2 lbs. nett
THE CHISWICK POLISH CO. LTD. CHISWICK. W.4

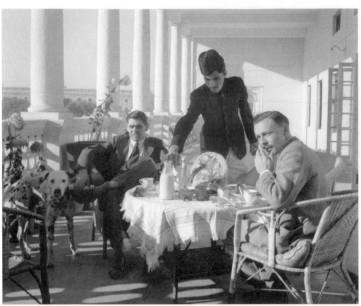

'For those who experienced it, nothing would ever again match the Anglo Indian household in its pomp.' With the exception of the *ayah*, most servants in the British Raj were men and each domestic job was accompanied by intricate distinctions of religion and caste.

Elizabeth Dashwood (E. M. Delafield) in 1935. Dashwood's columns on the travails of the 'Provincial Lady' captured the mood of the post-First World War woman who saw herself trapped between the demands of domesticity and recalcitrant servants and those of her own spiritual development.

Refugees from Austria and Germany scour the advertisements at Bloomsbury House in London for vacancies for domestics. By 1938, visa applicants no longer had to line up jobs in advance and block visas were issued to all women prepared to take up domestic work.

The British Housewives' League campaign against post-war rationing. 'Women have come into their own and realise that they have a brain', said a participant in a BBC discussion in 1946, 'and housework makes the brain just become stagnant'.

The Duke of Bedford pictured unloading dishes from the first Kenwood Fully Automated dishwasher, at the Ideal Home Exhibition of 1959. The Duke's grandfather had maintained until his death just nineteen years earlier a household of sixty indoor servants – all the parlourmaids standing at over five foot ten.

A modishly nostalgic 1969 kitchen. The book suggests that a copper, in which once the laundry would have been boiled over a fire, makes a striking feature when filled with geraniums. The cast-iron range, once laboriously cleaned and blacked each morning, is now a period accessory.

resident in London in the decade, saw this as an indication of English moral decline into the decadence of individualism. 'Now self-expression is the cry: the old moral code is scorned as prudery,' he wrote after the First World War. 'There is a deterioration in manners everywhere: men's dressing becomes slack – dress clothes, once obligatory for every evening function, are, as on the Continent, the exception rather than the rule.'[10] George V's son, the popular Prince of Wales, would become the pin-up for a more casual, sporty line in menswear, popularising Fair Isle pullovers, flat caps, plus-fours and diamond-patterned socks. The King harped on about Edward's solecisms: 'I hear you were not wearing gloves at the ball last night. Please see that it does not happen again.'[11] The Prince of Wales's clothes did not simply reflect a more relaxed attitude towards 'form', but also the fact that for most people in the country, the old standards of upper- and middle-class men's dress were no longer sustainable by anyone not in possession of a private laundry.

The valet often appeared a shadow of the gentleman himself, even wearing his old clothes. The author of *The Duties* makes clear that the valet must provide his own clothes for the job, not being a liveried servant like the footman, and should also expect to be in receipt of his master's clothes when he had finished with them. The valet therefore cut an almost clerkly figure in his dark suit, probably one of his master's cast-offs, or a 'salt and pepper' version, a dark grey, flecked suit. 'Every male member of staff,' remembered Stanley Ager, 'had one of these in his cupboard.'[12] The valet ensured that his master need never have to wonder where his toothbrush was, or worry about the temperature of his shaving water. After the Second World War, Winston Churchill's valet John Gibson found the former prime minister still quite unable to dress himself without assistance: 'He was social gentry . . . He sat there like a dummy and you dressed him.'[13]

Readymade clothes had been gaining ground in middle-class circles since before the First World War, but gentlemen lagged notably behind ladies in their willingness to take up clothes that could be bought off the peg, and their wardrobes therefore needed vigilant attention. 'He attends to his master's wardrobe and sees that everything is in repair and in order,' were the valet's instructions. It was a full-time job. If the wardrobe of the civilian gentleman was complicated, its upkeep was as nothing to the knowledge of ceremonial dress required by the mess servant. Former footman George Fox was a Steward, Second Class, on HMS *Arrogant* and HMS *Edward VII* between 1910 and 1914. He had to learn exactly what was required for every occasion: a frock coat for inspecting the men or for attendance at court martials, 'on fine occasions with a sword'. The gold lace on the ceremonial dress was actually gilded silver and had to be wrapped carefully in salmon-coloured tissue to preserve it and prevent the gold from flaking off. Each button was lacquered – not brass – so it did not need polishing, but each one had also to be wrapped in tissue.[14] Fox cleaned boots with blacking of the kind used to bring up a shine on old-fashioned kitchen ranges. The best boot trees were traditionally the foreleg of a deer – and these were also used for polishing boots.

The bugbear of the manservant (and it was often a footman's job where a valet was otherwise occupied) was cleaning hunting kit: it took hours. Hunting pink was ruinously expensive and needed expert care to keep it from speckling by first mud and then the black spots caused by the water reacting with the pink dye. Charles Dean remembered: 'It was when I graduated to pink that my worries started, for one slip and a coat can be ruined, since it's about the most expensive garment that a gentleman wears; a ruined coat leads to an unpopular servant.'[15] Most career valets had their own box of cleaning materials which they carried with them at all times. 'On the whole, [it was] quite expert work,' was the verdict of Stanley Sewell, who worked at Langton Hall in Yorkshire between the wars, and in whose testimony one hears the voice of a master craftsman:

If you're living in a county that isn't very limey, the water leaves white marks on a red coat, then you use rainwater. When I first came to Langton, we was drawing water from the brook, before the mains water was on and you had to use rainwater there, lime you see. They were washed every time they come in, straight in the tub, it's wonderful material. The colonel, he could have hunted seven days a week in a different coat. You can't dry them quick; fresh air and then finish them off in an airing cupboard, knock them back into shape when they're very wet, button them. The breeches, they were wool; you had to be very careful with breeches. Buckskin, of course, that's a job on its own. Took me nearly twelve months before I could say I was good at it, difficult job. Well, it's not getting your water too hot, keeping it quite soapy but not too soapy, because when they were wet they were slipping about the saddle. French chalk when they were nearly dry and keep polishing them with your hand on a flat table, dry them steadily else they'd be like drying a chamois leather; it would be as hard as a brick. Ridiculous thing buckskin is.[16]

The valet's training required him to be so discreet as to be self-effacing, carrying the idea of gentlemanly reticence to its extreme. Somewhere along the way, as the comrade-in-arms became a personal grooming assistant, the civilian valet (as opposed to his military counterpart) often became associated with sexlessness and softness. Charles Dickens scornfully described menservants as 'long and languid men, flabby in texture'.[17] According to Eric Horne, the valets he had worked with had 'a savour of a "dog at heel", a not entirely manly creature who spent too much time in the kitchen talking to the women'. Said Horne: 'I can just conjure a picture of mam'selle sitting on a window sill darning my Lady's stockings, and John the valet sitting opposite taking a lesson in French.'[18] Margaret Powell was also scornful. Despite his intimacy with the master, the valet in the Cutlers' South Kensington household Powell viewed with withering pity as being entirely unmarriageable. 'Now you would think that a valet would be a sort of kingpin in a household. I don't know whether it was always the same, but this one seemed so feminine. Whether it's the nature of their job (although valeting is not really an effeminate job), or whether it's because they're in domestic service and they're living so much with females I don't know, but we used to look on him as one of us. They all spoke and made jokes with him as if he was a woman. His hands were so soft, and he was so soft spoken, he didn't seem masculine. More like a jelly, somehow, to me.'[19]

Yet, despite its effeminate reputation in the servants' hall, a good valeting post brought opportunities to travel, to learn languages, to see the world. Charles Dean crossed the Atlantic twenty-eight times while he was working as valet for Prince Obolensky during the twenties. The chauffeur-valet, an increasingly popular double role, added some masculine independence and appeal to the job in the inter-war period. By 1921 there were 5,200 private chauffeurs in England and those ex-servicemen who had acquired mechanical and engineering skills in the war were greatly in demand. In his goggles, gaiters, flat cap and brass-buttoned livery, the chauffeur retained the impertinent, flash-Harry allure of his pre-war incarnation, and now he had increased in number. A kitchen visitation from a chauffeur was always a major excitement: 'To us, these chauffeurs looked simply wonderful, and to be actually able to speak to these hundred-percent men in leggings was something too glorious for words.'[20] The following advertisement from the columns of *The Times* in 1939 was typical of the type: 'Chauffeur-Valet, 37; intelligent man, Russian birth, speaks English well, some French and Hindustani; travelled; served as corporal in British Army; personal attendant 15 years to a General, and three years to invalid gentleman – strongly recommended by Canon Quirk, the Close, Salisbury.'[21]

The relationship between batman and officer who had served together during the war was a close one, giving the former batman or combatant's valeting job in peacetime another dimension. No civilian relationship could quite match the shared experience of wartime. Barbara Cartland recalled in her autobiography the common experience of getting into taxi cabs with young men in the 1920s, only to find the partition sliding back to reveal a wartime comrade driving the cab. Cartland remembered how the men on either side of the partition were so delighted to see each other that they forgot her presence completely; it was a fellowship she envied.

Yet for the most part the civilian valet, like the lady's-maid, was a casualty of the particular loneliness of the upper-servant: stranded somewhere between the camaraderie of the servants' hall and that of the drawing room. Stanley Ager, who was valet to Lord St Levan during the 1920s, reflected that the job left him 'neither up nor down . . . a very lonely person'.[22] The necessary daily intimacy of the job made it difficult to conceal defects. 'There's a saying that no man is a hero to his valet; of course it's true but it would be bloody dreary serving a hero all the time,' was George Washington's experience when he was valet to Ronald Tree at Ditchley Park. 'You get mutual understanding and trust between you and if you're sensible you leave it there.'[23]

But there was poignancy too in the lonely in-betweenness of the third-class traveller in the cast-off gentleman's clothes. 'Even when I travelled abroad with the family party, I felt alone,' wrote Ager. 'Everyone aboard ship knew that I was a servant; the odd passenger might speak to me – but only in the hopes that this would lead him to my employer. I had to stay aloof – if I'd been the least bit brash then his Lordship would have wondered about me.'[24]

Chapter 18

The Question of the Inner Life

Caroline Miniver, who became in the late 1930s the embodiment of English femininity under fire, made her first appearance in the comment pages of *The Times* on 6 October 1937 in a column entitled 'Swept and Garnished'. This presented its readers with an idyll, an image of the perfect synchronisation of domestic order and inner life. Mrs Miniver, walking home to her Chelsea house on an autumn afternoon, is moved by the beauty of the frost-burnished boughs in the park and in a moment of impulse purchases a bunch of chrysanthemums which will make a harmonious addition to her drawing room. Neither forbiddingly smart nor slavishly fashionable, the Minivers' home is warmed by the patina of the past, by the beauty of simple things made with care and loved for generations. Mrs Miniver's home, like Mrs Miniver's mind, is well stocked with the precious and antique fragments of a disappearing culture:

She rearranged the fire a little, mostly for the pleasure of handling the fluted steel poker, and then sat down by it. Tea was already laid; there were honey sandwiches, brandy-snaps, and small ratafia biscuits; and there would, she knew, be crumpets. Three new library books lay virginally on the fender stool, their bright paper wrappers unsullied by the subscriber's hand. The clock on the mantelpiece chimed, very softly and precisely, five times. A tug hooted from the river. A sudden breeze brought the sharp tang of a bonfire in through the open window. The jigsaw was almost complete, but there was still one piece missing. And then, from the other end of the square, came the familiar sound of the Wednesday barrel-organ, playing with a hundred apocryphal trills and arpeggios, the Blue Danube. And Mrs Miniver, with a little sigh of contentment, rang for tea.[1]

The creator of Mrs Miniver, Jan Struther, had been invited by the author Peter Fleming, an editor on *The Times*, to inject some femininity into the paper's comment pages. Fleming suggested that Struther might 'write about an ordinary woman who leads an ordinary sort of life – someone like yourself'.[2] Mrs Miniver was actually not at all like the hard-working, professional journalist Jan Struther, who left her husband during the war for a Viennese refugee thirteen years her junior; but the *idea* of Mrs Miniver and her gracious indomitability in the face of war and change came to define a certain kind of ideal Englishness. It was claimed that the publication in 1939 of the Mrs Miniver articles in book form and the production of the Oscar-winning film three years later, starring Greer Garson, helped galvanise American attitudes towards the war.

A *Times* editorial pinpointed for its readers the social context from which Caroline Miniver emerged: 'We know that she is in her early forties, that she is sympathetically rather than ecstatically married to Clement Miniver, a prospering (domestic) architect, who has kept his looks and his figure, and that their London house is in one of the smaller squares in the South-Western district, not far from the King's Road. In her seventeen years of married life she has had three children, conveniently spaced.' Mrs Miniver was, *The Times* went on, 'exquisitely feminine': not only did she take pleasure in the domestic details of the well-run home but her imagination was alive to nature, landscape and art; she enjoyed life's quiddities and its enchanting incidentals. While under the dentist's drill, Mrs Miniver is consoled by recalling the poetry of Donne. Altogether superior but in a carefully self-deprecating and un-intimidating way, Mrs Miniver is 'at once dainty and cosy and rather grand'.[3]

In other words, what an utterly desirable vision for the 1930s housewife, reading *The Times* over her breakfast, whose inner world is under constant siege from domestic disorder, the chief enemy of its flowering the departing servant. Readers of Struther's first column never found out who it is who answers Mrs Miniver when she rings for tea because the column ends tantalisingly at that moment. Yet to complete the image of perfection, the tea, so beautifully laid just at the moment when it is most required, must be delivered as it always has been delivered: on time, abundant and blessed by the loyal labour of the invisible hands that created it.

In 1934, P. L. Travers's Mary Poppins had flown in on her umbrella to bring magic and order to the Banks family in Cherry Tree Avenue, where chaos had ensued on the departure of their nanny. The quiet efficiency of a well-run household was the 1930s dream but in real life it was under threat, with servants difficult to secure and widely expected to leave at the drop of a hat, leaving catastrophe in their wake. Employers were no longer able to impose the conditions they once had done. Gretta Guy, a farmer's daughter from County Galway who came to England in 1938, went for an interview in Harley Street, and 'I said I must go to Mass on Sunday and her face changed'. Gretta's prospective employer got her stick and she pounded it on the floor: 'It would be against my principles to engage a Catholic and if you wish to come here, in no way can you go to Mass.' But the stick-wielding employer was now the loser: Gretta simply walked out and found work somewhere else.[4]

By 1937 there were 1.6 million unemployed in Britain, yet in middle-class English homes the departing servant was a defining anxiety of the inter-war years. Having to placate domestics, trembling in the face of their superior bargaining power, became a hallmark of a changing world. Women still saw themselves as martyrs to their servants' caprices, felt helpless and fearful in the face of bad food or sulkiness. In her London house, the paragon Mrs Miniver employs Mrs Adie the cook, a house-parlourmaid and Mrs Burchett the charlady, and there is a nanny for the children. In Starlings, the

Minivers' country home in Romney Marsh, there is a housekeeper, Mrs Downce, who with her husband looks after the house. But even for Caroline Miniver, the necessary daily routine cruelly throws up irritants that would have been all too familiar to her readers. 'Everything went wrong at once; chimneys smoked, pipes burst, vacuum cleaners fused, china and glass fell to pieces, net curtains disintegrated in the wash.' Worst of all, the people who could make it all better were themselves as subject to mechanical failing as machines: 'Nannie sprained her ankle, the cook got tonsillitis, the house-parlourmaid left to be married; and the butterfly nut off the mincing machine was nowhere to be found.'[5]

How was a woman to cultivate the important things of the mind, to water the flowers of learning and reflection, unless she could rely on another woman to take from her the wearisome burden of day-to-day domestic practicalities? Nearly one hundred years earlier, clever, sharp Jane Carlyle had tried not to be overwhelmed by the daily domestic struggle of life at the Carlyles' house in Cheyne Walk – and ended up making it the raw material of her correspondence. 'My goodness. Why make bits of apologies for writing about the servants – as if "the servants" were not a most important – a most fearful item in our female existence!' she wrote, witnessing a seemingly endless procession of maids through her cramped home, one drunk, one sulky, quite a few who simply left without a word.[6] It was not 'done' to talk about the servants, providing as they should merely the distant background hum of a well-managed household; but the relationship was a constant vexation to the woman in search of an intellectual life. Clever women found that any desire they might have for the focusing, unifying theme of a great purpose was constantly thwarted by the fragmenting realities of domestic management. 'I am daily dropped in little pieces and passed around and devoured and expected to be whole again next day and all days and I am never alone for a single minute,' was the experience of the American novelist Mary Hallock Foote in 1888.[7]

One answer was to make oneself an income by writing about it. As a seam of life among the upper-middle classes, the servant problem (and running alongside it the problem of the husband whose engagement with the business of the household was limited to a grunt of complaint about the breakfast eggs) touched on both the comic and the tragic. It was about women free and women emphatically not free – and that applied, in different ways, to both mistress and maid. In 1929 the journalist and novelist Elizabeth Dashwood, a veteran of the women's suffrage movement (and a former religious novice), penned the first of her 'Diary of a Provincial Lady' columns in *Time and Tide* under the pseudonym 'E. M. Delafield'. These weekly dispatches from the domestic battlefield of a 'new poor' upper-middle-class family in Devonshire are witty, sharply observed portraits of a certain kind of inter-war provincial life: the Provincial Lady is socially on a par with the trumpeting philistine Lady Boxe, the local grandee, but due to financial constraints (and too irreverent an estimation of the county status quo) hovers on the edge of ruin. Being of livelier intelligence than Lady Boxe, the Lady, as similar ladies had done before her, makes her predicament work for her by writing it down. Dashwood made her own domestic desperation into comedy: she too was married to a land agent (though he was surely not quite as glum as the Lady's husband Robert); both had children; both women were active in the Women's Institute and in local affairs and, crucially, both were professional writers who see literary opportunities in the small events and encounters of everyday life and between whose domestic and working existences there is often a hopeless muddle. 'As a matter of course, regardless of interruptions . . . All that I have tried to do is observe faithfully and record accurately, the things that have come within my limited range,' wrote Elizabeth Dashwood in her autobiography.

The Provincial Lady chronicles her financial hardship with light self-mockery; nonetheless, she never for one moment entertains the thought of willingly going without servants. Although she tells us that she can only afford baked beans for lunch and has to go without expensive new stockings, the family keeps a resident cook, a house-parlourmaid and a French governess ('Mademoiselle') who has exacting standards of elegance. Relationships with all of these are as delicate as eggshells and participants are always on the alert for offence taken or given: 'March 4 – Ethel, as I anticipated, gives notice. Cook says this is so unsettling, she thinks she had better go too. Despair invades me. Write five letters to Registry Offices.'[8] Like many women of her type, the Lady believes that it is she who is constantly at the disadvantage in the battle to keep servants. We read in another entry that she: 'Cannot hear of a house-parlour-maid. Ethel, on the other hand, can hear of at least one hundred situations, and opulent motor cars constantly dash up to front door, containing applicants for her services. Cook more and more unsettled . . .'[9]

The voice of the Provincial Lady, despite her clear-eyed take on the social scene, is that of the Englishwoman who will accept all sorts of social changes, who considers herself modern and free-spirited, but who is nonetheless conventionally helpless when it comes to domestic servants. When the Lady, unable to find a parlourmaid to replace the one who has flounced out, is offered a 'house-parlourman' she is 'completely amazed', and regards the new servant during his short tenure in Devon with suspicion: 'I must certainly make it crystal clear that the acceptable formula, when receiving an order, is not "right-oh".'

Respectability and deference were still the first requirement in a good servant. Not even a successful professional woman of progressive views wanted the lines between servant and master to get too blurred. Things did not go *smoothly* unless everyone knew where they stood. Faizur Rasul, who found himself happily employed in the early 1930s for the imam of a mosque (the first in Britain) in Woking, has left a memorable description of the middle-aged housemaid, Miss Bowden, who worked with him there. 'Having spent her working life under the middle-class ladies in the district she had acquired their habits, tastes and morals. She spoke better English, using such words as consequently, eventually, consolation, possessive, episode etc. and lady-dog for bitch and perspire for sweat, and she made abundant use of the word "respectable", and ended her sentences with a question mark which it took me some time to get used to . . . Miss Bowden didn't like "love" as a topic.'[10] What fun Mrs Miniver and the Provincial Lady would have had with such a housemaid and how much they would have liked to have employed Miss Bowden. But Miss Bowden was a period piece, as Rasul himself realises when he observes the way the other servants behave towards her. Miss Bowden's deep respect for her 'betters' was increasingly strange to the young girls reluctantly pressed into service in the thirties. The new domestic would probably be more like Ivy, the one maid remaining to old Mrs Powell in Lettice Cooper's *The New House*: 'When Ivy came in at ten o'clock to show them her new Marks and Spencer jumper, Mrs Powell said that she did not know her place. Ivy was nineteen, and belonged to a generation for whom this place hardly existed.'[11]

Mrs Miniver and the Provincial Lady observe their servants with a kindly detachment but nonetheless keep them at arms' length by ascribing to them colourful characteristics as befits their walk-on parts in the deeper, more complex psychological drama of their employers' lives. The features displayed by Mrs Adie, the Minivers' cook, for example, include extreme thinness, a 'wintry smile', a touching loyalty, and an amusing tendency to mix her metaphors. 'Well, well, we'll see,' Mrs Adie says darkly on one occasion, 'wedding cake and work basket, what will be will be and one thing leads to another.' To indicate the lady's superiority to her boorish county neighbours the Boxes, she pauses from studying 'the heraldic beauty of the pineapple' that had appeared during the Boxes' dinner party to 'speculate on the second footman's private life (he had a studious, enigmatic face and probably reads philosophy)'.[12]

'The mechanics of life should not be allowed to interfere with living,' Mrs Miniver observed in 'Mrs Miniver and the Khelim Rug'. But, alas, they so often did. While self-mockery provided some armour in the daily battle for solitude and harmony, others submitted to the choppy waters of the new domestic relationships with less grace. Mary Wylde was an occasional features writer for the *London Evening Standard* who, in her book, *A Housewife in Kensington* (1937), laid bare for her readers her fear, and theirs, of being browbeaten by domestics into irrevocable downward mobility. Many of the Wyldes' friends have moved into flats, facing down a shortage of servants and funds by downsizing. 'My usual reaction in times of domestic crisis is to long for a tiny service flat. We are almost the last of our circle to hang on to a house. Our friends have long ago given up the struggle to live spaciously. They squeeze themselves into flats, get rid of their furniture and are independent of maids and the worry they entail.'[13] But Mrs Wylde and her husband boldly strike out against the tide and upsize (their two children are at boarding school) to a large, unmodernised house in a pleasant square in Kensington. The refurbishment and maintenance of the house, together with the necessary upholding of appearances, is the subject of her book. Mrs Wylde wages a daily battle between the dream of home and the daily reality of running it. The house, 'late Georgian with cream stucco walls, blue front door, shining brass knocker, Dutch garden all abloom, and a window-box gay with pink ivy-leaf geranium', is, for Mrs Wylde, the perfect backdrop for the cultivation of the mind which she believes is her destiny. Yet Mrs Wylde is thwarted at every turn by dripping pipes, leasehold complications or the demands of a cook who has the temerity to telephone her about 'sausages' while she is in the middle of penning a topical lifestyle article.

When her cook storms out, Mrs Wylde is forced to make dinner herself – or rather to supervise the housemaid doing it. 'I peeled the potatoes using a large kitchen knife because I could not find the special peeler, which turned up the next day in the back of the drawer. Meanwhile I slowly struggled with an ordinary knife. I had no idea that peeling four potatoes could take so long,' she reported indignantly. Harried by the inadequacies and ignorance of her servants, Mrs Wylde remembers, or thinks she remembers, a pre-war golden age of competence, deference and superior household management. 'Time was when the cook put on a clean apron every day when I came to give the orders. This morning I was greeted by a cook with the dirtiest apron I ever hope to meet . . . yet her wages are double the pre-war rate. She goes to the cinema two or three times a week and spends every penny of her earnings.'[14] Caroline Miniver, whose delicacy of feeling, as transmitted by Jan Struther, is far more finely tuned than Mary Wylde's, spoke for her readers when she observes ruefully that 'the Servant Problem' was, maddeningly, more about people than practicalities: 'burst water mains are so much easier to deal with than injured feelings'.[15]

The higher occupation of leisure was still a challenge for those women who could afford it. Charitable work was always popular. 'All these people interested themselves in charities. They were all on this board or that board,' wrote Margaret Powell, working as a cook in South Kensington. Mr Cutler's job in the City required him to leave the house at ten and return at four, and Mrs Cutler ran a cake stall to raise funds for fallen women. 'Mrs Cutler was very keen on helping the fallen women, from a distance. Like a lot of people she could be generous when she wasn't involved.'[16]

Yet the inner life was a space jealously reserved for itself by the upper end of the middle classes. Post-war social shifts produced a creeping ambiguity about exactly where one stood socially, resulting in both awkwardness as to the definitions that underpinned the categorisations of class, and a desire explicitly to reinforce them. The suspicion that the lower-middle classes, those women now living in new suburban homes with built-in labour-saving devices, might themselves desire an inner life, was frowned upon, as though inner life would look like self-indulgence and idleness in people not educated to cultivate it appropriately.

In *The Lancet* in 1938, Stephen Taylor, the senior resident medical officer of the Royal Free Hospital, claimed to have diagnosed a widespread depressive condition called 'suburban neurosis'. Taylor sketched out a portrait of a lonely housewife he called 'Mrs Everywoman', the lucky recipient of a new home in a new estate, bought through a hire-purchase scheme by a clerkly 'hubby', and replete with new technology. Mrs Everywoman exhibits symptoms of listlessness, anxiety, weight loss, nagging headaches and insomnia. Taylor attributes these problems to what he terms a 'set of false values', his suburban woman presumptuously aspiring to a shallow materialism nourished by idleness. 'The suburban woman has made a fetish of the home,' he wrote, aiming at the kind of life successfully led by people to whom books, theatres and things of the intellect matter. 'To them, the home is a necessary part of life, but only a part. To her, because she does not see the rest, the home looks like isolation and she wonders why it does not bring her the happiness it appears to bring to them.'[17]

Taylor correctly nailed a problem, but the reason for it – that suburban woman might share Mrs Miniver's longings for a life not bound by domesticity – was distasteful to him. Certainly, the rapid increase in new magazines for women inculcated ideals of home and housewifery that were often at odds with the reality of suburban life. Monthlies like *Ideal Home*, which had first appeared in 1920, *Homes and Gardens*, *Good Housekeeping* and *Woman and Home* all reinforced an ideal of domestic perfection, stressing uplifting hobbies, beauty tips and relationship advice as well as dainty, man-pleasing meals and outfits that transformed the suburban wife into a wonder-worker. Two years after it first appeared in 1937, the new magazine *Woman* had a circulation of a quarter of a million.

It was no wonder then that lonely housewives struggled to reconcile the dream with the reality. The new housing estates were often far from friends, extended family and shops. A young wife found time hanging heavy on her hands. For Edith Broadway, a former millinery designer:

I had nothing to do, all day long stretching in front of me, what do you do with yourself when you've done all the housework and the things you've got to do and there's nothing and nobody . . .? I can remember the tears falling into the sink when I was doing the washing, filling the sink more than the tap, I think. There were the sheets and pillowcases and shirts and I hadn't got a clue where to start. You see I was creative and housework isn't very creative. Household chores were an absolute bore. I liked to see it looking beautiful but I really didn't want to do it. [My husband] did get me a resident person and that was a great help . . . I used to feel there was so much outside and here was I, trapped in this little street with this little narrow house, it wasn't enough for me, I wanted more. I wanted to be on the move and every day was deadly.[18]

By 1939, however, everything was on the brink of change. On 3 September, Britain declared war on Germany and Jan Struther's Mrs Miniver, her columns collected that year as a book, 'boxed and in a gay binding', approached her finest hour. Rosamond Lehmann reviewed the book in the *New Statesman* and found its heroine tiresome: 'One must look out for her next appearance with such feelings as the deserving poor must entertain for the local Lady Bountiful . . . It is not so much that we are irritated by her being pleased with herself: blissfully married, mother of three, well off, well read, she has a right to be pleased: is it perhaps the way she has of masking her colossal self-satisfaction with tender self-depreciation? "See what a silly I am!".'[19]

But Lehmann rightly spotted that Mrs Miniver and her real-life counterparts were approaching a moment of change both drastic and triumphant. The urgent demands of the inner life would be subsumed for the duration of the war by the more pressing and practical demands of the outer life: the domestic landscape of England was about to be altered completely. 'Now the war is upon Mrs Miniver,' wrote Lehmann, 'as it is upon all of us, but whoever is defeated, she'll come through. Having plenty of courage and common sense, she will cope successfully with evacuees and increased taxation, even if necessary with bombs . . . Inheriting . . . no long traditions, or rather inheriting only bits and pieces of outworn and debased ones, she will be adaptable and come up shaken and intact, whatever new society emerges.'[20]

Chapter 19

'Do They Really Drink
Out of Their Saucers?'

Towards the end of the 1930s, Monica Dickens, former debutante and descendant of Charles Dickens, decided to enter
domestic service for a lark, and to make some pocket money. As an
aspiring actress, she would have a chance to practise her dramatic
skills by presenting herself as a bona fide housemaid or
cook-general.

Like her predecessor Elizabeth Banks in the 1890s, Monica
scanned the Sits Vac columns for posts as a cook or cook-general,
and then entertainingly wrote up the different types she encountered in a book that was published in 1939. Although Monica's
experiences could never capture what it is like to labour in a kitchen
when you have no other choice, she observed with pitiless accuracy
the strain of social and domestic desperation that ran through the
English middle classes in the years immediately before the war. *One
Pair of Hands* is an examination of the housewife's abject dependence on a service both hard to find and difficult to keep. It is also a
vivid portrait of life in what Odette Keun described as a 'quite
unbelievable thing called a "basement"'. Keun had been appalled by
the living conditions of most servants in the 1930s: 'In this dank
sepulchre the English kitchen is situated, the English cook lives,
and often the English servant sleeps. Such accommodation has

resulted in the production of a species with which I was unacquainted before I came to London, and which I may call, refraining from comment, the London Troglodyte.'[1]

Monica did not find her experiences entirely troglodytic, but she did discover that the English basement kitchen was still, on the whole, damp, gloomy and inhospitable: modern boilers, where there actually were boilers, were prone to breakdown at any hint of exertion; the alternative – the still prevalent cast-iron ranges – took for ever to light and then suddenly went cold in the middle of a dinner party. Food was a great deal better and cheaper than it had been for most Edwardians. In 1934 Britain spent nine shillings per head per week on food, out of an average weekly income of thirty shillings. Cheaper, processed food was increasing in popularity (potato crisps had once been a foreign novelty; in 1928, over a million packets were sold in Britain) but was still frowned on by the upper-middles whose servants laboured at what one kitchen-maid called the 'eternal scrubbing, preparing and cooking vegetables, and washing-up that marked the daily round of meals'.[2]

Monica Dickens's employers exhibited a range of expectations and behaviours. In some houses she was treated with consideration, even friendliness, in others with the chilly hauteur judged appropriate for the relationship. We do not know if any of them guessed who she was (on a couple of occasions she found herself serving an acquaintance at a dinner party). She worked for a raffish socialite who slept in all morning and whose caddish boyfriend would make drunken lunges for Monica in the kitchen (she learned, after politely being handed her notice, that on these occasions, the boyfriend is rarely in the wrong). There was a helpless young wife who had not the first idea how to run her home, an insecure housewife who wanted to give a dinner party to impress her husband's employer, and a kindly, retired general trying to look after an invalid wife and three children. Most employers' ideas of service and standards exceeded their budget, and the dress designer who tripped down to the kitchen to count the eggs and the bottles of salad oil never seemed to have enough change on him to pay Monica back for the extra shopping she did for his fashionably last-minute supper parties.

Monica only took one country house job, as a cook on an estate in Devonshire, where a large household, run by a housekeeper, was trained in the traditional manner to serve one elderly couple. But already that world seemed like an anachronism even to a young debutante. Monica's experiences in service were largely of working for housewives who found that the energy required to find and keep staff was at least equal to the work that had to be done. Breakfast was always cooked, according to taste, a combination of kippers, bacon, eggs, toast, coffee, perhaps kidneys, mushrooms or tomatoes. The kitchen was often ill-equipped with even basic utensils. In her first kitchen, there was a refrigerator, but Monica, having never encountered one, did not realise that you had to close the door to keep it cold. For handy household dodges, she thumbed through *Home* magazine. Lunch was always at least two courses and dinner at least three. Tea, of course, also had to be factored in to a day's work and would include a homemade cake (never a shop-bought one). Puddings on an average, economical day were stodgy: spotted dick, sago, rice pudding or prune mould. Monica had to get up at dawn to clear up after cocktail parties where cigarette stubs had been ground into the carpet. While working as a cook-general she learned to whip up a hollandaise sauce at the same time as making sure the fires in the drawing room were still alight, and to remember to exchange her kitchen apron for some frilly confection every time she was summoned upstairs. (The hated mob cap, according to Albert Thomas, had been largely replaced during the thirties by 'a very small handkerchief of an apron and a bow tied saucily to the side of a maid's head'.[3])

Yet social awkwardness still dominated the relationship between mistress and servant in a small home. When Celia Fremlin made her foray into domestic service, posing as a maid at about the same time as Monica Dickens, it was to examine at first hand 'the science of everyday life'. Taking into consideration how formidable Fremlin herself may well have appeared, here is her account of a hideous interview with a young housewife in London:

There was a cat on the rug, with two kittens. Mrs X stooped and stroked them. 'They're my babies; aren't they sweet?' she said, and then stopped nervously. Evidently this was a little too familiar. So I stood in painful indecision as to whether to follow her first lead and stoop and stroke them or her second and say, 'Aren't they, Madam?' with a slight laugh. I chose the latter course, perhaps wrongly. Then we returned to the sitting-room and I decided that the wages were not enough. So we parted, after once more navigating the perilous, class-haunted journey through two doors, and ending up with the fearful indecision between 'good afternoon' (servant) and 'good-bye' (friend). I could almost hear her sigh of relief as I turned my back for good and all.[4]

For most women, the mainstay of domestic help came in the person of the charwoman. The char, who came to 'do the rough', was on the lowest rung of the domestic ladder: in the person of the char, there can be no pretence that scrubbing, scouring and mopping is a means of 'bettering' yourself, for the char could never progress upwards but was stuck for ever not only with the drudgery of her work but with the comic stereotype that was pinned upon her. Frank Swinnerton described the Char Type in a 1938 article in *Good Housekeeping*. 'On the stage,' he wrote, 'they are often film-struck or anaemic, and make audiences laugh by creeping dismally from wing to wing, sniffing or wiping their noses with the backs of their hands, leaving pails and mops to be tripped over, and uttering proverbial wisdoms with ridiculous mispronunciations.'[5] Edith Milton, an Austrian-Jewish refugee who arrived in England in 1938, remembered that the family she lived with had a daily char who did all the work. In Milton's autobiography, the woman is erased of all identifying features whatsoever. 'The charwoman, universally referred to as "the char" was an anonymous, shapeless and unmemorable bundle of clothes attached to a mop or a scrub brush, which she applied to the floors mid-morning after the two maids had got brass polish on them or the cook had spilled soup in the scullery.'[6]

When Mrs Miniver needs to find a char, she bravely makes a perilous journey to the 'towering, red-brick jungle' of slum dwellings on the wrong side of Chelsea. There she discovers the improbably cheery Mrs Burchett; many of Jan Struther's readers must have swooned with longing for such a paragon, 'obviously a pearl among women, a capable pearl'. The typical charwoman was sometimes a former servant who had known better days, had perhaps lost a husband in the war which left her no option but to go out for the daily 'rough' work. But Mrs Miniver was fortunate enough to find the charwoman that all her readers dreamed of, who might have stepped straight from a music-hall stage: an honest-as-the-day-is-long cockney who does not even char for money. Mrs Burchett chars because she *enjoys* it, thus relieving her mistress of any unpleasant feelings of guilt or embarrassment. 'I was just wishing summing like this would turn up,' Mrs Burchett tells Mrs Miniver. 'Not that I need to do cleaning at present, really, Burchett and the boys all being in work. In fact, my son, Len, 'e says I've no business to go out to work at all, when there's others wanting it more. But there – I don't know whatever I should do if I didn't. Every now and then I just feel I've got to 'ave a bit of a fling.'[7]

As part of her experience of the rough end of service Celia Fremlin made a study of charladies, taking on charring work to observe them closely, in the manner of an anthropological investigation into 'the vast, incomparable silence of chardom'. Before she embarked on her project she made a list of some of the assumptions made about chars, by that stage by far the most ubiquitous form of domestic service across the classes, by her contemporaries and acquaintances. 'Do they really drink out of their saucers?' asked one. And another: 'Haven't they a sort of superstition about cats being poisonous?' Many were contradictory: 'All the shouting and quarrelling that goes on must be terrible'; 'They're much nicer to each other than we are'; and: 'They all adore animals', was followed by: 'They've never been taught kindness to animals, that's the trouble.' Though Fremlin is sharp on the often self-deluding attitudes of the middle-class employers who were familiar to her, the deep and alien world of the poorest working class stumped her as absolutely as it had Mrs Wylde or the Provincial Lady. Here she relates

a Pinteresque dialogue during a chars' teabreak that is entirely
impenetrable to her:

> There, see, there's something funny under Mrs Biggs's chair.
> What is it?
> Dunno, funny, ain't it?
> Eh?
> Looks like a bit o' chocklit.
> That's funny.
> Pause.
> Pick it up and 'ave a look.
> That's right. Pick it up and 'ave a look.
> Lemme see, Mrs Biggs.
> What is it, Mrs Biggs?
> It's a bit o' chocklit. [8]

These educated adventures behind the baize door do not reveal
that life among the servants was always merry and subversive, but
there is nonetheless a spirit and gusto exposed by their investigations that makes Mrs Miniver's inner musings seem whimsical and
over-polished. 'I was crazy to go to London,' remembered Gretta
Guy, who wanted to live the high life in a big city.[9] Monica Dickens
enjoyed her riotous late evenings with a fellow maid polishing off
the dregs of the dress designer's party cocktails. She describes the
cheerful comings-and-goings in the basement of Hoover salesmen,
delivery boys and gas engineers. Doris, the general maid in a school-
master's household, had a passion for the theatre and went most
Saturday evenings to a show – though after watching an Edgar
Wallace thriller her employer had to escort her to bed as she was so
frightened of the dark landing.[10]

There were many servants too who had not been completely
bypassed by the political movements of the previous twenty years.
When Winifred Foley was reprimanded by her boss for talking to
one of the students when she was working as a kitchen-maid in a
teacher training college, she gave in her notice and 'sang the Red
Flag as loud as I dared among the clatter of pots and pans and

thought of my Dad and all the down-trodden workers of the world and nearly cried'.[11] The description by Margaret Powell of her life as kitchenmaid in the Cutlers' South Kensington kitchen has the effect only of making us feel how static, indolent and dull were the Cutlers' lives in comparison to those of Margaret and her fellow servants. 'You could generally get a job as a kitchen-maid,' wrote Powell; 'nowadays of course, they lay the red carpet for you, but even then there wasn't a queue for the job. The trouble with kitchen-maids, to anyone who wasn't a kitchen-maid, was that they were always larking about with the tradesmen. Like all the kitchen-maids I used to lark around with the tradesmen, especially the errand boys. They were one of the notable sights of London, the way they used to go through the streets with a bicycle laden sky-high, whistling all the latest tunes. And they were cheeky little devils.'[12]

Chapter 20

'Of Alien Origin'

In the late 1970s the oral historian Ronald Fraser attempted a psycho-exploration of his childhood half a century earlier by tracking down and interviewing all the remaining servants who had worked for the Frasers at Manor House in Amnersfield, Sussex. His father was a distant, sometimes brutal, foxhunting squire; his mother also distant but much younger, shy and diffident. In the course of his investigations, Fraser unearthed accounts and memories that, to his surprise, contradicted his own version of long-ago events. He was startled, for one thing, by the extent to which many of the servants employed by his parents had disliked and resented the family, telling him that it was only the dire unemployment of the late twenties and early thirties that sent them into service at all. The atmosphere was far pricklier and more politicised than the young Ronald had been able to understand at the time. The gardener told him how he had thought Fraser's high-handed father would have sacked him on the spot if he had known he voted Labour: 'We were no more than a heap of dirt in his eyes.' The former groom, who had left to join up in 1939, was still smarting that after seven years working at Amnersfield, the announcement of his departure aroused barely a reaction from Mrs Fraser.

Among the servants, two figures loomed large in Fraser's memory, both of them veiled in ambiguities. One of them was his German nanny Ilse, who was already *in situ* when he was born in 1930; the other was the family's Viennese cook, Nelly, who appeared in the Amersfield household just before the outbreak of war. Both women were refugees, part of the two main waves of refugee domestics who arrived in Britain between the wars. The first wave included Ilse, who came from Hamburg, where she had been forced into service in the late twenties by her mother's financial ruin. Ilse was just one of many German and Austrian girls, renowned all over Europe for their domestic industriousness, who were forced abroad to find work. The second wave was far larger and more influential, comprising Jewish refugees who secured visas to work in Britain as domestic workers as their only means of escaping Nazi-occupied Europe.

When Ronald Fraser tracked down Ilse, nearly fifty years later, she was still living in England. 'I felt myself to be more or less a servant,' she told him, describing her time working at Amersfield. 'Inferior, I don't know why. Perhaps it had to do with my past, with the fact that I had to go out to work,' she told him. 'I felt I shouldn't express opinions, that I had to hide my private life, be industrious, loyal and characterless.' Ilse was more educated than the other servants and they felt it; she eschewed the company of the servants' hall, spending her days off in London going to galleries and museums. Amersfield, in the rural Home Counties, she remembered as lonely, 'a world to itself', though she observed that the English treated their servants better than the Germans did. Often invited to dine with the Frasers in their dining room (yet another ambivalent aspect of Ilse's position which riled the other servants), she found the conversation between the beautiful, German-speaking Janey Fraser and her husband Alexander was almost exclusively concerned with horses and hunting. Life at Amersfield, thought Ilse, was a throwback, a very English kind of anachronism: 'All rather feudal, I thought, though Prussia was no doubt worse. The servants gave loyalty and devotion to their master and mistress because that was what was due from them. The young girls seemed quite happy in service without any cultural or even love life.'[1]

Conditions and pay for servants were poor in Germany, as Ilse had discovered, and Britain was therefore a popular destination for

young domestics. (It was not, however, the most popular destination: in the Netherlands, of 30,000 maids employed in 1930, 24,000
were German and 3,300 were Austrian.) The German maid was
praised all over Europe for her *Tüchtigkeit* (hard work and thor-
oughness) and particularly her reputation, born of necessity, for
being able to adapt herself to new circumstances. By the beginning
of the 1930s, a British domestic recruitment agency had opened a
branch in Vienna that led to an influx of Austrian maids. There
were no restrictions on this free traffic of domestics until 1931 when
the Ministry of Labour, keen in the middle of high unemployment
and an economic depression to encourage British girls into service,
closed the open door.

Refugee servants struggled for acceptance in British servants'
halls where they often became the very personification of the
Teutonic stereotype. 'She was a real regimental nurse, stomping
along,' is how one of Amnersfield's English maids remembered
Ilse. Compared to the cosy English nanny, 'she was a bit starchy,
like her uniforms. The other nannies were motherly, cuddly sort
of thing, there was an easy atmosphere around them.' Another
former housemaid found Ilse 'a bit military-like, you know', and
when Ilse asked her to sweep the nursery section of the stairs, she
deliberately swept the dust into the nanny's room: 'I meant to
show her that nobody's ever sat on me, even if I have to work for
my living.'[2] By the time Ilse left Britain in 1939, all the servants at
Amnersfield were convinced not only that she was a spy but that
they were sure they had overheard her making mysterious telephone calls or passing cryptically admiring comments about the
Führer.

By 1933 the government's restrictions on the free entry of
German and Austrian domestics were urgently revised in the light
of the political situation in Germany. British-Jewish leaders asked
the government to grant temporary asylum for German-Jewish
refugees in return for which they would undertake to guarantee
that no refugee would be a burden on the state. Householders wishing to employ a foreign domestic were then issued with a permit,
each household being granted a maximum of two permits each. To

avoid undercutting wages for homegrown labour, employers undertook to pay maids no less than £36 per annum.

Of the 55,000 refugees who arrived in Britain from Europe
during the 1930s, over half were women and over a third came to
work as domestic servants. By 1936 the number of foreign domestics coming to Britain had doubled to 8,849, and by 1937 it was
14,000. For at least 7,000 Jewish women, unable to enter Britain
unless they had secured a job, the Ministry of Labour scheme was a
lifeline. By 1938, when the events of *Kristallnacht* had alerted the
British government to the brutality of Nazi anti-Semitic legislation,
applicants no longer needed to line up jobs in advance and block
visas were issued to all women prepared to take up any domestic
work. (Marion Smith, a former refugee domestic originally from
Hamburg, told me that her employer in Sussex explained it was
Kristallnacht that convinced him to help get her mother out of
Germany – successfully, as it turned out.[3]) A third of all refugees
who came through the domestic service option arrived in 1938, in
the last months before Britain entered the war and the frontier was
finally closed. Among these was Cornelia, known as 'Nelly' (or
sometimes 'Cookie'), who was on the last train out of Vienna with
her young daughter Lisel. Nelly came to work at Amnersfield. It
was, she remembered, 'the most richest house I have ever seen in
England. My father was an antique dealer in Vienna and I understood correctly what was nice and what was not.'[4]

A network of friends and family in Britain was usually deployed
by refugees to find vacancies through agencies, or by placing advertisements in British newspapers; some wealthy Jewish families in
Britain acted as guarantors (children on the *Kindertransport*, the
British rescue mission that brought Jewish children out of Nazi-
occupied Europe in the final nine months before Britain entered the
war, were guaranteed to the sum of £50 per child). These criteria of
entry effectively excluded those without contacts and also those
who were unused to the reams of paperwork required for entry
visas. 'The effect of British official policy has been to exclude prac-
tically all working-class refugees,' pointed out the Labour MP Sir
Norman Angell in 1939, when just before the outbreak of war he

called for a lifting of all restrictions on incoming refugees.[5] Examples from the 'Refugee Advertisement' columns of the *Manchester Guardian* show how desperate the appeals for help had become by 1938. Applying via a contact in Hampstead Garden Suburb, a 'Tragic couple in Prague, must leave, urgently desire posts. Husband, chauffeur, gardener, handyman, wife a good cook and all household duties'; 'Hungarian solicitor's daughter, 29, cultured, trained musician, fluent French and German, desires hospitality as an au pair'; 'two Jewesses, must leave Prague, beg for Domestic Posts'; 'Who will take care of German-Jewish girl (13) until parents emigrate?'[6]

Hanna Fischl, from the small Czech town of Komotau in German-speaking western Bohemia, was twenty-five, fluent in German and English, and a secondary school teacher when she applied to enter Britain. With help from friends and colleagues with British connections, and after sending dozens of letters and applications to individuals, institutions, domestic employment agencies, newspapers, the Czechoslovak Committee for Refugees in London and the Ladies' League, she received on 15 January 1939 an acceptance for a nannying job in England. 'I want to shout and sing and jump for joy!' she told her diary. Her plan was eventually to go to Canada but Britain would be the first stop.[7]

Lore Groszmann, daughter of a Jewish accountant in Vienna, was aged just ten when Germany annexed Austria in 1938. Two months later, the Groszmanns' gentile maid Poldi had to leave them, for it was forbidden under the Nuremberg Acts of 1935 for Aryan women under forty-five to work for Jewish families. Shortly afterwards the SS commandeered the Groszmanns' flat and its contents. Moving from relative to relative, waiting for news of the visas that would take them out of Austria, the Groszmanns busied themselves learning practical skills that as professionals they had never imagined they would need. Jewish groups in Vienna had mobilised themselves in a remarkably short time and established workshops to teach practical crafts useful for survival in new countries. Lore's mother learned to translate her light, dinner-party cooking skills into ones suitable for large-scale catering; her father learned machine-knitting and leatherworking – he even took a course in massage. At the end of 1938, the Nazis closed down the workshops, but the lessons learned by those who attended them were to prove invaluable.

The Groszmanns finally managed to get Lore a place on the *Kindertransport*, one of 10,000 children to arrive in Britain in 1938. She was allotted a home with a Jewish family in Liverpool and from there she badgered the Domestic Bureau in London to grant her parents the domestic work permits that would enable them to join her. Her persistence paid off: the Groszmanns finally arrived, and travelled to rural Kent to take up jobs as cook and butler to the Willoughby family. They earned £1 a week between them and were given a small attic room above the Willoughbys' kitchen and a lumpy mattress to sleep on.[8]

The refugee domestics were largely middle class, professional, educated, many of them used to having servants of their own. It was easier for women to find domestic work, though many couples advertised themselves as available to work together as a cook-housekeeper and butler/driver/gardener. Twenty-five out of the twenty-seven couples advertising in the situations vacant columns of *The Times* on 22 December 1938 were from Austria. 'The highly specialised man seemed suddenly to be worthless and the psychological fact is that whatever may happen later will never eradicate the sense of frustration and bitterness once it takes root in the individual's heart,' wrote Gabrielle Tergit in the *Austrian Refugee Journal* after the war.[9] Lore Groszmann's elderly father was hopelessly unfit for manual work and struggled with the heavy trays he had to carry when waiting at table. Sidney and Elsa Schott, who arrived in Britain without a job lined up, could only find work as a domestic couple for a large house, for pocket money and keep. On their first day there, Sidney was given a white jacket and told to be the waiter at the family's Christmas party. When they later asked him where he had learned to do it so well, he replied: 'At the good hotels where we used to stay.'[10] Although a celebrated German actor took to his new role as a footman with style, dressing in full livery and playing the part to perfection, Walter Fulop, who was rescued by *Kindertransport* and who, like Lore, managed to get his parents out on a domestic permit, found 'the idea of my stepfather as a butler passed the realm of imagination'.[11]

The refugees found much was strange about the new country. They were amazed to discover, for example, that journalists, 'the lowest form of animal life in Germany', were 'highly respected' in England, as was 'business', recalled Gabrielle Tergit. They noted, too, the English suspicion of any education worn too obviously: 'a high degree of intelligence or scholarship is suspect. The tradition of the gentleman dilettante is the ideal.'[12] In Manchester, Inge Ader was nonplussed by the popularity of garden gnomes. But in many households, the presence of the new servants made for unease. At Amnersfield, remembered Betty, the youngest maid, Nelly the Austrian cook 'used to go around deep in thought ... Her face would be drawn and you could see how much she suffered.' Their attitude towards her was tinged with only a little more sympathy than it had been towards the German Ilse. 'She always wore a queer cap with strings to it, and some of her cooking I didn't take to. Peas and beans dripping in butter, wine in red cabbage which should have been pickled, and once she even cooked pea pods before they filled out.'[13]

Often it was just too difficult to make the effort to understand the sad-eyed newcomers with their histories of loss and terror – and an unthinking anti-Semitism was common. Margareta Burkill, secretary of a refugee committee in Cambridge, was amazed to find that 'dons' wives could treat somebody who was in every way as good as them in an absolutely terrible manner'.[14] Joyce Grenfell, while looking for a new cook, remarked to her diary: 'There's something a bit uncosy about a non-Aryan refugee in one's kitchen.'[15] Lotte Hümbelin, affronted by being treated in service as though she 'did not exist', later commented that it was in 'Democratic England' that she came to understand what class difference really meant. Embarrassed by the sight of Mr Groszmann, so frail and so obviously unsuited to waiting at table (he never could remember which side to serve the soup from), the Willoughbys chose simply to ignore their new domestics altogether. Mrs Groszmann's faltering attempts to explain that her husband, like Mr Willoughby, was an accountant, were met with frostiness. Mrs Willoughby thought herself generous: an egg was offered to the refugees for supper on their arrival, but they had to cook it themselves, and Mrs Groszmann, an accomplished musician, was permitted to play their piano, provided no-one else was in the house at the time.

The burden of gratitude was therefore sometimes difficult to bear and Mrs Willoughby's small acts of kindness were undermined almost in the same breath as they were bestowed. Lore was permitted to stay in the house when visiting from Liverpool but Mrs Willoughby insisted that she should not have the decent sheets that were used by the family, instead digging out some rust-stained old ones from the back of the linen cupboard. Other servants proved unfriendly for different reasons. Mrs Groszmann's efforts to befriend an English cook from a neighbouring family by making her an apple strudel were rebuffed when the visitor said she would eat nothing but Victoria sponge. One couple found their employer's lady companion 'cannot figure out where to put us socially. She is a bit put out.'[16] Hanna Fischl in Sheffield felt 'imprisoned by my ignorance and insecurity'. She observed that Mrs Anderson, mother of Hanna's fiendishly spoilt charge, was 'very particular about maintaining status'. It was complicated: 'When talking to subordinates, she refers to her daughters, aged seven and nine, as "Miss Jean" and "Miss Margaret", and that's the way the maid has to talk about them and address them . . . As nanny, I may call her Jean, but in talking about her to Nelly [the maid], I am to refer to this brat as "Miss Jean". Needless to say, I haven't yet let the words pass my lips!'[17]

Most painful of all was the revelation that many English families simply did not want to know about what was happening to Jews in Nazi-occupied Europe; some did not even know the difference between Germany and Austria. At Amnersfield, when Cookie fell into an unhappy reverie as the wireless played 'Tales from the Vienna Woods', the maid Betty shouted out: 'Blooming German rubbish!' Marion Smith's employer demanded that she wear a folksy German dirndl and apron. And Mrs Willoughby wondered why it was that the Groszmanns had not simply got on a train in Austria and 'come direct'. When they attempted to explain how difficult it was for the

Jews there, 'her eyes wandered. She did not want to know.' Several
refugees working in Jewish homes found that many British-Jewish
families were no less ignorant of what was happening in Europe.
Nathalie Huss-Schmickler went to work for a Jewish family in
Kensington and was given twenty-three rooms to clean – alone. 'My
hands were shaking,' she recalled, but her employer said to her: 'If it's
too much for her, I send her back to Hitler.'[18]

The new servants found themselves having to adapt to English
homes that seemed perversely old-fashioned in comparison to the
comfortable modern flats usual in German and Austrian cities.
English homes appeared to revel in discomfort and inconvenience.
Labour-intensive cleaning equipment and ancient lighting, heating
and cooking arrangements were a trial for the new domestics.
Central heating was common in German homes but still rare in
Britain. 'Our sponges froze in the washbasins,' remembered the
Schotts. Edith Argy even considered applying for a passport to
return to Vienna. 'I wasn't used to eating in the kitchen. Poor
though we were, we had all our meals, except perhaps for a hasty
breakfast, in the living room – nor was I used to eating alone. I
found the food very hard to swallow – quite tasteless; and I had
never had malt vinegar before. I missed my duvet. The thin blankets
seemed to provide no warmth at all.'[19]

Ilse Lewen from Wuppertal, working as a maid in Birmingham,
was surprised by her new employer when, 'on the first day, she
asked me to make toast. I looked for the electric toaster, but she
gave me a fork.'[20] Gertrude (Trudi) Ascher, a musician, was thirty-
nine when she took a job as a cook in a large house in Sussex. 'The
kitchen, and one room, in the attic, no comfort whatever, a difficult
job, as most things in the house were broken or dirty and I had not
the material for cleaning, especially for the kitchen, I had to cook
on an oil stove, the pans were always black with dirt. I had very
little hot water, no soap, no towels, really nothing to do a proper
job.'[21]

The food too was largely unappetising for those who had enjoyed
the best cuisine that central Europe had to offer. Kippers, tripe with
onions, custard powder and rehydrated soup were among the

horrors. Hanna Fischl's diet was typical: meat paste, beef dripping ('disgusting'), and enormous plates of boiled mutton, boiled cabbage and boiled onions (known as onion sauce); to say nothing of a 'rather solid something' known as 'a "bun"'. The new domestics had to remember that English tea was served with milk and teapots required tea cosies. Hanna watched in horrified fascination as Mrs Anderson showed her how to make coffee ('to demonstrate her *savoir faire*', Hanna thought): 'She filled a pot with a mixture of milk and water, added a heap of ground coffee and placed the mixture on the gas stove to boil, after which she stirred it all up and poured it through a sieve.'[22] For those lucky enough to be employed in the grander rural houses the food was generally in a different league: Cookie was amazed by the abundance of produce at Amersfield during the war, though Bronka Schneider, working with her husband on a freezing and remote Scottish estate, wondered why 'anyone could be bothered to eat something as tiny as a grouse'.[23]

Refugees who found compatriots living nearby formed groups and clubs. Mrs Groszmann and a former lawyer and his wife also working as a gardener/cook in Kent, would, remembered Lore, sit 'round the table talking, telling anecdotes of their preposterous "ladies". They spoke of their lost parents and relatives from whom they heard nothing beyond a rare twenty-five-word Red Cross letter. They sat and cried.'[24] Charlotte Singer, working as a char-woman in a block of bachelor flats in Birmingham, took in mending in her spare time. She waited for her husband Robert, a surgeon, to arrive in Britain, terrified all the while that it would be discovered that she had managed to slip into the country without a permit. She played the violin and 'the thing which most helped us to forget our sorrow was our music. We joined an orchestra of fellow refugees. I would rather have gone without my lunch to have the bus fare for this.'[25]

While some British families treated their refugee domestics as little more than cheap labour, as remarkable as the instances of unkindness and indifference are other stories of real tenderness and commitment. Cookie remembered receiving only consideration from the Frasers at Amnersfield. Her daughter Lisel's memories were more mixed, however: she recalled the children at the village school ostracising her and calling her 'Nazi'. Ronald Fraser, who by his own recollection was an unusually sensitive child, was shocked to learn that Lisel had found 'Master Ronnie' to be 'a very snooty boy who didn't say Good Morning, who wouldn't even answer when I spoke', who 'just pushed past'.[26] In some cases, children or adults taken in by British families became friends for life. Sometimes more than friends: family. When Hanna Fischl went to live with the Cunningtons in Manchester, she found everything changed. 'I feel like an adult human. It's wonderful,' she wrote in her diary.[27] Every evening she joined the family downstairs. The experience of Lily Crewe, who had arrived from Prague, aged just sixteen, in the nick of time in 1939 was also heartening. Her mother had sent her with a maid's uniform in black and white, with a cap, because she had heard that was what would be needed – 'but they weren't that sort of family at all ... anyhow, she laughed her head off when I unpacked it as you can imagine. We all ate in the kitchen, you know, I was one of the family.'[28] Then there is the story of Trudi Ascher and her friend Edith Wildorf, who arrived in Britain separately, then met and worked together as cook and parlourmaid for many years in a house in Windermere, 'where flowers were on the table and all was kindness and welcome'. In the evenings, Trudi played the piano for the family, Edith accompanying her on the violin.[29]

There was public hostility to the influx of foreign domestics, however, from many quarters. The National Union of Domestic Workers in 1938 protested that 'foreign nationals were making the bad conditions in domestic employment even worse'.[30] In the build-up to war, with tension mounting, the refugees began, to many people, to look like the very embodiment of the enemy within – and what is more, they were within the British home itself. Viscount Elibank told the House of Lords that women were well known to be much more effective spies than men: 'Today this country is ridden by domestic servants of alien origin ... And many of them are not trustworthy.'[31] No matter that of the 75,000 Germans living in Britain, 60,000 by this time were Jewish. The *Daily Mail* led the panic, calling for internment of enemy aliens. 'We are nicely honey-combed with little cells of potential betrayal,' warned the paper in April 1939; the 'paltriest kitchen-maid with German connections . . . is a menace to the safety of the country.'[32]

The government's internment policy was a muddle. At first categorised as low-threat C-grade aliens, domestics were not included in the first group of foreign nationals to be interned. In May 1940, however, with the tabloids ratcheting up the panic, C-class men were shunted up to B status and herded into holding camps to await transportation to the government's vast internment camp on the Isle of Man. When the Schotts moved into a more congenial home from the freezing house where they had been working as unpaid domestics, their previous employer informed the police that they were in the country illegally. Sidney was immediately interned and Elsa too was locked up, first in Winson Green Prison and then Holloway, for much of the time in solitary confinement; they were finally sent to the camp for married refugees on the Isle of Man. Women categorised as B-class, particularly domestics working in coastal areas, were forbidden to have in their possession maps, bicycles or vehicles of any kind. Bronka Schneider and her husband Joseph, stranded in the remote Scottish highlands, found the long walks that had been their chief pleasure were now forbidden. They were bitterly hurt when, although they had been given a C-class categorisation, their employers had locks fitted to all the doors, leaving them more or less trapped inside the servants' quarters.

The panic over the alien in the kitchen turned out to be short-lived, at least in part because the British housewife found herself prepared to take the risk of harbouring a Nazi spy if it meant help with the housework. By the start of 1941, of the 3,000 unemployed refugee women who had registered with the Domestic Bureau in London in November 1940, all but 500 were re-employed. The housewife was to be thwarted however as few of them returned to domestic service. Educated people with languages and clerical skills could now be more productively employed in war work and were much in demand. Mrs Smith, for example, went to work on the German-language newspaper that was run for refugees by the

Foreign Office. In the little community of Amnersfield, the Frasers were therefore fortunate to keep Cookie and she became increasingly close to the family.

But war changed everything: the fences would fall for ever between servant and master and between the big house and the village. It was, remembered Ronald Fraser, as if 'the Manor seemed suddenly to have opened its gates to the world'.[33]

PART V

A New Jerusalem

Chapter 21

'A New and Useful Life'

In 1942, aged fourteen, Christopher Falconer went to work on the local estate, still known in his rural community as the big house. He was to stay there for nearly fifteen years, one of seven gardeners 'and goodness knows how many servants in the house'. Interviewed twenty-five years later by Ronald Blythe in his portrait of the Suffolk village 'Akenfield', Christopher recalled a life that refused to bow to any alteration or interference from an outside world at war. Still wearing the green baize apron of the eighteenth-century gardener, Christopher and his colleagues played their roles in the elaborate pantomime of a great country house, while all around them Britain was mobilised for change. The gardeners drove a barrow of weeds half a mile round the grounds rather than risk being spotted by any guest or member of the family sitting on the terrace; the maids still turned their faces to the wall if they encountered their employers. 'Ladyship', as their employer was known, always graciously accepted compliments on the magnificent flower arrangements in the house, renewed every day, the components of which were grown, picked and arranged by someone else; the gentry never had to witness the fading or dying of a flower: 'It was as if, for them, flowers lived forever. It was part of the magic of their lives.'[1]

For 'Lordship and Ladyship' it was their patriotic duty to see that not by one jot would 'that dreadful man' in Germany change the feudal order of their piece of England. When the dining-room table was shuddered out of place by a stray bomb, the butler simply replaced it and the matter was never mentioned again. These islands of wilful tradition stuck the war out all over Britain. 'They seemed to think things shouldn't change, war or no war – which made me angry as I knew how my mother was struggling at home,' remembered Audrey King, who became a house-parlourmaid in 1939, of her employers, who from their Sussex home could watch the Battle of Britain raging overhead.[2] While most estates changed absolutely and for ever in the course of the Second World War, a few managed to continue as if nothing had happened. In one large country house, air-raid arrangements in the spacious network of cellars were organised along strict lines of precedence: 'First cellar: for the elderly owner and her guests; Wilton carpet, upholstered armchairs, occasional tables, a ration of best bitter chocolate, a bottle of expensive brandy, petit-beurre biscuits, thermos jugs, packs of cards, a Chinese lacqueur screen concealing an eighteenth-century commode. Second cellar: for female servants; wicker-work armchairs, an oak table, an old phonograph (complete with horn), a half-bottle of cheap brandy, plain biscuits, tea-making apparatus, a Japanese paper screen concealing sanitary accommodation of a bedroom type. Third cellar: for chauffeur, boot-boy, gardeners and stray neighbours; a wooden bench, wooden table, an electric bell connected with first cellar in case owner should wish to summon masculine moral support; water biscuits. No brandy, no screen.'[3]

How English class distinctions would or could survive the enforced and jostling proximities that were most people's experience of wartime was a popular media theme. In *Punch*, in 1939, a cartoon showed a tin-hatted butler at the door of an Anderson shelter, addressing a plus-foured couple: 'If you would wait on the steps sir, I will see if his Lordship is at home.'

In its own idiosyncratic fashion, the Royal Family led from the top, staunchly taking upon themselves the duties of coping with food shortages and other discomforts. The Queen Mother moved for the duration of the war to Badminton House, home of the Duke and Duchess of Beaufort, bringing with her a slimmed-down retinue of fifty courtiers and elderly servants, each wearing siren suits bearing the royal cipher. The Beauforts were relegated to the status of guests in their own home, Queen Mary demanding that the entire household suffer patriotic privations: napkins had to languish unwashed for a whole week (Queen Mary had a silver napkin ring made for this specific purpose) and Her Majesty became an enthusiast for Woolton Pie, the Food Ministry's notorious recipe for using up leftover vegetables. She took a keen interest in the husbandry of the Badminton woods, where logs were chopped for use in a local barracks, and to save petrol was taken there every afternoon on a bathchair resting on a farm cart that was carried aloft by her two chauffeurs.[4]

At the outbreak of war, of the nation's 4.8 per cent of resident servant-employing households, the largest country houses still took a lion's share of the numbers, leaving the smaller house struggling on with, at most, a cook-general or a daily char. It took some time for establishments to realise it was no longer tenable to keep able-bodied men, and women, at work in domestic situations. In the first weeks of the war *The Times* still carried confident advertisements for new staff by 'one gentleman (titled)', for example, in SW1 who kept twelve servants and wanted another.[5] In the Home Counties, two elderly ladies with a staff of nine wanted a third housemaid. As the war progressed and servants were called up or left voluntarily, most large houses that had not been requisitioned by the War Office or other institutions were manned by a skeleton staff at most. When James Lees-Milne was invalided out of active service he travelled round the great houses of England on behalf of the National Trust, finding most of them in varying stages of decreptitude, with state rooms shrouded in dust sheets and once immaculate gardens given over to weeds.

Following the introduction of conscription for women in 1941, employers of domestic servants were required, if they wanted to keep them, to submit a written justification to the Ministry of Labour. Most middle-class families were permitted one servant, but a large household might, at a pinch, claim for two or three. The resulting allotment seems often to have been startlingly uneven. At

Knole in Kent, for example, there remained just one housemaid to clean 250 bedrooms, yet when Jean Arnold went into service in 1943, aged fourteen, it was for 'the last surviving of three brothers' living in a large house in Kent where 'there was a butler, a cook and kitchen-maid and the housemaid and me'.[6] Many employers tried to cling on to staff, believing it a privation far worse than petrol rationing or butter shortages to be forced to live without them. Kay Allsop, a Mass Observation diarist, reported a conversation with Molly, a parlourmaid of her acquaintance, who had gone to the employment exchange to register for war work only to find that her employer had already telephoned the exchange and ordered them to 'let her off' for her 'own good', informing them that Molly's eyesight was under threat. Molly held her ground, writing to her employer later: 'It was cleaning your silver, I said, ruined my eyes, not the work.'[7] Nonetheless, in some rural areas old prejudices died hard: Jean Arnold's parents were resistant to her doing any other kind of work. 'I was told that if I went into service I would work for gentlemen but if I did shop work as I wished I would have to serve any old tramp.'[8]

Joyce Helps had gone into service in 1937 aged fourteen at Warleigh Manor, near Bath, home of a Miss Skrine. It was a defiantly old-fashioned establishment, remembered Joyce. No electricity, no running water in the bathrooms and sixteen bedrooms in which fires had to be kept lit to prevent damp. The estate was entirely patriarchal, the butler ringing a rope which in turn rang a bell on the roof which signalled lunch hour for the estate workers. 'The parties ended in 1939,' wrote Joyce, and the house was filled with evacuee families. 'There were very few guests, the parlourmaid left as she married the butler and he worked in the garden as well as the house. No more kitchen-maids, only the cook, who came in daily. I felt that I was all alone, looking after my lady and the big Manor.'[9] Shortly afterwards, Joyce herself went to work for the Admiralty.

Some foresaw early on the end of the primacy of the English landed estate, and with it the systemic hierarchy of servants that it supported. As early as 1939, the author of an article for the *Women's*

Institute Magazine envisaged a revitalised new Britain emerging from the wartime mixing-up of communities: the evacuees and workers who were moving about the country and also the presence of German and Austrian refugee maids. But the author also thought that the new uses to which country houses were being put, by banks, insurance companies, government offices and so on, would shift the locus of attention from cities to the regions. In this way, the shape of things would change and the great edifice of England's landed hegemony would be shattered for ever. 'Some of the great houses of England, in which no private person will ever again be able to live, might in this way find a new and useful life,'[10] the magazine observed.

The owners of many houses were turned out altogether or consigned to a single wing, while their home was requisitioned by sundry government ministries, barracks or intelligence-gathering operations. The buildings were often roughly treated by their new inhabitants and misrule descended where once there had been well-managed order. Reverence for the past was no longer as urgent as securing the future; it was not uncommon, in those houses that had no central heating, for the new residents to simply break up antique furniture, staircases and panelling and use them for firewood. Of the bustling townships that had once been the servants' halls of large houses, what remained resembled ghost towns, manned only by the very young, the very old or the chronically unfit. When Evelyn Waugh visited his wife's family home at Pixton Park in Somerset in 1939 he found, 'a household of fifty-four, including twenty-six evacuated children, six spinster "helpers" and most unexpectedly a neighbouring doctor and his wife; he had been struck by a mortal disease and had been brought here to die'.[11] Miss Ellery was cook-housekeeper during the war in a house that took in soldiers and evacuees: the young evacuees moved into the servants' rooms at the top and the servants moved into the guest rooms. In Laura Talbot's novel *The Gentlewoman* (written just after the war), Miss Bowlby, an obsessively genteel governess, finds employment in a country house now run by an assortment of misfits and is horrified that her employer's secretary is given one of the state rooms to sleep in.

The first large-scale evacuation of children, mothers and moth-
ers-to-be, Operation Pied Piper, began two days before Britain
declared war on 1 September 1939. For the most part it was argued
that it was better to put working-class children in working-class
homes, but pressure of numbers resulted in several large houses
being turned into huge evacuee dormitories. At Lyme Park a large
portion of the house became a war nursery. 'The billiard table in
the long gallery was covered over and they used it for the children's little night clothes. They were all labelled,' wrote one of the
surviving servants.[12] Tales abounded of evacuee misbehaviour.
James Money, working for a local evacuee station near Tunbridge
Wells, wrote that six East End boys 'of extreme wickedness' had
confined the owners of a large house to the servants' hall, 'then
proceeded to rearrange and redecorate the main part of the house
with obscene murals in soot'.[13] It was reported that bed-wetting
and vermin were besetting problems among younger evacuees.
The press whipped up a picture of classes locked in uncomprehending conflict. 'Their Ladyships and Butler Delouse their
Guests' ran a headline in *Life* magazine.[14] It also gave the mislead-
ing idea that most evacuees had been transplanted to stately homes
when, in fact, the majority of them were taken in by poor or
middling households.

Evacuees themselves were sometimes used as unpaid domestics.
In London, Dolly Davey was tipped off that her evacuated daughter, aged six, was being used for housework. She paid a surprise visit
to her in Plymouth and 'found her being treated like a housemaid.
She was in a mob-cap and apron, with a dustpan and brush in her
hand, when I met her.'[15] Evacuees were more of a burden for smaller
middle-class homes – and for those servants that still remained in
them. In fact, 'my maid will leave' was a popular excuse used to get
out of taking in any more children. Wild stories fuelled the general
opinion, widely put about by the press, that taking in evacuees was
an example in war of almost unparalleled heroism. Yet, wrote the
Member of Parliament, T. M. Sexton, 'people who in peaceful times
like jubilees and coronations are very much in the limelight, but
now when they have been called upon to do a real job of patriotic

work they have hardened their hearts and barred their doors to the evacuees from the poor areas'.[16]

Adapting to war was particularly difficult for those older women for whom the standards of a different age were hard to relinquish. Philip Mason's elderly mother 'wanted the house to run as it had always been and it caused her irritation amounting to distress if the Georgian silver teaspoons did not appear on the tea tray with the right Crown Derby teacups'.[17] But it was difficult too for many servants of the old school, whose working lives had been given over to the routines of the bell, of the unquestioned allegiance to the rule of 'knowing your place'. Mollie Panter-Downes, who wrote a weekly letter on English wartime life for *The New Yorker*, captured just such a discombobulated figure in her 1943 short story 'Cut Down the Trees'. In it, the patrician Mrs Walsingham adapts to change with spirit, even enjoyment, when her house is taken over by Canadian soldiers; it is Dossie, her elderly maid, now the only remaining servant, who is appalled: everything that gives her life dignity, derived from the dignity with which she invests the lives of the family she has served for so many years, has been abruptly taken from her. Dossie hates it that Mrs Walsingham no longer dresses for dinner – and eats that dinner in the kitchen. Mrs Walsingham even gives Dossie a trolley to use on those occasions when the too-casual Canadian officers come to dine, to wheel in the dishes that would once have been carried by a fleet of footmen.

The values of behaviour and form that Dossie thinks she has imbibed from her 'betters' are confounded by the realisation that her 'betters' no longer value them themselves. Panter-Downes understood how, in many ways, it was the Dossies who lost most in the social changes of wartime. For what is Dossie if she is not a servant? What is the value of her life's dutiful labour if it can be shrugged off so easily in the name of the new? When Mrs Walsingham's son comes to visit the house on leave, Dossie waits for him in the evening, her day's work not done until he has gone to bed. 'He was aware that Dossie was watching him anxiously, the old woman's eyes seemed to implore him to play their game for a little while longer, to pretend that things were just as they used to be, that their world, which had come to an end, could still be saved.'[18]

Yet assumptions about servants being part of the everyday fabric still dominated the general view of domestic life well into the war. When Eileen Whiteing opened her newly purchased diary for 1942, among recipes such as sugar-free Christmas pudding with grated potato, she was amused to see in its opening pages 'a section entitled "Household Law: Domestic Servants", which contained much useful information as to the engagement, dismissal and general treatment of servants – which only goes to show that even in the middle of war, some things had not changed!'[19] Women who had never had to do their own housework found themselves for the first time confronted by an inadequacy that often surprised them.

'It was as she stood in Mrs Loman's Registry Office for Domestic Servants that Rose Fairlaw suddenly realised what a useless and helpless woman she was. Up till that moment she had always assumed vaguely that she was a busy and useful member of society.' The opening paragraph of Winifred Peck's 1942 novel *House-Bound* sees her over-refined, otherworldly heroine embarking on the great adventure of managing alone her large old house in Edinburgh. Just as Rose begins to sink under the strain of the work, the employment agency sends her help in the form of a professional career servant, the former upper-servant Mrs Childe, who undertakes to train Rose in everything needed to make her a 'passable lower servant'. For the first time Rose sees how the upper-middle-class home, with its constant demands of perfection, order and regularity, is only maintained by backbreaking hard work: 'You know one dusts tables, but did you realise one ought to dust cornices and doors and tops of furniture and stair balustrades? I've put away most of the silver, but what there is goes black on me every other day. And the brasses! That doesn't just mean ornaments but all the door handles and the front door.'[20]

The writer and poet Nesca Robb worked on the Women's Employment Federation in 1940. She found that by far the most difficult women to place in employment were those middle-aged, intelligent and educated women, like Rose Fairlaw, who had no previous training or experience of work of any kind – except running a home which was itself cleaned and ordered by servants. Many had married young and never given a thought to future vicissitudes. Now the war, and its attendant money struggles, had thrown these women on the job market. The only work for which they were even remotely suited was that of a housekeeper in a private house, and those posts were few and far between. 'Neither marriage nor private means give any guarantee that a woman will never have to work for her living. The instability of human fortunes is more marked than it has ever been in our lifetimes; and the scales are weighted more heavily against the unqualified,' wrote Robb.[21]

Those accustomed to domestic hard labour, having a practical advantage, came to the fore in wartime. As is the case with the fictional Mrs Childe, the skills of career servants often proved invaluable. By 1942, the former kitchen-maid, parlourmaid and housemaid Jean Rennie, with her experience not only of cooking for large numbers but of budgeting, cleaning, ordering stocks and organising, was given the job of managing a large Red Cross canteen in Greenock for American servicemen. The hated costume of menials was in many cases now replaced by a uniform that demanded respect, and girls wearing the livery of war work were hailed as patriotic heroines.

As Winifred Peck's niece and fellow novelist Penelope Fitzgerald has noted, it is the routines of domestic life that Rose Fairlaw finds so irksome, so debilitating to the inner life. 'The endless day-in, day-outishness of her new life' had once been the comforting background to the well-ordered life.[22] Yet for those brought up with the endless 'day-in, day-outishness' of domestic service, routine was second nature. Most women began to look helpless in the face of their servants' superior practical skills and experience. When Frances Partridge's cook Joan left in 1941 to work in a munitions factory, Frances was thrown into confusion: 'If only I could cook!' – but she taught herself to do so with some success. At Cliveden, Lady Astor took up knitting socks for her sons at the front. Rose Harrison recalled: 'I was sent out to buy the most expensive wool and then had to cast it on to the knitting needles so that she could begin. She was hopeless at it, it was comic to watch her.'²³

Edith Milton, a young German-Jewish refugee from Karlsruhe, living with her foster parents the Harveys in Swansea, witnessed the sudden shattering of routine in the English home. There was 'a sense of sparseness, of things getting smaller, narrow and more dangerous', she remembered. Mrs Harvey, like so many middle-class women, had had no acquaintanceship with cooking except for the large copy of Mrs Beeton's *Book of Household Management* that, unread, had collected dust on her kitchen shelf since she was first married. But Edith noted that the habits which had character-ised life with servants continued even in their absence; indeed no-one could imagine life without the shape and discipline of domestic life, a discipline sharpened as the shortages started to bite. After the servants had left the Harvey household for war work, 'the routine of the household remained, dictating the life we lived as if it had been written on a stone tablet – not only because it had become habitual but because, like the Ten Commandments themselves, it made a great deal of sense. I suppose all of us who grew up there – in that household, in that culture, at that time – still find ourselves vacuuming weekly, having our three daily meals more or less on schedule, and changing the bed linen at regular but rather distant intervals as behoves those without washing machines.'²⁴

For many in a new generation of women, however, the sudden end of the age of service came as a relief, a cessation of a relationship that had grown uncomfortable. Many women had felt burdened by the presence of employees to whom they continued to feel an obligation but who represented arcane social rules and demarcations they no longer fully understood or cared about. Family relationships in smaller houses were freed at last from the pall of inhibition that had often hung over them: the important things that were left unsaid in case the servants would hear; the sudden silences that descended when the doorknob rattled or the tea tray was heard coming up the stairs. Many women found within themselves practical resources they had never thought they would need to acquire. 'My husband went to India and I was left with five children including an evacuee and a four-week-old baby. I found that all the things that he used to do, I had to do, I had to take over and pay the bills; look after the shopping and attend to all sorts of things that he'd done for me previously and manage the money,' remembered Margaret Wheeler.[25] And for the young, middle-class, married woman, it no longer seemed entirely strange or indeed humiliating to be having to do one's own housework. In fact, in some ways it was exciting, exhilarating, liberating. Elizabeth Jordan, who after the war would herself become a professional cook (and an author), found that the war released in her practical abilities and hard grafting of which she had never imagined herself capable: 'When during the war, Fiona and Elizabeth were born, it was as a matter of course that I looked after them single-handed, washing, scrubbing, cooking and gardening.'[26]

The shared experience of utility clothing, rationing, petrol shortages and, above all, work began slowly to level the tussocks of social difference that lay between the classes. Siren suits, after all, were unflattering on everyone. It was increasingly difficult to tell the difference between tailor-made and off-the-peg fashions. Rose Macaulay, working in bombed-out London in 1941, wrote in *The Listener* of the delightful freedom of living easily in slacks, woollen stockings and sturdy boots, and, above all, of not dressing for dinner. 'It saves trouble, money, time and gives us lazy, go-as-you-please feelings.'[27] Food-rationing books were introduced in the first months of 1940, special needs identified by different-coloured covers. Food was, for the most part, a social leveller: four ounces of butter and bacon, three and a quarter of cooked ham and twelve ounces of sugar constituted one adult's basic weekly ration. Most people had to endure extraordinary food-like concoctions such as Prem, Tang, Spam and Mor, and all the other dismal delights of wartime tinned and processed foodstuffs. Wartime privations did pull people together, and in the confines of small houses, employers and their servants were equal in rations and adversity. 'What a kind, loving Kate,' wrote Mrs Milburn, a housewife in Leamington Spa, in her diary when her housemaid returned from a visit to her breast-feeding sister with orange juice and milk from the sister's extra ration of seven pints a day to supplement the meagre one pint of the Milburns' allowance.[28]

Many women relished the opportunity to test their ingenuity after years of issuing orders to cooks. Theodora Fitzgibbon, who was then an artists' model in Chelsea but later became a celebrated food writer, was an expert at cooking rabbit: 'braised rabbit in dark beer with prunes, which made it taste vaguely like pheasant, or with cider and tomatoes; or with curry spices and paprika; or stuffed and baked rabbit, when we would pretend it was chicken; and, if it was very young, Peter would joint it and we would fry it in a crisp batter'.[29] At Carradale, Scottish home of the Mitchisons, they were lucky enough to grow much of their own food. Carradale, a large house with no source of electricity but a small generator, continued to maintain during the war a staff of ten, which included a shifting population of indoor servants. Upstairs and downstairs, or as Naomi Mitchison put it, 'Dining Room' and 'Kitchen', were not always at one on practical details, Dining Room apparently being more amenable to the vegetarian option than Kitchen. On 3 August 1940, Naomi Mitchison wrote: 'We have to cut down on cooking fat; but at present we have hardly any puddings other than jellies with our own fruit in them, water ice made with fruit pulp, occasional curds, and any amount of raw fruit. We don't have meat or (our own or gift) fish more than once a day, unless there are sausages for breakfast, when we may have it twice. Sometimes "Dining Room" has only vegetables, usually with cheese sauce, for meals, but "Kitchen" doesn't like that.'[30]

In 1940, with a new baby on the way, the Mitchisons employed a young Australian woman to run the house leaving Naomi time to devote to the wartime diaries – one million words of them – which she wrote for Mass Observation. Mitchison was beleaguered by a complicated relationship with her servants: she wanted their friendship, to share their relationship troubles, their aspirations, yet needed their labour to facilitate the freedoms she enjoyed as a left-wing, thinking woman, and to give her time to work on her literary projects. She both dreaded their leaving to take up war work and, often, encouraged it.

At Amnersfield, Janey Fraser, before the war so anxious and detached from the running of the house, donned a pair of old

overalls and learned (with great success) to keep chickens and milk
cows. Amnersfield breathed a new air of camaraderie. The Frasers'
groom, Bert, remembered Janey in those years: she 'changed so
much, so good I don't know how to describe it. Matey, pally, it was
like talking to the missus or my brother. She was a lot happier than
before . . . we all mucked in together sort of thing.'[31] Up and down
the social scale, the accoutrements of deference began to fall away.
As Jessie Cox, who had gone into service in 1934, and during the
war worked in an aircraft factory, observed: 'What a change!
Someone once said 1939 was the end of an era, and it was. Servants,
what few were left, became treasures rather than drudges.'[32] When
Mary Ann Mathias went to work as a housemaid for Doctor and
Mrs Mere in 1939, she addressed the doctor, as she would have
expected to do, as 'Sir' and his wife as 'Madam' and they called her
Mary Ann. But at some unspecified point during the war, she started
to call her employers Dr and Mrs Mere and they in turn referred to
her Mrs Matt. They used to do the washing-up together: 'all three
of us in the kitchen – we had a lovely time there'.[33] When, after the
war, Mrs Mere died, Mrs Matt stayed on and looked after the doctor
for many years, until he too died. By that time, she called him Dick
and he called her Mary.

In 1942, Winifred Peck had described, in the figure of Rose
Fairlaw's stuffy, ineffectual husband Stuart, the type of Englishman
who cannot conceive of life without a perfectly cooked breakfast.
Stuart is the hapless representative of an England stumbling into
oblivion in contrast to an American army major who sings the
liberating New World pleasures of refrigerators, dishwashers,
thermostats, gas stoves and superior plumbing. 'Unless you get
down to fundamentals and realise that your old world is as dead as
a flayed horse, I don't see that you have much hope of winning this
particular war,' the Major tells Rose.

The war had struck the final blow to the life of the English great
houses, their upholding of traditions whose source and purpose
had been long forgotten. Those houses that still managed to retain
such a life had become an insular parody of themselves and, to most
people, the servanted comforts of the past seemed as ghostly and

unreal as a stage set. Towards the end of the war, Jean Rennie found herself overseeing the catering for the offices of a government ministry situated in a house in Eaton Square, a few doors down from the house she had worked in during the 1920s and identical in every particular. Jean wrote:

> I cannot describe the feeling, a kind of ghostly shiver, as I walked in the front door and up to my office, which had once been the drawing room. There was still the remains of the white fireplace, one or two white doors, tall and wide and ornate ceilings. It was physical pain in my heart – *not* I must hasten to add a nostalgic pain – to go down to the basement where we kept rows and rows of files. Here was the servants' hall, here the butler's pantry, this dark little room was either the butler's room or the cook's. And this, this dark dungeon, with the long dresser and this great ugly stove, and the now rickety wooden table, worm-eaten, had been the kitchen where I, and others like me, had quite literally sweated away an existence that was accepted as 'that station in life'.[34]

Chapter 22

The Housewife Militant

'No-one in wartime can quite escape the illusion that when the war ends things will snap back to where they were,' wrote the novelist Sylvia Townsend Warner in 1946.[1] Few in 1945 imagined that the end of the Second World War would bring about an immediate transformation of living conditions in Britain, but the pre-war normality that people remembered and many longed for seemed inordinately slow to snap back into place. The years of the late 1940s were drab and pinched for housewives, characterised by disappointment and frustration. It is one thing to scrimp for victory, quite another to have to continue scrimping when you are the victorious. The ideal of the resourceful housewife had been one of the boosters of wartime morale. 'The nation at war is a thrifty housewife,' wrote the author of a Ministry of Labour pamphlet. But now that hostilities were over, eking out a thin supply of food substitutes was dreary rather than patriotic. 'Something has gone from a nation that thinks of "custard" as a concoction of coloured cornflower,' was the conclusion of a dispirited correspondent to *Housewives Today*.

After 1945 rationing became even tighter than during the war, exacerbated by a run of terrible harvests combined with freakishly bad winter weather with flooding and storms. In 1947 the average adult was reduced to a weekly three ounces of bacon, one and a half of cheese, six of butter and marge, one of cooking fat, eight of sugar, two pints of milk and one egg. Hated whale steaks were still on the menu at the Lyons Corner Houses and by the late 1940s attempts to convince people that tinned snoek, an aggressive, spiny tropical fish, was an adequate substitute for sardines, were met with weary disbelief. Fresh bananas, grapes, pineapples and oranges were still scarce and exotic. Queuing for basic foods took hours out of each day, and organising rations, quotas and allowances involved interminable form-filling and 'a tremendous amount of government interference . . . bread tickets, food tickets, clothes tickets, petrol tickets . . . My mother used to say there were snoopers everywhere and there was a ticket or a docket for everything,' said Mrs Mary Blakey, looking back forty years later.[2]

As it became clear that the end of the war would not bring a quick end to food shortages, British housewives mobilised themselves quite unexpectedly in 1945 into a formidable campaigning force under the leadership of Mrs Irene Lovelock, the wife of an Anglican clergyman in suburban London, who had been stung into action by the sight of women and children queuing yet again for food in the bitter cold of that year's winter. Members of Mrs Lovelock's British Housewives' League, who soon numbered in their thousands, campaigned against attempts to reduce still further the bread ration and even to remove for ever that ghastly wartime staple, dried egg. Splinter groups such as the 'Anti-Queue Association' were formed, taking their campaigning methods from the example of the suffragettes: Mrs Mary Were, for instance, appealed through the pages of the *Daily Sketch* for 'food protest officers'. Addressing a meeting of 700 women in Liverpool in 1946, League member Mrs Hill summed up the prevailing mood: 'We are suffering from mental exhaustion, irritation and frustration. The smiling mother of yesterday is the bad-tempered mother of today, and the understanding partner is now the nagging wife . . . we are underfed, under-washed, and over-controlled.'[3] The League had limited success when it came to shortages: bread, tea and jam rationing was not lifted until 1952 and a year later, the sweet ration, to the joy of children of everywhere, was also removed. The same year saw the end of the sugar ration, the egg ration and in 1954, fats, cheese and meat came off the list.

In the background there was the ever-present problem of domestic service. Were housewives always to battle alone at the frontline of domestic life? Could domestic service ever again be made a desirable job option, even a career? In 1940, Celia Fremlin had observed that 'the shop-girl or factory hand tends to regard the lifelong domestic worker not as an inferior but a crank. She tends to feel about her something as a normal business man might feel about a nudist colony or group of holy rollers.'[4] Post war that mood intensified. The government had attempted to persuade women and girls to engage in domestic war work by employing a booming home-front rhetoric of patriotic national domesticity. Domestic workers were called to be surrogate mothers in the service of the state. Motherhood, the highest of all female callings, was the guiding spirit in hospitals for the war wounded, in nursing homes, convalescent hostels and nurseries for the sick or with the elderly and children with handicaps. Even during the war, measures were taken to promote the idea that well-regulated domestic service would be a healthy career option after the conflict was over, a job whose representatives could hold their heads high. 'Wouldn't you agree that this job of looking after a home, if well done, is as important as any job in an office, shop or factory?' wrote the Labour MP Elaine Burton in 1944, calling for a minimum wage and a new programme of qualifications to encourage girls to return to domestic service. 'Let us get away from the old picture of eternal drudgery,' she added optimistically; 'there is more in running a house than cooking and washing-up.'[5]

As early as 1943, Ernest Bevin, then Minister of Labour, began to address the problem of post-war domestic service, primarily the inclusion of private domestic workers in the unemployment insurance from which they had been excluded after the First World War. Like his Ministry of Labour predecessors in the 1920s, Bevin commissioned a report, which turned out to be startlingly similar in its conclusions to those of the 1923 report: there must be regularisation of service, proper wages and the discipline by law of employers

whose servants' care and conditions fell below the required standards. The authors of the report, published in 1945, were Violet
Markham and Florence Hancock, old hands at the thorny questions of the mistress, the working woman and the slavey.

The two women themselves embodied a new spirit of fellowship among women of different backgrounds. Florence Hancock,
then in her late forties, was the daughter of a Wiltshire cloth
weaver, and had been all her working life a highly effective Labour
and trade union activist, and during the war the chief woman
officer of the Transport and General Workers' Union. She was one
of fourteen children and left home at the age of twelve to take up
work washing up in a café. But it was her employment in a non-
unionised factory where she was the only woman member of the
strike committee that sparked Florence Hancock's political
engagement. Violet Markham was twenty years older than her
colleague, a patrician with wealthy industrial roots (she was the
granddaughter of Sir Joseph Paxton) and an indefatigable believer
in the duties and responsibilities of privilege. She had been brought
up in the luxury and well-staffed comfort of Tapton House.
Neither woman had children (Florence Hancock married for the
first time a stevedore and fellow trade unionist in 1964, at the age
of seventy-one) though Markham 'never wavered in her belief
that women's chief joy in life was procreation'.[6] The provision of
childcare to women of all classes was central to the Markham and
Hancock report's conclusions.

In spirit, somewhat nostalgically, the 1945 'Report on Domestic
Service' paid tribute to Sir William Blackstone's 'first relationship':
'service between master and man and mistress and maid is the age-
long relationship stretching far back into history'. But its authors
understood that this relationship, while not quite dead, was in
urgent need of updating if the demands, not only of the war-weary
housewife, but of the professional woman, were to be met with
domestic support. Their report proposed the creation, capitalising
on the wartime status of women in the services, of a 'Domestic
Service Corps' of trained, uniformed girls working under a set of
rules governing membership and employment.

Like their 1923 predecessors, Hancock and Markham attempted to address too the education of both sides of the relationship, 'if the mistresses were thoughtless and inconsiderate, the maids were care-less and untrustworthy', and ways in which the insulting stereo-types of a slavey, 'with her cap askew and smut on her nose', could be banished. Their report recommended the regulation of hours and terms of service, the establishment of Ministry of Labour employment exchanges and a scheme of registered home-helps run by local authorities who would place them where they were most needed; trade union protection would be extended at last to private domestic employees. Their final recommendation was the founda-tion of a National Institute of Houseworkers where proper instruc-tion, examinations and qualifications, as well as the rigorous vetting of prospective employers, would ensure that domestic service was known as 'an entirely honourable and self-respecting institution for any woman and an occupation that fulfils an essential service to the community'.[7] Their most radical insight, however, was that work-ing-class women might themselves need some domestic service: that if they were provided with childcare they might be able to go out to work, perhaps even to give the professional woman some help in the house. For if women were to take advantage of the freedoms and experiences the war had brought them, then they could not be expected to bear the burden of domestic work as well. As Markham wrote in her autobiography: 'Women in large meas-ure fail to recognise how much their own future as independent beings turns on finding some solution to the problem of domestic help. For if all alike, whatever their individual capacities and gifts are forced unaided to grind their own corn and make their own oil – tasks that never fall to the men – neither in art, literature, nor the professions can they hope to find time to attain excellence.'[8]

Markham and Hancock's report also suggested the elevation of the private status of housework to a public service, a duty of citi-zenship. On the Institute of Houseworkers' courses, there were to be classes in specialist cooking, training by dietitians and nutrition-ists, and 'some measure of general and civic education, including the study of literature, economic history, citizenship etc., to be given by visiting tutors'. The prospect of a well-read housemaid with an expertise in vegetarian cookery was alluring to some readers, but others thought it was getting the relationship off to a bad start. Elaine Burton's 1944 proposal of a 'Domestic Workers' Charter' was set upon by furious housewives who complained bitterly to Mrs (later Baroness) Burton that the balance was unfairly weighted in favour of servants: 'It was all very well to talk of servants having a bad time, but before this war they could do as they liked. You gave them good furniture, wireless in their rooms and exactly the same food as yourself. What did they do? They broke the wireless, upset ink on the bedclothes and smashed your best china. If you said a word they walked out. Oh, no! Just before the war, maids were at a premium and knew it, surely in any scheme, the mistress must be safeguarded.'[9]

Few people, however, can have been entirely prepared for the extent to which working-class aspirations had changed during the war, and how the conditions in which many of them lived would change further under a post-war Labour government. In 1947, in a government survey, a representative sample of just under 6,000 households was asked if they had non-resident help (i.e. a charwoman). It turned out that over 94 per cent of the households had no help at all.[10]

In Marghanita Laski's 1952 novel *The Village*, an English village in the Home Counties, typical of hundreds, is the backdrop for a drama of disintegrating social certainties. The 'gentry' are now hopelessly impoverished by war; the last representatives of generations who have lived well but earned little, they are now scratching for pennies to keep large and incommodious houses functioning without staff. The lower-class villagers, however, those formerly employed in the big house and its orbit, are making sums beyond their wildest dreams in nationalised factories and leaving their damp and primitive cottages for new social housing developments with all modern conveniences. In the first wave of the new housing were the pre-fabs, assembled overnight from flat-packed sections: they were only supposed to last for ten years, but former housemaid Joyce Storey could not wait to get on the list for one in Grimsby:

A pre-fab was the desire and love of my life . . . The kitchen housed a number of labour-saving units, including a stove and a fridge along one wall, together with cupboard space and a delightful alcove for the breakfast area. In the lounge, windows which extended from the front round to the side gave light and brightness. The fire was an all-night Rayburn and provided warm air to the other two rooms through vents in the wall. Finally, a large airing cupboard in the hall was also heated by the master fire and when the doors were left open, the hall would be warm and cosy too. A large garden front and back was also a feature that appealed to me. Over the cute little porch, I could picture roses and honeysuckle. I wanted one of those prefabs more than anything else in the world.[11]

Another former housemaid, Winifred Foley, now married with two children, went out charring during the war and lived in a damp tenement. When, in the late 1940s, she and her husband were given the keys of a new council flat in a just-built block, she found it kitted out more luxuriously than many of the houses of her employers; furthermore, new hire-purchase schemes offered the promise of more bounty. The Foleys' flat had three bedrooms, a communal laundry, piped hot water, a lounge-diner, a fridge, an electric stove and an inside bathroom and lavatory. In the late 1940s, a sixty-six-year-old charwoman, paid at a rate of half a crown an hour, and who got up to work at 4.30 every morning, told the sociologist Ferdynand Zweig that she was the proud owner of a semi-detached house, an electric washing machine, which cost her £78, and an immersion heater; and she was saving up for a particularly new and expensive luxury: a television.[12]

Many women had spent the six years since 1939 dreaming of laundered napkins, bountiful teas produced, like Mrs Miniver's, at the ring of a silver bell, and a cheerful cook creating delicious meals three times a day without complaint. Surely this idyll would be their reward for the hardship of the war years? However, 'Still no Mrs Mop,' sighed Maggie Joy Blount in 1947, noting that it some-times took eight weeks to get a job advertisement published in the Sits Vac columns, such was the demand. In their 1949 study on the middle classes, the Conservative MP Angus Maude and his co-author Roy Lewis thought the first concern for the government should be the struggling middle-class housewife who had to slum it: she 'normally insists upon a rather higher standard of feeding than – at any rate – the urban working-class wife. She may not spend more money on food; she tends to expend more time and care on buying; to prepare and cook more food at home; to produce, with the aid of a stock pot, more soups and stews, as well as making more jam, bottling more fruit, and so forth. The house or flat that the middle-class housewife has to run is normally larger, and contains more belongings. Often special rooms must be looked after, such as a husband's study, studio or consulting rooms and generally a nursery.'[13]

Maude and Lewis were among those (Violet Markham too) who worried that civilised values themselves would be under threat if the ruling classes, the guardians of those values, had no time in which to cultivate them. The contribution to public service made by the servant-employing classes entirely justified the help of the state in seeing that the housewife got the domestic help she needed. They did, however, accept that government intervention on the matter would be impossible to implement fairly: 'Yet there is no acceptable system which shall provide that this professional man and his wife deserve a domestic servant and will get one, while that business man does not and won't.'

It sometimes looked as though the labour of lovely things outweighed the pleasure of them, if all the effort of looking after them fell to one person. The pursuit of the perfectly run home began to seem like the enemy of promise. Even Winifred Foley felt slightly oppressed by her new flat, which needed so little cleaning and maintenance after the slum dwelling she had left behind; and she understood why it was that so many re-housed tenement dwellers expressed regrets at leaving for the new blocks. 'The flat had gone to my head and partly covered my heart. After living in the tenement I never felt at home in the flat, but more like a daily cleaner. Not a speck or spot of dirt or dust, nor any sort of muddle would I tolerate. Our old furniture and second-hand rugs and mats were simply not good enough for our new grandeur, and I was determined to replace them.'[14]

In *Return Passage*, her autobiography published in 1953, Violet Markham reflected on the years and the changes in domestic life and expectations since her childhood. 'The life I knew when a girl at Tapton, with its large well-trained docile staff, has gone forever. In a period of peace and security before the internal combustion engine had destroyed the basis of a static society, it was possible for a generation, un-tempted by a whole range of new and exciting adventures, to devote time and effort on the scale I have set forth, to the minutiae of housekeeping. But even so, I feel it was a terrible waste of human effort. As a housekeeper I am not fit to look at my mother's shoes, but I too have my own standards of good food, good drink, cleanliness, and order.'[15]

In April 1946, Markham chaired a round-table discussion for a BBC radio broadcast; entitled 'Help for Housewives', it addressed the question of the future of domestic service with speakers from all sides of the question. 'This is a very serious problem we're up against,' is how Markham started the debate. Miss Nancy Adam represented the National Union of Domestic Workers while Mrs Adam, Mrs Blandford, Mrs Serpel and Mrs Montgomery Smith were employers; Mrs Proctor and Mrs Silver were working-class housewives; and Miss Dunkley, Miss Mitchell and Miss Ayris were domestic workers. Courtesies were maintained at all times – but it was clear that on many sides of the debate there was little room for manoeuvre. The employers proved, unsurprisingly, more cautious about giving up the old separations. When the ever-contentious question of uniform cropped up and Mrs Blandford thought it quite correct that a servant should be asked to wear something 'dark and plain', Miss Dunkley, the domestic worker, responded that 'it isn't right to keep another woman deliberately in the background by making her dress in dark colours'. Miss Dunkley upheld the dignity of service: 'Domestic work is creative. You can see something growing under your fingers: the well-polished floor, the beautiful brass, the well-kept china and all those hundred and one details which go to make the home not merely a house or domestic museum.' Her suggestion, however, that wages should be set by law at the same rate as those paid to girls working in factories was met with dismay by the employers' faction, who pointed out that they made up the difference 'in kind' with food and other provisions.

The middle-class housewives, as predicted, saw themselves drowning under the impossible demands of domesticity. Mrs Montgomery Smith complained: 'I can't even get daily help. I only got nanny after about a three months' wait,' and Mrs Serpel (bearing out Violet Markham's previous warning that women would stop having babies if they were not guaranteed some help about the house) said: 'When you're trying to cope with two toddlers, trying to bring them up to become more or less rational citizens, it's almost impossible to cope with all the housework yourself.' She told the group that she couldn't possibly have more than two children if the shortages of servants continued: 'Women have come into their own and realise they have a brain,' and 'Housework makes the brain just become stagnant.' To this the working-class housewife Mrs Proctor retorted: 'I'm just a working man's wife and I'm on seven or eight different committees, social welfare, chairman of schools and so on. I've had two children – I'll admit there's twelve years between them – but it never dawned on me that I wanted help.' Furthermore, Mrs Proctor, thoroughly agreeing that the brain might stagnate with housework, added a proposition surely unthinkable before the Second World War, to whit that in order to stop the stagnation, working-class housewives could use some help about the house too.

Violet Markham put to the group some of her suggestions for a healthy renewal of domestic service for a modern world, 'no longer on any basis of condescension or rank, but on terms of justice and mutual respect and independence . . . So that service will cease to be considered a badge of inferiority but will find its true place as a princely motive for the enrichment of life.' Markham put a trusting faith in the public-spiritedness of women who might want to do part-time work as local authority home-helps in such a world. She mentioned that she had heard that in America teenagers could be recruited to help with looking after neighbours' children, taking their homework to other peoples' houses after school to 'babysit'.

But it was Mrs Proctor who, characteristically and because she knew something more of the realities of working-class aspiration than Violet Markham, put her finger on the problem. 'Sounds nice,' she sniffed, 'but where are the women for these home-helps coming from? Where are you going to get enough people?'[16]

Chapter 23

'The Change: It Must Have Been Terrible for Them'

In 1945, P. G. Wodehouse looked out on what had been Bertie Wooster's England and wrote to a friend: 'I wish I could get the glimmering of an idea for a novel. What the devil does one write about these days, if one is a specialist in country houses and butlers, both of which have ceased to exist?'[1]

With the war, the great cobweb of social dependency that had knitted the heart of English life disappeared for ever. The changes were so rapid that many saw the world they had grown up in vanish in twenty years. The groom Alfred Tinsley, last of generations of estate workers and domestic servants, was one of them: 'After the Second War, the gentry had to start looking after themselves, almost. My boss, the present Colonel B, was brought up by servants, and wasn't allowed to do a thing for himself: if there was anything to be done the servants did it, no matter what. And now he maybe just has someone to help out in the mornings. It must have hurt the gentry, the change: it must have been terrible for them.'[2]

Country houses and their owners buckled under the weight of post-war taxation and death duties. Many of the houses had been left in ruinous states by their wartime occupants and the number of properties secured by the National Trust, including many of England's greatest country estates, was accelerated between 1939 and 1945. Many owners could not afford the repairs required after six years of occupation by the armed forces or by schools or institutions. Others, like the Hoares of Stourhead (whose only son had been killed in the First World War), had simply run out of heirs. In 1946, after exactly 700 years of the Legh family's residence there, Lord Newton gave Lyme Park to the National Trust. For those long-serving estate workers and domestics, many of them the last of generations, the wrench was considerable. Jim Sidebotham refused to leave Lyme and was re-employed by the Trust. 'I could never leave here. Dig me up and root me up after a lifetime? It would have been as bad for me to have left as it was for his Lordship when he went to Hampshire. No my home was here. Lord Newton was our gaffer. What shall I say again? He was our bread and butter.'[3]

But the myriad of niche skills that had once sustained, and themselves been sustained by, the great estates were more or less finished. Jimmy Rumbsy at Somerleyton Hall, born the son of an estate gardener and raised into service, nonetheless found himself, as a boy, arriving to work at the Hall after the war at a time of uncertainty. Jimmy had learned how to polish silver, to valet and to wait at table under the butler at Somerleyton but by the time he had reached an age to become a butler himself, the Crossley family no longer needed one. The munificent hospitality that was part of pre-war life at Somerleyton was a thing of the past. So Jimmy ended up doing something of everything: cleaning shoes, a bit of valeting, helping out with the washing-up. Although he was an indispensable member of the household right up to his retirement in the 1980s, his official status remained hazy and was, in the end, and by the standards of the old-fashioned servants' hall, diminished by the odd-jobbing nature of his work. The decline of the career manservant was reflected in a new ambiguity about his job title: he was known by some as the butler and by others as the 'odd man', a job previously reserved for the lowest-ranking servant. These distinctions, once so vital to the hierarchy of the big house, gradually ceased to have importance as domestic service itself became generalised, fluid, flexible, divorced from the old dependencies of the village and the estate.[4]

Yet a sometimes melancholy desire to do things correctly by the old standards still hangs over accounts of the final years of the great estates. When, in 1947, James Lees-Milne visited Ham House, the Surrey seat of the Tollemaches, the door was opened to him by a middle-aged man: 'He had red hair and a red face, carrot and port wine. He wore a tail coat and a starched shirt front which had come adrift from the waistcoat. "The old alcoholic family butler," I said to myself.' It turned out that the seedy butler was in fact Sir Lyonel Tollemache's son who was running the place completely alone, acting as cook, cleaner and manservant while his father, immaculately attired, received visitors in the drawing room.[5]

Only in Britain's remaining colonies did something approximating the old-fashioned ideal of service continue, an increasingly bizarre manifestation of the last years of the Empire. When Lesley Lawrence married in 1944, her husband was stationed in Sudan, where they were 'waited on by male Arab servants who, from the days of Kitchener, had absorbed much of the household lore which in England had mostly been forgotten. In our own home, on Nile steamers, in the bush where we seldom failed to dress for dinner, we ate delicious steak and kidney pies or plum duff, regardless of the climate.'[6]

In this new world, the news, in November 1952, that a young footman called Harold Winstanley, in the employ of the Earl and Countess of Derby at Knowsley Hall, had run amok with a shotgun, murdering a butler and an under-butler, was given a mournfully surreal aspect by the revelation of the legions of Edwardian staff maintained by the Derbys. Winstanley's intended victim, Lady Derby (he shot her in the neck), was eating supper alone in front of the television when he rushed in. The delivery of the TV supper had involved two butlers and a footman, and the incident further involved a lady's-maid, a valet, two housemaids and a chef whose tall white hat was riddled with bullets during the attack.[7]

The older members of the Royal Family, in their inimitable way, although they maintained the ostentatious frugality of their war years, also continued to employ a vast staff. Queen Mary followed to the last letter the regulations laid down by the Ministry of Food, royal rations somewhat eased by reinforcements not only from Sandringham and Windsor but by packages of tinned delicacies sent by worried well-wishers from all over the Commonwealth. At Marlborough House, where she had moved after the war, Queen Mary called out of retirement her old chef Gabriel Tschumi, who had lost his job in George V's 1932 purge of the royal household. Tschumi's duties included cooking not only for the Queen Mother herself but also for the sixty upper-servants who ate every day in the steward's room; the sixty lower servants at Marlborough House were catered for in separate kitchens on their own level.

A new generation of royals were more relaxed and low key, at least by the standards of their parents. Tschumi was disappointed by the modesty of the wedding breakfast that celebrated the 1947 wedding of Princess Elizabeth and Lieutenant Philip Mountbatten. 'With restrictions demanded by the food industry', the meal was very simple fare compared to the gastronomic excesses of King Edward VII,* being merely 'a fish course (filet de sole Mountbatten), a meat course (perdreau en casserole) served with beans, small new potatoes and salad, an ice cream dish with patisserie, and fruit'.[8] Ernest King, who now worked as a butler for Princess Elizabeth and her new husband, was equally unimpressed by the couple's taste for plain, even proletarian, food. 'I never saw sole, salmon, smoked salmon on the menu. It was mostly fillets of plaice,' he complained. John Gibson, former valet to Winston Churchill, was at one time a footman to the royal couple at Kensington Palace: Prince Philip's favourite meals, he reported aghast, were fish and chips and bangers and mash – 'Can you imagine!'[9]

Nonetheless, for the older generations of royals, the world of the court continued for the most part as if sealed for ever from the social changes that were taking place in the world around it. Peter

---

* In his Edwardian heyday, Tschumi recalled ruefully, he had been charged with making a wedding cake for Queen Alexandra's lady-in-waiting that required: 'Forty eggs, three-and-a-half pounds of butter, one pound of peeled almonds, three pounds of orange and lemon peel, four pounds of brown sugar, five pounds of flour, a bottle of brandy and other vast quantities of ingredients.' (Tschumi, *Royal Chef*, p. 65.)

Russell, butler to the Duke and Duchess of Kent during the 1950s, observed the complicated processional that had to be engaged whenever Queen Mary wanted to go to the lavatory. 'It was the practice of the Queen or the Queen Mother that if they wanted to use the loo, they informed the Duchess, who in turn told me. I then told the head housemaid, who arranged for a housemaid to stand near the door, holding a hand towel for appearance sake. The house-keeper would tell me when all was at the ready. I would tell the Duchess who discreetly would inform Her Majesty.'[10] Russell reported that the Duke of Kent insisted that his breakfast routine be carried out to the last detail: three rashers of bacon with the rinds and gristle cut off and a fried egg on fried bread. The egg and the bread had to be cut in the same circular shape – carefully trimmed to fit by the cook using a serrated pastry cutter. Lunchtime potatoes had to be exactly the same size, the kitchen-maid laboriously shaving them for hours to get them exactly right; cheese and biscuits were another favourite of the Duke's, but the biscuits had to be served at exactly the correct temperature. The Royal Family, never characteristic of any other social group, were thus the last repositories of the manners and habits of a disappearing age.

Apart from the eerie aquarium of royal life, for most people, even if they were able to afford them, servants of the old school were now very difficult to find. Most people remembered them now as absences, sometimes painfully so. In Mollie Panter-Downes's novel *One Fine Day*, Stephen Marshall returns from active service in the war to find that the invisible mainstays of his world are gone: 'All his life he had expected to find doors opened if he rang, to wake up to the soft rattle of curtain rings being drawn back, to find the fires bright and the coffee smoking hot every morning, as though household spirits had been working while he slept. And the strings had been dropped, they all lay helpless as abandoned marionettes with no-one to twitch them.'[11]

It became necessary to trawl overseas for the employment of butlers, maids and cooks. The post-war years saw a surge in immigrant domestics from countries where unemployment was high, such as Malta, Spain or Portugal. At the 'Akenfield' big house, the

British butler was replaced by a Maltese butler who commuted every day from Ipswich, knocking off work at five. In 1946 the Ministry of Labour granted 7,622 permits for private domestic service; in 1955, the number had risen to 18,614. The solution to dire post-war unemployment in the remote Atlantic island of St Helena, for example, was the opening of a domestic employment agency. Helenian Pat Duncan, who arrived in Britain to work as a servant in the 1950s, remembers how the closure of the island's flax mill, established by the government in 1903 to give employment on St Helena, led to a mass exodus in search of work abroad: 'There was nothing, no food, no work.' The establishment of the domestic agency was the idea of an enterprising islander called Jack Thorpe who initially supplied the British military base on Ascension Island with mess stewards, cooks and porters. Willing Helenians then travelled further afield and prospective employers contacted Jack Thorpe's agency direct; the islanders were only permitted work permits to come to Britain if they had a job already lined up, but the large houses of England were only too happy to oblige.

Pat Duncan came over with his cousin and found himself in a residential job at a large house that had been leased to a girls' boarding school: 'Most of the posh people in England, as soon as one had a Helenian, they asked where they got one and they wanted one too.' Pat and his friends earned £1.50 a week and brought their own uniform with them. Pat was astonished by snow: 'It scared the life out of me. I couldn't understand it. Everything was froze up – I thought "What's going on?".'[12] Other migrant domestics found Britain less old-fashioned than they had thought it would be. Pearl Scott, a nanny and housekeeper who in 1959 accompanied the British family she had worked for in Trinidad, saw an electric iron for the first time (in Port of Spain, she had still been heating one over hot coals): 'There were no Hoovers in Trinidad when I left.'[13]

For most people, however, a Helenian butler, even if one could be secured, was an unimaginable luxury. Elizabeth Jordan thought herself lucky to have a part-time charwoman she could barely afford and whose every demand she acceded to for fear of her departure. In 1945, Elizabeth's husband Terrance had returned from the war a stranger to his wife and small daughters. He had been so traumatised by his experiences that he appeared to be entirely unsuited for civilian employment – and, as it turned out, for marriage. Elizabeth, who, in common with so many women, had learned to cook scratch meals from challenging ingredients during the war years, found herself the family's sole breadwinner. And as she had anyway to cook meals every day for herself, her daughters, their governess and Mrs Price the charwoman, she thought she would put her talents to good use in the evenings and earn some pin money. When the Jordans separated, on her shoulders fell the task of providing for her daughters and making enough money to pay Mrs Price her £3 a week. Elizabeth decided to try her luck as a professional cook, signing on with 'The Do-All Agency' in London. She was inundated with offers of work – though she rarely earned more than the cost of retaining Mrs Price – and her ingenuity was tested to the hilt in a period of the tightest rationing. She learned cunning ruses to conceal the dreaded dried egg, and also that smelts, when liberally battered, could, at a pinch, pass for whitebait.

Elizabeth Jordan's experience of London kitchens during the lean times of the late 1940s was grimly familiar: grubby basements still dependent on unreliable and ancient boilers, or stoves that needed to be lit hours before any actual cooking could begin. Vegetables, when she could find them, were usually withered and past it; meat was even more suspect. Summoned to cook a dinner party for two particularly mean brothers living near Sloane Square, Elizabeth found waiting for her in their kitchen, 'a few potatoes, two onions, a very old-looking cauliflower, five soft carrots, and a pitiable cabbage. I brought the whole lot out to the sink, wondering how I could make any of them taste anything but uneatable. The sink contained several cups and plates, a vast quantity of tea leaves, and a minute torn rag which I supposed was to serve as dishcloth. It was situated in a passage between the back door and the kitchen. The place appeared to be exceedingly drab and dreary. On the kitchen table I found a few apples and a newspaper parcel. In the midst of the sodden paper was one tattered piece of stringy steak.'[14]

The brown and over-boiled dreariness to which English cooking had become consigned since the war was lifted by Elizabeth's own, uncommon, deployment of garlic and fresh herbs, nearly five years before Elizabeth David revealed their Mediterranean magic to her hungry English readers. Exotic foreign ingredients were beginning to make an appearance in English shops and Elizabeth Jordan was thrilled to find one place in London that stocked '*jaghourt*'; she returned from a skiing holiday in the Alps smitten by a magical breakfast dish she had encountered there called *mousslé* ('an ambrosial mixture of different fruits, Nestlé's milk, porridge oats and sugar').[15]

Elizabeth Jordan was one among many middle-class women who took advantage of the domestic shortage, and in adventurous spirit launched themselves on the job market. The 'lady-help', thanks to the efforts of Universal Aunts, was no longer the sad and impoverished companion of caricature but an energetic, well-educated type looking for opportunities to travel and see a bit of life. 'At that time, people who hadn't been brought up to run a house were absolutely desperate,' remembers Ann Stallard, who left school and signed up for employment with Country Cousins, another agency which specialised in placing 'well-born ladies with no money, employed to pick children up from planes and accompany them to school'. Her first employer, a wealthy, raffish woman in Essex, was both helpless, domestically speaking, and 'mean as mean'. She had never had to do anything for herself, and kept freezers (then a luxurious rarity) filled with long-out-of-date foodstuffs. When she laid the table for tea, she put out cups without saucers: 'She had no idea!'[16]

The position of the new lady-helps was still sometimes ambiguous. In most of her jobs, Ann Stallard laid herself a place at the table on the first day and let her employers know that that was how it was to be, but former debutante Marigold Hay, who took a job as a 'lady cook' in a stately home while her husband was stationed in Ghana, clearly relished the larks of being below stairs rather as though she were in an out-of-the-way diplomatic posting. 'Conversation at tea at Chestnut Hall that evening was slightly forced – until Lord Bainsworth appeared. He blew in, surrounded by dogs, in his gardening clothes. On being introduced to him his first remark was: "Well, well, Mrs Hay, How do you do? Are you as frightened of being a lady cook as we are of having one?" This splendid remark completely took the wind out of my rather droopy sails, but I bravely smiled, and said "Oh, no, of *course* not Sir George".'[17]

Uneasy social divisions as usual were delicate territory. Elizabeth Jordan stood at the door of her employer's drawing room and announced that 'dinner is served Madam', but noted with embarrassment that many of the guests looked like people she might know. One of her hosts even brought her a cocktail in the kitchen – something that didn't happen very often for a cook. The parlourmaid called her 'Madam' when Elizabeth came for tea with her friend and prospective employer, but addressed her as 'Mrs Jordan' when she turned up to work in the kitchen. As it became clear that fewer women could count on having full-time or resident cooks, cookery courses actually became fashionable among upper-class girls. By the time Elizabeth Jordan had earned enough money by working as a plain cook to attend a smart and expensive cooking school for a course in French cuisine, she found that the school had introduced a two-hour midday break in order to accommodate the long luncheon engagements of the debutante students.

Gradually (though not without resistance), the approach to home comforts became influenced by ideas from across the Atlantic. There were many Americans in London after the war and they came to represent to their British counterparts both glorious, unrationed excess and domestic shiftlessness (Ernest King had worked as a valet for an American, Mr Hill, who spent £1,000 at a time on silk underwear). English homes were rapidly absorbing American technologies but, for many, the American way of life still aroused the English suspicion that labour-saving devices led to laziness and sloppy habits. Elizabeth Jordan thought the Petersens, an American family she worked for, were horribly slovenly and slapdash. They seemed to have oodles of money coupled with low expectations of quality. Their extravagance, after the years of English penny-pinching, seemed monstrous and they took as a matter of course, she reported, those lazy domestic shortcuts that Roy Lewis and Angus Maude thought so antithetical to the high standards of the middle-class British housewife. The Petersens were strangers to fresh air and never opened the windows, but they were so addicted to cold drinks that they put ice in their claret. When they had a dinner party it was a relaxed affair, only two courses, and Elizabeth Jordan, to her amazement, was told to make *hamburgers*: 'To this day I am not really clear what hamburgers really are, but I did my best and whether I made them correctly or not is doubtful.'[18]

American babies, it was commonly thought by English nannies, were overfed and allowed an unrestricted supply of sweets. Particularly extraordinary to Elizabeth Jordan was the fact that the Petersens' youngest daughter was still in nappies at nearly two years old; her own children, she marvelled disapprovingly, had started potty-training at nine months. 'Potting! What a perform-ance,' wrote Nanny McCallum, who had started work as a nurse-maid in the mid-1920s: 'This was the high spot of our day or the most important event in it. Or events rather, because it happened incessantly. All through the morning, afternoon and evening, regu-lar as clockwork, out came the pots. They were put on the pot before the end of the first month. Out of nappies by ten months, it was the beginning, the very fundament of their training.'[19]

The 1950s, however, saw the beginning of the decline of many traditional routines, including those that had so dominated chil-dren's upbringing in the first half of the century. Potty-training had once been a crucial skill in the armament of a professional nanny; but now that nannies were less in evidence, the whole business of measuring the child's day by rules and regularity slipped, never fully to return.

Chapter 24

The Shape of Things to Come

The Homes and Gardens Pavilion was the most visited exhibition space in the 1951 Festival of Britain. Engineered under the auspices of the Council of Industrial Design to lift the spirits of a nation grown tired of the frugality and monotone of the war years, the pavilion was an airy display of light, colour, wood, plastic and, of course, technology; a celebration both of post-war design and traditional Englishness. Capsule rooms, in the area marked 'Home of the Future', were designed with a range of inhabitants in mind: a room for an old lady; one for a family of four; another for a farmer. There were bathrooms, kitchens, sitting rooms and areas for 'hobbies' in which there might be a sewing machine (for her), a work table (for him) and a chess board for both of them. In a cosy space called an 'entertainments' room, chairs were grouped companionably around a television. Surfaces were laminated, smooth and easy to wipe clean.

The pitted wooden kitchen table which was scrubbed every day with soda and boiling water was now replaced by a 'surface', probably made from a material such as the ubiquitous Formica, a heat-resistant, brightly coloured covering of thermal-set resin which had been invented in the United States. 'We covered everything we could with Formica. It was very, very fashionable and you didn't need to do anything with it. All you did was cut out the size you wanted for your cabinets and stick it on top,' recalled a newlywed housewife.[1] The 'Farmers' Home' in the Pavilion had a serving hatch and a 'dining recess', but its rural roots were now aesthetic rather than strictly practical, a fireplace of artfully exposed brick, a shelf of modern pottery jugs and the now inevitable Aga in the kitchen. There were American-influenced imports such as the breakfast bar, which hinted at fast food eaten on the hoof, and, of course, the trolley. Furniture was designed to make the most of space and avoid clutter and fustiness: storage was key; chairs were stackable; lamps were anglepoise; tables came in easily tidied-up nests or folded up completely.

What visitors to the Homes and Gardens Pavilion did not realise was that early in the morning, before the admissions gates opened, a team of girls in black and white uniforms swarmed all over these new rooms cleaning, polishing and sweeping the home of the future into perfection. The girls were students of the newly formed Institute of Houseworkers based near London, at Deyne Court, Harrow. The brainchild of Violet Markham and Florence Hancock had finally come to fruition in 1948 and Joy Evans, then aged fifteen, was among the girls who 'did' in the Home of the Future. Joy, like most girls of her age, had not particularly wanted to go into domestic service, which by the last years of the 1940s, despite the best efforts of the Ministry of Labour seemed particularly retrograde even if you had few qualifications. 'I didn't have much choice – only a secondary modern to go to. Employment officers came to the school to find jobs for school leavers and my grandmother insisted I went into service.' Joy had been adopted, but her birth mother had been a chambermaid and 'my adopted grandmother thought I'd better stick to my background'. Thus it was that she found herself at Deyne Court, with forty other girls, learning how to be a domestic servant – or, as they were now encouraged (without much success) to call it, a 'houseworker'.[2]

It was a nine-month pre-diploma class and they all received sixteen shillings a week in pocket money.[3] In her exercise book, Joy carefully logged her lessons and activities. They studied a mixture of old and new cleaning techniques (when taught washing-up, for example, they used old-fashioned soda rather than new detergent), and more newfangled technical expertise (on one occasion, they had a visit from a representative from the Hoover factory who demonstrated the latest model from the company's range of vacuum cleaners). The students at Deyne Court were still instructed to scrub the doorstep with whitener before breakfast, but they also watched films produced by the Ministry of Information which showed them a brave new world of social housing, with modern flats built to the highest specifications of modern science to replace the slums and tenements of pre-war Britain. 'How the scientists were trying to make it soundproof etc.', Joy noted for one film. The girls also received a government pamphlet about a man who had 'changed the slums of a town into a decent community'.

Some of the lessons were pleasingly off-beam: Mrs Gentry, for example, gave them a talk, based on her own experience, on the care of a foundling owl. Joy learned how to do patchwork and mending and watched a United Dairies film about milk pasteurisation. 'Also it made me sit up and think,' she wrote, 'when one of the customers in the film put out dirty bottles until he learned how unhygienic it was.' When Joy and her fellow houseworkers visited the 'Safety in the Home Exhibition' at the Festival of Britain, a female health and hygiene expert answered questions sent in from all over the country ranging from: 'Should toy guns that fire missiles be banned from shops?' to: 'Would horrific photographs on posters help to prevent accidents?' to: 'Are high heels a source of accidents?' and: 'Would it be desirable to have automatically locking gas taps?' Among the skills the Deyne Court students had to display for their final exam was that old favourite: the creation of the perfect sponge cake. 'My mixture curdled', was Joy's one-line report on her performance.

Joy Evans did get a job – with a kindly family in Harrow who were interviewed and vetted by the Institute. But she had no intention of staying in service and left after only a few years. Despite the exhortations of the Institute of Houseworkers and other schemes to encourage domestic service, the 1950s brought new opportunities for girls who had never had opportunities before – and cleaning other people's houses was not the most attractive of them. A closer look at a typical working-class housewife's day makes this hardly surprising. In 1950 this woman submitted a minute-by-minute breakdown of her day for the Mass Observation survey:

7.15 Got up and washed myself
7.30 Did the grate out
7.45 Prepared the breakfast
8.00 Had breakfast
8.30 Cleared away and got the children ready for school
8.45 Ironed a couple of small things
9.00 Made beds and had a good tidy round
10.30 Went out shopping
11.15 Got back and started to prepare the lunch
12.00 Did some washing
12.30 Had lunch
1.15 Sat and read the paper
1.45 Washed up
2.15 Finished the washing and hung it out – while listening to the radio
2.45 Washed the floor – ditto
3.10 Wrote a couple of letters
3.45 Sat and did a crossword in the paper
4.00 Machined a dress for daughter
4.45 Prepared the tea
5.00 Had tea (while watching TV)
5.30 Cleared away the tea things (ditto)
6.00 Did some more dressmaking
7.45 Prepared supper for the children
8.00 Washed son
8.15 Gave the children their supper
8.45 Put son to bed
9.00 Put daughters to bed and gave husband his supper
9.15 Tried on the dress had been making
9.30 Tidied round and washed up
10.00 Put the finishing touches to the dress
10.30 Got some milk for husband
10.45 Did a bit of knitting

11.30 Had a cup of milk

11.45 Went to bed.[4]

With the exception of a snatched half-hour reading the paper and fifteen minutes for the crossword, this anonymous housewife's day is packed tight with monotonous physical work. The belief, much beloved of those who had servants, that civilised English values were promoted by healthy labour, the craft of housework and the care of lovely 'old, discrepant things' nonetheless remained at the heart of the English idea of home. Angus Maude and Roy Lewis feared that what they called 'gracious living', a Mrs Miniverish combination of refined inner life and beneficent household and social order, would be sacrificed to bleak utilitarianism unless domestic service could be reinstated at the heart of English daily life. 'The sort of life which used to be comprehended in the term "gracious living",' wrote Lewis and Maude,

> is not desired by everyone, nor will it – in the foreseeable future – be available to everyone who desires it. But it is still considered by some to be a worthwhile goal to aim at, and egalitarians should not underestimate either the strength of the aspiration or the adverse effects that might result from its being quenched. Those who hold it may sometimes feel that, if they must restrict their families to the size which can be accommodated in a service flat; if they must cut themselves off from leisure activities, however useful, outside the home; if their music and drama are to be purveyed to them only through the radio; if good furniture, good silver and good pictures (all of which need careful maintenance) are to be banished for ever to museums; and if entertaining is to be permanently restricted for all but Cabinet Ministers, then emigration to Eire or South Africa seems the only hope.[5]

The emergence of the 'new housewife' of the 1950s redefined the perception if not the actuality of domestic labour. If middle-class women were going to have to do their housework for themselves, then the housewife must be remodelled in the public's mind as a dainty creature in an impossibly clean apron, pulling a Pyrex casse-role dish from her new electric oven as her husband returns home from work. Kay Smallshaw, a former editor of *Good Housekeeping*, made a brave stab at suggesting in her book *How to Run Your Home Without Help* (1949) that the dynamic of the traditional household could and should change; that even men might pitch in to help with the housework. Smallshaw's standards remained punishingly high: she approached housework with alarming effi-ciency and enthusiasm. 'Let's see how the day is going,' she cajoles her readers: '1–2½ hours for the daily tidying; 3–4 hours for shop-ping, cooking and washing-up and 2–3 hours for house-cleaning, washing and other big jobs.' Then, 'on your side, do remember that your husband's work has its strains and stresses too, not the least of them being rush-hour travelling. When he gets in, let him rest and relax, with a drink or tea. Then, when he has changed and feels refreshed, have dinner ready without any waiting, even though it has meant some sacrifice on your part to keep to the timetable. He'll help you clear away with much better grace because of your understanding when he came in.'

Even children can be roped into the domestic business: 'at five years old they are eager to help, even if their attempts are not very practical, let them take a share. Don't differentiate between boys and girls. Both should learn how to cook a simple meal, and to clear it away, before the teens are reached. Although grumbles are natu-ral, no youngster was ever any the worse for doing a share of the household chores. In fact, it's noticeable that in the happiest fami-lies, everyone "pitches in", even if it is, very rightly, mother who does the lion's part and keeps the whole machine running sweetly.'[6]

The parlourmaid was now a rarity, as were the housemaid and the cook-general. The charwoman, generally a middle-aged woman who had perhaps herself once been in grander service, filled in the gaps. The new housewife might whisk a duster over the antiques, but in the interests of preserving the space for reading, reflection and personal maintenance that 'gracious living' demanded, the scrubbing of the kitchen floor would be best left to a daily cleaner. Thus, many women who had quite possibly a high degree of training in the skills of looking after beautiful things often found themselves consigned to the drudgery of 'the rough'. As 'Mrs A. D.' remembered: 'One thing about those days, you never cleaned windows and you never done washing, not like since the war.'[7]

The opening in 1946 of the celebrated florist Constance Spry's new domestic science college at Winkfield Place, Berkshire, captured the mood of the new housewifery: it was really just an extension of the old-fashioned finishing school. A course at Winkfield included needlework, flower-arranging, bookbinding, gardening and cookery. All was pretty, feminine: the dressing tables in the bedrooms had organdie flounces; the girls learned how to make evening bags from parachute silk and sequins, and to bake Victoria sponge cakes in tins lined with geranium leaves. The journalist Beverley Nichols, after a visit to one of its cooking demonstrations, thought that Winkfield turned 'tiresome ex-debutantes' into brisk, efficient young women thrilled by the romance of domesticity – and not yet disillusioned by its reality. After the war years, Winkfield was an island of excess, a *Petit Trianon* of housewifery. In 1953 the 'austerity table' at the school's graduation party of that year was groaning with delectable homemade breads and cheeses arranged on an artisanal gingham-checked tablecloth. A demonstration of dinner-party culinary skills included consommé flecked with gold leaf and hand-made cellophane swans filled with sweets.[8]

The old British resistance to household technology gradually began to break down during the fifties. Although, according to the 1961 census, 22 per cent of the country's homes still had no running hot water, by 1948, 86 per cent of them were at least wired for electricity. A new kind of home was taking shape. Fridges, vacuum cleaners and televisions became cheaper and were widely available across the classes. But the beginning of the age of domestic consumerism was viewed with concern in some circles. In 1953, members of the House of Lords wondered if a display in the Warrington showroom of the Electricity Board could be considered blasphemous: it featured the Three Wise Men bearing gifts of a washing machine, an electric cooker and a refrigerator.[9]

A lingering distaste for quick-fix housework was now outweighed by the urgency of getting things done. In 1949, the arrival of the first self-service laundry (for which appointments had to be booked in advance) changed for ever the labour of most women's working week. The proliferation by the early 1950s of new dry-cleaning outlets, though welcomed by many, was considered (and probably quite rightly) to have damaging effects on clothes and carpets. The Mass Observation diarist Herbert Brush reported: 'I used to think my corduroy trousers were everlasting, but now I have changed my mind. Just now I was walking along the rhubarb patch when my left trouser leg caught on a marking stake and it tore a hole from the calf to the ankle. The material has been absolutely rotten since it went to the cleaners.'[10]

Anyone, however, who remembered the unceasing pre-war battle against textile moths hailed the introduction of the latest pest control, DDT. 'Housekeeping was far more complicated before the days of DDT. You couldn't just cover things and leave them for the winter because the moths would eat the covers off them,' recalled Lady Burrell. 'My first winter at Knepp, the tennis balls were all eaten, and unless all your clothes were beaten and put in moth-proof bags, in six months they would probably have had it.'[11] The hostess trolley, viewed with such snobbish derision in the 1920s, increased in popularity, as did the hotplate, the electric percolator and the 'teasmade'. Violet Markham had envisaged a system of state-supported, properly paid domestic training which would free women from the enslavement of hard labour, releasing them into a kind of mutual self-help society; housekeeping and its attendant chores taking their proper place in the background of the larger pursuit of intellectual endeavour, charitable work, political engage-ment and public service. In 1951, Markham wrote that labour-saving devices brought that vision closer. 'Every sort of mechanical and labour-saving device will replace the bucket and brush of my youth. Kitchens will no longer be equipped with Moloch-like ranges, devouring coal and human effort in equal proportions. A wilderness of underground cubby holes and passages will be replaced by compact reconstructed units, lighted and heated by electricity.'[12]

In 1947, Maggie Joy Blount visited the 'Britain Can Make It' exhibition in London and was enthralled by its panoramic vision of the domestic future: 'Here is the brave new world, the Shape of Things to Come, the sweeping lines, the pastel-coloured walls, the curves and candy pillars, fabric-swathed ceilings, the cunningly concealed and directed lighting, the air-conditioning and central heating, glitter of plastics and light metals – all that one expects and fears of the underground world of tomorrow.'[13] In reality, however, the British home took longer to adapt itself to needs that now centred round a nuclear family of only four or five members rather than the loose accommodation of individuals, some family, some extended family, some servants, that had been the pattern of the past. Kay Smallshaw's recommendations for altering a small Victorian house suggest that the kitchen, once hidden in the lower depths of the house, should be raised to pavement-level – a first step for its progress from the basement to the centre of the family home. 'All the old kitchen fitments were obsolete and work-making,' reported Smallshaw of her own newly refurbished terraced house, 'so these were not moved into the new quarters. Instead, factory-made units, all uniform depth were chosen.' Smallshaw's old kitchen space was converted into a 'den', or masculine place for storing tools: where the modern man in fact might try his hand at a bit of the newly popular 'Do-It-Yourself'. Smallshaw's house contained a washing machine, a 'dining niche' in what used to be the scullery and a 'utility room'. Hospitality, once so demandingly proscriptive, began to take on a more relaxed and ad hoc flavour and the home was now a reflection of its inhabitants' modern and fashionable informality. But, as always, for the family without help, running a home, however sophisticated its ergonomics, meant work. Smallshaw counselled her readers that even casual entertaining required considerable effort:

Few of us live in monastic seclusion or want to. Half the fun of having a home is being able to invite other people in. But entertaining, however simple, means another cake, or fresh trolley cloths, or some more glasses to wash. Extra work again. The same with the finishing touches, the little things that add so much to the enjoyment of the home. Flowers make all the difference to a room, and can add anything from a few minutes to an hour on the schedule. Altering the furniture round, experimenting with the pictures, rearranging the books or gramophone records – well, you can't call them work, but a whole evening can easily be whiled away in such pleasant pottering, while the mending basket remains untouched.[14]

Even with the promise of regulation, qualifications, professionalism and inclusion in unemployment benefit schemes (introduced for domestic servants in 1948), the 1950s demonstrated that, despite small oases of survival, the old forms of domestic service were by and large gone for good. The number of domestic servants more than halved during the decade: in 1951 there were 250,000 people employed as domestics in Britain; by 1961 this had dropped to just 100,000.

In 1959, in a final flourish to the changing domestic face of the fifties, the annual Ideal Home Exhibition was opened by none other than the Duke of Bedford. The Duke, whose grandfather only thirty years before had forbade the workers to look directly at him while they were installing electricity at Woburn, was photographed in his shirtsleeves and smiling broadly, as he carefully loaded plates into a brand-new and fully automated Kenwood dishwasher.[15]

PART VI

'We Don't Want *Them* Days Again'

Chapter 25

'We've Moved to the Front'

In 1965, Catherine Mary Kirk, then in her late fifties, who had spent all her working life in domestic service, was still in demand among a host of clients for part-time cooking work. Mrs Kirk relied on Masseys, the London domestic agency that had been established in 1845 and was still going strong (as it is to this day) to find work suited to her requirements. Her employers tended to be elderly or middle-aged women who had slipped through the social changes of the last twenty years and were unaccustomed to daily cooking or any domestic chores. In 1965, for example, Masseys sent Mrs Kirk particulars of a post 'which may be of interest to you': Lady Hulse needed a cook, two or three evenings a week, 'for two in family, electric cooker'. Another woman that year wrote to Mrs Kirk in panic that her mother-in-law had engaged a cook who had walked out the very next day.

With many of her employers, Mrs Kirk's correspondence suggests a friendly relationship of some affection; they ask kindly about her children, their health and their progress with recorder practice. In 1972, at the age of sixty-six, Mrs Kirk received from a regular employer, Mrs Chamberlayne, a letter, one of many in which she fretfully calls upon the cook for help. Mrs Chamberlayne writes:

Dora will be here, as she and her sisters are going to have a little 'London Season' to look after our flat while we're away. I'm sorry we shall have no housemaid from next week – shall have to manage with some good 'outside help' 2 mornings a week. Our tiresome house-parlourmaid has let us down rather badly and suddenly decided she must go back to Hungary immediately. I had offered to make it worth her while to wait – but unfortunately we cannot get anyone in her place. Though I had tried, I expected we're better without her. She's a good worker but it's the second time she has let us down at an awkward time.

The letter concludes with a fervent: 'We shall be so pleased to see you again!'

When it came to running her home, Mrs Chamberlayne was stranded in the chasm between the generations. Her letters to Catherine Kirk depict the mild domestic battleground of the post-war upper-middle-class home, between the foreign domestic workers that were available to her and the standards and expectations of an earlier age. Deference, for one thing, was no longer to be unquestioningly relied upon; Mrs Chamberlayne was shocked to find how ripe the new foreign girls' language was and how unabashed they were about using it in front of her.[1]

Mrs Kirk, however, was enjoying the freedoms of a new world. She no longer wore a servant's uniform; the 'badge of servitude' was gone for ever. She owned her own house, was mistress of her own time, could manage her own hours, and dictate, should she wish, her own employment terms. Her cooking skills, learned in large houses before the war, were much in demand for dinner parties or special occasions. She was typical of the servants of her generation in manner and experience and had become a prized resource in modern Britain. As Margaret Powell noted, after the war, career servants were so valuable that they would be snapped up even without a reference – or you could just 'pretend your previous employer had died' and a new employer was usually too desperate even to check. The reluctant trickle of young British girls, and boys, going into domestic service had shrunk to almost nothing. The steep decline in the numbers of skilled domestic career servants was reflected in the dramatic disappearance of domestic employment registries. In the small Leicestershire town of Market Harborough, for instance, they had once flourished: in 1895 there were eighteen, in 1912 there were sixteen, in 1922 eleven, 1947 six, 1957 three; but by 1966 there were none at all.[2]

Most middle-class British homes from the 1950s onwards, at least those that could afford help, were largely reliant on foreign workers. Even the supply of deferential Helenians had in 1961 been reduced by the Union-Castle shipping line's decision to cut out passenger calls at St Helena, leaving the islanders stranded. Helenians, as the *Evening Standard* noted, had been 'coming in scores' to work in Britain's larger private homes as maids, chauffeurs, gardeners and cooks; 'now they will be as captive as Napoleon was'.[3] Ex-servicemen were still much in demand for cleaning jobs, but were now more often taking up part-time work, employed on an hourly rate or with contract cleaning agencies. The continuing success of agencies such as 'Doorsteps', which had been set up in 1925 to employ war veterans as cleaners, was followed by the establishment of many more.

Violet Markham and Florence Hancock's attempts to raise the status of domestic service, to make it a regulated profession rather than simply unregulated labour, proved to be largely unsuccessful. The efforts of the League of Skilled Houseworkers' first chairman, Dorothy Elliott, 'to turn out a domestic worker skilled in her craft: and to give that worker a sense of confidence in herself as a member of the community, breaking down the idea that domestic workers are a race apart',[4] were not embraced by the spirit of the new age in Britain. Spartan training centres and all-female environments were off-putting to 1950s girls who were elsewhere encouraged by the prospects of a range of other jobs. The old-fashioned maid no longer had a context, and where that context still existed, few working-class women wanted a place within it.

Demand for domestic help, particularly now by women going out to work and for families that needed two incomes, therefore far outstripped supply. In 1950, in the *Observer*, the columnist Alison Settle found signs of encouragement in the Home Helps Service, initiated by the government and run by local authorities with some success as part of the new National Health Service. That year, she reported, there were 15,000 part-time and 4,000 full-time members of the scheme. Settle noted approvingly that in Sweden they had managed what in Britain succeeding generations had found so difficult: the development of a trained, respected and professionalised domestic workforce: 'The Swedish method is to use only specially trained women, none under twenty years.' When the organiser of the Swedish scheme visited Britain, she was of the opinion that the British version was cumbersome, bureaucratic, suffering from too much red tape and too little investment.

The fact was that the British had with extraordinary speed devalued the status of paid domestic work; it was too bound up with the servile pantomime of the past and was now anathema to a generation that not only did not want to launder other women's clothes but fully expected to own a washing machine for their own laundry. Any work, it seemed, was better than working in another woman's house. 'We don't want *them* days again,' the researcher Pearl Jephcott was told when she conducted interviews among young women factory workers in Bermondsey.[5]

In the early 1950s, foreign domestics were still popular, being considered more in the traditional deferential style. Between 1945 and 1991, an estimated 13,000 Filipinos moved to London to work in domestic service.[6] Once general domestic work had lost its association with particular and defined skills and training, however, the door was opened to the most common of all post-war household helps: the au pair. In 1962, the *Sunday Times* reported on this new and increasingly ubiquitous brand of help for harassed mothers, comparing the au pair favourably to other demanding foreign workers who 'will not be happy with £4 a week if she knows the girl next door is getting £5'. The paper went on, approvingly: 'The au-pair girl on the other hand, has a different attitude. She may even regard it as useful training to have to manage on £2 a week (living in of course and 'all found'), but she will rightly object if not given time off to attend a language school, to meet people of her own age and in general to explore and develop as any teenager should.'[7]

The au-pair scheme had been founded after the First World War to foster peacetime European collaboration and took its name from the French for 'share and share alike'. It had originally been designed as an exchange programme that would encourage the learning of languages and the experience of other European cultures and accommodation and keep was offered in exchange for light child-care. It was not until after the Second World War that the scheme really took off and in 1964 alone, an estimated 20,000 women were brought to Britain by private agencies to work as au pairs, some of them as young as fifteen.[8] For most of them, the experience was, inevitably, mixed.

Young Margit Latter came from Germany in 1960 to au pair for a family on the south coast and found herself used as a general dogsbody. Her complaints were all too familiar: the British, as exemplified by her host family, had no taste, hideous clothes and houses and whining, spoilt children. Margit was treated more or less as a general servant and nurserymaid and often made to eat alone in the kitchen where she had to cope with the mysteries of riddling the temperamental Aga. The washing machine was so primitive that every morning she was forced to pick bits of pyjama cord out of its filter. Worst of all, there was the disgusting English frugality of saving old fat and dripping in which to fry the chips for supper. Then on top of everything, the woman of the house told Margit that she smelled (not surprising considering the hours she had to work and the notorious national parsimony with hot water) and instructed her to shave her armpits in the English style.[9]

Hanging often over the au-pair relationship, certainly on the English side of the divide, was the cultural memory of the master-servant relationship (or, in the case of many families, the *idea* of that relationship). It was difficult to negotiate the new terms of engagement and all too often it became prickly and difficult; what was intended to be cultural exchange degenerated into misunderstanding and exploitation. Yolande Dykes, a young New Zealander who had come to Britain in 1954 to 'see a bit of the world', found work as an au pair in Orpington, and although the job was far more lucrative than working in an office, as she told a reporter on the *Wellington*

Evening Post, the risk was of being treated 'with marked condescension'.[10] Added to which, the advent of the foreign au pair gave
rise to a whole new stereotype of domestic sexual temptation,
almost eclipsing that of the pert and frisky maid of the previous
century.

As early as 1953, the plot of Dorothy Whipple's novel *Someone
at a Distance* concerned a hard and mercenary French au-pair girl
who cold-heartedly sets out to steal the husband of her employer's
neighbour and wreck a happy English marriage. The theme was
apparently inexhaustible. In Monica Ware's 1967 *Au Pair*, Jacqueline
cuts a swathe through the hearts of wide-eyed young Englishmen
while, just to shake up the theme, in Andrew McCall's *Au-Pair Boy*
(1969), creepy Jacques does the same with the wide-eyed Chelsea
girls he encounters (though in actual fact it was not until 1998 that
the au-pair scheme was expanded to include boys). The influx of
Scandinavian au pairs in the late sixties and seventies brought with
it and into the home itself a titillating popular fantasy of new and
foreign sexual freedoms.

Piecemeal, daily domestic help was good business for Universal
Aunts, still thriving after the Second World War, and similar agencies such as Country Cousins. Trained nannies too were still available, though in increasingly short supply. A professional nanny had
cachet. Muriel Binding became an untrained nanny/dogsbody in
Kent in the early 1960s, caring for three children under four and in
charge of cleaning the house from 6.45 in the morning to seven in
the evening: 'After deductions for my food and laundry, I was left
with £3.3s a week.' Her employers liked Muriel to wear a blue
nylon housecoat during the day, 'but, if any distinguished guests
were expected I had to dress up like a nurse in the "correct" uniform
of a children's nanny', in starched collar and cuffs and short cape.[11]

Nannies could be found through agencies or the employment
departments of their training colleges or by advertising in *The
Nursery World*, or in the national dailies, but those moral and social
mores that were once the backbone of the cross-class relationship
had to be overlooked now that supplies of residential childcare
were scarce. Unmarried mothers, for example, who just a

generation ago would almost certainly have been sacked on the spot if found to be pregnant, were now courted by promises of tolerance and compassion. 'If you ring one of the big London domestic agencies, asking hopefully for a nanny or mother's help, you may be asked if you will consider employing an unmarried mother who wants to keep her own child with her,' explained *The Times* in 1960. Some employers were advised to go to the National Council for the Unmarried Mother and Child, whose members were often looking for residential work. But in a radical shift of moral attitudes, the employer might actually have found herself the one considered unsuitable in such an arrangement: 'Here you will have to submit to a more searching inquiry as to your suitability for employing such a girl.'[12]

Forms of communal living with residential service continued to be widely used: shared 'digs' with breakfast and dinner provided by a landlady were popular right up to the end of the 1970s. (Celia Fremlin, the researcher who had infiltrated the world of domestic service in the 1930s, turned her hand after the war to writing popular thrillers, where she used to the full her beady observations on domestic life, setting many of her fictions in the small and often murderous domestic world of the bed-sitting-room establishment.) Blocks of service flats also thrived. In the Mayfair residential block where Ivy Provine's parents had worked as cook and valet since the 1920s, fashionable new residents included sixties stars Terence Stamp and Jean Shrimpton.

The purveyors of interior designs and technology continued to tempt the housewife with new appliances – not quite yet the robotic housemaid of science fiction, but there seemed increasingly a machine to fulfil every possible household need, including those needs that no-one had anticipated. Now that the housewife and her home were no longer a centre of manufacture, they became voracious agents of consumption: cooking, cleaning and daily chores were outsourced to the market where an ever-growing list of processed foods and appliances were available to buy outright or on hire purchase. Rather than being relegated to the dark passages where domestics had once toiled, unseen, the everyday labour of the home was now on display, in the front room, in the kitchen-diner and in shiny new equipment that proudly proclaimed its utility.

'The most interesting thing about kitchens is how they have come up in the world,' proclaimed the *Woman's Own Book of Modern Homemaking* in 1967. 'Two generations ago they were dark, dreary and very much "below stairs", or pushed to the back of the house in any odd corner the builder could spare between the front hall and the back . . . Today, in any modern house, the kitchen is usually the nicest room in the place, the centre of family life, and the area in which they have spent most money and thought. Architects and builders, with housewives jogging their elbows, are now providing more space for kitchens, usually double the area they thought adequate in the 1930s.' Kitchens were being brought out 'of the back regions into the main part of the house, giving them a chance of sunshine and a good view from the sink. Walls between kitchen and dining room are coming down and being replaced by counters and cupboard units. Sometimes the kitchen is moved into the area once occupied by the traditional "front room", or it is linked with the open-plan living room so that whatever she is doing about the dinner, the hostess is never shut out from the conversation or the television news.'[13]

Indeed the television, which by 1963 was a crackling presence in 82 per cent of British homes, changed, as no other piece of technology, the way the average home operated: once, the parlour, the front room, the sitting room, had been almost exclusively reserved for the admission and hospitality of visitors; now it was more often than not where the family gathered to watch the box. A factory shop-steward noted in 1961 the changes in his own family home: 'In our previous house the front door was never meant to be used; we had a settee across it. Everyone, including the postman, called at the back door. Now it is different. We've moved to the front.'[14]

Fashions in entertaining reflected the shortage of domestic help. Service became self-service and the buffet an increasingly popular form of the dinner party. The hotplate and the serving hatch, which had made their first appearance in the late 1920s, became ubiquitous in the sixties and seventies. The *Woman's Own Book of Modern*

Homemaking hailed the end of the sheer labour of entertaining:

> Traditional shapes and canteens are still available and you can, if you like, buy table 'silver' that is an exact copy of your grandmother's, even to the rat-tailed spoons and real ivory-handled knives. But more likely you will look at stainless steel in six- and seven-piece table settings, not just because this is newer, but because it is *sensible* . . . and specifically designed for eating a meal! Few things we use about the house have changed more than tableware . . . go to buy some new ones and you find yourself in the middle of a small domestic revolution. The cutlery and china which young people buy today doesn't even pretend to look like the stuff their parents use. The linen has almost vanished. From the material and the design to the method of selling, everything is different. And in most cases, very much better.[15]

Napkins and table linen were drip-dry or even paper, and napkin rings a practical commonplace rather than a wartime necessity. Sleek stainless steel, washable and rust-resistant, became the material of choice for knives and other kitchenware, and a shining and gleaming expanse of steel or Formica worktops made a stark contrast to the wooden counters of the old galley kitchen. For most homes, it was the end of (on all but special occasions) bone-handled knives that needed laborious sponging, and of 'the footman's bugbear' of daily plate polishing. Even the nostalgic appeal of garlic plaits, quarry tiles or bunches of herbs hanging from the ceiling was decorative rather than necessary, a comforting nod to a bucolic rural past. A guidebook to the modern kitchen, published in 1969, shows an old copper like Mrs Praga's being praised as a 'period feature' and filled with geraniums. The Aga, resembling the comforts of the traditional range in appearance, was now generally gas-fired and ignited by the flick of a switch. The home's very utility, its spanners and engines, had become, for the first time, a statement of personal style.

What few had anticipated was that domestic appliances, while they undoubtedly made many daily chores a great deal easier, in other ways actually added to the burden of housekeeping. The first

labour-saving devices were invented to be used by servants: someone still had to make them work – and if it was not a servant, it was
almost certainly a woman. The presence of the washing machine, so
apparently quick and easy, resulted in a daily wash where once a
weekly washday was sufficient. Food processors, vacuum cleaners,
tumble driers and dishwashers are a constant reproach to the untidy
house: many found that housework simply expanded to fit the
hours made available by labour-saving technology. In 1950 a survey
of full-time housewives showed that they spent an average of
seventy hours a week on housework; in a survey in 1970 that average had risen to seventy-seven hours.[16]

Middle-class women were on the whole now working these
hours without help. During the late 1960s the demand for domestics fell sharply, prompted partly by economics and partly by ideology. In 1968–9, more than 10,000 people received work permits to
work in Britain as domestic servants, but by 1972 the number had
dropped to 8,000. The tidy little wife in a pinny opening the door of
her brand-new oven, ready for her husband's return, was a despised
symbol of 1950s subservience and for the seventies' feminist the
untidy house was often a badge of pride in hard-won independence. Domestic regularity and routine, the binding glue of the
households of the past, were now viewed as cramping the spirit and
individuality of women. Suzanne Gail, a middle-class housewife in
the 1960s, felt trapped at home with a small child, not because she
did not have help in the house but because the very routines that for
previous generations had seemed as reassuring as natural order was
no longer a haven but a prison: 'The thought of those millions of
women performing exactly the same gestures as me, enclosed in
their little circular activities, and perhaps with no possibility ever of
escaping, depresses me more than I can say.'[17]

The increasing participation of men in the day-to-day raising of
children was another major shift. 'In my days a man pushing a pram
would have been a laughing-stock; now you see a great many men
pushing their pram proudly,' a factory worker told Ferdynand
Zweig in 1961.[18] Yet in the 1970s many radical feminists took a line
on long-distance, paid and regulated childcare that turned the

child-centred years of the thirties on their head. Privacy, which had for a century been the cornerstone of the English sense of home, was even viewed as a danger to those within it. 'The housewife-mother is a backward, conservative force,' wrote the feminist psychoanalyst Juliet Mitchell in 1971; 'her work is private and because it is private and for no other reason it is unsupervised'. Taking a line on childcare that would surely have met with some agreement from generations of Victorian and Edwardian upper-middle-class parents, Mitchell went on to praise the collective methods of child-rearing in the Israeli *kibbutzim*, where 'the child who is reared by a trained nurse . . . does not suffer the backwash of typical parental anxieties and thus may positively gain from the system'.[19]

Chapter 26

'I'd Never Done What I Liked . . .
Never in All My Life'

For former career servants, the new world must have seemed bewildering. The standards of display, deference, ritual and order in which they had been schooled were ghostly relics of an era in which a new generation no longer believed, or even respected. Many of the older servants, such as Catherine Kirk, went into part-time service, working for those of their own generation who had never helped themselves, for whom the world of the washing machine and the eat-in kitchen was alien. Employer and servant often found themselves in an alliance of the old guard, with friendships forged in adversity and mutual dependence.

Many other old servants (and not so old: after all, a girl who went into service aged fourteen in 1930 was only forty-four at the beginning of the sixties) found work in different sectors of domestic employment. Miss Ellery, who had started her kitchen career skinning hares and fashioning angelica flowers in the stillrooms of inter-war country houses, became a school cook, before retiring in the late seventies at the age of sixty. She mourned the loss of cooking skills and knowledge, the insipid joylessness of the heated-up ready-meal. The final blow for her was the introduction of soya as padding for school dishes. 'When they started putting soya stuff in fish pies and mixed with minced meat and all that – that wasn't my

line,' she told an interviewer in the early 1980s. 'You're brought up
to do the best you can with whatever you've got . . . You can make
something out of nothing. It makes me cross when I see somebody
doing a quickie, I think, with so many eggs and a quarter pint of
cream and all things like that . . . I mean, when you live on pension
you think to yourself: "Well, how stupid. They want a quarter pint
of cream and so many eggs and so much and so much – and so much
cheese, at the price it is . . ." Any fool can make "quickies" out of
them sort of things. But it's when you've got to make something
out of nothing.'[1]

Other former servants retired, supported, if they were lucky, by
housing and pensions supplied by their former employers, and if
they were not, by the state. Laundress Annie Wilkinson, who for
forty years had toiled with goffering irons and on bleaching lawns
at Castle Howard, found her skills unwanted after the war with the
advent of dry-cleaning and the popularity of washing machines and
drip-dry fabrics. Like many other former servants, she took work
as a general residential domestic:

> Well, you know when the Second World War came, they didn't want
> laundry maids. They shut up all the laundries, so I'd to take anything.
> So I took [work with] a parson's widow that I knew. I couldn't cook,
> but I thought I'd try. I was her maid for ten years. Then I left it, I
> thought I'd do without. And I got a little cottage in Terrington, and
> believe me, all of you, you couldn't believe how happy I am. I could
> do what I liked. I'd never done what I liked in my life – never in all
> my life; but I did then and I do now. So you can guess – I've been
> nearly twenty years in it, and I've loved it. It's a little old place, and
> I've a cat and me garden takes as much doing in the summer as me
> housework. It's nice to do it – it's nice to have your own place.[2]

Traditional service had emerged from a world which had been
dealt its final blow by the Second World War, and was now regarded
by most people as an historical anachronism, another theatrical
tableau in the English pageant of class and the country estate.
However, in the largest country houses, the royal household and

for the very rich, where silent and unobtrusive luxury was still highly prized, service continued to survive in something resembling its old form. In 1974, Andrew Barrow interviewed some 'proper' servants of the old school for *Harpers & Queen*. A sixty-year-old housemaid, 'tall with an aristocratic aura and bearing', had absorbed, seemingly without question, the tastes and mannerisms of her employers. For pleasure she read the *Tatler*, travelled first class on her holidays and stated that she liked 'to work for people who have breeding . . . When I started you were really a servant, whereas now you're more of a friend. They come and thank you more.' Another of Barrow's interviewees, a middle-aged butler working for a multi-millionaire, had 'a brisk efficient manner'; he was a model of discretion and 'laid out tea every day with three or four different kinds of cake and bread and butter and china'. A younger, part-time, butler was of a different ilk altogether: he was more professional, did not feel demeaned or deferential towards his wealthy employers, and was, like his predecessor at Cliveden, Edwin Lee, 'startlingly upper class in manner and appearance'. The interviewees saw themselves as a dying breed – and took pride in it. A cook interviewed by Barrow regarded the other staff as untrained and rather common types: they wanted to watch *Come Dancing* on television, 'which I just couldn't bear'.[3]

Some domestics continued in residential jobs less for the money and prestige than for the security, the 'sense of community' that a large house run on traditional lines could still offer, even in reduced circumstances. During the 1970s, June Morris and her husband worked in a house with a small estate in North Wales; she did the sewing and ironing and he was head gardener. They went into service because they had 'itchy feet' and it gave them a chance to travel to beautiful parts of the country and live in a tied cottage. There was also an under-gardener, a cook and three daily servants, and a butler would be 'borrowed' for evening parties. Their employer was, like Mrs Chamberlayne, adamantly not one of those who had embraced the throwaway spirit of the paper napkin. When June Morris arrived at the house they had not had anyone for a while to do the ironing and there were forty pillowcases waiting to be pressed: 'She was very particular – ironing the table napkins had to be perfect.'[4]

In that vast and splendid mausoleum, Blenheim Palace, where Consuelo Vanderbilt had once suffered the agonising boredom of dinner waited on by fleets of indifferent staff, life also continued curiously unchanged, like a galleon oblivious to the whirling social currents beneath it. Pat Duncan, the Helenian who had come to Britain as a young manservant after the war, married his English wife Jenny in the early 1960s. By the end of the decade the Duncans took up work as gardener-handyman and lady's-maid to Laura Canfield in Buckinghamshire, who in 1972, at sixty-two, became the wife (he was her fourth husband) of Consuelo's son, the tenth Duke of Marlborough, then aged seventy-five. Mrs Canfield herself maintained old-fashioned standards of perfection. Jenny was required to turn out her mistress's handbag and wash her loose change every night. The maintenance and laundering of her clothes took hours ('her dresses were fantastic – every layer needed a different iron setting'). But she thought her employer 'a lonely kind of a person. She never really did a lot for herself and she never realised that things got messy because everything was always clean.'

Nothing, however, prepared the Duncans for the world they found still in existence at Blenheim. All the ranks of the staff maintained the strictest separation – even eating separately and each level with its own different menu – all catered for by a fleet of kitchen staff and cooks. The servants were so numerous that the Duncans (their status elevated by Jenny's role as lady's-maid to the new Duchess) were allotted two maids of their own. When they invited the other servants to a party the upper-servants refused to attend when they learned that staff belonging to the lower ranks were also to be there. The Duke was presented with a menu of fourteen choices every day, for every meal, as his father and grandfather had been before him. During the industrial power cuts of the seventies the palace was lit by nothing but candles; Jenny remembers: 'Blenheim was so creepy! It was frightening!' When the Duke died, two months after the marriage, the Duncans and the Duchess were unceremoniously asked to leave and, not without a sigh of relief, they returned to Buckinghamshire. Laura, Duchess of Marlborough, eventually died in London in the care of two Filipino maids, while the Duncans moved into a council house (having never had a chance to buy a house of their own) in Rickmansworth. Jenny became a cleaner, a job she does still, and to the highest standards: 'I'm very good at ironing – sheets over everything, tissue paper in the bodice to keep it puffed up!'[5]

On rural estates, in particular, old attitudes stuck for longer. The Oxfordshire shepherd Mont Abbot tells of an encounter with his employer, Miss Bruce, in 1966, by then an old woman:

> Her were getting a bit wandery. The police had picked her up several times at night walking miles away from home. Her were getting unpredictable in her behaviour. She invited me in one afternoon to come and have a drink. I didn't like to thwart her: her be still aristo-crat. But I warn't used to drinking in the middle of the day. I felt uncomfortable stuck among the valuable knick-knacks in her front room in my old shepherding gear drinking whisky from a crystal glass. I were wanting to get back to my flock. She set me next to a posh silver ornament with polished rams' horns 'so you'll feel at home'. She called it a mull. It were part of the grandeur of her Scottish childhood.[6]

Many in a new generation of estate owners struggled to reconcile the economic demands of a new world with an old world's patrician responsibilities. As sporting and agricultural fiefdom became corporate business, the laird of a Scottish estate reported in the 1970s that form-filling and employment regulations got in the way of the old relationship: 'It's a hard job to keep pace with bureau-cracy today and no longer possible to play the game by the rules.' The harassed heir said that while he could not distribute the largesse among his employees as his father had done, he felt the anxiety of dependence: 'If I go under financially it will not be only myself and my family who will suffer.' The new laird was holding on by his fingernails to something, an idea as well as a place, that he felt guilty about letting go. His social awkwardness was compounded by the shadow of the past and the expectations it aroused: 'I don't go round the estate at Christmas and the New Year wishing everyone the compliments of the season (as my father did), but I do try to convey my best wishes to those who live and work on the estate through the various departmental heads.'[7]

Chapter 27

'We Like It Because the Past Is Not So Worrying as the News'

The age of the butler and mob-capped housemaid was barely over before it was transmuted into stories of an English golden age. How golden depended largely on which side of that age you belonged. In many memoirs written after the war, a veil of nostalgia for old certainties hung over a tumultuous modern present. The decline of standards that came with machines was a common complaint, the hazy longing for what one of Marghanita Laski's fictional heroines calls, 'the glaze that laundries gave good linen', in the age of the self-service launderette and the dry-cleaner.

By the 1960s the era of the country house servant had assumed an anthropological distance and several former servants set down their recollections in autobiographies that became bestsellers. Margaret Powell – mouthy, indignant and sharp-eyed – is still the most celebrated of all the former servant-memoirists of the late sixties. The reluctant cook, with her size nine feet and seething radical politics, wrote her autobiography, *Below Stairs*, in 1968, and it was published that year to instant acclaim. Margaret soon became a television regular, producing several more books throughout the seventies, including a novel and a cookbook. Among the more poignant of Powell's memories were those involving her struggle to get an education. Her employers, she recalled, were often quite happy to lend her books from their libraries, but they were almost always amazed that a servant might actually want to read one. 'They knew that you breathed and you slept and you worked, but they didn't know that you read. Such a thing was beyond comprehension. They thought that in your spare time you sat and gazed into space or looked at *Peg's Paper* or the *Crimson Circle*. You could almost see them reporting to their friends. "Margaret's a good cook, but unfortunately she reads. Books you know."'[1]

By the 1970s, as that world slipped into a historical past, the reading public's appetite for the details of nine-course Edwardian dinners, of silver-polishing, curtseying and lace-trimmed caps, seemed unlimited. Margaret Powell's book was closely followed by *Every Other Sunday* by Jean Rennie and then by Winifred Foley's series of accounts of her childhood of rural poverty in the Forest of Dean and life as a maid and cleaner – books that made her into a celebrated and prolific writer up until her death in 2009. While the books of Rennie, Foley and Powell are spirited, observant and striking, most servants from the 'upper' end of service tended to maintain the discreet and unquestioning carapace of the old-fashioned retainer. Former butlers became popular as authors of guides to etiquette or how to give a dinner party, proving that social change had not entirely extinguished social insecurity. Retired valet Stanley Ager published *Ager's Way to Easy Elegance*, and then joined forces with his employer's daughter to co-write *Butler's Guide: Clothes Care, Managing the Table, Running the Home and Other Graces*. Arthur Inch (later to be technical advisor on Robert Altman's film *Gosford Park*) produced *Dinner is Served*. And Eileen Balderson, one of the few women servant memoirists who seemed genuinely to have revelled in life as a country house domestic, came out of retirement in 1982 to pen *Backstairs Life in a Country House*, with a co-writer who remembered that she was 'passionately determined to get it right' after noticing all the errors made by television period dramas. Other former servants noted how such dramas often got the smallest details wrong. An Oxfordshire woman who had been a maid between the wars found costume designers overly keen on elaborate, beribboned headwear: 'Oh no, we didn't have those flowing things – that's only on the television.'[2]

No contemporary cultural phenomenon, however, has laid the template of our idea of below-stairs life quite so completely as the ITV television series *Upstairs, Downstairs*, which, over four years (1971–5), and sixty-eight episodes, reached an estimated one billion viewers worldwide. Its creators, actresses Jean Marsh and Eileen Atkins, were themselves the children of former domestics (Marsh's mother a housemaid, Atkins's father an under-butler). *Upstairs, Downstairs* was originally to be titled 'Behind the Green Baize Door', and to have been a tale primarily of below stairs. But it was the close interweaving of the story of the Bellamy family upstairs and their servants below, and the crucial changes in that relationship through the first thirty years of the century, that gave the show its dramatic layers and its authenticity. As Jean Marsh told the broadcaster Russell Harty: 'The mistress of the house held their fate in her hands. Her rule over the servants' lives was as complete as any dictator.'[3] The original storyline, which included Lady Marjorie Bellamy as a one-time chorus girl and Rose the housemaid as a repressed lesbian, was toned down and the first episode, by Fay Weldon, was praised for the accuracy of its portrait of Edwardian life: one reviewer remarked how the maids were correctly depicted putting petrol on the muddy hems of their skirts, which then had to be hung outside because of the smell.

Much of the inside information for the drama was supplied by former servants, including Jean Rennie and Margaret Powell, who worked as consultants on the programme. Gordon Jackson, who played Mr Hudson, the Bellamys' butler, remembered taking advice from a professional butler, but found the 'do nots' so constraining to the character of Hudson that he jettisoned many of them. 'The butler, as head of the domestic staff, never took off his jacket in front of the other servants,' Jackson observed, 'and he always ate alone below stairs, probably in a little room adjoining the pantry. I didn't agree with all this, so in the end I gave up the research and played Hudson by ear. I tried to project him as a good man, not a bully or a tyrant, and being able to play him with my own Scots

accent gave me great confidence, as though he were a Scottish ghil-
lie, given a chance in town.'[4] It is an interesting illumination of the
extent to which upstairs-downstairs values, so apparently discarded
by the 1970s, continued their deep hold, that when filming began
on the series the actors who played 'upstairs' were allotted the finest
dressing rooms with showers, while the 'downstairs' actors, including Jackson and Angela Baddeley (Mrs Bridges, the cook), who
were at the time far better known and established, were furious to
find that they had been given the inferior ones.

The nearest most people now will come to service of the *Upstairs,
Downstairs* kind is in an expensive hotel. The Ritz hotel in London
saw out the Second World War by maintaining rigidly the exclusiv-
ity that its residents paid for. 'In the Palm Court every afternoon all
the tea tables were marked "Reserved". In this way the waiter could
politely explain to any he deemed undesirable that unfortunately
no tables were vacant.'[5] A system of lights summoned service at the
press of a button: valets were on a red light, yellow for the maid and
green for room service. Even in the 1970s many of the maids at the
Ritz had been there for over forty years, standing sentinel at each
end of the corridor.

The standards of the country house weekend party are still applied,
with a flattering personal touch: 'A client didn't have to ask for
breakfast. The staff already knew the order. Toast, buttered or not,
porridge with salt or sugar,' recalled a hall porter in 1999. In that year,
the Ritz employed seven floor housekeepers, two assistant housekeepers, fourteen full-time maids, two evening maids, four house-
men and five night cleaners. The following details of a 9 a.m. staff
meeting at the Ritz demonstrate the extraordinary service that money
can buy: 'Mr G is to have a traditional car to go sightseeing. Mr B, a
repeat client from Switzerland, is having Room 622 as always. Mr A,
a client from Jordan, has requested a specific room but this might be
an opportunity to show him new rooms ... Mr L likes his window
free of furniture and does not like petit fours, so there must be a bowl
of fruit but no bananas. Mr and Mrs D need a valet and a maid to
unpack. The Bibles must be removed from the rooms of a party from
Brunei, as must the alcohol from the minibars.'[6]

Such quiet luxury and attention is in the tradition of the absolute discipline that was the pride of grand English hospitality. As the sybaritic American journalist, Nathaniel Parker Willis, wrote in the 1840s: 'An arrival at a strange house in England seems to a foreigner almost magical. The absence of all bustle consequent on the same event abroad – the silent respectfulness, and self-possession of the servants – it is like the golden facility of a dream.'[7] Some of the large houses of the past have been transformed into institutions catering for particularly modern requirements. Tapton House in Chesterfield, the childhood home of Violet Markham, is now part of Chesterfield College, with an 'innovation centre' in its grounds, where clients can partake of 'executive stress services' including simulated golf and Indian head massage. In 1985 the former Astor home, Cliveden, became a luxury country house hotel, leased by an international hotel chain from the National Trust.

The market for private career domestics is small but lucrative, catered for by a series of specialist employment agencies who offer an updated version of the services of their Edwardian counterparts. 'Greycoat Placements', a domestic recruitment agency, occupies a few slightly shabby rooms in Victoria, London, overlooking the railway station. Greycoat's public face is threadbare but discreet, suggesting an establishment of long standing; in fact the agency was founded in 1996. Tradition, or the suggestion of tradition, is still an attraction for those able to afford housekeepers, butlers and valets. At Greycoat, however, the word 'servant' is frowned upon: the management prefer to talk of 'clients' and 'candidates', but on the whole the style is old-school, because old-school sells among the international super-rich, the 'high-net-worth individuals' for whom the agency caters. A house journal, *Discretion*, carries advice on grooming and personal appearance for would-be professional career domestics in the language of twenty-first-century managerese: wheels must be oiled, busy clients spared from stress, feathers soothed, people's whims and needs 'facilitated'. Ex-servicemen can be found on the books at Greycoat: continuing a tradition started after the First World War, they are greatly in demand for valet and butler work. People with experience of domestic service, or what at Greycoat they call 'the industry', also include former flight attendants, hotel caterers, even funeral directors – those accustomed to the deft efficiency and the self-effacing hush of good service.

In place of the small areas of skilled expertise that were formerly the preserve of large servants' halls, there is much talk of 'multi-skilling' and 'business hubs'. The most desirable servant is a flexible general factotum, who can turn his or her hand to most jobs. Nowadays the duties of a butler – or as they might now be titled, a 'household manager' – will probably include, say Greycoat, those of 'organising flights and downloading the Blackberry'. A butler's employer may well have properties all over the world which require continual management and organisation. For this work an experienced butler can expect to earn more than £50,000 a year.[8]

A popular mystique still surrounds the English aristocratic tradition of service, nourished by a worldwide appetite for English period television dramas. The Greycoat agency has a number of clients, particularly the Chinese new-rich, looking for a British butler (and he must be British) who will tell them what cutlery to use and when to use it. Underlining everything is still the absolute superiority of the hand-made, the particular, the individual, over the processed, the packaged and industrial. 'Try to draw the line at pre-packaged tea bags,' advises the website of the Butlers' Guild.

Traditional service of this kind has become affordable only to the ultra-rich. Norland nannies, still wearing their familiar brown uniforms, hats, gloves and capes, can command large salaries all over the world; English 'governesses' (now with obligatory teacher-training qualifications) are in great demand in Russia, and lady's-maids (commonly now called wardrobe managers) in the Middle East. A 'house steward', in an interesting reinvention of a role that had largely died out at the turn of the twentieth century, might nowadays be in charge of overseeing the use of his employer's house for 'corporate events'. These are the visible servants. Below them there are invisible hordes. In an echo of the Duke of Portland's underground network at Welbeck Abbey, One Hyde Park, the most expensive residential housing block in London, completed in

2011, boasts tunnels that will bring its billionaire residents food from its onsite restaurants, ensuring that the maids and waiters are entirely hidden from public view.

It is a world both new and old for Britain's longest-serving butler, Horace Mortiboy. Mr Mortiboy was still at work in 2007, aged eighty-eight, having begun his career in 1937 at the age of nineteen. From his neat modern house in Fontmell Magna, Dorset, he wonders at the lowering of standards in a world that once judged one on little else: 'Some of the people I work for now would have their breakfast in the kitchen. That would have been unheard of in the past.' The new butler-employing types, the pop stars and media moguls and billionaires, are not to his taste. During the seventies, Mr Mortiboy tried to get out of service, but found, like many male servants, that his experience left him qualified for little else, so he ended up working as a steward at the Ministry of Defence. He has also taught domestic science to students in an establishment outside Oxford. This was followed by some butlering work on the judges' circuit near Winchester. 'The people today who want people like me have not been trained to deal with people in personal life because they haven't had the staff to show them how to do it,' he says. Now he finds regular employment as a part-time butler, helping out at dinner parties or weekend house parties. But Mr Mortiboy laments the decline of standards. Anything goes now: 'You should be in the drawing room to welcome your guests when they arrive. You shouldn't expect them to be served champagne by the butler while you are in the bath.' As for accepting mobile phone calls during dinner: 'there's no suppose about it. It's wrong!'[9]

In 1981, Lavinia Smiley, writing about her Edwardian childhood, looked back in wonderment at just how densely peopled was the Edwardian home. 'I never cease to marvel at the astonishing lack of privacy which, in modern times, we would find so intolerable. You could not arrive or leave any big house without being let in or let out by some unfortunate menial who had to stay in – or stay up – for the purpose.'[10] As houses and living spaces have become smaller and expectations of personal space greater, modern employers who live with nannies and au pairs often jostle together, sharing bathrooms and living spaces, in an intimacy that resembles more the servants of the eighteenth century than the recent past. In 2005, in an article in the *Guardian*, the middle-class employers of an au pair talked about the inhibiting effect of the lack of privacy and the tension of it, and admitted to censoring their behaviour when the au pair was around: 'I think it's unsettling for her to hear us arguing, especially because her whole employment is based on the foundations of our relationship.' At best the relationship is negotiable because, unlike that of the traditional servant, it is designed to be temporary, short term, not a life-defining career choice but a mutually beneficial unprofessional arrangement convenient for modern working families. Clover Stroud, a single mother of two, wrote in 2006 of her Slovakian au-pair boy: 'I did not really care if I had to cook him a four-course cordon bleu meal every evening, as long as he could keep the children happy long enough for me to do some work.'

It is as difficult as it has always been to negotiate by law the relationships of the private home. Residential domestic service is still the most difficult to monitor, and the hours worked remain long: an average housekeeper living in, according to Greycoat, will work a twelve-hour day, from seven to seven, whereas the non-residential counterpart works from eight until six. Residential employees are often asked to sign a waiver on the working-time directive of forty-eight hours a week for reasons of 'flexibility'.

For the British worker, memories of the restriction and the indignities of the old service are burned deep in the collective memory. In the 1980s an English professional woman reported that she had to 'pluck up the courage' to tell her mother she had a cleaner, as to have one seemed a betrayal of her working-class roots and was 'totally alien to my background'. In the last two decades the service economy has grown beyond all expectations. For those lifestyles not catered for by the Greycoat agency, service may not look quite as it did, but it still fulfils the basic requirements that the fastest and newest appliance cannot: the daily demands of cleaning, washing, cooking and childcare in an age of two-income families. More than two centuries ago Voltaire observed that 'the comfort of the rich depends upon an abundant supply of the poor'. Now rich nations import servants from the poorer countries to fill the space left by a decline in service at home and to facilitate the freedom of work and education that their women enjoy. The historian Pamela Horn estimates that between 1996 and 1997 between 100,000 and 200,000 migrants came to Britain to work as domestics, and according to the Office for National Statistics, in 2011 household expenditure on domestic service has quadrupled in real terms since 1978.[11]

Some estimates suggest that there were as many domestics in London in 2011 as there were in the nineteenth century. Furthermore, the modern innovations that have removed visible labour from the good life are still underpinned by an unseen army of workers, a high percentage of them migrants. 'The cheapness and readiness with which the products of the factory can be obtained, whether for the purposes of food or clothing, has to a large extent removed [from the housewife] the desire to exercise these arts herself, especially from the woman whose time can be otherwise employed to her financial advantage in industrial pursuits,' Alice Ravenhill wrote in 1910. In the twenty-first century, these domestic requirements are met in large part by a growing service economy, with labour increasingly outsourced to industrial kitchens where workers produce pre-washed bags of salad, microwaveable plastic tubs of mashed potato or ready-to-heat pancetta-wrapped salmon.

The influx of European migrants and the increasing demand over the last twenty years for casual cleaning labour has become for the large part an unregulated system. The privilege of employing a domestic in the developed West reflects the economic hardship of the country from which that domestic originates. Few women would choose to enter domestic service as a cleaner: it entails long hours and low wages. Some do it because it provides a short-term solution to an economic problem or an opportunity to live abroad and send money home; for others it is a life sentence to which there is no alternative. The demand for domestic service has increased not just because people have got richer, but because of the availability of so many poor women who have no option but to take up domestic work. Many women, particularly from the Philippines or Brazil, would rather do cleaning or housekeeping work than childcare, which they find too painful because they have left their own children behind – and may not see them again for years. Many, having arrived on tourist visas, must duck and dive in constant fear that they may be deported.

Loose, woolly, difficult, sometimes embarrassing, the domestic relationship of employer and employee is one of the most testing, most intimate and one of the hardest relationships to define. Domestic service is both underpaid and undervalued, the skills of its practitioners considered remedial rather than creative. In 1925, Ernestine Mills wondered why domestic work, an occupation and preoccupation shared at some level by most people, should be looked down on with such disdain: 'Why cleaning a house should be considered more unproductive than cleaning a motor car or a golf course has yet to be explained.'[12] She has still not received an answer.

Notes

PART I: THE SYMBOLIC PANTOMIME
Chapter 1: 'A Sort of Silence and Embarrassment'

1 *The Private Life of the King by One of His Majesty's Servants*, London, 1901, p. 18.
2 A. F. Winnington-Ingram, *Fifty Years' Work in London*, London, 1940, p. 32.
3 *The Times*, 10 July 1902.
4 Francesca Wilson, *Strange Island: Britain Through Foreign Eyes, 1395–1940*, London, 1955, p. 173.
5 Susan Tweedsmuir, *The Lilac and the Rose*, London, 1952, p. 93.
6 Diana Cooper, *The Rainbow Comes and Goes*, London, 1958, p. 35.
7 H. G. Wells, *Tono-Bungay*, London, 1908, pp. 245–6.
8 Charles Jennings, *Them and Us: The American Invasion of British High Society*, Stroud, 2007, p. 51.
9 N14421796, 'In Service', Oxfordshire History Centre, interviews 1975.
10 Lady Cynthia Asquith, 'In Front of the Green Baize Door', in Noel Streatfeild (ed.), *The Day Before Yesterday: First-hand Stories of Fifty Years Ago*, London, 1956, p. 110.
11 Georgina Green (ed.), *Keepers, Cockneys and Kitchen Maids: Memories of Epping Forest 1900–1925*, London, 1987, p. 24.
12 M. J. Loftie, *Comfort in the Home*, London, 1895, p.149.
13 Maureen Dillon, *Artificial Sunshine: A Social History of Domestic Lighting*, London, 2001, p. 29.

14 Elizabeth Banks, *Campaigns of Curiosity: Journalistic Adventures of An American Girl in Late Victorian London*, London, 1894, p. 35.

15 'An Old Servant', *Domestic Service*, London, 1922, p. 10.

16 Cooper, *The Rainbow Comes and Goes*, p. 37.

17 Gordon Grimmett, 'The Lamp-Boy's Story', in Rosina Harrison (ed.), *Gentlemen's Gentlemen: My Friends in Service*, London, 1976, p. 22.

18 G. K. Chesterton, *Autobiography*, New York, 1936, p. 25.

Chapter 2: The Dainty Life

1 Quoted in Leonore Davidoff, *The Best Circles: Society, Etiquette and The Season*, London, 1973, p. 44.

2 QD/FLWE/MUC/2028, University of Essex.

3 C. F. G. Masterman, *The Condition of England*, London, 1909, p. 21.

4 'An Old Servant', *Domestic Service*, p. 14.

5 Mrs Alfred Praga, *Appearances: How to Keep Them Up on a Limited Income*, London, 1899, p. 14.

6 E. Royston Pike, *Human Documents of the Age of the Forsytes*, London, 1969, pp. 161–5.

7 T. W. H. Crosland, *The Suburbans*, London, 1905, p. 40.

8 V. S. Pritchett, *A Cab at the Door: An Autobiography*, London, 1968, p. 148.

9 Pike, *Human Documents*, p. 70.

10 Ibid., p. 75.

11 Beryl Lee Booker, *Yesterday's Child, 1890–1909*, London, 1937, p. 23.

12 Letter, *The Lady*, 26 July 1900.

13 'Conditions of Servants' Quarters', *The Lancet*, 24 March 1906.

14 J. E. Panton, *From Kitchen to Garret: Hints for Young Householders*, London, 1888, p. 3.

15 Quoted in Witold Rybcynski, *Home: A Short History of an Idea*, London, 1987, p. 17.

16 Tweedsmuir, *Lilac*, p. 107.

17 Quoted in John Burnett, *A Social History of Housing 1815–1985*, London, 1986, p.194.

18 Pritchett, *A Cab at the Door*, p. 142.

19 Eric Horne, *More Winks: Being Further Notes from the Life and*

Adventures of Eric Horne (Butler) for Fifty-Seven Years in Service with the Nobility and Gentry, London, 1932, p. 77.

20 Banks, *Campaigns of Curiosity*, p. 30.

21 Margaret Thomas, 'Behind the Green Baize Door', in *Day Before Yesterday*, pp. 82–3.

22 Mrs Eustace Miles, *The Ideal Home and it's Problems*, London, 1911, p. 74.

23 Quoted in Victoria Kelley, *Soap and Water, Cleanliness, Dirt and the Working Classes in Victorian and Edwardian Britain*, London, 2012, p. 147.

24 Quoted in ibid., p. 12.

25 *Norland Quarterly*, June 1911, Norland Institute Archives, Bath.

26 N14421796, Oxfordshire History Centre.

27 D/DX173/1, University of Reading.

28 Miles, *Ideal Home*, p. 6.

Chapter 3: 'A Seat in the Hall'

1 N14421796, Oxfordshire History Centre.

2 William Plomer, *Curious Relations*, London, 1945, p. 19.

3 Samuel Mullins and Gareth Griffiths, *Cap and Apron: An Oral History of Domestic Service in the Shires, 1880–1950*, Leicester, 1986, p. 7.

4 QD/FLWE/MUC/2028, University of Essex.

5 John Burnett (ed.), *Useful Toil: Autobiographies of Working People from the 1820s to the 1920s*, London, 1974, p. 216.

6 Quoted in Davidoff, *Best Circles*, p. 61.

7 Edith Waldemar Leverton, *Servants and their Duties*, London, 1912, p. 63.

8 Banks, *Campaigns of Curiosity*, p. 69.

9 Leverton, *Servants*, p. 64.

10 Quoted in Adrian Forty, *Objects of Desire: Design and Society Since 1750*, London, 1986, p. 85.

11 Eveline Askwith, *Tweeny: Domestic Service in Edwardian Harrogate*, Bridgwater, 2003, p. 20.

12 Quoted in Davidoff, *Best Circles*, p. 42.

13 Ibid., p. 46.

14 Anonymous, *The Manners and Rules of Good Society*, London, 1910, p. 30.

15 Philip Mason, *A Shaft of Sunlight: Memories of a Varied Life*, London, 1978, p. 18.

16 Ann Gander, *Top Hats and Servants' Tales: A Century of Life on Somerleyton Estate*, Wenhaston, 1998, p. 19.

17 Pike, *Human Documents*, p. 39.

18 Violet Markham, *Return Passage: An Autobiography*, London, 1953, p. 9.

19 Banks, *Campaigns of Curiosity*, p. 68.

20 Burnett (ed.), *Useful Toil*, p. 218.

21 Arnold Bennett, *Elsie and the Child: A Tale of Riceyman Steps*, London, 1929, p. 17.

22 D/DX173/1, University of Reading.

23 Markham, *Return Passage*, p. 36.

24 Lesley Lewis, *The Private Life of a Country House*, Newton Abbot, 1980, p. 46.

25 Pamela Sambrook, *Keeping Their Place: Domestic Service in the Country House*, Stroud, 2005, p. 90.

26 Charles Dean, 'The Hall-Boy's Story', in Harrison (ed.), *Gentlemen's Gentlemen*, p. 206.

Chapter 4: Centralising the Egg Yolks

1 Albert Thomas, *Wait and See*, London, 1944, p. 40.

2 Ernest King, *The Green Baize Door*, London, 1963, p. 89.

3 Consuelo Balsan, *The Glitter and the Gold*, London, 1953, pp. 62, 76.

4 Oxfordshire History Centre, N14421796.

5 King, *Green Baize Door*, p. 8.

6 Miss E. E. T., *The Domestic Life of Thomas Hardy*, Beaminster, 1963, p. 27.

7 Bennett, *Elsie and the Child*, p.10.

8 Asquith, 'In Front of the Green Baize Door', in *Day Before Yesterday*, p. 106.

9 Oxfordshire History Centre, N14421796.

10 Sarah Sedgewick, 'Other People's Children', in *Day Before Yesterday*, pp. 16–18.

11 Paul Thompson, *The Edwardians: The Remaking of British Society*, London, 1975, p. 94.

12 Sedgewick, 'Other People's Children', in *Day Before Yesterday*, p. 21.

13 Asquith, 'In Front of the Green Baize Door', in ibid., p. 118.
14 Sedgewick, 'Other People's Children', in ibid., p. 21.
15 Quoted in Penelope Stokes, *Norland: The Story of the First One Hundred Years*, Hungerford, 1992, p. 49.
16 Norland Institute Archives, Bath.
17 H. G. Wells, *Marriage*, London, 1912, p. 47.

Chapter 5: Popinjays and Mob Caps

1 Quoted in Duncan Crow, *The Edwardian Woman*, London, 1978, p. 128.
2 Charles Kightly, *Country Voices: Life and Lore in Farm and Village*, London, 1984, p. 148.
3 QD/FLWE/MUC/2028, University of Essex.
4 Interview, T1442R, British Library Sound Archive.
5 Kightly, *Country Voices*, p. 146.
6 Horne, *More Winks*, p. 217.
7 Margaret Llewelyn Davies (ed.), *Life as We Have Known It*, London, 1931, p. 18.
8 Askwith, *Tweeny*, p. 23.
9 Quoted in Phillis Cunnington, *The Costume of Household Servants from the Middle Ages to 1900*, London, 1974, p. 60.
10 Cunnington, *Household Servants*, p. 69.
11 Ibid., p. 77.
12 Horne, *More Winks*, p. 76.
13 Eric Horne, *What the Butler Winked At: Being the Life and Adventures of Eric Horne (Butler), for Fifty-seven Years in Service with the Nobility and Gentry*, London, 1924, p. 154.
14 Frederick Gorst, *Of Carriages and Kings*, London, 1956, p. 88.
15 Burnett (ed.), *Useful Toil*, p. 211.
16 Harrison (ed.), *Gentlemen's Gentlemen*, p. 230.
17 Gorst, *Carriages and Kings*, p. 112.
18 Thomas, 'In Front of the Green Baize Door', in *Day Before Yesterday*, p. 88.
19 Mrs C. S. Peel, *A Hundred Wonderful Years: Social and Domestic Life of the Century, 1820–1920*, London, 1926, p. 74.
20 'A Butler's View of Men-Service', *The Nineteenth Century*, Vol. XXXI, 1892.
21 King, *Green Baize Door*, p. 21.

Chapter 6: The Desire for Perfection

1 QD/FLWE/MUC/2028, University of Essex.
2 Markham, *Return Passage*, p. 56.
3 N14421796, Oxfordshire History Centre.
4 Rosina Harrison, *Gentlemen's Gentlemen: My Friends in Service*, London, 1978, p. 150.
5 Charles Dean, interviewed in 1975, in Geoffrey Tyack, 'Service on the Cliveden Estate Between the Wars', *Oral History*, Vol. 5, No. 1, Spring 1977.
6 Lewis, *Private Life*, p. 45.
7 Mullins and Griffiths, *Cap and Apron*, p. 15.
8 Daphne Fielding, *Before the Sunset Fades*, Longleat, 1953, p. 17.
9 QD/FLWE/MUC/2028, University of Essex.
10 Leverton, *Servants*, p. 7.
11 QD/FLWE/MUC/2028, University of Essex.
12 'The Page-Boy's Story', in Harrison (ed.), *Gentlemen's Gentlemen*, p. 116.
13 King, *Green Baize Door*, p. 9.
14 Frank V. Dawes, *Not in Front of the Servants: A True Portrait of Upstairs, Downstairs Life*, London, 1973, p. 64.
15 King, *Green Baize Door*, p. 152.
16 'An Old Servant', *Domestic Service*, p. 92.
17 William Lanceley, *From Hallboy to House Steward*, London, 1925, p. 161.
18 Thomas, *Wait and See*, p. 42.
19 King, *Green Baize Door*, p. 80.
20 Osbert Sitwell, *Tales My Father Taught Me: An Evocation of Extravagant Episodes*, London, 1962, p. 77.
21 Quoted in Sambrook, *Keeping Their Place*, p. 113.
22 Gorst, *Carriages and Kings*, p. 41.
23 Horne, *More Winks*, p. 119.

Chapter 7: 'Some Poor Girl's Got To Go Up and Down, Up and Down . . .'

1 H. G. Wells, *Kipps: The Story of a Simple Soul*, London, 1905; Penguin edition, 2005, p. 3.
2 Mullins and Griffiths, *Cap and Apron*, pp. 151–2.

3 Interview 2225, University of Essex.

4 Helen Dendy Bosanquet, *Rich and Poor*, London, 1898, p. 30.

5 Clarice Stella Davies, *North Country Bred*, London, 1963, p. 56.

6 Walter Southgate, *That's the Way It Was: A Working-Class Autobiography 1890–1950*, Centre for London History, 1982, p. 65.

7 Burnett (ed.), *Useful Toil*, pp. 215–16.

8 Bosanquet, *Rich and Poor*, p. 34.

9 D/DX173/1, University of Reading.

10 Burnett (ed.), *Useful Toil*, p. 220.

11 Banks, *Campaigns of Curiosity*, pp. 10–21.

12 Horne, *More Winks*, p. 76.

13 Elizabeth Roberts, *A Woman's Place: An Oral History of Working-Class Women 1890–1940*, Oxford, 1995, p. 242.

14 Stephen Caunce, 'East Riding Hiring Fairs', *Oral History*, Vol. 3, No. 2, Autumn 1975.

15 Mullins and Griffiths, *Cap and Apron*, p. 10.

16 Lanceley, *Hallboy to House Steward*, p. 20.

17 Oxfordshire History Centre, D/DX173/1.

18 Quoted in Anna Davin, *Growing up Poor: Home, School and Street in London, 1870–1914*, London, 1996, p. 88.

19 Margaret Powell, *Below Stairs*, London, 1968, p. 2.

20 Sheila Stewart, *Lifting the Latch: A Life on the Land, Based on the Life of Mont Abbott of Enstone*, Oxford, 1987, p. 62.

21 Quoted in Simon Nowell-Smith (ed.), *Edwardian England 1901–1914*, Oxford, 1964, p. 145.

22 Leverton, *Servants*, p. 9.

23 Banks, *Campaigns of Curiosity*, pp. 27–9.

24 Booker, *Yesterday's Child*, p. 20.

25 Quoted in Alistair Service, *Edwardian Interiors, Inside the Homes of the Poor, the Average and the Wealthy*, London, 1982, p. 67.

26 Panton, *Kitchen to Garret*, p. 157.

27 Mullins and Griffiths, *Cap and Apron*, p. 10.

28 Correspondence with author.

29 Burnett (ed.), *Useful Toil*, p. 217.

30 Edith Hall, *Canary Girls and Stockpots*, Luton, 1977, p. 31.

31 Edna Wheway, *Edna's Story: Memories of Life in a Children's Home and in Service, in Dorset and London*, Wimborne, 1984, p. 38.

32 Kedrun Laurie (ed.), *Cricketer Preferred: Estate Workers at Lyme Park, 1898–1946*, Disley, 1981.

33 *The Lady*, 27 September 1900.

34 D/DX173/1, University of Reading.

35 Lewis, *Private Life*, p. 96.

36 Interview 2000/156, University of Essex.

37 Mullins and Griffiths, *Cap and Apron*, p. 18.

38 King, *Green Baize Door*, p. 16.

39 John Burnett, *Destiny Obscure: Autobiographies of Childhood, Education and Family from the 1820s to the 1920s*, London, 1994, p. 293.

40 Quoted in Tony Rivers et al, *The Name of the Room: History of the British House and Home*, London, 1992, p. 199.

41 Lewis, *Private Life*, p. 99.

42 D/DX173/1, University of Reading.

43 Ibid.

44 Wheway, *Edna's Story*, p. 42.

45 Special Collections, Somerset Museum of Rural Life.

46 *Costume: Journal of the Costume Society*, 1969.

47 Laurie (ed.), *Cricketer Preferred*, pp.19–20.

48 Kathleen Woodward, *Jipping Street*, London, 1928, p. 12.

49 Interview 213, University of Essex.

50 Roberts, *A Woman's Place*, p.140.

51 See Judith Flanders, *Consuming Passions: Leisure and Pleasure in Victorian Britain*, London, 2006.

52 See Marghanita Laski's essay 'Domestic Life' in Nowell-Smith, *The Edwardians*.

53 Pike, *Human Documents*, p. 26.

54 Rose Harrison, *My Life in Service*, London, 1975, p. 64.

55 Pike, *Human Documents*, p. 171.

56 E. S. Turner, *What the Butler Saw: Two Hundred and Fifty Years of the Servant Problem*, London, 1963, p. 202.

PART II: THE SACRED TRUST
Chapter 8: The Ideal Village

1 Banks, *Campaigns of Curiosity*, p. 5.

2 Quoted in Kelley, *Soap and Water*, pp. 7–8.

3 1906 Annual Report, Barnardo's Archives, Barkingside.

4 Quoted in Standish Meacham, *Regaining Paradise: Englishness and the Early Garden City Movement*, New Haven and London, 1999, p. 30.

5 George Sturt, *Change in the Village*, London, 1912, p. 111.
6 Ibid., pp. 230–9.
7 E. V. Lucas, *Encounters and Diversions*, London, 1924, p. 8.
8 Mason, *A Shaft of Sunlight*, p. 20.
9 Powell, *Below Stairs*, p. 83.
10 Quoted in June Rose, *For the Sake of the Children: Inside Dr Barnardo's – 120 Years of Caring for Children*, London, 1987, p. 44.
11 Eileen Whiteing, *Anyone for Tennis? Growing up in Wallington Between the Wars*, Sutton Libraries, 1979, p. 20.
12 Rose, *For the Sake of the Children*, p. 51.
13 Mrs Richmond Ritchie, *Upstairs and Downstairs*, London, 1882, p. 200.
14 Ibid., p. 66.
15 Interview 740, Sound Archive, Imperial War Museum, London.
16 Mullins and Griffiths, *Cap and Apron*, p. 29.
17 Dolly Davey, *A Sense of Adventure*, Southwark People's History Project, 1980, p. 7.
18 'The Working Girl of Today', *The Nineteenth Century*, May 1888.
19 *Pall Mall Gazette*, 7 July 1885.
20 Quoted in Lydia Murdoch, *Imagined Orphans: Poor Families, Child Welfare and Contested Citizenship in London*, New Jersey, 2006, p. 58.
21 Ibid., p. 139.
22 Norman Wymer, *Father of Nobody's Children: A Portrait of Dr Barnardo*, London, 1954, p. 18.
23 Rose, *For the Sake of the Children*, p. 52.
24 Hall, *Canary Girls*, p. 29.
25 Banks, *Campaigns of Curiosity*, p. 4.
26 Quoted in Standish Meacham, *A Life Apart: The English Working Class 1890–1914*, London, 1977, p. 189.
27 Interview 132, University of Essex.
28 Green, *Keepers, Cockneys*, p. 19.
29 Quoted in Crow, *Edwardian Woman*, p. 100.
30 Quoted in Murdoch, *Imagined Orphans*, p. 47.
31 Charles Booth, *Life and Labour of the People in London*, London, 1892–7, Vol. 4.
32 Kightly, *Country Voices*, p. 147.
33 Crosland, *The Suburbans*, p. 82.
34 Correspondence with author.
35 Interview 153, University of Essex.
36 Interview 213, ibid.

37 Quoted in Davin, *Growing up Poor*, p. 78.

38 T. S. Eliot, 'Morning at the Window' (1917), in *Prufrock and Other Observations*, London, 1920.

39 Interview 153, University of Essex.

Chapter 9: 'Silent, Obsequious and Omnipresent'

1 'Female Emigration to South Africa', *The Nineteenth Century*, January 1902.

2 Pamela Horn, *Life Below Stairs in the Twentieth Century*, Stroud, 2001, pp. 192–3.

3 Ibid., p. 194.

4 Quoted in Gina Buijs (ed.), *Migrant Women: Crossing Boundaries and Changing Identities*, London, 1996, p. 171.

5 Buijs (ed.), *Migrant Women*, p. 14.

6 Santha Rama Rau, *Home to India*, London, 1945, p. 8.

7 Lawrence Fleming, *The Last Children of the Raj: British Childhoods in India*, London, 2004, Vol. I, p. 112.

8 W. H. Dawes, *Beyond the Bungalow*, London, 1888, p. 19.

9 Jon and Rumer Godden, *Two Under the Indian Sun*, 1964, p. 30.

10 Quoted in David Burton, *The Raj at Table: A Culinary History of the British in India*, London, 1993, p. 69.

11 Rau, *Home to India*, p. 45.

12 Dawes, *Bungalow*, p. 9.

13 Quoted in Mary Procida, *Married to the Empire: Gender, Politics and Imperialism in India*, Manchester, 2002, p. 89.

14 Quoted in Margaret MacMillan, *Women of the Raj*, London, 1996, p. 26.

15 Maud Diver, *The Englishwoman in India*, London, 1909, p. 34.

16 Fleming, *Last Children*, p. 197.

17 Quoted in Hilton Brown, *The Sahibs: The Life and Ways of the British in India as Recorded by Themselves*, London, 1948, p. 218.

18 Brown, *Sahibs*, p. 70.

19 Rau, *Home to India*, p. 15.

20 Charles Allen, *Plain Tales from the Empire*, London, 2008, p. 336.

21 Ibid., p. 338.

22 V. K. R. Menon, *The Raj and After: Memoirs of a Bihar Civilian*, New Delhi, 2000, p. 97.

23 Faizur Rasul, *Bengal to Birmingham*, London, 1967, p. 78.

24 Powell, *Below Stairs*, p. 122.

25 Rasul, *Bengal*, p. 159.

26 Interview with Happy Sturgeon, British Library Sound Archive/ George Ewart Evans Collection.

27 Ethel Savi, *Birds of Passage*, London, 1939, p. 97.

28 Brown, *Sahibs*, p. 211.

Chapter 10: 'Bowing and Scraping'

1 *The Times*, 29 November 1911.

2 Quoted in William Watkin Davies, *Lloyd George 1863–1914*, London, 1939, p. 379.

3 *The Times*, 29 November 1911.

4 D/DX173/1, Oxfordshire History Centre.

5 Thomas, *Wait and See*, p. 9.

6 Sir William Blackstone, *Commentaries on the Laws of England*, 1765.

7 Robert Roberts, *A Ragged Schooling: Growing Up in the Classic Slum*, Manchester, 1976, p. 88.

8 E. P. Thompson, *The Making of the English Working Class*, London, 1963, p. 31.

9 Dolly Scannell, *Mother Knew Best: An East End Childhood*, London, 1974, p. 29.

10 Thomas, *Wait and See*, p. 21.

11 Interview in Thompson, *The Edwardians*, p. 54.

12 D/DX173/1, Oxfordshire History Centre.

13 707/455/1–2, University of Essex.

14 Interview 213, University of Essex.

15 Kightly, *Country Voices*, p. 168.

16 Thea Thompson, *Edwardian Childhoods*, London, 1981, p. 195.

17 Harrison, *My Life in Service*, pp. 19–20.

18 *The Times*, 21 January 1911.

19 Charles Cooper, *Town and County: Or Forty Years in Private Service with the Aristocracy*, London, 1937, p. 47.

20 Alice Osbourn diaries.

21 Davey, *Adventure*, p. 7.

22 Tyack, 'Service on the Cliveden Estate'.

23 Markham, *Return Passage*, p. 37.

24 852, Lady Lewis Collection, Bodleian Library.

25 Auguste Schlüter, *A Lady's Maid in Downing Street*, London, 1922, p. 51.

26 Quoted in Philip Ziegler, *Osbert Sitwell*, London, 1998, p. 160.

27 Merlin Waterson, *The Servants' Hall: A Domestic History of Erddig*, London, 1980.

28 Quoted in Jessica Gerard, 'Lady Bountiful, Women of the Landed Classes and Rural Philanthropy', *Victorian Studies*, Vol. 30, No. 2, 1987.

29 Burnett, *Destiny Obscure*, p. 40.

30 'An Old Servant', *Domestic Service*, p. 24.

31 Stewart, *Lifting the Latch*, p. 53.

32 N14421796, Oxfordshire History Centre.

33 2,541, Burnett Archive, Brunel University.

34 Quoted in Dawes, *Not in Front of the Servants*, p. 29.

35 707/455/1–2, University of Essex.

36 QD/FLWE/MUC/2028, University of Essex.

37 Horn, *Life Below Stairs*, p. 12.

38 Panton, *Kitchen to Garret*, p. 90.

39 Tweedsmuir, *Lilac*, p. 97.

40 Powell, *Below Stairs*, p. 36.

41 Quoted in Alison Light, *Mrs Woolf and the Servants*, London, 2007, p. 142.

42 Llewelyn Davies, *Life As We Have Known It*, p. 29.

43 Panton, *Kitchen to Garret*, p. 84.

44 Quoted in Dillon, *Artificial Sunshine*, p. 180.

45 Thompson, *The Edwardians*, p. 82.

46 Miles, *Ideal Home*, p. 265.

47 Willoughby de Broke, *The Passing Years*, London, 1924, p. 99.

48 Thompson, *The Edwardians*, p. 47.

49 Lewis, *Private Life*, p. 47.

50 Viola Bankes, *A Kingston Lacy Childhood*, Wimborne, 1986, p. 28.

51 Frances Partridge, *Memories*, London, 1981, p. 19.

52 Tweedsmuir, *Lilac*, p. 93.

53 Schlüter, *Lady's Maid*, p. 30.

54 Thompson, *The Edwardians*, p. 48.

55 Service, *Edwardian Interiors*, p. 149.

56 Private recording.

57 Thomas, *Wait and See*, p. 102.

58 C. V. Butler, *Domestic Service: an Enquiry by the Women's Industrial Council*, London, 1916, p. 34.

59 Tweedsmuir, *Lilac*, p. 80.

60 'A Four-inch-Driver', *The Chauffeur's Handbook*, London, 1909, p. 31.
61 Lewis, *Private Life*, p. 15.
62 Hall, *Canary Girls*, p. 32.
63 Butler, *Domestic Service*, p. 96.
64 Thompson, *The Edwardians*, p. 168.
65 George Dangerfield, *The Strange Death of Liberal England*, London, 1935, p. 14.
66 Private papers.
67 Quoted in Waterson, *Servants' Hall*, p. 178.

PART III: THE AGE OF AMBIVALENCE
Chapter 11: 'Out of a Cage'

1 Kightly, *Country Voices*, p. 97.
2 Mrs C. S. Peel, *How We Lived Then*, London, 1929, pp. 22–3.
3 *The Times*, 8 October 1916.
4 Osbourn diaries.
5 Horne, *What the Butler Winked At*, p. 19.
6 Alison Adburgham, *A Punch History of Manners and Modes 1841–1940*, London, 1961, p. 18.
7 Peel, *How We Lived*, p. 22.
8 Ibid., p. 23.
9 Gabriel Tschumi, *Royal Chef: Forty Years with Royal Households*, London, 1954, p. 142.
10 Quoted in Kenneth Rose, *King George V*, London, 1983, p. 260.
11 Arthur Marwick, *The Deluge: British Society and the First World War*, London, 1965, pp. 91–2.
12 *The Times*, 8 December 1915.
13 Quoted in Gail Braybon and Penny Summerfield, *Out of the Cage: Women's Experiences in Two World Wars*, London, 1987, p. 39.
14 Interview 693, Imperial War Museum.
15 *The Times*, 11 October 1915.
16 *The Times*, 8 December 1915.
17 Osbourn diaries.
18 Laurie, *Cricketer Preferred*, pp. 32–3.
19 Horne, *What the Butler Winked At*, p. 1.
20 Merlin Waterson (ed.), *The Country House Remembered: Recollections of Life Between the Wars* London, 1985, p. 33.
21 Horn, *Life Below Stairs*, p. 32.

Chapter 12: 'Don't Think Your Life Will Be Any Different to Mine'

1 Private papers.

2 Harrison (ed.), *Gentlemen's Gentlemen*, p. 59.

3 Leslie Baily, *Scrapbook for the Twenties*, London, 1959, p. 196.

4 Quoted in David Mitchell, *Women on the Warpath: The Story of the Women of the First World War*, London, 1965, p. 90.

5 Quoted in Judy Giles, *Women, Identity and Private Life in Britain 1900–50*, Basingstoke, 1995, p. 5.

6 Quoted in Gail Braybon, *Women Workers in the First World War*, London, 1981, p. 189.

7 *Daily Mail*, 14 September 1915.

8 Turner, *What the Butler Saw*, p. 226.

9 John Clarke et al (eds), *Working Class Culture: Studies in History and Theory*, London, 2007, p. 124.

10 Burnett (ed.), *Useful Toil*, p. 221.

11 Davey, *Adventure*, p. 9.

12 Osbourn diaries.

13 Brian Braithwaite, *Ragtime to Wartime: The Best of Good Housekeeping 1922–1939*, London, 1986, p. 15.

14 Joyce Storey, *Our Joyce*, Bristol, 1987, p. 80.

15 Ibid., p. 86.

16 Jean Rennie, *Every Other Sunday*, London, 1955, p. 100.

17 Ibid., p. 120.

18 Quoted in Susan Kingsley Kent, 'The Politics of Sexual Difference: World War One and the Demise of British Feminism', *The Journal of British Studies*, Vol. 27, No. 3 (July 1988), pp. 232–53.

19 Robert Graves and Alan Hodge, *The Long Weekend: A Social History of Britain 1918–1939*, New York, 1941, p. 66.

20 Harrison (ed.), *Gentlemen's Gentlemen*, p. 207.

21 Mrs Lily Frazer, *First Aid for the Servantless*, Cambridge, 1913, p. 207.

22 Ernestine Mills, *The Domestic Problem, Past, Present and Future*, London, 1925, p. 36.

23 Mrs C. S. Peel, *Waiting at Table*, London, 1929, p. 40.

24 Quoted in Dale Spender (ed.), *Time and Tide Wait for No Man*, London, 1984, p. 216.

25 Correspondence with author.

26 Rennie, *Every Other Sunday*, p. 141.

27 Spender, *Time and Tide*, p. 213.

28 Quoted in Horn, *Below Stairs*, p. 83.

29 Pamela Horn, 'Ministry of Labour Female Training Programmes between the Wars, 1919–39', *History of Education* (2002), 31:1.

30 Thomas Jones, *A Diary with Letters*, Oxford, 1954, p. 286.

31 F. A. F. Livingston, 'Household Economy and Cookery in Relation to Poverty', in *The New Survey of London Life and Labour*, Vol. 6, London, 1930–35, pp. 299–333.

32 Quoted in Steve Humphries et al (eds), *A Century of Childhood*, London, 1988, p. 97.

33 Interview with Happy Sturgeon, British Library Sound Archive.

Chapter 13: 'It Was Exploitation But It Worked'

1 Baily, *Scrapbook*, p. 84.

2 Winifred Foley, *A Child in the Forest*, London, 1974, pp. 156–7.

3 Private collection.

4 Horne, *More Winks*, p. 12.

5 Private collection.

6 Quoted in Ruth Adam, *A Woman's Place 1910–1975*, London, 1975, p. 91.

7 Harrison (ed.), *Gentlemen's Gentlemen*, p. 94.

8 Naomi Mitchison, *You May Well Ask: A Memoir 1920–1940*, London, 1979, p. 19.

9 Ethel Mannin, *Young in the Twenties: A Chapter of Autobiography*, London, 1971, p. 17.

10 Ibid., p. 18.

11 Harrison, *My Life in Service*, p. 20.

12 Paul Berry and Alan Bishop (eds), *Testament of a Generation: the Journalism of Vera Brittain and Winifred Holtby*, London, 1985, p. 94.

13 Quoted in Marion Shaw, *The Clear Stream: A Life of Winifred Holtby*, London, 1999, p. 127.

14 Vincent O'Sullivan and Margaret Scott (eds), *The Collected Letters of Katherine Mansfield*, Oxford, 1984–2008, p. 111.

15 Ronald Blythe, *The Age of Illusion, England in the Twenties and Thirties, 1919–1940*, London, 1964, p. 20.

16 Thompson, *The Edwardians*, p. 210.

17 Quoted in Margaret Horsfield, *Biting the Dust: The Joys of Housework*, London, 1999, p. 73.

18 Violet Firth, *The Psychology of the Servant Problem, A Study in Social Relationships*, London, 1925, pp. 7–25.
19 Partridge, *Memories*, p. 128.

Chapter 14: 'Tall, Strong, Healthy and Keen To Work'

1 Rose Mary Crawshay, *Domestic Service for Gentlewomen*, London, 1876, p. 26.
2 Quoted in Alice Renton, *Tyrant or Victim? A History of the British Governess*, London, 1991, p. 113.
3 *The Times*, 2 January 1920.
4 *News Chronicle*, 7 June 1937.
5 Kate Herbert-Hunting, *Universal Aunts*, London, 1986, p. 22.
6 Ibid.
7 Foley, *Child in the Forest*, p. 231.
8 Universal Aunts archives.
9 *The Lady*, 27 March 1902.
10 Brian Masters, *Great Hostesses*, London, 1982, p. 91.
11 Herbert-Hunting, *Universal Aunts*, p. 27.
12 E. V. Lucas, *Advisory Ben*, London, 1923, p. 9.
13 Quoted in Waterson, *Country House Remembered*, p. 35.
14 Universal Aunts archives.

Chapter 15: The Mechanical Maid

1 Mannin, *Young in the Twenties*, p. 46.
2 Randal Philips, 'The Servantless House', *Country Life*, Vol. 52, 1922.
3 Quoted in Philip Hoare's *Dictionary of National Biography* entry for Syrie Maugham.
4 Mills, *The Domestic Problem*, p. 69.
5 Ibid., p. 70.
6 Quoted in Jerry White, *London in the Twentieth Century: A City and its People*, London, 2001, p. 18.
7 Interview 96.45, Museum of London.
8 Thomas, *Wait and See*, p. 66.
9 Interview 96.45, Museum of London.
10 2.51, Burnett Archives, Brunel University.
11 Burnett, *Social History of Housing*, p. 262.
12 Caroline Haslett, *Household Electricity*, London, 1939, pp. 7–8.

13 Quoted in Forty, *Objects of Desire*, p. 187.
14 Interview T1434WR, British Library Sound Archive.
15 Frazer, *First Aid*, p. 44.
16 Braithwaite, *Ragtime*, p. 39.
17 Dorothy Scannell, *Mother Knew Best*, p. 24.
18 Daisy England, *Daisy, Daisy*, London, 1981, p. 100.
19 Correspondence with author.
20 Dawes, *Servants*, p. 7.
21 Hall, *Canary Girls*, p. 16.
22 Braithwaite, *Ragtime*, pp. 40–1.
23 Odette Keun, *I Discover the English*, London, 1934, p. 45.
24 Lettice Cooper, *The New House*, New York, 1936, p. 147.

PART IV: OUTER SHOW AND INNER LIFE
Chapter 16: 'A Vast Machine That Has Forgotten How To Stop Working'

1 Clough Williams-Ellis, *England and the Octopus*, London, 1928, p. 80.
2 Waterson, *Country House*, p. 16.
3 Ibid., p. 187.
4 Duke of Bedford, *A Silver-Plated Spoon*, London, 1959, p. 15.
5 Interview with author.
6 Powell, *Below Stairs*, p. 48.
7 Waterson, *Country House*, p. 69.
8 Lewis, *Private Life*, p. 110.
9 Correspondence with author.
10 Lewis, *Private Life*, p. 111.
11 Dawes, *Servants*, p. 97.
12 D/DX173/1, University of Reading.
13 Masters, *Hostesses*, p. 70.
14 D/DX173/1, University of Reading.
15 Ibid.
16 Rennie, *Every Other Sunday*, p. 22.
17 Correspondence with author.
18 Quoted in Norman Longmate, *How We Lived Then: A History of Everyday Life during the Second World War*, London, 1971, p. 37.
19 D/DX173/1, University of Reading.
20 Ibid.
21 Laurie, *Cricketer Preferred*, p. 28.

22 Eileen Balderson, *Backstairs Life in an English Country House*, Newton Abbot, 1982, p. 17.
23 Harrison, *My Life in Service*, p. 38.
24 Sir Philip Gibson, *The New Man*, London, 1913, p. 81.
25 *The Times*, 29 January 1925.
26 *The Times*, 6 March 1925.
27 *The Times*, 10 January 1930.
28 Harrison (ed.), *Gentlemen's Gentlemen*, p. 210.
29 Rennie, *Every Other Sunday*, p. 62.
30 Thompson, *Edwardians*, p. 45.
31 Balderson, *Backstairs Life*, p. 119.
32 Waterson, *Country House*, p. 90.
33 Rennie, *Every Other Sunday*, p. 40.
34 D/DX173/1, University of Reading.
35 Rennie, *Every Other Sunday*, p. 36.
36 Quoted in Alun Howkins, *The Death of Rural England: A Social History of the Countryside Since 1900*, London, 2003, p. 59.
37 Powell, *Below Stairs*, p. 218.
38 Correspondence with author.
39 Ibid.
40 Celia Fremlin, *The Seven Chars of Chelsea*, London, 1940, p. 34.

Chapter 17: 'Bachelor Establishments Are Notoriously Comfortable'

1 Philip Mason, *The English Gentleman: The Rise and Fall of an Ideal*, London, 1982, p. 145.
2 Peel, *Waiting at Table*, p. 8.
3 Braithwaite, *Ragtime*, p. 29.
4 George Criticos, *The Life Story of George of the Ritz*, London, 1959, p. 27.
5 Jeremy Lewis, *Penguin Special: The Life and Times of Allen Lane*, London, 2005, p. 172.
6 Leverton, *Servants*, p. 31.
7 Pike, *Human Documents*, p. 56.
8 Quoted in Allen, *Plain Tales*, p. 327.
9 Harold Nicolson, *George V, His Life and Reign*, London, 1952, p. 54.
10 Wilhelm Dibelius, *England*, Stuttgart, 1922, p. 9.
11 Quoted in Rose, *George V*, p. 292.

12 Stanley Ager and Fiona St Aubyn, *The Butler's Guide to Running the Home and Other Graces*, London, 1980, p. 13.
13 Interview 24708, Imperial War Museum.
14 Interview 751, Imperial War Museum.
15 Harrison (ed.), *Gentlemen's Gentlemen*, p. 228.
16 Mullins and Griffiths, *Cap and Apron*, p. 36.
17 Quoted in Turner, *What the Butler Saw*, p. 213.
18 Horne, *More Winks*, p. 118.
19 Powell, *Below Stairs*, p. 73.
20 Ibid., p. 80.
21 *The Times*, 30 December 1939.
22 Ager, *Butler's Guide*, p. 53.
23 Harrison (ed.), *Gentlemen's Gentlemen*, p. 230.
24 Ager, *Butler's Guide*, p. 53.

Chapter 18: The Question of the Inner Life

1 *The Times*, 6 October 1937.
2 'Jan Struther', *Dictionary of National Biography* entry by Nicola Beauman.
3 *The Times*, 19 May 1938.
4 Interview with author.
5 *The Times*, 19 June 1939.
6 Quoted in Thea Holme, *The Carlyles at Home*, London, 1965, p. 162.
7 Quoted in Ruth Schwartz Cowan, *More Work for Mother: The Ironies of Household Technology from the Open Hearth to the Microwave*, New York, 1983, p. 43.
8 E. M. Delafield, *The Diary of a Provincial Lady*, London, 1930, p. 127.
9 Ibid., p. 165.
10 Rasul, *Bengal to Birmingham*, p. 95.
11 Cooper, *New House*, p. 102.
12 *The Times*, 26 November 1937.
13 Mary Wylde, *A Housewife in Kensington*, London, 1937, p. 45.
14 Ibid., p. 36.
15 *The Times*, 19 May 1938.
16 Powell, *Below Stairs*, p. 84.
17 Stephen Taylor, 'The Suburban Neurosis', *The Lancet*, 26 March 1938.
18 Humphries, *Century of Childhood*, pp. 95–7.

19 Quoted in Jenny Hartley (ed.), *Hearts Undefeated: Women's Writing of the Second World War*, London, 1995, pp. 342–3.
20 Ibid., p. 343.

Chapter 19: 'Do They Really Drink Out of Their Saucers?'

1   Keun, *I Discover the English*, p. 47.
2   Correspondence with author.
3   Thomas, *Wait and See*, p. 77.
4   Fremlin, *Seven Chars*, p. 24.
5   Braithwaite, *Ragtime*, p. 178–79.
6   Edith Milton, *The Tiger in the Attic: Memories of the Kindertransport and Growing Up English*, Chicago, 2005, p. 17.
7   *The Times*, 24 February 1938.
8   Fremlin, *Seven Chars*, p. 170.
9   Interview with author.
10 Correspondence with author.
11 Foley, *Child in the Forest*, p. 80.
12 Powell, *Below Stairs*, p. 70.

Chapter 20: 'Of Alien Origin'

1   Ronald Fraser, *In Search of a Past*, London, 1984, pp. 13–15.
2   Ibid., p. 33.
3   Interview with author.
4   Fraser, *In Search of a Past*, p. 133.
5   Norman Angell and Dorothy Buxton, *You and the Refugee: The Morals and Economics of the Problem*, London, 1939, p. 8.
6   Quoted in Zoe Josephs, *Survivors: Jewish Refugees in Birmingham, 1933–1945*, Oldbury, 1988, p. 138.
7   Hanna Spencer, *Hanna's Diary, 1938–1941*, Ontario, 2001, p. 71.
8   Lore Segal, *Other People's Houses*, London, 1964, p. 82.
9   Gabrielle Tergit, *Austrian Jewish Refugee (AJR) Newsletter*, 1951.
10 Josephs, *Survivors*, p. 140.
11 Bertha Leverton and Shmuel Lowensohn (eds), *I Came Alone: The Stories of the Kindertransports*, Indiana, 1990, p. 61.
12 Tergit, *AJR Newsletter*.
13 Fraser, *In Search of a Past*, p. 144.

14 Werner E. Mosse (ed.), *Second Chance: Two Centuries of German-Speaking Jews in the United Kingdom*, Tubingen, 1991, p. 567.

15 Mosse, *Second Chance*, p. 574.

16 Leverton and Lowensohn, *I Came Alone*, p. 97.

17 Spencer, *Hanna's Diary*, p. 93.

18 AJR 'Refugee Voices' Archive, Wiener Library.

19 Ibid.

20 Josephs, *Survivors*, p. 139.

21 Exs/2, German Institute, University of London.

22 Spencer, *Hanna's Diary*, p. 86.

23 Bronka Schneider, *Exile: A Memoir*, Ohio, 1998, p. 80.

24 Segal, *Other People's Houses*, p. 120.

25 Josephs, *Survivors*, p. 143.

26 Fraser, *In Search of a Past*, p. 146.

27 Spencer, *Hanna's Diary*, p. 100.

28 AJR 'Refugee Voices' Archive, Wiener Library.

29 Exs/2, German Institute.

30 Mosse, *Second Chance*, p. 577.

31 Ibid., p. 574.

32 Quoted in Pat Kirkham and David Thoms (eds), *War Culture: Social Change and Changing Experience in World War Two*, London, 1995, p. 17.

33 Fraser, *In Search of a Past*, p. 151.

PART V: A NEW JERUSALEM
Chapter 21: 'A New and Useful Life'

1 Ronald Blythe, *Akenfield: Portrait of an English Village*, London, 1969, p. 119.

2 Interview with author.

3 Quoted in Norman Longmate, *The Home Front: An Anthology of Personal Experience, 1938–1945*, p. 35.

4 John Martin Robinson, *The Country House at War*, London, 1989, p. 27.

5 Quoted in Turner, *What the Butler Saw*, p. 211.

6 Correspondence with author.

7 Quoted in Angus Calder, *The People's War: Britain 1939–1945*, London, 1992, p. 88.

8 Correspondence with author.

9 Ibid.

10 Penny Kitchen, *For Home and Country: War, Peace and Rural Life as Seen Through the Pages of the W.I. Magazine, 1919–1959*, London, 1990, p. 55.

11 Quoted in Robinson, *Country House at War*, p. 225.

12 Laurie, *Cricketer Preferred*, p. 24.

13 Quoted in Robinson, *Country House at War*, p. 190.

14 Quoted in E. S. Turner, *The Phoney War on the Home Front*, London, 1961, p. 269.

15 Davey, *Adventure*, p. 26.

16 Turner, *The Phoney War*, p. 254.

17 Mason, *A Shaft of Sunlight*, p. 219.

18 Mollie Panter-Downes, *Good Evening, Mrs Craven: The Wartime Stories of Mollie Panter-Downes*, London, 1999, p. 80.

19 Eileen Whiteing, *Some Sunny Day: Reminiscences of a Young Wife in the Second World War*, Sutton Arts and Libraries Services, 1983, p. 8.

20 Winifred Peck, *House-Bound*, London, 1942, p. 26.

21 Nesca Robb, *An Ulsterwoman in England 1924–1941*, Cambridge, 1942, p. 89.

22 Penelope Fitzgerald, Afterword to *House-Bound* (2007 edition), p. 4.

23 Harrison, *My Life in Service*, p. 171.

24 Milton, *Tiger in the Attic*, p. 33.

25 Quoted in Angela Holdsworth, *Out of the Doll's House: The Story of Women in the Twentieth Century*, London, 1988, p. 190.

26 Elizabeth Jordan, *As Cooks Go*, London, 1950, p. 11.

27 Quoted in Hartley, *Hearts Undefeated*, p. 292.

28 Clara Milburn, *Mrs Milburn's Diaries: An Englishwoman's Day to Day Reflections, 1939–45*, London, 1979, p. 33.

29 Leonora Fitzgibbon, *With Love: An Autobiography, 1938–46*, London, 1982, p. 57.

30 Naomi Mitchison, *Among You Taking Notes: The Wartime Diary of Naomi Mitchison*, Oxford, 1986, p. 35.

31 Fraser, *In Search of the Past*, p. 142.

32 Correspondence with author.

33 Interview 409, University of Essex.

34 Rennie, *Every Other Sunday*, p. 34.

Chapter 22: The Housewife Militant

1 David Kynaston, *Austerity Britain, 1945–1951*, London, 2007, p. 109.
2 Quoted in Christina Hardyment, *Slice of Life: The British Way of Eating Since 1945*, London, 1995, p. 26.
3 Quoted in James Hinton, 'Militant Housewives: the British Housewives League and the Attlee Government', *History Workshop Journal*, 38:1 (1944).
4 Fremlin, *Seven Chars*, p. 48.
5 Elaine Burton, *Domestic Work: Britain's Largest Industry*, London, 1944.
6 'Violet Markham', *Dictionary of National Biography* entry by Helen Jones.
7 Violet Markham and Florence Hancock, *A Post-War Report on Domestic Service*, London, 1945, p. 59.
8 Markham, *Return Passage*, p. 33.
9 Burton, *Domestic Work*, p. 5.
10 Caroline Davidson, *A Woman's Work is Never Done: A History of Housework in the British Isles, 1650–1950*, London, 1982, p. 238.
11 Joyce Storey, *Joyce's War*, Bristol, 1990, p. 142.
12 Ferdynand Zweig, *Women's Life and Labour*, London, 1952, p. 141.
13 Roy Lewis and Angus Maude, *The English Middle Classes*, London, 1949, p. 250
14 Winifred Foley, *Shiny Pennies and Grubby Pinafores: How We Overcame Hardship to Raise a Happy Family in the 1950s*, London, 1977, p. 71.
15 Markham, *Return Passage*, p. 32.
16 *The Listener*, 23 April 1946.

Chapter 23: 'The Change: It Must Have Been Terrible for Them'

1 Jennifer Jenkins and Patrick James, *From Acorn to Oak Tree: The Growth of the National Trust 1895–1994*, London, 1994, p. 144.
2 Kightly, *Country Voices*, p. 168.
3 Laurie, *Cricketer Preferred*, p. 35.
4 Gander, *Top Hats*, p. 98.
5 James Lees-Milne, *Some Country Houses and Their Owners*, London, 2009, p. 34.

6 Lewis, *Private Life*, p. 7.

7 *The Times*, 7 November 1952.

8 Tschumi, *Royal Chefs*, p. 153.

9 Interview 24708, Imperial War Museum.

10 Peter Russell, *Butler Royal*, London, 1982, p. 153.

11 Mollie Panter-Downes, *One Fine Day*, London, 1947, p. 169.

12 Interview with author.

13 Ibid.

14 Jordan, *As Cooks Go*, p. 16.

15 Ibid., p. 110.

16 Interview with author.

17 Marigold Hay, *Beyond the Green Baize Door*, Ilfracombe, 1975, p. 21.

18 Jordan, *As Cooks Go*, pp. 69–77.

19 Quoted in Jonathan Gathorne-Hardy, *The Rise and Fall of the British Nanny*, London, 1972, p. 172.

Chapter 24: The Shape of Things to Come

1 Quoted in Miriam Akhtar and Stephen Humphries, *The Fifties and Sixties: A Lifestyle Revolution*, London, 2001, p. 19.

2 Correspondence with author.

3 Interview with author.

4 Bulletin 42, Mass Observation.

5 Lewis and Maude, *English Middle Classes*, pp. 356–7.

6 Kay Smallshaw, *How to Run Your Home Without Help*, London, 1949, pp. 171–78.

7 N14421796, Oxfordshire History Centre.

8 Sue Shephard, *The Surprising Life of Constance Spry*, London, 2010, pp. 252–3.

9 Quoted in Christina Hardyment, *Slice of Life*, p. 163.

10 Simon Garfield (ed.), *Our Hidden Lives: The Remarkable Diaries of Post-War Britain*, London, 2004, p. 251.

11 Waterson, *Country House*, p. 53.

12 Markham, *Return Passage*, pp. 32–3.

13 Garfield, *Hidden Lives*, p. 291.

14 Smallshaw, *How to Run Your Home*, p. 89.

15 Akhtar and Humphries, *The Fifties and Sixties*, p. 28.

PART VI: 'WE DON'T WANT *THEM* DAYS AGAIN'
Chapter 25: 'We've Moved to the Front'

1 FL671, Women's Library, London Metropolitan University.
2 Mullins and Griffiths, *Cap and Apron*, p. 10.
3 Turner, *What the Butler Saw*, p. 298.
4 Quoted in Horn, *Life Below Stairs*, p. 253.
5 Pearl Jephcott, *Married Women Working*, London, 1962, p. 18.
6 White, *London in the Twentieth Century*, p. 141.
7 *Sunday Times*, 11 November 1962.
8 Celia Briar, *Working for Women? Gendered Work and Welfare Policies in Twentieth-Century Britain*, London, 1997, p. 111.
9 Correspondence with author.
10 *Wellington Evening Post*, 27 March 1954.
11 Correspondence with author.
12 *Sunday Times*, 11 November 1960.
13 Quoted in Grace Lees-Maffei, 'From Service to Self-Service: Advice Literature as Design Discourse, 1920–1970', *Journal of Design History*, Vol. 14, No. 3 (2001).
14 Ferdynand Zweig, *The Worker in an Affluent Society: Family Life and Industry*, London, 1961, p. 5.
15 Lees-Maffei, 'From Service to Self-Service', p. 188.
16 Ann Oakley, *Housewife*, London, 1974, p. 7.
17 Ellen Malos (ed.), *The Politics of Housework*, London, 1980, p. 91.
18 Zweig, *The Worker in an Affluent Society*, p. 32.
19 Adam, *Woman's Place*, p. 306.

Chapter 26: 'I'd Never Done What I Liked . . . Never in All My Life'

1 D/DX173/1, University of Reading.
2 *Costume: The Journal of the Costume Society*, 1969.
3 *Harpers & Queen*, June 1974.
4 Correspondence with author.
5 Ibid.
6 Stewart, *Lifting the Latch*, p. 175.
7 Roderick Grant, *Strathalder: A Highland Estate*, London, 1978, p. 20.

Chapter 27: 'We Like It Because the Past Is Not So Worrying as the News'

1 Powell, *Below Stairs*, p. 18.
2 N14421796, Oxfordshire History Centre.
3 Richard Marson, *Inside Updown: The Story of 'Upstairs, Downstairs'*, Bristol, 2001, p. 37.
4 Ibid., p. 45.
5 Criticos, *Life Story*, p. 3.
6 Marcus Binney, *The Ritz Hotel*, London, 1999, pp. 18–19.
7 Quoted in Jeremy Musson, *Upstairs and Downstairs: The History of the English Country House Servant*, London, 2010, p. 141.
8 Interview with Stephanie Rough and Laura Hurrell of the Greycoat Agency.
9 Interview with author, 2007.
10 Lavinia Smiley, *A Nice Clean Plate: Recollections, 1919–1931*, Salisbury, 1981, p. 32.
11 *Economist*, 17 December 2011.
12 Mills, *The Domestic Problem*, p.19.

Select Bibliography

Archives

Transcripts, manuscripts and recordings from 'The Edwardians: Family Life and Experience Before 1918' and the 'Colchester Recalled' Archives at the University of Essex (Albert Sloman Library); the Burnett Archive of Working-Class Autobiographies at Brunel University, London; the TUC Library Collections and the Women's Library Collections at London Metropolitan University; the Wiener Library, London; Special Collections at the Somerset Museum of Rural Life, Glastonbury; the Oral History Collection at the Museum of London; the British Library Sound Archive; Reading University Special Collections at the Museum of Rural Life, Reading; the Sound Archive and other collections at the Imperial War Museum, London; the Oxfordshire History Centre Collections; the Barnardo's Archive, Barkingside; the Universal Aunts archive (private collection).

Articles

'A Butler's View of Men-Service', *The Nineteenth Century*, Vol. XXXI, 1892

'A Four-inch-Driver', *The Chauffeur's Handbook*, London, 1909

Dean, Charles, in Geoffrey Tyack, 'Service on the Cliveden Estate Between the Wars', *Oral History*, Vol. 5, No. 1, Spring 1977

Caunce, Stephen, 'East Riding Hiring Fairs', *Oral History*, Vol. 3, No. 2, Autumn 1975

Franklin, Jill, 'Troops of Servants: Labour and Planning in the Country House 1840–1914', *Victorian Studies*, Vol. 19, No. 2 (December 1975), pp. 211–39

Gerrard, Jessica, 'Lady Bountiful: Women of the Landed Classes and Rural Philanthropy', *Victorian Studies*, Vol. 30, No. 2 (Winter 1987), pp. 183–210

Higgs, Edward, 'Domestic Servants and Households in Victorian England', *Social History*, Vol. 8, No. 8 (May 1983), pp. 201–10

Hinton, James, 'Militant Housewives: The British Housewives' League and the Attlee Government', *History Workshop Journal*, 38:1 (1994), pp. 129–56

Horn, Pamela, 'Ministry of Labour Female Training Programmes Between the Wars, 1919–39', *History of Education*, 31:1 (2002), pp. 71–82

Kent, Susan Kingsley, 'The Politics of Sexual Difference: World War One and the Demise of British Feminism', *The Journal of British Studies*, Vol. 27, No. 3 (July 1988), pp. 232–53

Lees-Maffei, Grace, 'Accommodating "Mrs Three-in-One": Homemaking, Home Entertaining and Domestic Advice Literature in Post-War Britain', *Women's History Review*, Vol. 16, Issue 5 (November 2007), pp. 723–54

——'From Service to Self-Service: Advice Literature as Design Discourse, 1920–1970', *Journal of Design History*, Vol. 14, No. 3 (2001), pp. 187–206

Todd, Selina, 'Domestic and Class Relations in Britain 1900–1950', *Past and Present*, 203 (1) (2009), pp. 81–204

Published Sources

Adam, Ruth, *A Woman's Place 1910–1975*, London, 1975

Adams, Samuel and Adams, Sarah, *The Complete Servant*, London, 1825

Adburgham, Alison, *Shops and Shopping 1800–1914: Where and in What Manner the Well-Dressed Englishwoman Bought Her Clothes*, London, 1989

——*A Punch History of Manners and Modes 1841–1940*, London, 1961

Addison, Paul, *Now the War is Over: A Social History of Britain, 1945–51*, London, 1985

Ager, Stanley and St Aubyn, Fiona, *The Butler's Guide to Running the Home and Other Graces*, London, 1980

Akhtar, Miriam and Humphries, Steve, *The Fifties and Sixties: A Lifestyle Revolution*, London, 2001

Allen, Charles, *Plain Tales from the British Empire: Images of the British in India, Africa and South-East Asia*, London, 2008

Allingham, Margery, *The Oaken Heart*, London, 1941

Angell, Norman and Buxton, Dorothy, *You and the Refugee: The Morals and Economics of the Problem*, London, 1939

'An Old Servant', *Domestic Service*, London, 1917

Anon., *The Ideal Servant-Saving House by an Engineer and his Wife*, London, 1918

——*Mistresses and Maids: A Handbook of Domestic Peace*, London, 1904

——*Commonsense for Housemaids*, London, 1853

——*The Manners and Rules of Good Society*, London, 1910

Askwith, Eveline, *Tweeny: Domestic Service in Edwardian Harrogate*, Bridgwater, 2003

Baily, Leslie, *Scrapbook for the Twenties*, London, 1959

Balderson, Eileen, *Backstairs Life in a Country House*, Newton Abbot, 1982

Balsan, Consuelo, *The Glitter and the Gold*, London, 1953

Banks, Elizabeth, *Campaigns of Curiosity: Journalistic Adventures of an American Girl in Late Victorian London*, London, 1894

Bankes, Viola, *A Kingston Lacy Childhood*, Wimbourne, 1986

Barker, Paul, *The Freedoms of Suburbia*, London, 2009

Barrie, J. M., *The Plays of J. M. Barrie*, London, 1947

Bateman, Robert, *How to Own and Equip a House*, London, 1925

Bedford, John Robert Russell (Duke of), *A Silver-Plated Spoon*, London, 1959

Bennett, Arnold, *Elsie and the Child: A Tale of Riceyman Steps*, London, 1929

Binney, Marcus, *The Ritz Hotel*, London, 1999

Blythe, Ronald, *Akenfield: Portrait of an English Village*, Harmondsworth, 1972

——*The Age of Illusion: England in the Twenties and Thirties*, 1919–1940, Harmondsworth, 1964

Booker, Beryl Lee, *Yesterday's Child, 1890–1909*, London, 1937

Booth, Charles, *Life and Labour of the People in London* (17 Vols), London, 1892–7

Bosanquet, Helen Dendy, *Rich and Poor*, London, 1898

Bostridge, Mark and Berry, Paul, *Vera Brittain: A Life*, London, 1995

Bradbury, D. J., *Welbeck Abbey and the Fifth Duke of Portland*, Mansfield, 1989

Braithwaite, Brian, *Ragtime to Wartime: The Best of Good Housekeeping 1922–1939*, London, 1986

Branson, Noreen, *Britain in the 1920s*, London, 1975

——*Women Workers in the First World War*, London, 1981

Braybon, Gail and Summerfield, Penny, *Out of the Cage: Women's Experiences in Two World Wars*, London, 1987

Brendon, Vyvyen, *Children of the Raj*, London, 2005

Briar, Celia, *Working for Women: Gendered Work and Welfare Policies in Twentieth-Century Britain*, London, 1997

Briggs, Asa, *Victorian Things*, Harmondsworth, 1990

Brittain, Vera, *Testament of Friendship: The Story of Winifred Holtby*, London, 1940

——*Testament of Youth: An Autobiographical Study of the Years 1900–1925*, London, 1933

de Broke, Willoughby, *The Passing Years*, London, 1924

Brown, Hilton, *The Sahibs: The Life and Ways of the British in India as Recorded by Themselves*, London, 1948

Buijs, Gina, *Migrant Women: Crossing Boundaries and Changing Identities*, Oxford, 1996

Burnett, John, *A Social History of Housing 1815–1985*, London, 1986

——*Destiny Obscure: Autobiographies of Childhood, Education and Family from the 1820s to the 1920s*, London, 1982

——*A History of the Cost of Living*, Harmondsworth, 1969

——*Plenty and Want: A Social History of Diet in England from 1815 to the Present Day*, Harmondsworth, 1968

——(ed.) *Useful Toil: Autobiographies of Working People from the 1820s to the 1920s*, London, 1974

Burnett, John, Mayall, David and Vincent, David, *The Autobiography of the Working Class: An Annotated, Critical Bibliography*, Brighton, 1984

Burton, David, *The Raj at Table: A Culinary History of the British in India*, London, 1993

Burton, Elaine, *What of the Women: A Study of Women in Wartime*, London, 1941

——*Domestic Work: Britain's Largest Industry*, London, 1944

Butler, C. V., *Domestic Service: An Enquiry by the Women's Industrial Council*, London, 1916

Calder, Angus, *The People's War: Britain 1939–45*, London, 1992

Cannadine, David, *Ornamentalism: How the British Saw Their Empire*, London, 2001

——*Class in Britain*, London, 2000

——*Aspects of Aristocracy: Grandeur and Decline in Modern Britain*, London, 1995

——*The Decline and Fall of the British Aristocracy*, London and New Haven, 1990

Carey, John, *The Intellectuals and the Masses: Pride and Prejudice Among the Literary Intelligentsia*, London, 1992

Cartland, Barbara, *I Reach for the Stars: An Autobiography*, London, 1984

Chesterton, G. K., *Autobiography*, New York, 1936

Clarke, John, Critcher, C. and Johnson, Richard, *Working Class Culture: Studies in History and Theory*, London, 2007

Cohen, Deborah, *Household Gods: The British and their Possessions*, London, 2006

Compton-Burnett, Ivy, *Manservant and Maidservant*, London, 1969

Conekin, Becky, *The Autobiography of a Nation: The Festival of Britain*, Manchester, 2003

Cooper, Charles, *Town and County: Forty Years in Service with the Aristocracy*, London, 1937

Cooper, Diana, *The Rainbow Comes and Goes*, London, 1958

Cooper, Lettice, *The New House*, New York, 1936

Cowan, Ruth Schwartz, *More Work for Mother: The Ironies of Household Technology from the Open Hearth to the Microwave*, New York, 1983

Crawshay, Rose Mary, *Domestic Service for Gentlewomen*, London, 1876

Criticos, George, *The Life Story of George of the Ritz*, London, 1959

Crosland, T. W. H., *The Suburbans*, London, 1905

Crossick, Geoffrey, *The Lower Middle Classes in Britain 1870–1914*, London, 1977

Crow, Duncan, *The Edwardian Woman*, London, 1978

Cunnington, Phillis, *The Costume of Household Servants from the Middle Ages to 1900*, London, 1974

Dangerfield, George, *The Strange Death of Liberal England*, London, 1935

Davey, Dolly, *A Sense of Adventure*, London, 1980

Davidoff, Leonore, *The Best Circles: Society, Etiquette and The Season*, London, 1973

Davidson, Caroline, *A Woman's Work is Never Done: A History of Housework in the British Isles, 1650–1950*, London, 1982

Davies, Clarice Stella, *North Country*, London, 1963

Davies, William Watkin, *Lloyd George 1863–1914*, London, 1939

Davin, Anna, *Growing up Poor: Home, School and Street in London, 1870–1914*, London, 1996

Dawes, Frank V., *Not in Front of the Servants: A True Portrait of Upstairs, Downstairs Life*, London, 1973

Dawes, W. H., *Beyond the Bungalow*, London, 1888

De Broke, Lord Willoughby, *The Passing Years*, London, 1922

Delafield, E. M., *The Diary of a Provincial Lady*, London, 1930

Devereaux, G. R. M., *Etiquette for Men*, London, 1902

Dibelius, Wilhelm, *England*, Stuttgart, 1923

Dickens, Monica, *One Pair of Hands*, London, 1939

Dillon, Maureen, *Artificial Sunshine: A Social History of Domestic Lighting*, London, 2001

Ditchfield, P. H., *The Manor Houses of England*, London, 1910

Diver, Maud, *The Englishwoman in India*, London, 1909

Driver, Christopher, *The British at Table 1940–1980*, London, 1983

E. E. T., Miss, *The Domestic Life of Thomas Hardy*, Beaminster, 1963

England, Daisy, *Daisy, Daisy*, London, 1981

English, Deirdre and Ehrenreich, Barbara, *For Her Own Good: Two Centuries of the Experts' Advice to Women*, New York, 2005

Fielding, Daphne, *Before the Sunset Fades*, Longleat, 1953

Firth, Violet, *The Psychology of the Servant Problem: A Study in Social Relationships*, London, 1925

Flanders, Judith, *Consuming Passions: Leisure and Pleasure in Victorian Britain*, London, 2007

——*The Victorian House: Domestic Life from Childbirth to Deathbed*, London, 2003

Fleming, Lawrence, *The Last Children of the Raj: British Childhoods in India* (2 Vols), London, 2004

Foley, Winifred, *Shiny Pennies and Grubby Pinafores: How We Overcame Hardship to Raise a Happy Family in the 1950s*, London, 1977

——*Full Hearts and Empty Bellies: A 1920s Childhood from the Forest of Dean to the Streets of London*, London, 2009

——*A Child in the Forest*, London, 1974

Forty, Adrian, *Objects of Desire: Design and Society Since 1750*, London, 1986

Four Inch Driver, *The Chauffeur's Companion*, London, 1909

Franklin, Jill, *The Gentleman's Country House and its Plan, 1835–1914*, London, 1981

Fraser, Ronald, *In Search of a Past*, London, 1984

Frazer, Mrs Lily, *First Aid for the Servantless*, Cambridge, 1913

Fremlin, Celia, *The Seven Chars of Chelsea*, London, 1940

Gander, Ann, *Top Hats and Servants' Tales: A Century of Life on Somerleyton Estate*, Wenhaston, 1998

Gardiner, Juliet, *Wartime Britain 1939–45*, London, 2004

Garfield, Simon (ed.), *Our Hidden Lives: The Remarkable Diaries of Post-War Britain*, London, 2004

Gathorne-Hardy, Jonathan, *The Rise and Fall of the British Nanny*, London, 1972

Gerard, Jessica, *Country House: Family and Servants 1815–1914*, Oxford, 1994

Gibbs, Mary Ann, *The Years of the Nannies*, London, 1960

Gibbs, Philip, *The New Man: A Portrait Study of the Latest Type*, London, 1913

Gibson, Sir Philip, *The New Man*, London, 1913

Giles, Judy, *The Parlour and the Suburb: Domestic Identities, Class, Femininity and Modernity*, Oxford, 2004

——*Women, Identity and Private Life in Britain 1900–50*, Basingstoke, 1995

Girouard, Mark, *Life in the English Country House: A Social and Architectural Survey*, London, 1979

Godden, Rumer and Jon, *Two Under the Indian Sun*, London, 1964

Gorst, Frederick, *Of Carriages and Kings*, London, 1956

Gradidge, Rodney, *Dream Houses: the Edwardian Ideal*, London, 1980

Grant, Roderick, *Strathalder: A Highland Estate*, London, 1978

Graves, Robert and Hodge, Alan, *The Long Weekend: A Social History of Great Britain 1918–1939*, New York, 1941

Green, Georgina (ed.), *Keepers, Cockneys, Kitchen Maids: Memories of Epping Forest 1900–1925*, Woodford Bridge, 1987

Green, Henry, *Loving; Living; Party-Going* (combined Penguin edition), London, 1993

Grenville, Anthony, *Jewish Refugees from Germany and Austria in Britain, 1933–1970: Their Image in AJR Information*, London, 2010

——*Refugees from the Third Reich in Britain*, Amsterdam, 2002

Hall, Edith, *Canary Girls and Stockpots*, Luton, 1977

Hardwick, Mollie, *The World of Upstairs, Downstairs*, Newton Abbot, 1976

Hardyment, Christina, *From Mangle to Microwave: The Mechanisation of Household Work*, Cambridge, 1998

——*Slice of Life: The British Way of Eating Since 1945*, London, 1995

Hare, Augustus, *The Story of My Life* (6 Vols), London, 1896

Harrison, Rosina, *My Life in Service*, London, 1975

——(ed.), *Gentlemen's Gentlemen: My Friends in Service*, London, 1976

Hartcup, Adeline, *Below Stairs in the Great Country Houses*, London, 1980

Hartley, Jenny (ed.), *Millions Like Us: Women's Fiction of the Second World War*, London, 1997

——(ed.) *Hearts Undefeated: Women's Writing of the Second World War*, London, 1995

Haslett, Caroline, *The Electrical Handbook for Women*, London, 1934

——*Household Electricity*, London, 1939

Hay, Marigold, *Beyond the Green Baize Door*, Ilfracombe, 1975

Heath-Stubbs, Mary, *Friendship's Highway: Being the History of the Girls' Friendly Society, 1875–1925*, London, 1926

Herbert-Hunting, Kate, *Universal Aunts*, London, 1986

Holdsworth, Angela, *Out of the Doll's House: The Story of Women in the Twentieth Century*, London, 1988

Holme, Thea, *Carlyles at Home*, London, 1965

Holtby, Winifred, *Women and a Changing Civilisation*, London, 1934

Horn, Pamela, *Flunkeys and Scullions: Life Below Stairs in Georgian England*, Stroud, 2004

——*Life Below Stairs in the Twentieth Century*, Stroud, 2001

——*The Rise and Fall of the Victorian Servant*, Stroud, 1990

Horne, Eric, *More Winks: Being Further Notes from the Life and Adventures of Eric Horne (Butler) for Fifty-seven Years in Service with the Nobility and Gentry*, London, 1932

——*What the Butler Winked At: Being the Life and Adventures of Eric Horne (Butler), for Fifty-seven Years in Service with the Nobility and Gentry*, London, 1923

Horsfield, Margaret, *Biting the Dust: The Joys of Housework*, London, 1999

Howard, Ebenezer, *Garden Cities for Tomorrow*, London, 1902

Howkins, Alun, *The Death of Rural England: A Social History of the Countryside Since 1900*, London, 2003

Hughes, Kathryn, *The Short Life and Long Times of Mrs Beeton*, London, 2005

Humphries, Steve et al (eds), *A Century of Childhood*, London, 1988

Humphries, Steve and Gordon, Pamela, *A Labour of Love: The Experience of Parenthood in Britain 1900–1950*, Plymouth, 1992

Jackson, Alan, *The Middle Classes 1900–1950*, Nairn, 1991

——*Semi-Detached London: Suburban Development, Life and Transport, 1900–39*, London, 1973

James, John, *Memoirs of a House Steward*, Holt, 1949

Jenkins, Jennifer and James, Patrick, *From Acorn to Oak Tree: The Growth of the National Trust, 1895–1994*, London, 1994

Jennings, Charles, *Them and Us: the American Invasion of British High Society*, Stroud, 2007

Jennings, Mrs H. J., *Our Homes and How to Beautify Them*, London, 1902

Jephcott, Pearl, *Married Women Working*, London, 1962

——*Some Young People*, London, 1954

——*Rising Twenty: Notes on Some Ordinary Girls*, London, 1948

Jermy, Louise, *Memories of a Working Woman*, Norwich, 1934

Jordan, Elizabeth, *As Cooks Go*, London, 1950

Josephs, Zoe, *Survivors: Jewish Refugees in Birmingham 1933–1945*, Oldbury, 1988

Keating, P. J., *Into Unknown England: Selections from the Social Explorers*, Manchester, 1976

Kelley, Victoria, *Soap and Water: Cleanliness, Dirt and the Working Classes in Victorian and Edwardian Britain*, London, 2010

Keun, Odette, *I Discover the English*, London, 1934

Kightly, Charles, *Country Voices: Life and Lore in Farm and Village*, London, 1984

King, Ernest, *The Green Baize Door*, London, 1963

Kirkham, Pat, and Thoms, David (eds), *War Culture: Social Change and Changing Experience in World War Two*, London, 1995

Kitchen, Penny, *For Home and Country: War, Peace and Rural Life as Seen through the Pages of the W.I. Magazine, 1919–1939*, London, 1990

Kushner, Tony, *The Persistence of Prejudice: Anti-Semitism in British Society during the Second World War*, Manchester, 1989

Kynaston, David, *Family Britain, 1951–1957*, London, 2009

——*Austerity Britain, 1945–1951*, London, 2007

Lanceley, William, *From Hallboy to House Steward*, London, 1925

Laski, Marghanita, *The Victorian Chaise Longue*, London, 1953

——*The Village*, London, 1952

Laurie, Kedrun (ed.), *Cricketer Preferred: Estate Workers at Lyme Park, 1898–1946*, Disley, 1981

Lees-Milne, James, *Caves of Ice*, London, 1983

——*Midway on the Waves*, London, 1983

——*Prophesying Peace*, London, 1977

——*Ancestral Voices*, London, 1975

Letwin, Shirley, *The Gentleman in Trollope: Individuality and Moral Conduct*, London, 1982

Leverton, Bertha and Lowensohn, Shmuel, *I Came Alone: The Story of the Kindertransport*, Indiana, 1990

Leverton, Edith Waldemar, *Servants and their Duties*, London, 1912

Lewis, Jane, *Labour and Love: Women's Experience of Home and Family, 1850–1940*, Oxford, 1986

Lewis, Jeremy, *Penguin Special: The Life and Times of Allen Lane*, London, 2005

Lewis, Lesley, *The Private Life of a Country House*, Newton Abbot, 1980

Lewis, Roy and Maude, Angus, *The English Middle Classes*, London, 1949

Light, Alison, *Mrs Woolf and the Servants*, London, 2007

——*Forever England: Femininity, Literature and Conservatism between the Wars*, London, 1991

Llewelyn Davies, Margaret, *Life As We Have Known It: The Women's Cooperative Guild 1883–1904*, London, 1931

Lloyd, Valerie, *The Camera and Dr Barnardo*, London, 1974

Loftie, M. J., *Comfort in the Home*, London, 1895

London, Jack, *People of the Abyss*, London, 1903

London, Louise, *Whitehall and the Jews 1933–48: British Immigration Policy, Jewish Refugees and the Holocaust*, Cambridge, 2000

Long, Helen, *The Edwardian House: The Middle-Class Home in Britain, 1880–1914*, Manchester, 1991

Longmate, Norman, *The Home Front: An Anthology of Personal Experience, 1939–1945*, London, 1981

——*How We Lived Then: A History of Everyday Life during the Second World War*, London, 1971

Lucas, E. V., *Encounters and Diversions*, London, 1924

——*Advisory Ben*, London, 1923

Lurie, Alison, *The Language of Clothes*, London, 1981

MacMillan, Margaret, *Women of the Raj*, London, 1996

Malet, Marian, and Grenville, Anthony, *Changing Countries: the Experience and Achievement of German-Speaking Exiles from Hitler in Britain, from 1933 to Today*, London, 2002

Malos, Ellen (ed.), *The Politics of Housework*, London, 1982

Mandler, Peter, *The Fall and Rise of the Stately Home*, New Haven, 1997

Mannin, Ethel, *Young in the Twenties: A Chapter of Autobiography*, London, 1921

Markham, Violet, *Duty and Citizenship: The Correspondence and Political Papers of Violet Markham*, London, 1984

——*Collected Stories*, London, 1981

——*Friendship's Harvest*, London, 1956

——*Return Passage: An Autobiography*, London, 1953

Markham, Violet and Florence Hancock, *A Post-War Report on Domestic Service*, London, 1945

Marshall, Dorothy, *The English Domestic Servant in History*, London, 1969

Marson, Richard, *Inside, Updown: The Story of Upstairs Downstairs*, Bristol, 2001

Marwick, Arthur, *The Deluge: British Society and the First World War*, London, 1965

Mason, Philip, *The English Gentleman: The Rise and Fall of an Ideal*, London, 1982

——*A Shaft of Sunlight: Memories of a Varied Life*, London, 1978

Masterman, C. F. G., *The Condition of England*, London, 1909

Masters, Brian, *Great Hostesses*, London, 1982

Maxstone-Graham, Ysende, *The Real Mrs Miniver: Jan Struther's Story*, London, 2001

Mayhew, Henry, *London Labour and the London Poor* (Vols 1–4), London, 1864

McBride, Theresa, *The Domestic Revolution: The Modernisation of Household Service in England and France, 1820–1920*, London, 1976

McCrum, Robert, *Wodehouse: A Life*, London, 2004

Meacham, Standish, *Regaining Paradise: Englishness and the Early Garden City Movement*, New Haven and London, 1999

——*A Life Apart: The English Working Class 1890–1914*, London, 1977

Menon, V. K. R., *The Raj and After: Memoirs of a Bihar Civilian*, New Delhi, 2000

Milburn, Clara, *Mrs Milburn's Diaries: An Englishwoman's Day-to-Day Reflections, 1939–45*, London, 1979

Miles, Mrs Eustace, *The Ideal Home and its Problems*, London, 1911

Mills, Ernestine, *The Domestic Problem, Past, Present and Future*, London, 1925

Milton, Edith, *The Tiger in the Attic: Memories of the Kindertransport and Growing Up English*, Chicago and London, 2005

Mitchell, David, *Women on the Warpath: The Story of the Women of the First World War*, London, 1965

Mitchison, Naomi, *Among You Taking Notes: The Wartime Diary of Naomi Mitchison*, Oxford, 1986

——*You May Well Ask: A Memoir 1920–1940*, London, 1979

——*Small Talk: Memories of an Edwardian Childhood*, London, 1973

Mosse, Werner E. (ed.), *Second Chance: Two Centuries of German-Speaking Jews in the United Kingdom*, Tübingen, 1991

Mullins, Samuel and Griffiths, Gareth, *Cap and Apron: An Oral History of Domestic Service in the Shires, 1880–1950*, Leicester, 1986

Munby, Arthur Joseph, *Faithful Servants: Epitaphs and Obituaries Recording their Names and Services*, London, 1891

Murdoch, Lydia, *Imagined Orphans: Poor Families, Child Welfare and Contested Citizenship in London*, New Jersey, 2006

Musson, Jeremy, *Upstairs and Downstairs: The History of the English Country House Servant*, London, 2010

Muthesius, Stephen, *The Terraced House*, London, 1982

Nicolson, Juliet, *The Great Silence: 1918–1920: Living in the Shadow of the Great War*, London, 2010

Noakes, Daisy, *The Town Beehive: A Young Girl's Lot in Brighton, 1910–34*, Brighton, 1991

Nowell-Smith, Simon, *Edwardian England 1901–1914*, Oxford, 1964

O'Sullivan, Vincent and Scott, Margaret (eds), *The Collected Letters of Katherine Mansfield, 1888–1923*, Oxford, 1984–2008

Oakley, Ann, *Housewife*, London, 1974

Oldfield, Sybil, *This Working Day World: Women's Lives and Culture(s) in Britain 1914–1945*, London, 1994

Oliver, Paul, *Dunroamin: The Suburban Semi and its Enemies*, London, 1981

Pakenham, Valerie, *The Noonday Sun: Edwardians and the Tropics*, London, 1985

Panter-Downes, Mollie, *One Fine Day*, London, 1947

——*Good Evening, Mrs Craven: The Wartime Stories of Mollie Panter-Downes*, London, 1999

——*London War Notes 1939–1945*, London, 1972

Panton, J. E., *From Kitchen to Garret: Hints for Young Householders*, London, 1888

Partridge, Frances, *Memories*, London, 1981

——*A Pacifist's War*, London, 1978

Peck, Winifred, *House-Bound*, London, 1942

Peel, Mrs C. S., *Waiting at Table*, London, 1929

——*Life's Enchanted Cup: An Autobiography*, London, 1923

——*A Hundred Wonderful Years: Social and Domestic Life of the Century, 1820–1920*, London, 1926

——*How We Lived Then*, London, 1929

Phillips, Randal, *The Servantless House*, London, 1923

Pike, E. Royston, *Human Documents of the Age of the Forsytes*, London, 1969

Pleydell-Bouverie, Millicent, *The Daily Mail Book of Post-War Homes*, London, 1944

Plomer, William, *Curious Relations*, London, 1945

Powell, Margaret, *Climbing the Stairs*, London, 1969

———*Below Stairs*, London, 1968

Praga, Mrs Alfred, *Appearances: How to Keep Them Up on a Limited Income*, London, 1899

Pritchett, V. S., *A Cab at the Door: An Autobiography*, London, 1968

Procida, Mary, *Married to the Empire: Gender, Politics and Imperialism in India*, Manchester, 2002

Rasul, Faizur, *Bengal to Birmingham*, London, 1967

Rau, Santha Rama, *Home to India*, London, 1945

Ravenhill, Alice, *Household Administration: Its Place in the Higher Education of Women*, London, 1910

Reeves, Maud Pember, *Round About a Pound a Week*, London, 1913

Rennie, Jean, *Every Other Sunday*, London, 1955

Renton, Alice, *Tyrant or Victim? A History of the British Governess*, London, 1991

Richards, J. M., *Castles on the Ground: The Anatomy of Suburbia*, London, 1946

Ritchie, Mrs Richmond, *Upstairs and Downstairs*, London, 1882

Rivers, Tony et al, *The Name of the Room: History of the British House and Home*, London, 1992

Robb, Nesca, *An Ulsterwoman in England, 1924–41*, Cambridge, 1942

Robbins, Bruce, *The Servant's Hand: English Fiction From Below*, New York, 1986

Roberts, Elizabeth, *A Woman's Place: An Oral History of Working-Class Women 1890–1940*, Oxford, 1995

Roberts, Robert, *A Ragged Schooling: Growing up in the Classic Slum*, Manchester, 1976

———*The Classic Slum: Salford Life in the First Quarter of the Century*, London, 1973

Robinson, John Martin, *The Country House at War*, London, 1989

Rose, Jonathan, *The Intellectual Life of the British Working Classes*, London and New Haven, 2001

Rose, June, *For the Sake of The Children: Inside Dr Barnardo's – 120 Years of Caring for Children*, London, 1987

Rose, Kenneth, *King George V*, London, 1983

Russell, Peter, *Butler Royal*, London, 1982

Ryan, Deborah, *The Ideal Home through the Twentieth Century*, London, 1997

Rybczynski, Witold, *Home: A Short History of an Idea*, London, 1987

Sambrook, Pamela, *Keeping Their Place: Domestic Service in the Country House*, Stroud, 2005

Scannell, Dolly, *Mother Knew Best: An East End Childhood*, London, 1974

Schlüter, Auguste, *A Lady's Maid in Downing Street*, London, 1922

Schneider, Bronka, *Exile: A Memoir*, Ohio, 1998

Scott-Moncrieff, M. C., *Yes, Ma'am: Glimpses of Domestic Service 1901–51*, Edinburgh, 1984

Segal, Lore, *Other People's Houses*, London, 1964

Service, Alastair, *Edwardian Interiors: Inside the Homes of the Poor, the Average and the Wealthy*, London, 1982

Shephard, Sue, *The Surprising Life of Constance Spry*, London, 2010

Sheridan, Dorothy, *Wartime Women: A Mass-Observation Anthology*, London, 2002

Sissons, Michael and French, Philip (eds), *Age of Austerity*, Harmondsworth, 1963

Smallshaw, Kay, *How to Run Your Home Without Help*, London, 1949

Smiley, Lavinia, *A Nice Clean Plate: Recollections, 1919–1931*, Salisbury, 1981

Smith, Hubert Llewellyn, *The New Survey of London Life and Labour* (9 Vols), London, 1930–5

Smith, Virginia, *Clean: A History of Personal Hygiene and Purity*, Oxford, 2007

Southgate, Walter, *That's The Way it Was: A Working-Class Autobiography 1890–1950*, Centre for London History, 1982

Spencer, Hanna, *Hanna's Diary, 1938–1941*, Ontario, 2001

Spender, Dale (ed.), *Time and Tide Wait for No Man*, London, 1984

Spring Rice, Margery, *Working-Class Wives: Their Health and Conditions*, Harmondsworth, 1939

Steedman, Carolyn, *Labours Lost: Domestic Service and the Making of Modern England*, Cambridge, 2009

——*Master and Servant: Love and Labour in the Industrial Age*, Cambridge, 2007

——*Dust*, Manchester, 2001

Stewart, Sheila, *Lifting the Latch: A Life on the Land, Based on the Life of Mont Abbot of Enstone*, Oxford, 1987

Stokes, Penelope, *Norland: The Story of the First One Hundred Years*, Hungerford, 1992

Storey, Joyce, *Joyce's Dream: The Post-War Years*, London, 1995

——*Our Joyce*, Bristol, 1987

——*Joyce's War*, Bristol, 1990

Strachey, Ray and Rathbone, Eleanor, *Our Freedom and its Results*, London, 1936

Streatfeild, Noel (ed.), *The Day Before Yesterday: First-hand Stories of Fifty Years Ago*, London, 1956

Struther, Jan, *Mrs Miniver*, London, 1989

Stuart, D. M., *The English Abigail*, London, 1946

Sturt, George, *Change in the Village*, London, 1912

Summerfield, Penny, *Women Workers in the Second World War: Production and Patriarchy in Conflict*, London, 1989

Thackeray, William Makepeace, *The Memoirs of Mr Charles J. Yellowplush*, London, 1898

Thomas, Albert, *Wait and See*, London, 1944

Thompson, E. P., *The Making of the English Working Class*, London, 1963

Thompson, Paul, *The Edwardians: The Remaking of British Society*, London, 1975

Thompson, Thea, *Edwardian Childhoods*, London, 1981

Tschumi, Gabriel, *Royal Chef: Fory Years with Royal Households*, London, 1954

Turner, E. S., *What the Butler Saw: Two Hundred and Fifty Years of the Servant Problem*, London, 1963

——*The Phoney War on the Home Front*, London, 1961

Tweedsmuir, Susan, *The Lilac and the Rose*, London, 1952

Veblen, Thorstein, *The Theory of the Leisure Class*, Oxford, 2009

Waterfield, Giles and French, Anne, *Below Stairs: 400 Years of Servants' Portraits*, London, 2003

Waterson, Merlin (ed.), *The Country House Remembered: Recollections of Life Between the Wars*, London, 1985

——*The Servants' Hall: A Domestic History of Erddig*, London, 1980

Wells, H. G., *Tono-Bungay*, London, 1908

——*Kipps: The Story of a Simple Soul*, London, 1905; Penguin edition, 2005

——*Marriage*, London, 1912

——*An Experiment in Autobiography: Discoveries and Conclusions of a Very Ordinary Brain (Since 1866)*, London, 1984

Wheway, Edna, *Edna's Story: Memories of Life in a Children's Home and in Service, in Dorset and London*, Wimborne, 1984

Whipple, Dorothy, *Someone at a Distance*, London, 1953

——*The Priory*, London, 1939

White, Jerry, *London in the Twentieth Century: A City and Its People*, London, 2001

Whiteing, Eileen, *Anyone For Tennis? Growing up in Wallington Between the Wars*, Sutton Libraries, 1979

Williams-Ellis, Clough, *England and the Octopus*, London, 1928

Wilson, Elizabeth, *Only Halfway to Paradise: Women in Post-War Britain, 1945–68*, London and New York, 1980

Wilson, Francesca, *Strange Island: Britain through Foreign Eyes 1395–1940*, London, 1955

Winnington-Ingram, A. F., *Fifty Years' Work in London*, London, 1940

Woodward, Kathleen, *Jipping Street*, London, 1928

Wright, Lawrence, *Clean and Decent: The Fascinating History of the Bathroom and the Water Closet*, London, 1960

Wylde, Mary, *A Housewife in Kensington*, London, 1937

Wymer, Norman, *Father of Nobody's Children: A Portrait of Dr Barnardo*, London, 1954

Ziegler, Philip, *Osbert Sitwell*, London, 1998

Zweig, Ferdynand, *The Worker in an Affluent Society: Family Life and Industry*, London, 1961

——*Women's Life and Labour*, London, 1952

——*Labour, Life and Poverty*, London, 1948

Acknowledgements

I am indebted to all those who took the time to share their memories of work and life in service or who introduced me to the recollections of friends and relations. Not everyone appears in the book by name but all have been invaluable in adding pieces to the background jigsaw. My thanks therefore to those I interviewed in person: Ann Stallard, Joy Schreiber, Marion Smith, Enid Fields, Gretta Guy, Peter Telford, Pearl Scott and Horace Mortiboy; Jenny and Pat Duncan I came to know through Pamela Hatfield; Colin Lee was introduced to me by Rosalind Morrison and Fred Collett by Dorothy Bell RSCJ. Hazel Munting invited me to read the journals of her great uncle Ernest Squire and Jackie Best to listen to the recorded memories of her mother Margaret Flockhart; Luz Bansil and her sister told me about their experiences of thirty years of housekeeping in London. The insights provided by many correspondents were also invaluable. My thanks to Jean Arnold, Hope Gilbert, Doreen Warwick, Ann Humpage, K. M. Hayles, Barbara Worman, June Morris, Peter Rankilor, Joan Crook, Eileen Sayer, Mary Woodhouse, Dennis Parratt, Dorothy Schulz, Jackie Day, Chris Noonan, Wallace Giddings, Elva Lipscomb, Joyce Helps, J. E. Bratton, Robert E. Reece, Bairnie Henderson, Margit Latter, Audrey King, Roger Kingsley (who had written his memories of 'Marieken'), June Morris, Winifred Hadland and Anne Baird.

Piers and Vyvyen Brendon, Giles Waterfield and Alison Light let me pick their brains in the early stages of the project, as did Dr Anthony Grenville of the Association of Jewish Refugees. It was my friend Crispin Jackson who discovered the diaries of Alice Osbourn; Andrew Barrow sent me the tape recording of his interview with a servant in the royal household; Miriam James told me of the letters of Gwendoline Rush in the Bodleian; and Penelope Billyeald let me read her unpublished thesis, *What the Butler Did Not Do: The Function of the Domestic Servant in the Crime and Detective Fiction of the Golden Age*; Phil Baker put me on to *Curious Relations*. Many thanks also to Stephanie Rough and Laura Hurrell of Greycoat Placements, Rebekah Frankcom of the Norland Institute and Angela Montfort-Bebb of Universal Aunts.

Many friends have in different ways been instrumental in the making of the book. Jeremy Lewis is, as always, a fount of invigorating enthusiasm and to the generosity of both Jeremy and Petra I owe much. Selina O'Grady, Tony Curzon-Price, Jane O'Grady, Kathy O'Shaughnessy and Daniel Jeffreys were unstinting in their encouragement. As was Claudia Fitzherbert: my thanks to her and to Fram Dinshaw for their months of hospitality. Simon and Jenny Haviland are the most generous of friends and neighbours and, Kiloran Howard and Sarah Cole uncomplainingly put me up at short notice and at all hours. Thanks also to Jane Mulvagh, Tessa Boase and Nick Glass.

My wonderful editor Michael Fishwick must at times have wondered if I would ever finish, so many thanks to him, to Simon Trewin, and to the brilliant Bloomsbury team who brought everything to fruition with such patience and polish: Anna Simpson, Paul Nash, Phillip Beresford, Oliver Holden-Rea, Kate Johnson, Catherine Best and David Atkinson. I would also like to thank Amy Cherry and Anna Mageras of W. W. Norton in New York, whose help and suggestions have been invaluable; and my thanks also to George Lucas of Inkwell Management.

Finally, my family have been unfailingly supportive over the vicissitudes of the last five years and I owe them more than I could possibly put into words. My sister Anna is my beadiest critic and I am very grateful for all her support and encouragement. The love of my parents is the foundation of the writing of this book – and it is for them.

Index

A Note on the Author

Lucy Lethbridge has written for a number of publications and is also the author of several children's books, one of which, *Who Was Ada Lovelace?*, won the 2002 Blue Peter Award for non-fiction. She lives in London.